THE SPANISH BLUE DIVIS FRONT, 1941–1945

M000223318

War, Occupation, Memory

Xosé M. Núñez Seixas

In 1941, the Franco regime established the Spanish Division of Volunteers to take part in the Russian campaign as a unit integrated into the German Wehrmacht. Recruited by both the Fascist Party (*Falange*) and the Spanish army, around 47,000 Spanish volunteers joined what would become known as the "Blue Division."

The Spanish Blue Division on the Eastern Front, 1941–1945 explores an intimate history of the Blue Division "from below," using personal war diaries, letters, and memoirs, as well as official documents from military archives in Spain, Germany, Britain, and Russia. In addition to describing the Spanish experience on the Eastern Front, Xosé M. Núñez Seixas takes on controversial topics including the Blue Division's proximity to the Holocaust and how members of the Blue Division have been remembered and commemorated. Addressing issues such as the behaviour of the Spaniards as occupiers, their perception by the Russians, their witnessing of the Holocaust, their commitment to the war aims of Nazi Germany, and their narratives on the war after 1945, this book illuminates the experience of Spanish combatants and occupied civilians.

(Toronto Iberic)

XOSÉ M. NÚÑEZ SEIXAS is a professor of modern European history at the University of Santiago de Compostela.

XOSÉ M. NÚÑEZ SEIXAS

Translated by Andrea Blanch, Daniel Blanch,
and Craig Patterson

The Spanish Blue Division on the Eastern Front, 1941–1945:

War, Occupation, Memory

UNIVERSITY OF TORONTO PRESS
Toronto Buffalo London

© University of Toronto Press 2022
Toronto Buffalo London
utorontopress.com
Printed in Canada

ISBN 978-1-4875-4165-1 (cloth)   ISBN 978-1-4875-4168-2 (EPUB)
ISBN 978-1-4875-4166-8 (paper)   ISBN 978-1-4875-4167-5 (PDF)

Library and Archives Canada Cataloguing in Publication

Title: The Spanish Blue Division on the Eastern Front, 1941–1945 : war,
   occupation, memory / Xosé M. Núñez Seixas ; translated by Andrea
   Blanch, Daniel Blanch, and Craig Patterson.
Other titles: Camarada invierno. English
Names: Núñez Seixas, Xosé M. (Xosé Manoel), 1966– author.
Series: Toronto Iberic ; 72.
Description: Series statement: Toronto Iberic ; 72 | Translation of: Camarada
   invierno : experiencia y memoria de la División Azul (1941–1945). |
   Includes bibliographical references and index.
Identifiers: Canadiana (print) 2021037750X | Canadiana (ebook)
   20210377569 | ISBN 9781487541651 (cloth) | ISBN 9781487541668 (paper) |
   ISBN 9781487541682 (EPUB) | ISBN 9781487541675 (PDF)
Subjects: LCSH: Germany. Heer. Infanteriedivision (1941–1943), 250. |
   LCSH: Germany. Heer. Infanteriedivision (1941–1943), 250. – Biography. |
   LCSH: World War, 1939–1945 – Campaigns – Soviet Union. | LCSH:
   World War, 1939–1945 – Spain. | LCSH: World War, 1939–1945 –
   Regimental histories – Germany.
Classification: LCC D757.32.N86 C3613 2022 | DDC 940.54/1343–dc23

We wish to acknowledge the land on which the University of Toronto Press
operates. This land is the traditional territory of the Wendat, the Anishnaabeg,
the Haudenosaunee, the Métis, and the Mississaugas of the Credit First Nation.

University of Toronto Press acknowledges the financial support of the
Government of Canada, the Canada Council for the Arts, and the Ontario Arts
Council, an agency of the Government of Ontario, for its publishing activities.

**Canada Council Conseil des Arts
for the Arts   du Canada**

ONTARIO ARTS COUNCIL
CONSEIL DES ARTS DE L'ONTARIO
an Ontario government agency
un organisme du gouvernement de l'Ontario

Funded by the   Financé par le
Government   gouvernement
of Canada   du Canada

MIX
Paper from
responsible sources
FSC® C016245

Contents

Illustrations

(AA: Author's archive; AGA: Archivo General de la Administración, Alcalá de Henares)

Maps

Abbreviations

AK	Armeekorps
AOK	Armeeoberkommando
BD	Blue Division
DEV	Divisón Española de Voluntarios
DGS	Dirección General de Seguridad (Spanish State Police)
DNE	Delegación Nacional de Excombatientes (National Office for War Veterans)
FE-JONS	Falange Española de las JONS
FET-JONS	Falange Española Tradicionalista y de las JONS
FdJ	Frente de Juventudes (Youth Front; section of Falange)
Frontovik	Soviet front soldier
Gestapo	Geheime Staatspolizei (German Secret State Police)
Guripa	Soldier of the BD (colloquialism)
NKVD	Narodnyi Komissariat Vnutrennikh Del (People's Commissariat for Internal Affairs)
NSDAP	Nationalsozialistische Deutsche Arbeiterpartei (Nazi Party)
OKH	Oberkommando des Heeres (High Command of the German Army)
OKW	Oberkommando der Wehrmacht (High Command of the German Armed Forces)
OT	Organization Todt
SD	Sicherheitsdienst (German Security Service)

Acknowledgments

In the years it has taken for this book to mature, I have received help from several institutions and countless individuals: colleagues, friends, collectors, scholars, and descendants of Blue Division veterans, who made unpublished material available to me. Firstly, my thanks to the staff of the archives that I have accessed, who have so efficiently and decisively responded to my requests for material, as well as the librarians at the University of Santiago de Compostela and Ludwig Maximilian University of Munich. Chasia Bornstein-Bielicka, Alexandre Blumstein, José Manuel de Cárdenas, Xosé Fernández Naval, Emilia García, Carlos Gil-Andrés, Jordi Gracia, Juan C. Jiménez de Aberasturi, Carmelo de las Heras, Hans-Jürgen Kugler, Juaco López, J.A. López Covarrubias, Antonio C. Moreno, Jorge M. Reverte, Fernando Rebollo, Ana Romero, Adrian Shubert, Ricardo Silva, Raúl Soutelo, and Pavel Tendera kindly provided access to materials, diaries, letters, and pamphlets, some of which were nearly impossible to obtain. The HISPONA research group of the University of Santiago de Compostela provided financial support,

Discussions with interested colleagues on the cultural history of war and violence at seminars and conferences in Germany, Switzerland, Britain, Canada, Russia, and Spain also helped to refine my perspectives, identify focus areas, correct factual errors, and incorporate ideas. Though I cannot hope to do justice to everyone, I would particularly like to acknowledge Ángel Alcalde, David Alegre, Birgit Aschmann, David Bankier, Martin Baumeister, Jörg Baberowski, Oleg Beyda, Gustavo Corni, Jens Ebert, José M. Faraldo, Stig Förster, Ferran Gallego, Nicola Guerra, Alexander Hill, Boris Kovalev, Marco Mondini, Sönke Neitzel, Javier Rodrigo, Andreas Stucki, and Joan M. Thomàs.

Parts of the original manuscript were read by Ángel Alcalde, David Alegre, Andrés Antolín-Hofrichter, Miguel Cabo, and Henrike

Fesefeldt. Maps were adapted for this edition by Alfonso Iglesias and José C. García Vega. However, the author assumes full responsibility for all errors or omissions. Finally, thanks to my wife Henrike and my daughters, Sara and Irene, who patiently put up with the writing of this hefty tome.

The original version of this book was published by Editorial Crítica, Barcelona, in 2016 (*Camarada invierno. Experiencia y memoria de la División Azul, 1941–1945*, 2nd paperback edition 2017). A German version was also published in 2016 by Aschendorff, Münster (*Die spanische Blaue Division an der Ostfront, 1941–1945: Zwischen Kriegserfahrung und Erinnerung*). This adapted and substantially updated English version has benefitted enormously from the very constructive remarks and suggestions of the three external referees who evaluated the manuscript for University of Toronto Press. I also thank the editorial team of University of Toronto Press and History editor Stephen Shapiro for welcoming the original proposal and assisting the process with such consideration and professionalism.

Munich, summer/fall 2015;
Santiago de Compostela, May 2021

THE SPANISH BLUE DIVISION ON THE EASTERN FRONT, 1941–1945

1 Introduction: The Blue Division, the Franco Regime, and the Second World War

Placing the Blue Division within New Military History

The history of the Spanish Division of Volunteers, known from its inception as the Blue Division (BD), now qualifies as a classic subject in Spanish historiography. Internationally, however, it is perhaps less well known. This largely voluntary expeditionary force was formed in June/July 1941 to fight with the German Army on the Eastern Front in the Soviet-German War, immediately following the German invasion of the USSR on 22 June. In November 1943, the Spanish dictator, General Francisco Franco, ordered its retreat and sent instead the Spanish Legion of Volunteers, the "Blue Legion." That corps remained on the front until its definitive retreat in early March 1944.

Spanish participation on the Axis side in the Second World War did not end there. In 1944–5, several hundred Spanish soldiers – ex-Blue Division and Blue Legion combatants, new volunteers, and civilian workers in Germany – joined Wehrmacht and Waffen-SS units of their own initiative, assisting the struggle until the definitive fall of the Third Reich. Some even fought amidst the ruins of Berlin in April/May 1945. From 1941 to 1945, some five hundred to six hundred Spanish combatants were taken prisoner by the Red Army and remained in Soviet camps until 1954. In late March of that year, the Red Cross chartered the ship *Semíramis* to return 248 of them to Spain, along with four "war children" (who had been evacuated by the Spanish Republic in 1937 and taken in by the USSR). There were also thirty-one Spanish aviators and sailors who were loyal to the Republic and had been detained against their will in Soviet territory since 1939. In the air, dozens of Spanish pilots fought alongside the Luftwaffe, assisted by "Blue Squadron" ground support personnel (15. Spanische Staffel), through which around a hundred pilots passed over four periods. At sea, a group of

Spanish sailors served in the German Navy as part of a co-operative agreement that included training Spanish Navy officers in Kriegsmarine units, from November 1942 until the summer of 1943.[1]

The main objective of this book is to reconstruct the experience of Blue Division ground combatants and their direct or indirect successor units, from inception through May 1945. This group included around forty-seven thousand men; nearly five thousand of them fell in combat, while more than forty-two thousand of them returned to Spain. Among them were Fascist volunteers and idealists, or those who, due to age or geography, had missed the chance to fight for their beliefs in the Spanish Civil War. Some soldiers were enlisted or coercively recruited; others were civilian volunteers in search of adventure, extra pay, or even a chance to desert and join the Red Army. There were non-commissioned officers (NCOs) driven by anti-communism or the desire to build a military career as well as professionally or ideologically motivated army officers. A relatively high proportion of university students, young lawyers, and even university lecturers joined ranks alongside industrial and unskilled workers, employees, civil servants, shopworkers. and illiterate day labourers.

In Spanish post-war society, BD veteran profiles were equally varied: from writers and artists to professional soldiers, ministers, workers, policemen, or migrants to Argentina or Germany. Some even became anti-Francoist activists during the 1950s and 1960s. With such inter-class diversity, the BD memory permeated much of the social spectrum. Unlike the memory of other Western European expeditionary forces that fought alongside the Wehrmacht against the USSR, remembrance of the Blue Division was not circumscribed by far-right political tendencies or neo-fascist cult specificities. Spanish veterans from the Eastern Front were not stigmatized "collaborators" with the Nazis, in contrast with those returning to Norway, Denmark, or France. These conditions also prevented the memory of the Blue Division from being relegated to absolute public silence. From 1945 to 1954, Spanish veterans from the Eastern Front were treated as rather inconvenient heroes by the Franco dictatorship, as it attempted to "whitewash" over its earlier sympathies towards Nazi Germany and reposition itself in the Western Bloc against the Soviet Union.[2] The memory of Spanish participation in the Eastern campaign became something diffuse and ubiquitous: not forbidden or persecuted, but scarcely encouraged by the Francoist regime. This endowed it with a great capacity to endure.

The same dynamics also generated a kaleidoscopic memory of the Blue Division in Spanish post-war society. For some, it was a corpus of somewhat confusing memories, anecdotes, and stories about a relative or a neighbour who fought in Russia for unknown causes. For others, it was a benchmark of ideological integrity for non-conformist Falangism or anti-communist commitment, a professional posting in a brilliant military career, or a youthful adventure fuelled by the desire to see the world beyond the Pyrenees. The Blue Division was an uncomfortable memory for the Francoist regime, and the subsequent constitutional monarchy (restored in 1975–8) was not keen to commemorate it.

Occasionally, the Spanish democratic state has implicitly or explicitly equated the Blue Division and its combatants with the hundreds of Spanish Republican soldiers who fought with the Allies. This has given rise to intense moments ofand controversy. In October 2004, an ex-BD member and a former prisoner of the Soviets stood on the presidential podium as representatives of the Blue Division Foundation, together with a representative of the Spanish 9th Company (la Nueve) of the Régiment de marche du Tchad, part of the 2nd Armoured Division (Division Leclerc), who were loyal to General Charles de Gaulle and the Allies. The socialist minister of defence, José Bono, had invited them to attend as part of the 12 October (Spanish national holiday) military parade.[3] This attitude persists among members of the Spanish armed forces and in military academies, which still teach and idealize the "heroic deeds" of the Blue Division. In October 2020, a leak to the daily press informed that a police operation against alleged Russian connections with Catalan nationalist leaders in relation to the failed independence referendum in October 2017 had been given the code name "Operation Volkhov," recalling the first battle involving Spanish troops on the Eastern Front. It shows that the BD memory in post-francoist Spain still suffers from a lack of proactive, state-sponsored politics of democratic memory. After half a century, some wounds of the dictatorial past remain open and insufficiently adressed by public institutions.

Numerous books have been published about the Blue Division, mostly in Spain. Its exotic subject matter has inherent appeal: a sense of adventure, Southern Europeans lost in an immense frozen landscape, an accumulation of extraordinary experiences (the journey there, contact with the German Army, fighting on a distant front, returning), and the hazy impression that the Blue Division experience left on Spanish society after 1944–5. At least until the first decade of the twenty-first century, most Spaniards knew someone whose father, uncle, or grandfather had joined the Blue Division.

While commemorative writing on the Blue Division abounds, along with apologetic and descriptive approaches interested in recalling the most insignificant details, the historiographic relevance of such literature is meagre at best. However, the history of the Blue Division has also been amply treated in professional historiography. Most approaches have sought to understand the role of the BD within the framework of the diplomatic, economic, and cultural relations between the early Franco regime and the Third Reich. Accordingly, Francoist and post-Francoist historians regarded the Blue Division as a concession made by the Franco regime to fulfil its obligations with Nazi Germany, which was pressing Spain to side with the Axis powers and enter the war. From this perspective, the Spanish BD soldiers were the "blood price" that Francoism paid to maintain its "non-belligerency" in the Second World War.[4] Thus, their sacrifice had not been in vain: they had shielded Spain from the horrors of a new war, and even the threat of German invasion: Spanish heroism on the Eastern Front had shown Hitler what his troops could expect if they tried to invade Spain.[5]

Since the 1980s, some authors have taken the opposite view and argued that sending the Blue Division to the Eastern Front revealed the deeply Germanophile nature of Francoist officials and supporters, who would enter the war at any cost to see their fascist, totalitarian project fulfilled. The Blue Division thus constituted the purest expression of the most wholehearted Falangist sectors and much of the military, along with many traditionalists, Catholics, and conservatives who sincerely admired the anti-communist stance and military performance of the Third Reich, at least until 1944.[6]

Recent research has shed some new light on the the relationship between the Franco regime and Nazi Germany, adding to the contributions of diplomatic historians since the 1990s. It assigns the Blue Division a small part in the diplomatic game that was unfolding on Spanish soil from 1940 to 1945. Franco and most of his government certainly wished to enter the war on the Axis side but not without some kind of reward. Franco wanted the Germans to hand over a great part of the French colonial possessions in Africa to Spain, including French Morocco, parts of Algeria, and Cameroon. This would have been unacceptable to Vichy France. The Iberian Peninsula played only a minor role in Third Reich war strategy from early 1942 on. As its army and resources were almost negligible to German eyes, the German chancellor did not need Spain on his side at any price. Keeping Vichy France as a loyal ally and not pushing Marshal Philippe Pétain to side with the Allies was more important to Hitler than winning the full support of Franco's Spain. This was mainly why the meeting between Franco and Hitler at the rail station of Hendaye (23 October 1940) ended in failure: Hitler prioritized ties with Vichy France and Franco returned to Spain with no tangible wins.

Hitler's interest in Spain dramatically decreased after that, as other theatres of operation required his attention. Meanwhile, British diplomacy in Spain was playing its cards by systematically bribing generals and high officials to keep the country from intervening in the war on the German side. The government crisis of September 1942 and subsequent appointment of the Anglophile Count Jordana as the minister for foreign affairs marked a move towards full neutrality in Spanish diplomacy. Steady distancing from Berlin (and Rome) became more accentuated throughout 1943 and 1944. The debilitated Falangists were unable to avoid this strategic move and their projects to estabish a fully fascist "new State" in Spain faded away. Until August 1945, however, General Franco himself stuck to the theory of "three wars," which described the world war as three separate conflicts. In the first, between Germany and the Western democracies (Great Britain, the US, and France), Spain was neutral. In the second, between Germany and the Soviet Union, Francoist Spain enthusiastically allied itself with the Third Reich against a common enemy. In the third, between the US and Japan, the Franco dictatorship increasingly backed the US but never actually declared war on Japan.[7]

Unlike Nazi agents and members of the Nazi Party's foreign branch in Spain, pragmatic German diplomats in Madrid wanted Spain to remain neutral to better exploit what they considered its most interesting contribution to the Axis war effort: the regular supply of wolfram and other strategic raw materials. Francoist Spain maintained its peculiar position of "non-belligerency" until 1943, but with open preference for the Axis. This enabled Spain to provide some logistic support while avoiding involvement in military operations or declaring war on any of the belligerent countries, including the Soviet Union. The regime moved towards full neutrality in 1943, under direct pressure from the Western Allies. Meanwhile, German diplomacy acted to preserve the Third Reich's influence on Spanish public opinion by subsidizing publications, magazines, and propaganda in an effort to present Nazi Germany in an acceptable way to Catholics and conservatives. Above all, German diplomacy attempted to maintain control and secure access to the Spanish resources deemed crucial to their war effort. German influence was remarkable in many spheres of Spanish society and culture until 1945, and still lingered for decades in areas such as Spanish civil law and the organization of the Falange single party. As the Cold War set in, however, Germanophile attitudes were conveniently archived and the Franco regime managed to adapt to new circumstances.

After mid-1944, when all Spanish soldiers had returned from the Eastern Front (excepting a few hundred who continued to fight for the Third Reich on their own initiative), Francoist ministers and diplomats began portraying the sending of the Blue Division three years prior as a merely Catholic and anti-communist initiative, devoid of any proactive sympathy towards the Axis. This ran parallel to efforts by the regime, beginning with Catholic thinkers and certain Falangist leaders, to detach its founding principles from anything resembling fascism. Francoism was now presented as a Catholic, traditionalist, and anti-communist world view, which was devoid of any totalitarian, racist, or imperialist ambition.

Some studies focused almost exclusively on the "heroic deeds" of the Blue Division, the battles and operations it took part in, its overall evolution, recruitment practices, and composition. These monographs provided noteworthy reconstructions of the BD trajectory from highly diverse perspectives such as traditional military history, diplomatic history, and even economic history. Most were written from an enthusiastically pro-Francoist point of view and tried to present a benevolent, acritical image of the Blue Division. Such hagiographic, revisionist approaches by authors nostalgic for the Franco regime coexist alongside extremely positivist perspectives on the history of military operations, local histories attempting to showcase the contributions of their province and region to the expeditionary corps, and highly detailed and descriptive works on specific sections and branches of the Blue Division, from military chaplains to sappers and medical corps.[8] Common to nearly all of them is their endogenous self-sufficiency, accompanied by a flagrant lack of dialogue with war studies, new military history approaches, and international historiography concerning the Eastern Front. Most of these studies also displayed blatant ignorance of the contributions and debates from the comparative history of violence and modern warfare.

Approaches that have attempted to focus on the actual experience of BD members are far scarcer. These look at the ordinary men in uniform (Wolfram Wette), their motivations and reactions, their reasons for fighting, and how they were affected by participating in a war that differed substantially from prior conflicts. The Soviet-German War was an armed confrontation that began as huge display of technological and strategic modernity, but within a few months it was characterized by its extreme cruelty and high cost in human lives, and its extremely harsh climate and environmental conditions. Combat became increasingly brutalized amidst ever-growing numbers of civilian casualties, with mass killings of civilians and partisans in the rearguard.[9]

The Spanish volunteers in the summer of 1941 believed that they were embarking on a brief military adventure that many saw as a continuation of the Spanish Civil War. They were not always aware that they were participating in a conflict unlike many that had preceded it: a war of extermination. In English- and German-speaking spheres, this conflict is receiving renewed historiographical attention in new military history and the cultural history of violence.

This book addresses a series of basic questions concerning war as a complete social reality. Why do soldiers fight? What is the difference between volunteers and conscripts? To what extent do ideology, values, and the prior socialization of combatants influence their willingness to kill? Does the image of the enemy correspond more to pre-existing cultural constructions and images of the other, or to indoctrination in service, propaganda, and the desire to avenge dead comrades following the brutalization of combat? Is violence innate in people and more likely to be activated in environmental circumstances, featuring cumulative radicalization and brutalization of combat conditions? What is the role of comradeship and loyalty to fellow soldiers with whom relationships of complicity and mutual dependence are established? Bonds forged in blood and battle are often cemented in experiences that cannot be transferred beyond the primary combat group. How do individuals experience war and how does it affect their subsequent path? To what extent does it create a new war culture, understood here as a set of cultural perceptions concerning a soldier's own side, the enemy, and combat, which become pervasive in civil society during and after the war?

Within the sphere of "new military history," which is largely inspired by social history, new cultural history, and more recently by gender history and the transnational turn,[10] this book also endeavours to update and enrich current debates on Spanish wars of the modern period, from the colonial conflicts of Cuba and Morocco to the Spanish Civil War. The social and cultural history of violence has undergone a late renewal in Spain.[11] Traditional military historiography in Spain was acnhored to the exhaustive study of the Spanish Civil War (1936–9) and the subsequent mass repression by the winning side. As a result, military historians in Spain have only recently joined the tansnational methodological and theoretical debates concerning the Great War and the Second World War. Thus, for example, much of Spanish historiography and foreign historiography on twentieth-century Spain saw the ordinary combatants of both armies (Republican and insurgent or Francoist) during the Civil War as passive protagonists of an armed confrontation. The primary agents were great ideologies, world views in conflict, political parties and trade unions, great political leaders and military chiefs. Therefore, it was implicitly assumed that both sides were already drawn up in July/August 1936. However, the fact is that many soldiers became convinced of the cause they were fighting for during the course of the war. Conviction was an outcome of their war experience and the impact of martial culture in their units, and therefore in their minds.[12] This would also apply to the Blue Division.

Spanish military archives suffer from a scarcity of personal sources or ego-documents such as war diaries and soldiers' letters, even in war censorship collections, that handicaps any approach involving these subjective and everyday dimensions of the conflict. Analytical categories such as "war culture" were scarcely known or empirically assessed in Spanish historiography until the second decade of the twenty-first century. War culture correlates to a key concept in the formulation of this book: war experience and military experience in general, as a rite of passage that irreversibly modifies the perceptions, world view, and basic values of individuals who take part in war. In itself, the experience of war is individually constructed and conditioned by the sociocultural background, values, perceptions, and prior socialization of each combatant. While combat has a similar impact or immediate impression on all participants; the experience reflected by combatants hours or days later in letters or diaries will display palpable differences that reveal diverse encounters with fighting, mental landscapes, and formative background. How each individual summarizes that experience and transmits it weeks or years later will vary even more.[13]

In applying these concepts to the Blue Division, it becomes evident that studying the war experience of Spanish soldiers on the Eastern Front, in the war of extermination unleashed by the Third Reich against the Soviet Union, is inevitably a transnational and comparative endeavour. This perspective involves consulting sources in diverse archives, comparing mutual images of friends and foes, and constantly questioning whether the Spaniards were so typically different from the Germans and their allies as has been claimed in much of pro-Blue Division literature. South of the Pyrennees, this is the prevailing vision in the public sphere regarding Spaniards on the Russian Front, even among critics. It must be continuously contrasted with contributions from professional historiography concerning the experience of German, Soviet (still one of the least-studied aspects, even in Russian historiography), Italian, Dutch, Romanian, Finnish, or Hungarian soldiers on the Eastern Front from 1941 to 1945.

While military operations are not the main object of this study, they are intrinsec to the subject matter. The operational aspects necessary to provide an overview will be addressed mainly from the perspective of German military documentation, to gain a sense of the relative importance of the Blue Division within the armies, army corps, and army groups of the German Ostheer under which it served. This also implies acknowledging that the Spanish soldiers were never an autonomous island on the Volkhov Front and in the siege of Leningrad. Alongside German, Norwegian, Flemish, Baltic, and Dutch combatants, they shared visions of the enemy, experiences or exchanges with the civilian population, and encounters with rearguard societies in Russian, Baltic, or German military hospitals. They endured the climate, the combat conditions, and the dynamics of violence and destruction, from anti-partisan warfare to the deportation of Jews in the rearguard, the shooting of political commissars, and reprisals against civilian populations. These aspects shall be examined comprehensively, focusing on combatants in land units such as infantry and artillery. The experiences of Spanish airmen, seamen, or prisoners of war will not be addressed here. Seamen were a very reduced group, and the war experience of airmen was entirely different, given the nature of their combat conditions.[14] Similarly, prisoners of war in Soviet camps were also a limited group with limited sources, most of which are located in Russian archives.[15]

Whatever their motivation, political adherence, ideas, and experiences, soldiers do not always fight in the same way and for the same reasons. In modern warfare, bravery or heroism are problematic variables, difficult to trace and easy to idealize. Motivation, however, is more constant. Generally speaking, most soldiers enlist for a war – nearby or far away – out of sweeping principles or great ideals. They are borne along in a climate of enthusiasm or by a group of friends or comrades to defend their home or their surrounding environment, to see the world, or to earn a living. A few weeks after entering combat, most combatants keep fighting for their own survival and that of their combat group – from the platoon to the company and the "trench community." Idealist motives lose importance but do not always disappear. The efficiency of a military unit depends largely on motivation and morale, training and skill, the quality of their commanders, and equipment.

The Blue Division was just that: an infantry division of the Wehrmacht. It never covered a sector of the front greater than a few dozen kilometres, which nonetheless often exceeded average BD manpower. The Spanish units performed modestly in combat, but no better or worse than most other military units fighting alongside or against them. Though never a major cog in the strategic machinery of Army Group North, the BD was another tile in the mosaic of the Volkhov Front and the siege of Leningrad. For the German command, always captive to its own prejudices, the Spanish soldiers were individually brave, highly motivated combatants; but they were only reliable for passive defence tasks, coups de main, and small-scale or guerilla fighting. These were considered typically Spanish ways of making war. As a military collective, the Germans saw Spanish soldiers as a badly trained and insufficiently organized unit, led by unprepared officers and NCOs who could not grasp the requirements of modern warfare on the Eastern

Front. The Spanish Blue Division was a constant annoyance to the German high commanders but one they had to tolerate, partly due to diplomatic imperatives, and partly because German human and material recources were continually decreasing from late 1941 on. Though not particularly welcome, Spaniards could not easily be replaced with fresh German troops. However, the German military had no greater appreciation for other foreign legions and units, from Italians to Norwegians (Germanic or otherwise). Spaniards were not undesirable soldiers, but they were not desired.

The evolution of German-Spanish relations from 1941 to 1945 is well known and serves here as a background for discussing the history of the Blue Division.[16] Here, the magnifying lens is applied to military history from below, to the experiences, perceptions, and reinterpretations of cultural models and political slogans by individual combatants, within a general framework determined by war circumstances.[17] Testimonies are crucial to the reconstruction of these perceptions. Key sources include letters, war diaries, unpublished and published memoirs, even fictional accounts based on the author's war experience.[18] Press articles sent from the Russian Front to local and provincial journals constitute a complementary source. These were less subject to censorship and often digressed from the idealized combat rhetoric found in contemporary testimonies of the more prominent BD members: the writers, journalists, and political leaders.

This brings us to the ongoing dialectics between history and memory, between lived experience and war narratives. What many combatants wrote about years and decades later concerning their war experience – training in Germany, the journey to the front, being in the forefront or the rearguard – does not necessarily coincide with what they wrote during the war, in their letters to home or in their war diaries. The BD memory that was cultivated on the Spanish "home front" found its first expression in the cult to fallen soldiers in distant Russian locations, then in the codification of a collective account concerning the BD war experience, and later in the commemorations and activities of veterans' associations, partly endorsed by the Francoist state institutions. It was one shard of the diffuse memory of the Eastern Front that prevailed throughout Europe after 1945. It varied greatly from one country and period to another, encompassing competition between the legacy of Stalingrad and the Auschwitz syndrome, idealization of the Great Patriotic War, comparison of the "two occupations" (German and Soviet), and the (Italian) construction of a "benign occupier" myth.[19]

This book also discusses the specificity and variations of the role of Spain in this transnational memory, which was highly conditioned by two circumstances. First was the exceptional longevity of the Franco regime, a dictatorship with fascist origins. It welcomed the combatants back from the Eastern Front without stigmatizing or judging them, while in other European countries they were seen as traitors. The Franco dictatorship had no qualms about remembering the veterans' heroic deeds in public places and ceremonies. However, this ran parallel to the regime's efforts to realign Spain with Western powers in the context of the Cold War. To this end, the adventures of the Blue Division in Russia were portrayed as a second chapter or an epilogue of the Spanish Civil War, a purely anti-communist endeavour devoid of any association with Nazi extermination policies. Second was the tolerance of the successive democratic governments towards the remnants of that memory from 1977 onwards. Ultimately, they assimilated many features of the positive memory of the Blue Division that had been generated during the previous regime, without engaging in a critical review of its role in the German war of extermination in the East. This persisted in Spanish post-Francoist historical culture and in the public sphere through the first decade of the twenty-first century.

Enemies and Friends: Russia, Germany, and Spanish Fascism (1917–41)

From the Imagined Russian to the Real Russian (1917–41)

Russia constituted an almost unknown land in the Spanish popular imaginary prior to the Revolution of 1917. There were a few exceptions stemming from diplomatic relations between Spain and the Tsarist empire during the first half of the nineteenth century, and more particularly from the literary impressions transmitted by the travel novelist Juan Valera in his *Cartas desde Rusia* (Letters from Russia) in 1857.[20] Thirty years later, these sketches acquired dimension with the dissemination of what is now considered classic Russian literature from authors such as Lev Tolstoy and Fyodor Dostoevsky, along with an analysis of Russian society by the diplomat and historian Julián Juderías. Nevertheless, during the first two decades of the twentieth century, there were few direct mediators between Russia and the Spanish public sphere.[21]

Valera, Juderías and other authors reproduced the image based on the icon of alterity, backwardness and exoticism that characterized the empire of the Tsars in Western popular opinion during the final quarter of the nineteenth century: the pseudo-Asian, fanatic Russia, capable of unimaginable suffering. This neo-romantic vision of Eastern Europe, enhanced by a fascination with the exotic, was itself based on clichés forged by eighteenth-century French Enlightenment authors.

The lasting stereotypes that they consolidated made Russia the realm of barbarians, in contrast with a civilized Europe.[22]

From the early 1920s on, Spanish travellers and visitors to the fledgling Soviet Union transmitted a different image: an exemplary vision of the new "homeland of the proletariat," resurgent from the darkness. Nuances varied according to the ideological leanings of the travellers (socialists, communists, anarchists, or bourgeoisie), but almost all saw the USSR as the construction of a *new* world and an idealized, classless society. Soviet propaganda in Spanish, reports in the workers' press, and radio broadcasts from 1933 on solidified the Soviet myth among much of the left wing.[23]

This representation contrasted with the iconic image crafted by the counter-revolutionary European right wing from 1917–18 on. It superimposed ideological rejection of communism on updated images of alterity, fanaticism, and exoticism, aided by the spread of Russian literature classics from Pushkin to Maxim Gorki. Though some translations had begun to circulate in Spanish magazines in the mid-nineteenth century, most Russian writers found their way into Spanish based on French editions from the 1910s and 1920s and enjoyed notable popularity. The generic terms of this icon of alterity meant that the *Russian* as such was absent from the Spanish public sphere. The typical White Russian refugees of the *belle époque* in Paris did not appear in Spain until the Civil War.[24]

The stereotype corresponded to a familiar typecasting: Soviet communism, in alliance with Freemasonry and Judaism, would destroy Western and Christian civilization, using God's favourite nation – Spain – as a bridgehead. This discourse was updated with the advent of the Second Spanish Republic and spread more intensely after the end of 1935, when the anti-Republican right wing began accusing all Popular Front parties of having sold out for "Moscow gold." *Russia* was identified with the USSR, the incarnation of Evil. It began with a deep resemanticization of the counter-revolutionary image of liberalism and the French Revolution, seasoned with conspiracy theories.[25] By 1936, this icon was fully formed in Spanish fascism, which saw a fundamental continuity between the "oriental" essence of tsarist despotism and the materialist *Russia* that threatened to devour Western civilization.[26]

In a complementary manner, this image of *Russia* also corresponded to a national *other*. However, during the Spanish Civil War, the second function of this mobilizing myth – that of Russia as an adversary of the nation – reached an intensity superior to what had been its first function until then: to incarnate the Antichrist. This melded with the image of the enemy within and semantically reinforced its alterity.[27]

The war nationalism of the insurgents in the 1936–9 Spanish conflict began dehumanizing the enemy via denationalization.[28] Members of the *other* Spain had stopped being Spaniards by betraying the essences of the Homeland, disregarding tradition and national history, selling out to foreignizing ideologies. The traitors could thus be generically categorized as Spaniards infected with a foreign virus. The *other* was defined in moral patriotic and collective terms, but seldom as an explicit social group. The metaphor of *Russians* as communist foreigners reinforced the more general stigmatization of the enemy as *Reds*. Though several dozen Russian anti-communist volunteers, most of them arriving from France, joined forces with the insurgents,[29] the term *Russian* became autonomously effective for bolstering the perception of the conflict as a war against an invader. The ambition of Russia, which "had dreamed of digging its bloody, emblematic sickle into this lovely piece of Europe," had unleashed a war: "the communist and socialist masses of the earth, united with Freemasons and Jews" would use Spain as "a golden stepping-stone to global triumph." The war thus became a new *Reconquista*, a reconquest like that of the Middle Ages.[30]

Though the Civil War had at first been described as an uprising to restore full Spanishness to a Republican regime that had surrendered to "Russian-type anarcho-communist ideals," the involvement of the USSR transformed it in the eyes of Francoist propagandists into a war for national liberation. Spain represented nationalism resisting communism, a global conflict between "the vital reality of the nationalities" and an internationalist ideology. If it prevailed, the world would no longer be divided into nations.[31]

If proletariat internationalism turned into an invading power, all Spanish communists could be considered *Russians*. The features of this conversion were not described in ethno-cultural, but ideological terms.[32] The Republican militia were frequently represented as rough men with Soviet military caps, and Republican loyalists as undercover Russian agents. "Russia" and "Russian" also served as perfect metaphors of all the collective vices that characterized the Republican side from the perspective of the insurgents: poverty, chaos, lack of patriotism, moral vacuity … In their most Catholic version, it simply was the realm of Satan.[33]

The "Russians," however, lacked any specific physical features. Despite the substantial weaponry supplied by the USSR, no more than twenty-two hundred Soviet technicians, pilots, military consultants, and political police set foot on Spanish soil during the Civil War. There was little chance of actually meeting authentic Russians on the front, though insurgent propaganda depicted Republican prisoners with faces like Lenin as exponents of a "poor, decadent race" or as the "Mongol Cossack."[34] In their letters, rebel soldiers quite often alluded to their adversaries as "Russians,"[35] and the stereotype continued circulating into the early post-war years. Catholic writer José María Salaverría described the Russian as a "tavern thug," made doubly undesirable by his impenetrable exoticism and innate deceitfulness, predetermined by the "complexity of his racial make-up, which frequently borders on savagery." When word came of the invasion of the Soviet Union on 22 June 1941, the weekly paper *Mundo* reminded its readers that Spain already knew its adversary, "Russia, which personified its capacity for criminal induction and Satanic complicity."[36]

Hitler, German Nazism, and Spanish Fascism (1930–41)

Italian and German Echoes (1924–36)

In the initial stages of Spanish fascism, the influence of National Socialism was meagre. The first groups drawn to fascism in Madrid and Barcelona in the 1920s were attracted by the shining image of Mussolini's fascism after the March on Rome (October 1922), its removal of liberal political elites, and its mix of revolutionary appeal, avant-garde aesthetics, and charismatic leadership. The prolific intellectual Ernesto Giménez Caballero introduced fascism to the literary avant-garde in Spain after a trip to Rome in 1928. A common appeal to the classic heritage of the Roman Empire also made Spanish fascists feel that they were part of a new resurgence of Catholic-infused Mediterranean Europe. Italy's resurgence became a kind of Holy Grail that awoke in Spanish intellectuals the dream of antiliberal rebirth for the nation.[37]

However, the founders of the first fascist groups in the 1930s, Ramiro Ledesma and Onésimo Redondo, belonged to a younger generation. The rise of NSDAP in Germany from 1929 on decisively coloured their political views, and they were familiar with German language and culture. Ledesma spent four months in Heidelberg in 1930. A self-taught intellectual, he was influenced by the doctrines of Friedrich Nietzsche, Martin Heidegger, and Oswald Spengler. Redondo spent an academic year (1928–9) as Spanish reader at the High School of Commerce in Mannheim, dedicated to the analysis of the political strategies set in motion by German Catholicism. He regarded Hitler as a defender of Christianity against Marxism and advocated an alliance of Hitler with the Zentrum (Catholic Centre Pary) to confront German communism.[38]

From the first issue of his new weekly *La Conquista del Estado* (March 1931), Ledesma gave increasing attention to the trajectory of German National Socialism. Nonetheless, the Juntas de Ofensiva Nacional Sindicalista (JONS), which he founded in October that year, were heavily inspired

by Mussolini's social corporativism. Redondo and his followers in Valladolid, where he had been publishing the weekly journal *Libertad* since June
1931, were also strongly influenced by the Italian corporativist model.
Redondo's group had a more Catholic imprint but voiced anti-Semitic
slogans from the very beginning. The aggressive language and some of
the metaphors they used clearly recalled the tone of Nazi journals such as
Der Stürmer. However, the anti-Semitic content usually remained within
the limits of Catholic anti-Jewish prejudice, which mainly found fault
with the Jewish religion rather than the biological origins of Jews.

Though the echoes from Rome resounded with greater strength in
the ears of Spanish fascists, National Socialism came onstage as a spec-
tacular model of national resurgence. It was grounded in Hitler's hyp-
notizing charisma as a leader who had captured the heart of the people,
as well as his ability to win votes and members from both extremes of
the political spectrum.[39] Fragments of *Mein Kampf* were first translated
in the pages of *Libertad*, which was particularly interested in Nazi agitation strategies.[40]

From February 1933 on, admiration for Hitler spread across the
entire Spanish anti-Republican right wing, from Catholics to monarchists. They saw the new German chancellor as the standard-bearer
of a united anti-Marxist and nationalist front that transcended party
lines. Ledesma considered Hitler a genius of political agitation and a
pragmatic statesman, who had seized power with fewer concessions
to the Church and the conservatives than Mussolini had made earlier.[41]
Spanish fascists most admired how national solidarity had been orches-
trated around a charismatic leader, but they also envied Hitler's bold-
ness in imposing his political will over the constraints of international
law. Germany's rebirth shone as an example for a decadent Spain,[42] and
the first explicitly fascist Spanish weekly journal, *El Fascio*, appeared
in Madrid in March 1933. The journal gathered around it a number of
intellectuals and political activists from the radical right who saw the
Nazi power grab as proof of the irresistible modernity of fascism.[43]

Nazi racism and "paganism" indeed posed a dilemma for some
admirers of Hitler. While detaching themselves from biological anti-
Semitism, some attempted to elaborate a metaphysical theory of national-socialist racism by equating it with the cultural and historical
foundation of nationality. This made it exportable to other countries.[44]
Spanish fascists claimed that Spanish people disliked the Jews and expressed their understanding of the German interpretation of a universal *problem*, which in Spain manifested itself simply as a confessional
issue. Thus, they displayed a benevolent attitude towards the first seg-
regationist measures adopted by the Nazi regime against the Jews.[45]

The first Spanish parafascist and fascist travellers to Nazi Germany propagated similar views.[46] The conservative writer and university professor Vicente Gay visited Germany in 1933. Though he mistrusted biological racism and expressed his preference for a "milder" authoritarianism, he also justified establishment of the first concentration camps as institutions to "re-educate" bad Germans.[47] One year later, Falangist legal expert Juan Beneyto also advocated the need to "delimit" the influence of Jews and Catholics in public affairs as a strategy to "nationalize politics." He saw the new Germany as a new dimension of European identity. The Nazi struggle to overcome "bourgeois" notions of a national state merged with the new idea of race that fed into a new meaning of the term "empire."[48] Other visitors to the Third Reich agreed on that point. Ramón de Rato was a student from a middle-class background who regarded National Socialism as a promising future for European youth, who were besieged by Marxism. Furthermore, the Spanish people were hardly qualified to make moral judgments on Nazi anti-Semitism, because the "Jewish problem" had been absent from Spanish life since 1492.[49] In any event, the Falangist journal Libertad insisted in 1934, the German Führer's anti-communism redeemed his pagan errors:

So far ... the Hitler regime has not won the confidence of the Christian Western world. Yet, all Catholics can at least concede with it that Bolshevic atheism and merciless barbarianism are diametrically opposed to Christ's cause. Since we all agree that the reality of Hitler's presence is a strong barrier against Communist hell: ... Let us Catholics advocate the conversion of protestant or pagan National Socialism, but not its collapse![50]

From January 1933 on, most of the right-wing anti-Republican press was equally sympathetic towards Hitler. The monarchists, proto-fascists, and traditionalists who gathered around the journal Acción Española were good proof of it. German "national rebirth" and the modernity of Nazi mass performances also fascinated Spanish right-wing radicals. They admired how Nazism prioritized the national community over other values.[51] Some members of Acción Española even subscribed to Nazi eugenics theories, but most had reservations about Nazi "paganism" and anti-capitalist rhetoric. They also disliked how the NSDAP had come to power through the ballot boxes; Spanish anti-Republicans preferred a military coup d'état.[52]

Nonetheless, most Spanish fascists still saw the Italian model as the most appropriate option for a Catholic country. Accordingly, the Falange Española (Spanish Phalanx) party (1933–6) devoted much more attention to Italy, and even France, than to Germany. The main Spanish fascist

leader from October 1933, José Antonio Primo de Rivera, was invited by
the NSDAP to visit Germany in May 1934. He met briefly with some of its
leaders, including Hitler himself and Alfred Rosenberg, who recalled the
meeting in his diary two years later. The young Spanish fascist, "clever
and clear-minded; Catholic, not clerical; nationalist, not dynastic," had
impressed him. However, Rosenberg also noted that "the young Primo
de Rivera" had avoided any comment on the Jewish question.[53] On his return to Spain, José Antonio Primo de Rivera was actually rather sceptical
about National Socialism.[54] However, other Spanish fascists also reversed
their initial admiration for National Socialism after having visited Germany. The journalist Antonio Bermúdez-Cañete, who joined the JONS
in 1931 and later abandoned the group, had been attracted by Hitler and
embraced anti-Semitic tenets. After his time (from 1932 to January 1935)
as press correspondent in Berlin, Bermúdez-Cañete ended up repudiating
racism, atheism, and the "socialist" tendencies of National Socialism.[55]

Both the Falange and the combined FE-JONS party after merging
with the JONS (February 1934) looked to Rome rather than to Berlin, especially when they needed external financing. The Falangist poet Federico de Urrutia worked as a journalist for the newspaper *Informaciones*,
which had received subsidies from Berlin since 1934 to propagate anti-Semitic and pro-Nazi propaganda articles.[56] Some German consulates
also distributed Nazi leaflets and books in Spanish to local Falangist
groups. Though strong links also existed between Falangist groups and
local chapters of the NSDAP Foreign Organization branch,[57] German
diplomacy had little if any direct contact with the Falangist leaders. Reich diplomats in Spain were ignorant of the conspiracies to overthrow
the government in the spring of 1936. Meanwhile, Mussolini was making generous donations of money and arms to the military conspiracy
and several of the monarchic and traditionalist leaders involved in it.

Fascinated by the Third Reich (1936–41)

The outbreak of the Spanish Civil War marked a turning point in this
story. It is well known that the military insurgents were able to deliver
their demand for help directly to Hitler in Bayreuth by 25 July 1936.
Germany first sent airplanes, military supplies, and an expeditionary
corps: the Condor Legion, composed mainly of aviators and ground
support personnel. Later on, Germany also provided financial and diplomatic support.[58]

The finest hour of Nazi influence on Spanish fascism was from 1937 to
1942, in tandem with increasing economic, cultural, and diplomatic cooperation between the "new" Spain and the Third Reich. For the Germans,

the relationship was a strategic one. Hitler and his ministers hoped to include Spain in the economic frame of the New European Order, under German guidance. Culture and ideology played a minor, though not irrelevant, role in this, so exchanges increased. Dozens of Falangist leaders and party officials began travelling to Germany in 1937 to strengthen ties with the NSDAP. They used the Nazi Party press and propaganda, along with the youth and women's sections as a model for the Frente de Juventudes (Youth Front) in 1940. The Spanish relief organization Auxilio Social (Social Aid) was also greatly inspired by the German Winterhilfe, and the Bund Deutscher Mädel became a template for enhancing their Female Section.[59] Spanish visitors were usually fascinated by German welfare and social discipline, by the mass rallies, the new motorways, and everything related to technological progress. Their perceptions of German modernity resembled those of many British travellers at that time.[60]

Intellectual exchanges multiplied until 1944: German university towns became a common destination for Spanish academics, such as health experts who spent long periods in Berlin, Munich, or Vienna.[61] The Nazi state attempted to increase its influence on Spanish public opinion by subsidizing daily newspapers and radio stations. Leaflets were distributed presenting Hitler as the saviour of Europe against Bolshevism and a modern Christian knight-protector of civilization.[62] Strong links were forged with Francoist cultural institutions, such as the Instituto de Estudios Políticos (Institute of Political Studies, 1939), through which Nazi ideas on political theory, the social sciences, and, particularly, the philosophy of law could penetrate Spain. These measures had a lasting influence on several of the intellectuals who laid the theoretical foundations of the Francoist "New State."[63]

Strategic cooperation and ideological agreement implied that a portion of the Francoist political and intellectual elite was in tune with the Third Reich. This did not necessarily entail full-fledged identification with German strategic interests, as most Falangists preferred full belligerency. For many supporters of Franco, Germanophile attitudes were not synonymous with National Socialism. Among portions of the Spanish social elites, the military, and the Catholic right there was deep-rooted sympathy for Germany, which could be traced back at least to the First World War. This was reinforced by the political admiration that most of them felt for Hitler, as well as their fascination with the Wehrmacht, but it was not without contradictions. In September 1939, many Falangists were shocked by the signing of the Molotov-Ribbentrop Pact and expressed their disapproval of the Nazi invasion of Catholic Poland.[64]

However, these reservations quickly vanished after the German conquest of France in June 1940. Fascination with the Wehrmacht infected

Falangists, the military, and even many anti-Falangist army officers, who longed to enter the war on the Axis side.[65] Some traditionalists regarded Hitler as the gatekeeper of Christian European civilization against the communist threat. Thousands of "provisional" lieutenants and ensigns, those poorly trained NCOs who had fought in the Francoist army during the Civil War, shared similar views. Most of them adhered to basic values such as tradition, religion, and hierarchy.[66] They admired Germany's military might, which was now directed against France and Great Britain, the alleged "historical enemies" of Spain.

Praise for National Socialism and Hitler multiplied in Falangist propaganda during the early 1940s. He was regarded as a brilliant soldier and a clairvoyant strategist. Anti-Semitic tones were not absent from that rhetoric.[67] The Nazi propaganda machinery continued to fund newspapers, novels, and books. Radical Falangists sometimes approached the German consulates and institutions in search of recognition, while several Falangist groups adopted Nazi symbols and launched boycotts against British interests.[68] One such group, the "Crusaders against Russia," sent a long memorandum to the German ambassador in Madrid in July 1941, asking for Nazi help.[69] As fervent nationalists, however, radical Falangists were reluctant to serve as instruments for German interests. Even those who approached the Third Reich in search of political support hardly dared question Franco's leadership and insisted on preserving the Christian character of Spanish fascism.

In fact, hardly any Spanish National Socialists in Spain in the early 1940s would go so far as to question the mainstream tenets of Catholic fascism. Their radicalized rejection of Jews was still confessional and traditional, but not biologically based. A few authors succumbed to the influence of German eugenics theories and managed to merge biopsychology with the tenets of Cesare Lombroso. Military psychiatrist Antonio Vallejo-Nágera, for example, tried to demonstrate the Semitic origins of the Spanish left and reconcile his sense of biological determinism with an overarching concept of *Hispanidad* – Spanishness – based on culture and religious confession.[70]

In 1939–40, there were many "ordinary Spaniards" from different social and political backgrounds who openly sympathized with the Third Reich. Dozens of them took it upon themselves to write to the German embassy in Madrid on the occasion of the Führer's birthday (20 April) in 1940 and 1941. Several more letters arrived at the embassy after the German conquest of France. These moments coincided with Spanish declarations of non-belligerency and the Falangist offensive to increase its power within the regime. Many more letters were received after 22 June 1941, when the Wehrmacht invaded the Soviet Union. The senders of these missives belonged to the middle and lower-middle classes: liberal professionals, civil servants, civilian employees, and blue-collar workers.[71] Many of them were Civil War veterans of the Francoist army and had been victims of "Red Terror." They saw Hitler as their avenging angel. Such expressions of pro-German enthusiasm suggest that German propaganda efforts found a sympathetic audience "from below," and not only in radical Falangists.[72]

Certainly, the letters fit with the general climate of scepticism towards liberal democracy, the admiration for German power, and the confused expectations of authoritarian regeneration that spread across continental Europe during the second half of 1940.[73] In non-belligerent Spain, this trend had its own particular flavour. Some were grateful for German support during the Spanish conflict. Others acknowledged that the Third Reich was about to defeat Spain's main "historical enemies." Still others regarded the German Führer as the architect of a European New Order that Spain would enrich with its Catholic imprint.[74] Many also adhered to the fight against liberal democracy and "Judaism," which they equated with international capitalism.[75]

"Popular" Spanish enthusiasm for Hitler climaxed at the beginning of Operation Barbarossa, though the motivations of Germanophiles before and after 1941 scarcely changed. Spanish fascists ratified their earlier admiration for Hitler. Radical Falangists still expected that joining the German war effort would enable them to fulfil their aspirations of wielding full power within the regime. Catholics and some monarchists regarded the Wehrmacht as God's instrument to slay the "reincarnation of Lucifer" (communism) and teach Britain a hard lesson. They also hoped that through this fight against the Antichrist, Nazi Germany would redeem itself from the original sin of its pagan nature. Once "the Beast" had been destroyed, the Third Reich would experience religious conversion.[76] Carlist traditionalists, the most reluctant to accept Nazi atheism, also joined the pro-Germany fervour in hopes of "annihilating communism" alongside the rest of the "Christian world."[77] The world war represented a fight between democracy, as the cradle of communism, and the nations who understood their "historical destiny."[78] Unlike the Falangists, however, the Carlists insisted on their Germanophile stance during the Second World War but avoided reference to the charismatic leadership of Hitler, who was now merely regarded as the Kaiser's heir.[79]

2 Russia Is Guilty!

Extermination and Brutalization: Operation Barbarossa and a Different Kind of War

On 22 June 1941, 19 armoured divisions, 14 motorized divisions, and 119 infantry divisions of the Wehrmacht and the Waffen-SS, along with some Romanian troops, invaded the Soviet Union without warning. Altogether, 3,300,000 men, 3,325 armoured vehicles, 600,000 vehicles, and 625,000 horses participated in the Axis campaign. It began with strikingly different features from those of other fronts where the German Army was or had been engaged. Until then, on the Western Front and in Norway, North Africa, and part of the Balkans, the Wehrmacht had generally complied with the norms of the Geneva Convention. On the Eastern Front, however, the Third Reich unleashed a qualitatively different type of war against the communist world view, which it sought to eradicate by exterminating its defenders. It was a war against a people or a set of peoples – Russians, Slavs, and others – considered racially inferior based on biological postulates. After eliminating the "excess" portion of the population, the remainder would be reduced to semi-slavery and to provisioning the Third Reich with raw materials or food. Meanwhile the Jewish population, which had been shut into ghettos, would be killed en masse. After adoption of the "Final Solution" in January 1942, this involved systematic deportation to extermination camps.[1]

The armed units under direct Nazi command – the SS and the task forces or Einsatzgruppen – were not the only ones responsible for the extermination. The regular Wehrmacht forces also participated in this ethnic cleansing, and not always in a secondary capacity. In Berlin on 30 March 1941, Hitler himself had informed almost 250 Wehrmacht generals, the commanders of the troops committed to Operation Barbarossa, of his war plans. These included the generals in command of the three Army Groups (Heeresgruppen) of the Ostheer (North, Centre, and South), the Luftwaffe groups, the commanders of the armoured corps and the Chiefs of the General Staff. Hitler explained his racial world view and revealed that the campaign would be one of extermination, as the "Bolshevik commissars and the communist *intelligentsia*" had to be eliminated. The Wehrmacht should not consider the Bolshevik as a "comrade, as was usual on other fronts." This was a war of "two opposing world views" and would have a completely different nature.[2] Most of the generals demonstrated conformity; though few were Nazis, they shared a demonized vision of Bolshevism and a cultural contempt for the Slavic peoples. Additionally, they saw that the conquest of the Eastern Empire – a vision they had cherished since the end of the nineteenth century – was finally within their reach.[3]

Hitler's intentions were summed up shortly after in a series of instructions that were issued to the troops just prior to invasion, which a historiographer later dubbed as the "criminal orders." They had originated in directives dictated by the Führer on 18 December 1940 – there were four in the final version – which were discussed on several occasions by the High Command of the Wehrmacht (Oberkommando der Wehrmacht, OKW) and the High Command of the Army (Oberkommando des Heeres, OKH).[4] These involved the following:

1. The regulation of Einsatzgruppen activity, or task forces under the SS and SD. This collaboration agreement was communicated to the troops on 28 April 1941. Based on their partnership since the conquest of Poland, the Einsatzgruppen were authorized to operate freely within the areas controlled by the Wehrmacht. These units carried out the execution of certain population groups, Jews in particular. They could act with complete autonomy, answering to the regular army only in matters of basic logistics (lodging and supplies). Operation Barbarossa constituted the final thrust towards the irreversible radicalization of anti-Semitic politics in the Third Reich. The large Jewish populations living in occupied territories led the Nazi leaders to ponder what was to be done about them. This became yet another stepping stone on the path that had been initiated in the spring of 1939. At that time, Hitler had authorized the annihilation of physically and mentally disabled people in the Reich, then approved "savage euthanasia" programmes. Tens of thousands of Polish civilians were executed, in a process that apparently culminated one year later with plans to exterminate the millions of Soviet citizens caught up in Operation Barbarossa.

In July 1941, Hitler informed Reinhard Heydrich that the time had come for the definitive extermination of the Jews. These execution orders involved the serious logistical challenge of killing tens of thousands of people efficiently. Therefore, a new step was taken. Several experiments were carried out with prisoners of war from September to December 1941. Camps and crematoriums were prepared, and transportation was organized to implement the objective of annihilating all the Jews in the European territory dominated by the Third Reich. Operations would begin in January 1942, involving a process of systematic deportation and murder that would utilize the camps designed specifically for this purpose, along with special extermination units in Soviet territory.[5]

As Operation Barbarossa was unleashed, the Einsatzgruppen corps, composed of some three thousand men distributed into four areas (A, B, C, and D) followed in the rearguard in order to identify, gather, and execute all Jewish males affiliated with the Soviet regime.[6] Soon their objective expanded to include all Jews. The clear majority of Soviet Jews were killed during the first nine months of the war, before the extermination camp system became operative. The number of Einsatzgruppen victims was certainly no fewer than three hundred thousand people, along with another fifty thousand victims of the SS and Order Police (Ordnungspolizei). Added to these were the victims of the Wehrmacht units, local occupying authorities and auxiliary forces, Jewish war prisoners, thousands of Jewish civilians killed through starvation and disease in the ghettos, and more than 150,000 victims in the territory under Romanian control.[7]

To what degree did the soldiers of the Wehrmacht participate in the killing and mass deportation of the Jewish population in the East? All combatants knew that the ethnic community to which Nazism aspired excluded the Jewish people, and all were exposed to a constant barrage of propaganda equating communism with Judaism and Asian barbarism.[8] Annihilation was therefore an option. This representation of reality took root among many soldiers. When combined with the state of war and brutalizing conditions, it paved the way for the transition from order to execution.[9] There was close collaboration among German civil and economic administrations, the police, the SS, and Wehrmacht command.[10]

2. Prior to invasion of the USSR, German troops received the "Directives for Troop Conduct in Russia" ("Richtlinien für das Verhalten der Truppe in Russland"), from the OKW on 19 May 1941. These directives defined Bolshevism as "the mortal enemy of the German national socialist people," thereby justifying "forceful and ruthless procedures" against "agitators, guerrillas, saboteurs and Bolshevik Jews" and "total elimination of all passive or active resistance." In

addition to specifying who was to be eliminated (Jews, Communist Party members, partisans), these orders instructed German soldiers to treat prisoners of the Red Army ruthlessly: a portion of them were to be killed, and the rest were to be exploited to exhaustion. Such treatment of captives relaxed somewhat after May 1942, partly because of the growing need to utilize prisoners as a workforce for the Reich. By that time, Soviet prisoner deaths due to mistreatment, executions, malnourishment, and illnesses numbered between 1.6 and 1.9 million (out of 3.5–3.8 million total).[11]

3. The "Guidelines for the Treatment of Political Commissars" or "Commissar Order" (Kommissarbefehl), dated 8 June 1941, stated that Red Army commissars were to be "disposed of" immediately following their capture, after being separated from the rest of the prisoners. Such a procedure was justified by stating that these were members of the Communist Party: not just soldiers, but "central to the resistance," leaders of an all-out war with no rules. The execution of commissars ended up being operationally counterproductive, but the order was only revoked on 6 May 1942, after several thousand commissars had been executed. By then, those who remained had lost influence in the Red Army and had become radicalized in their pugnacity, aware that they would receive no mercy from the Germans.[12]

4. The "Decree of the Führer regarding the Exercise of Military Jurisdiction in the Barbarossa Area," dated 13 May 1941, was communicated orally to German officers, who were given freedom of action regarding partisans and civilians suspected of aiding them. Officers would judge whether the soldiers' abuse of civilians endangered military discipline and punish them accordingly. To avoid pillaging, this order was not immediately communicated to the combatants; instead, it was disseminated hierarchically from the division command down to the lower units as they advanced into conquered territory.[13]

Just a few division generals, as well as Marshall Fedor von Bock, resisted complying with these orders.[14] Throughout the campaign, the instructions were supplemented with orders enacted by the heads of the military corps. They painted a dehumanized and racially prejudiced image of the enemy, associated Judaism with Bolshevism, and urged the combatants to act without mercy. The Ostheer High Command, with a few exceptions, participated in the war of extermination, allowed others to do so, or turned a blind eye. The "criminal orders" significantly affected the ordinary soldiers. Propaganda directed at the troops communicated anti-Semitic and anti-Slavic leitmotifs; the trench journals habitually insisted on the need to annihilate the "Red subhumans" and clear Europe of Jews. German soldiers were not to forget that they exemplified a superior race that aspired to dominion over other peoples.[15]

Four out of every five German soldiers fought on the Eastern Front from 1941 to 1944. It was the scene of a murderous war, both in its conception and execution. Adding to the brutality of battle were harsh physical conditions and the bitter resistance of the Red Army, which slowed and then halted German progress in October–November 1941, less than one hundred kilometres from Moscow. At this point, the invaders were faced with a new set of obstacles: an intolerably cold winter followed by snowmelt that turned roads to mud; the constant presence of partisans in the rearguard; and a war of positions that ended the comparative advantage that the Wehrmacht had hitherto enjoyed. They had concentrated firepower in small areas and made swift advances with motorized and armoured divisions, thereby surrounding their enemies. The brutal fighting conditions surpassed those experienced in 1914–18. The number of casualties from enemy fire, frostbite, and illness far surpassed anything the German Army had previously experienced. By the end of 1941, Wehrmacht reserves were considerably reduced.

The brutalization of warfare was apparent in how the German soldiers treated civilians and resulted in a departure from military discipline. The intense Nazi indoctrination had made the soldiers particularly receptive to viewing the Slavic people as *Untermenschen*: subhumans.[16] Two main positions exist in the recent historiographic debate on the subject. Some authors argue that the increasingly miserable combat conditions, the brutality of what had become a war of attrition, and the camaraderie among German soldiers decisively precipitated the spiral of increasing violence in the East. From this situationist perspective, the environmental conditions on the Eastern Front did greater damage than any ideological predisposition of the soldiers towards violence against civilians or dehumanization of the enemy. It led to cumulative radicalization of war violence in practice.[17] For other authors, the deciding factor in the increasing radicalization of violent practices by regular Wehrmacht combatants was their perception of the conditions on the Eastern Front. As this perception had been conditioned by years of Nazi socialization and indoctrination, the soldiers were already relatively predisposed (compared to other national contingents) to dehumanizing their enemy based on biological-racial postulates and to treating both civilians and prisoners (Slavs or Jews) violently.[18] Alternatively, some historians have suggested that combat units treated civilians and prisoners differently according to situational factors. Though not an exclusive pattern, brutality towards non-combatants tended to increase with more brutal combat conditions.[19]

Allies in the "European Crusade against Bolshevism"

The troops participating in Operation Barbarossa were not exclusively German. Finnish and Romanian allies, motivated largely by territorial interests, provided no less than seven hundred thousand soldiers from the start of the campaign. The Finnish Army saw the German attack against the USSR as an opportunity to recover territory that had been lost to the Red Army in the Winter War of 1939–40. The Helsinki government sided with Hitler and declared war on the USSR on 25 June 1941.

Finnish intervention was mainly restricted to the northern flank in the siege of Leningrad, which contributed to blocking off the city. This participation was presented as a second act (the "Continuation War") to the Soviet aggression of 1939. For this reason, the Finnish Army exhibited no interest in advancing beyond their former border. Although the Helsinki government sent around three hundred thousand armed men to assist the Axis powers and made relevant logistical contributions in the Karelian region and in the siege of Leningrad, Finnish troops refrained from advancing into Soviet territory. In September 1944, following the siege of Leningrad, Finland signed its own peace accord with the USSR, renounced its claim to the territories lost in 1939–40, and assumed high reparation costs. Around eighty-four thousand Finnish soldiers and civilians lost their lives in this conflict; they were subsequently hailed as heroes.[20]

For the pro-fascist regime of Marshal Ion Antonescu in Romania, participation in Operation Barbarossa fit two objectives: reconquering the region of Bessarabia, which had previously been annexed by the USSR, and showing support for Hitler's New Order. This would ensure a favourable disposition in Berlin to Romanian territorial claims against their neighbours, as the northern third of Transylvania had been surrendered to Hungary the prior year, and a part of Dobrogea to Bulgaria. The OKW was highly sceptical about an army with such outdated weaponry but needed Romanian cooperation to invade Ukraine. They chose to create a combined Army Corps to which Romania contributed over 325,000 soldiers. Its main role was to clear the rearguard following the advance of German motorized units. In the fall of 1941, Romanians conquered Odessa and annexed the region of Transnistria, between the Bug and Dniester Rivers, which was much larger than the territories of Northern Bukovina and Bessarabia. The Romanian army also was requisitioned for the offensive of the summer of 1942. In this way, the Antonescu regime tied its fate to that of the Third Reich. In the Battle of Stalingrad, the Soviets obliterated two Romanian armies stationed at the Don Front. From then until their capitulation in September 1944, Romanian troops were tasked with defensive efforts.[21]

Within a few days after Germany invaded the USSR, Hungary, Italy, and Slovakia began to demonstrate interest in dispatching troops to the East. Puppet states and allies of the Third Reich wanted to play their part in hopes of receiving territorial shares in the envisioned "reordering" of the Continent under German control. Helping to exterminate the common enemy provided fascist governments with support for their own imperialist or irredentist dreams. It also dissuaded neighbouring countries from attempting to reclaim territories at their expense.[22]

Mussolini was first; he had been preparing to participate from the moment he learned of the plans for invasion. In August, the Corpo di Spedizione Italiano in Russia entered combat in Ukraine. Originally consisting of 62,000 men and 82 planes, when reinforcements from the 8th Italian Army arrived at the Don Front, well equipped with light and heavy artillery, they numbered 229,000 men altogether.[23] Slovakia, a satellite state, declared war on the USSR and sent nearly fifty thousand men to the Eastern Front, organized into two infantry divisions and one motorized brigade. Most of these men were removed at the end of July; those who remained were dispatched to the antipartisan fight in Byelorussia (today's Belarus) or to a "mobile division" in Crimea.[24] The puppet state of Croatia also dispatched to the East a symbolic contingent of five thousand soldiers. They were incorporated into the German 6th Army, which arrived at the front in late August 1941. Fear that Italy would be rewarded with territories in the Adriatic acted as a strong incentive for Croatia to demonstrate war merit.

The authoritarian regime of Miklós Horthy in Hungary did not participate in the invasion, but it declared war on the USSR several days later. Horthy and the Hungarian fascists feared that the Antonescu regime would demand devolution of Northern Transylvania in reward for Romanian participation in the war effort. As many as 93,115 soldiers were dispatched to the Eastern Front in August 1941, but heavy losses in the first month led the OKW to send the Magyars to fight against the partisans instead. However, faced with the depletion of his reserves in early 1942, Hitler requested a larger deployment of Hungarian troops to reinforce his summer offensive. The Hungarian 2nd Army, composed of 210,000 soldiers, was deployed on the Don Front. Lacking adequate equipment and experienced officers, the Hungarians were crushed by a Soviet offensive in January 1943. Some forty thousand men lost their lives and sixty thousand more were captured. Though this decreased the confidence of the German command in their allies, it did not prevent them from dispatching ninety thousand more soldiers to the Eastern Front through August 1944. Magyar participation increased after the German occupation of Hungary in March 1944. The Hungarian

1st Army was deployed to defend its borders in April and May, and 950,000 Hungarian soldiers fought the Red Army in September 1944.[25]

Although German troops were always a majority in the invaders' army during the Eastern campaign, allied troops of the "anti-Bolshevik" coalition contributed significantly, at times accounting for almost a fourth of total troops. In some sectors of the front corresponding to Army Groups Centre and South, non-Germans represented almost half of the men. In September 1942, the number of non-German invading soldiers reached 648,000. German troop in the Eastern forces ranged from 82.74 per cent in 1941, to 72.3 per cent in June 1942, to 88.55 per cent in July 1943, and 74.77 per cent in June 1944. The percentage of German combatants climbed to 95.7 per cent in January 1945, no longer joined by Hungarians or Romanians.[26]

Many officers of the Axis-allied armies were fiercely anti-Semitic and carried out their own ethnic cleansing projects. In mid-December 1941, the Romanian army began deporting and exterminating the Jewish population with the help of auxiliary Ukranian and German forces and Einzatsgruppe D. Several concentration camps were built for the Jews of mainland Romania, with victims numbering from 250,000 to 400,000. Since late 1942, Antonescu authorized the emigration of Romanian Jews to Palestine, but also sent thousands to work camps.[27] Several Hungarian units also participated in executing Soviet Jews, though not systematically.[28]

European Volunteers against Bolshevism: Myth and Reality

While Third Reich ally and satellite states contributed regular troops to the Eastern campaign, large numbers of foreign volunteers from Northern and Western Europe also joined the Axis forces. Nazi propagandists brandished defence of European civilization against "Asian" Bolshevism as their leitmotif in propaganda directed at fascist, ultranationalist, and anti-communist circles throughout Europe. They justified invasion of the USSR as a "preventative" measure against Stalin's probable plan to conquer Europe.

Foreign SS brigades and divisions were the object of much fascination and mythification in the post-war period. Neo-fascist propagandists and veterans have presented them as direct predecessors to NATO, as they were both "European" and "anti-communist." In reality, the actual contribution and combat capacity of these foreign units varied greatly. Nazi Europeanism was rhetorical: the goal of continental unity was subordinated to the envisioned hegemony of the Third Reich. Though Hitler, Himmler, and the rest of the Nazi hierarchy pursued the primary objective of a German empire extending to the

Urals, the Europeanist label served as a useful propagandistic tool for fostering goodwill outside of Germany.[29] From the beginning of Operation Barbarossa, Minister of Propaganda Joseph Goebbels clearly saw the possibilities associated with anti-communist public opinion across the Continent.[30] The war thus became, according to a proclamation of the Ministry of Foreign Affairs in late June 1941, a "European crusade against Bolshevism," which included "allies, neutral countries, and even those who had recently crossed swords with Germany."[31]

The New European Order program was developed in 1939–40 and accepted in political and intellectual circles sympathetic to the Third Reich. The "Anti-Komintern" pact, which was renewed in Berlin on 25 November 1941, presented the "anti-Bolshevik crusade" as a common endeavour from which a new Europe would emerge, united under German hegemony. Nazi Europeanist doctrines consisted mainly of generic ideas that the fascist intelligentsia adapted to their own world view. Using German slogans such as "living space" and "Christian West," they reimagined the specific roles of their respective countries from diverse positions within this New Order.[32] For many anti-communists, fascists, or fascistized conservatives across the Continent, participating in the invasion of the USSR presented an opportunity to cement their alliance with the Third Reich and gain greater influence within their own countries. This "crusade" also swayed many anti-communists who saw Hitler as an instrument for wiping out the Soviet threat, despite their distrust of Nazi atheism. Catholicism was a common trait among many European volunteers, along with the belief that communism had been created by Jews, freemasons, and inferior peoples.

Individual and collective enlistment first surprised the OKW and the Ministry of Foreign Affairs. On 30 June 1941, several representatives of the Ministry of Foreign Affairs, the OKW, the NSDAP, and the SS met in Berlin. They agreed that it was politically beneficial to accept these volunteers. At first, they were given German uniforms and placed within national units. However, a clear ethnonational hierarchy was established. Beginning in 1940, Nordic and other "Germanic" volunteers (such as the Dutch and Flemish) were incorporated into the Waffen-SS – the SS armed units (Schutzstaffel or assault brigades) under Heinrich Himmler.[33] Spanish and Croatian volunteers were placed into homogenous units in the Wehrmacht. French and Walloon volunteers were more challenging to resolve, but Czech, "White" Russian, and non-Russian USSR volunteers were refused. One week later, the OKW established some guidelines for the formation of foreign volunteer units.[34]

Following the stabilization of the Eastern Front, mobilization stemming from the "European crusade against Bolshevism" allowed the

Third Reich to recruit soldiers from almost all occupied or neutral European states. Their slogans continued to exalt the defence of European civilization against "Asian" communism, and on a second tier, against Judaism as a threat to European nations.[35] Hundreds of volunteers were recruited for the Russian Front, under the control of national fascist parties and even the regular army in some cases.[36] The Legion of French Volunteers (LVF) drew its recruits from sympathizers and members of the main fascist and collaborationist parties. This unit never exceeded four thousand men; it was only used in late November 1941 for some front-line fighting, and then moved to the antipartisan fight. Walloon volunteers were mostly sourced from the autochthonous Rexist Party, a fascist and Catholic movement led by Léon Degrelle. The 373rd Walloon Infantry Battalion initially numbered barely a thousand and entered combat as part of Army Group South. By September 1941, a total of twenty-four thousand French, Spanish, Walloon, and Croatian volunteers had joined the Ostheer forces. Over 70 per cent of them were Iberian.

Twelve thousand more volunteers originating from "Germanic" peoples were assigned to the ranks of the SS. By April 1940, Himmler had received permission to create the multinational SS Wiking Division. A total of 1,564 Germanic volunteers in this division were organized into the Nordland (Nordic countries) and Westland (Flemish and Dutch) regiments. Beginning in 1940, several dozen Finnish volunteers were also incorporated into the SS Das Reich Division. These modest contingents numbered far fewer than Nazi leaders had expected. In June 1941, the SS Reichsführer set the Waffen-SS European expansion project in motion. Himmler's model also incorporated political indoctrination, by which the soldiers became propaganda agents for the New Order upon returning to their countries. As a result, the influx of Germanic volunteers increased notably but never drastically. There were two recruitment paths: one by which certain groups were directly conscripted into the Waffen-SS, and another by which combatants were drafted into national legions under the SS umbrella. Collaborationist parties from occupied territories were more prominent in the latter group. This gave rise to the Dutch, Flemish, Norwegian, and Danish legions. By the end of 1941, 4,814 Dutchmen, 2,399 Danes, 1,882 Norwegians, 1,571 Flemish, 1,180 Finns, 39 Swedes, and 135 Swiss and Liechtensteiners had been included in the Waffen-SS, along with 6,200 ethnic Germans recruited from Eastern and Central Europe, Luxembourg, Alsace-Lorraine, and Denmark.

Until September 1943, preference was shown for "Germanics" and Scandinavians. By the end of 1941, over thirty-six thousand foreign volunteers from around Europe had enlisted in the Wehrmacht and

Waffen-SS, not counting ethnic Germans. This was not a large contribution in military terms, amounting to barely 1 per cent of troops stationed on the Eastern Front. Germanic and especially ethnic German volunteers (*Volksdeutsche*) increased in 1942 and 1943. The Waffen-SS had recruited 27,314 combatants from Western and Northern Europe by late 1943.[37] Through May 1944, Dutch troops numbered between 20,000 and 23,000, along with 10,000 Flemish and almost 6,000 Danish and 6,000 Norwegian recruits. Italians within the Waffen-SS numbered over 15,000.[38] While they certainly never constituted more than 10–12 per cent of the total corps, estimates vary regarding the global contingent of volunteers from Western and Northern Europe who fought in the Wehrmacht and Waffen-SS during the war. Including Spaniards, who comprised more than 40 per cent of the volunteers, the total number could be situated at around 115,000 men. This represented 1.15 per cent of total invading soldiers between 1941 and 1945. However, one estimate states that up to 400,000 of the 900,000 soldiers composing the Waffen-SS contingent were foreigners, separated into two categories: around 200,000 "ethnic Germans," and volunteers from Western and Northern Europe (61,000 as of January 1944) along with Eastern and Balkan Europe, the Caucasus, and other non-Russian areas of the Soviet Union.[39]

The operational efficiency of the new "crusaders" was questionable. They were all under surveillance to impede desertion or espionage. The Germans often imposed restrictive medical exams and attempted to "Germanize" their command as much as possible. Political rivalries among different fascist and collaborationist factions also chipped away at the internal cohesion of some volunteer corps. Adventurers, military men motivated by nationalism and anti-communism, and fascist fanatics all coexisted within these units. Transylvanian Germans, for one, were attracted by the idea of good salaries, anti-communism, and being members of an elite corps.[40]

Himmler gained the control of the foreign volunteer units in mid-1943, with the intention of turning the Waffen-SS into a pan-Germanic army.[41] Several regiments were reconverted into units with pompous names that had little to do with their actual numbers.[42] Volunteer SS formations, or legions, of Danes, Norwegians, Dutchmen, and Flemish soldiers thus became part of a "Germanic" Panzer Corps and were divided accordingly into the Panzergrenadier-Division Nordland (Danes and Norwegians), the SS-Brigade Nederland – which became the 34th SS Landstorm Division after February 1945 – and the Langemarck Assault Brigade, which later became the 27th SS Langemarck Division (Flemish). Wallonia was considered a "Frenchified Germanic" region and the Walloon Division, commanded by Degrelle, was incorporated in November 1944. These were followed by other nationalities, mainly Latin peoples, recruited through the usual channels and assigned to legions, SS brigades, and divisions. The French volunteer unit coexisted with a new Assault Brigade, and the combined remains of both units (along with some new recruits) became the Charlemagne Division eleven months later. The 1st Italian SS Brigade also became a division in March 1945.

In addition to pay and subsidies to the families of volunteers, SS propaganda from 1944 on emphasized the European nature of the war and cast volunteers as examples of anti-communist, Europeanist, and in some cases anti-Semitic self-sacrifice.[43] However, apart from fascists and anti-communists flocking to the ranks of the Waffen-SS, many recruits from 1943 on enlisted for more prosaic reasons. There were zeitgeist adventurers caught up in the clash of civilizations, common delinquents, convicts seeking to reduce their sentences, French and Belgian prisoners of war, and many foreign workers in Germany – mainly French, Dutch, Walloon, or Flemish – who saw an opportunity to improve their status and salary by joining the Waffen-SS. Fascist parties and collaborationist groups from France, Belgium, Holland, and Italy seeking refuge in German territory from 1944 on became the final pool for reserves. Until the Battle of Berlin (April/May 1945), many of these parties had no other recourse than to tie their fate to that of the Third Reich.

The non-Germanic peoples came next. A Croatian SS Division consisting mainly of Bosnian Muslim volunteers (1st Croatian Handschar Division) and some Kosovars was created in February 1943 to combat partisans. Later, an Albanian unit was formed (the Skanderberg Division), mainly recruited from Albano-Kosovars, which the Nazis viewed as a pseudo-Germanic warrior race.[44] Non-Russian peoples under Soviet dominion were also accepted and became the largest, most relevant group from a military perspective. The fates of the separate USSR nationalities in the New Order had already been decided. Hitler had no intention of giving the Baltic countries back their independence, and their recruits were subsumed into the Reichskommisariat Ostland, nor did he envision sovereignty for the Ukraine. The need for troops and auxiliary units in the rearguard drove the Nazis to recruit these "inferior" nationalities into the *Ostheer* and later the Waffen-SS. By the second half of 1941, the occupying forces were attempting to recruit non-Russian Soviet prisoners as well, thousands of whom seized the opportunity to escape an otherwise blighted fate. Some of these men joined antipartisan bands, others helped to exterminate Jews.[45]

The Turkmens, Crimean Tatars, and other Caucasians were initially incorporated into German divisions and placed under the command of

German officers. They began to form their own units in mid-1942 and numbered over 150,000 by 1943. Baltic and Ukrainian combatants were then admitted into the Waffen-SS.[46] A Turkic Division was formed that included Muslims in Soviet territory, including Crimean and Volga Tatars, Azeris, and Turkmen, along with two more Ukrainian divisions and another Waffen-SS Division recruited from Ukrainian nationalists. Around 150,000 Estonians, Latvians, and Lithuanians were also conscripted to serve in the rearguard and in the antipartisan fight. There were even some exotic units, including Hindu and Buddhist volunteers in the Wehrmacht and Waffen-SS. An Armenian legion was formed in the summer of 1942 that fought in the Caucasus, followed by a Georgian unit.[47]

The Cossacks became the ethnic group that contributed most combatants to the Wehrmacht. Hoping to create an independent republic, they fought partisans until 1943, when Hitler authorized the formation of a Cossack Division. Some thirty-thousand Cossacks fought on the front, and two hundred thousand more served as auxiliary troops.[48] Finally, the Russian Liberation Army (RLA) was originally composed of prisoners and mercenaries under the command of General Andrey Vlasov, who had been captured in 1942. With the consent of Nazi leaders, Vlasov created a Committee for the Liberation of the Peoples of Russia in December of the same year, as he envisioned an anti-communist Russia. Despite Hitler's reluctance, in September 1944 Vlasov gained the support of some SS intellectuals and even Himmler. Two newly formed RLA divisions were dispatched to Prague in March 1945; two months later, they sided with the Czechs against the Germans. However, after being subdued by the Soviets, most were executed or condemned to forced labour.[49]

Spanish Volunteers against the USSR: Recruitment, Sending, and the Nature of the Blue Division

Francoist Spain was not about to be left behind in the wave of anti-communist enthusiasm that swept through neutral and occupied Europe. On the night of 21 June 1941 – just before the German invasion of the USSR – Foreign Minister Ramón Serrano-Suñer dined with Falangist leaders Dionisio Ridruejo and Manuel Mora-Figueroa in Madrid. Serrano, who knew of the imminent German attack, disclosed his project: to create an "expeditionary corps of volunteers to fight Russia" the moment war broke out. Ridruejo and Mora-Figueroa were both favourable to this plan but wanted to confer more than mere anti-communist symbolism on the troops, so details were discussed. At six in the morning, Serrano Suñer received the official German statement.[50]

Events moved quickly.[51] Serrano presented the project to Franco, who approved it. The German ambassador was subsequently informed of the Spanish design to contribute with "some Falangist units" to the "fight against the common enemy, in remembrance of German fraternal aide in the Spanish Civil War," though Spain would not officially abandon non-belligerency. Rumours had already been circulating for several days and the Spanish military was restless. As Operation Barbarossa was anticipated to be another blitzkrieg, a Falangist initiative would politically reinforce the most radical sectors of the single party, who saw this as an opportunity to overcome the defeat they had suffered in the ministerial reordering of May 1941. The rise of José Luis de Arrese to general secretary of the FET-JONS (the new single party after the unification of the Fascist FE-JONS with Traditionalists in March 1937) had undermined the Falangist totalitarian project, which had lost out to Franco's consolidation of personal power and that of the Catholics, supported by most of the military. However, participation in the Russian campaign would strengthen Serrano Suñer's position, so several military commanders expected to meet with Franco in hopes of swaying his opinion.[52]

The Spanish proposal was accepted two days later in Berlin. The Germans subsequently expressed to Serrano their desire for Spain to declare war on the USSR, as Italy had done.[53] Pressure from military leaders created friction with the Falange; Army Minister General José E. Varela wanted to send a regular unit without any specific political colour. The Falange Political Council was divided on this issue. In the end, they expressed preference for a contingent of twenty thousand Falangists: "70% ex-combatants, 10% trustworthy personnel affiliated with the single party." The remainder was left undefined and military ranks were granted to leaders who volunteered.[54] Serrano Suñer wanted clear Falange prominence but was concerned that such a decision might lead the Allies to declare war on Spain.

Franco chose an intermediate solution. The Council of Ministers gathered on 23–4 June and approved the creation of a Spanish Division. It would consist of no more than fifty thousand men, led by army officers, with troops recruited by the FET Militia from among Falangist volunteers and others.[55] The entire Spanish Air Force officer corps volunteered together for the Russian Front and Air Force Minister General Juan Vigón offered to send forty-five trained pilots along with land personnel. The navy minister also visited the German ambassador to offer troops to the Reich.[56]

Once again, events unfolded quickly. On 24 June, the Falange organized a demonstration that crossed Madrid to the party headquarters,

where Serrano Suñer rallied the demonstrators with a fervent improvised speech stating that "Russia is guilty." Guilty of what? Of José
Antonio Primo de Rivera's death in November 1936, and of causing the
Spanish Civil War. The communist "Russian" was close to capitulation;
now was the time for definitive retaliation. Many of the demonstrators
made their way to the British embassy, where they damaged property,
then moved on to the German consulate to declare their support. Similar incidents occurred in other cities as well. Parallel Falange-organized
demonstrations took place in other cities and towns on the same
afternoon of 24 June and carried on through the next day. Although
public attendance was scarce in Santa Cruz de Tenerife, the numbers in
Seville, Málaga, and Alicante reflected great enthusiasm, according to
the German consuls.[57]

On the night of 25 June, all provincial FET leaders were issued instructions to organize recruitment for an expedition to the Russian Front as
soon as possible. Volunteers should preferably be selected from among
the best Falangists, whether in terms of military training or political-moral
fibre. Army officers with "a Falangist spirit" were also welcome. Combatants had to be twenty to twenty-eight years of age and pass a medical
exam. Preference was given to men with military experience, though the
original quota established a ratio of 75 per cent ex-combatants and 25
per cent ex-prisoners (in the Republican zone during the Civil War) and
politically trustworthy volunteers. Career military personnel wishing to
volunteer were required to do so within forty-eight hours, but Falangists
were given until 2 July. Theoretically, if multiple candidates presented
themselves for a military post, the most experienced men would be chosen. Everyone believed the final victory to be near.[58]

Instructions to request volunteers were also sent to the Military District Commands and troops in Northern Morocco. A provision on 28
June increased the personnel quota that the army was permitted to recruit: three-fourths of non-commissioned officers (NCOs) and specialized personnel, and as many troops as needed if civilian volunteers
were insufficient. General Agustín Muñoz-Grandes was chosen to command the Division. This veteran from the Moroccan war had directed
the so-called Assault Guard during the Second Republic and had served
as secretary general of the FET-JONS for a time.[59] He was a charismatic
military man of popular origin and in good standing with Falangists.
Serrano had no great liking for him but accepted him nonetheless. Officially christened as the Spanish Division of Volunteers, the unit was
popularly known as the *División Azul*, the Blue Division, in allusion to
its Falangist political colour. Apparently, FET Secretary General Arrese
came up with the name. Ridruejo, who had first outlined the plan of

dispatching volunteers to Russia, found it "somewhat ridiculous" but predicted it would "be a success."[60]

The Spanish declaration of war on the USSR never materialized, partly because Great Britain did not react to provocation. The London government was prudent enough to keep the Spanish regime from joining the war as an ally of the Axis. Thus, the Spanish expedition was presented as a purely anti-communist enterprise of retaliation for the Civil War, without a clear indication of alignment with the New European Order. Serrano Suñer stated to the *Deutsche Allgemeine Zeitung* that Spanish participation in the war against the USSR was a return to arms against their 1936 enemy and part of an European crusade "against Asian barbarity," to reorganize the Continent and achieve enduring peace with the British and Americans. Another propagandistic motive was added: the liberation of nine thousand Spanish children who had been "stolen" by the USSR in 1937 and never returned.[61]

The Spanish contingent was to be integrated into the Wehrmacht and would adopt its organizational structure, equipment, and uniform – along with a national badge on the sleeve – for its members to be legally recognized as combatants. Spanish soldiers received double pay in Spanish and German wages, a *Wehrsold* campaign bonus, and payment for time on the front. Civilian volunteers also maintained their regular salaries. The administration of justice proved the most complicated aspect of this integration. It was finally agreed that the BD would be placed under Spanish command but subject to the strategic dispositions of German High Command. The Division would use its own code of military justice, that of the Spanish Army. Any persons detained by the German military police were to be handed over to the relevant BD authorities and convicts would be transported back to Spain to complete their sentence, except for cases of espionage for Allied forces other than the USSR. General Keitel sanctioned these rules in mid-September on behalf of the OKH.[62]

The first Division advance guard was scheduled to leave on 8 July to prepare troop quarters at the Grafenwöhr training camp in the Upper Palatinate. The first contingent of troops and officers would leave by train on 13 July.[63] From the outset, issues surfaced in adapting the Spanish contingent to the Wehrmacht logistical priorities and organizational model. There were too many officers in proportion to non-commissioned officers. Furthermore, the Spanish Army could not provide motorized vehicles (three hundred lorries and four hundred motorbikes) to transport their troops to the front. However, partly due to pressure from the German Ministry of Foreign Affairs, the OKW acquiesced; the Spanish troops were accepted without transportation and the excess personnel was integrated.[64]

The initial four regiments were named after their colonels: Rodrigo (Madrid), Vierna (Valencia), Esparza (Seville), and Pimentel (Valladolid). The volunteers were distributed among different barracks in the various military regions. They then received general instructions and a Spanish Army uniform, which had been partly improvised with garments taken from the Republican Army: it also included a red beret, and usually a blue shirt with Falangist markings. Some thirty White Russian ex-combatants, most of them members of the Spanish Foreign Legion and volunteers of the Francoist Army in the Spanish Civil War, were also integrated into the Spanish contingent to serve as translators.[65]

In Madrid, volunteers were gathered in barracks and in the university district, where they performed some training exercises. Housing conditions were often unsanitary. Falangist Luis Aguilar noted that his barracks had fewer mattresses than soldiers, and that the food was bad and "dirty."[66] The first expeditions left their military command headquarters for Russia on 12 July. Very emotional scenes could be witnessed in train stations such as those of Madrid, Valladolid, and Seville. Serrano Suñer, the German ambassador, and other authorities attended the multitudinous send-off at the North Station in Madrid on 13 July. The more subdued scenes in Barcelona and Valencia, as well as the reception for convoys from other points of origin in Zaragoza, reflected the regime's lack of popularity in those regions.[67]

These expeditions had to change trains in Hendaye, the first train station in France. From there, the German occupying forces assumed responsibility for the volunteers.[68] The first thing they experienced outside their country was a collective shower and uniform disinfection, before continuing their journey to Germany in passenger carriages. They encountered many displays of hostility from the French railroad workers and civilians, who aimed insults, obscene gestures, and rocks at them. Minor altercations arose whenever the trains stopped.[69] Such scenes would repeat themselves for the next two years.

The outlook changed as the troops arrived in Alsace, which was under Third Reich dominion, and particularly as they pulled into Karlsruhe Station, in German territory. The troops were moved by the enthusiastic welcome that the German civilian population offered their exotic allies. The trains arrived at the Grafenwöhr military training camp complex in the Upper Palatinate region between 17 and 23 July. The modern, comfortable training camps seemed like paradise to the BD volunteers. They spent five weeks there – a third of the standard German training period for soldiers – training hard in unpleasant, rainy weather, with occasional outings into the surrounding areas.

Though the troops arrived in acceptable health overall, as many as four hundred of the men had contracted venereal diseases prior to leaving or from "unhealthy women" – prostitutes – aboard the trains during the journey. After being treated in Grafenwöhr, 285 afflicted volunteers were repatriated on 4 August, along with 62 men deemed unfit for service, and one sergeant of African origin. The Division lacked non-commissioned officers specializing in cavalry or transportation, and the reinforcements requested by Muñoz Grandes did not arrive before the departure for the front.[70] The Spanish soldiers were assigned bilingual instructors, received German equipment, and accustomed themselves to Wehrmacht barracks rules: reveille at 5:30 a.m., cold dinner in the afternoon, early nights. The volunteers found it more difficult to adjust to a new diet than to the rigorous physical training with live ammunition that they endured under the German motto, "sweat saves blood." Different meal hours, spartan daily rations, food such as pearl barley that was foreign to southern palates, beer instead of wine, and blond tobacco were common themes in letters and journals from the volunteer troops. Dionisio Ridruejo complained of the "outlandish but not always complete meals which we must endure."[71] Aside from the food, other causes for concern included the lack of mail from Spain, and the "discipline and ruthless … treatment" by officers and sergeants.[72] Falangist leaders who had been reduced to simple privates communicated their displeasure to the Spanish embassy in Berlin. However, the lack of political solidarity was even more disturbing than their treatment; despite recommendations from German diplomat Eberhard von Stohrer, the Falangist BD leaders scarcely had any contact with NSDAP delegations apart from one formal visit on 17 August by Robert Ley, the director of the Deutsche Arbeitsfront, and the Bayreuth *Gauleiter*.[73]

In late July, the Spanish Division of Volunteers underwent internal organizational restructuring in an attempt to adapt it to the *old* Wehrmacht model. The Replacement Regiment – which generally remained in Germany – was incorporated into the other three to be deployed on the front. There would also be a mobile reserve battalion (the 250th) with senior staff and three companies – two infantry and one mixed – that would remain in the immediate rearguard until needed. Thus, the BD officially became the 250th Wehrmacht Division (Spanischen Freiwilligen Division). The original four BD regiments became three, each composed of three battalions and two additional companies under the commands of Colonel Pedro Pimentel (262nd Regiment), José Vierna (263rd Regiment), and José Martínez Esparza (269th Regiment). The fourth colonel, Miguel Rodrigo, was posted as second head of the

Division. The BD also included an artillery and a sappers' regiment along with anti-tank, transmission, exploration, transportation, medical, logistical, and veterinary groups, military police, couriers, senior staff, and general staff. Total BD personnel was estimated at nearly eighteen thousand.[74]

Dispersed throughout the vast rearguard that stretched from Russia to Spain, small Spanish detachments were distributed to provide auxiliary services to the relief expeditions, march battalions, and the more reduced contingents of soldiers who were wounded, repatriated, or on leave. In addition to BD offices in Hof, Berlin, Königsberg, Vilnius, Riga, and Madrid, military police posts were created in May 1942 in Germany, the Baltics, and at several transit points in French territory and in the occupied Soviet rearguard. Two other mobile groups were given intelligence or counter-espionage work, with headquarters in Riga and Berlin.[75] Finally, a network of Spanish hospitals – sections of German military hospitals – was established in the immediate rearguard on the front, including the field hospital in Porkhov (later Mestelevo), those of the distant rearguard in Riga, Vilnius, Hof, and Königsberg, and the convalescent hospital in Berlin.[76] All of them were at least partially staffed by Spanish military doctors and medics, as well as volunteer nurses from the army, the Red Cross, the FET Women's Section, and local auxiliary personnel. However, in the years that followed, Spanish wounded and convalescents could be found in German military hospitals from Bromberg to Vienna.

Similarly, and in consonance with the importance given to the "spiritual care" of the Wehrmacht troops, the Spanish Division troops began to write their first trench journals. In Grafenwöhr and during the marches, they were pasted on walls. On the front, these irregular bulletins became a regular trench journal, the *Hoja de Campaña*, which was first published in Grigorovo, then in Riga, and finally in Tallinn until early March 1944. It featured contributions from Falangist BD intellectuals, such as international law professor Fernando Castiella and writer Álvaro de Laiglesia.[77]

On 31 July 1941, in formation under the German and Spanish flags on the Kramerberg field, the bulk of the Blue Division swore allegiance to the "head of the German Army Adolf Hitler in the fight against communism," before "God and on your honour as Spaniards." The Wehrmacht oath was adapted to avoid the word Führer and introduced the nuance that loyalty was linked to the fight against communism. Presiding over the ceremony with Muñoz Grandes were General Conrad von Cochenhausen and General Friedrich Fromm, commander in chief of the reserve army. In his speech, Cochenhausen emphasized the themes of an anti-Bolshevik crusade and the defence of European civilization against Judaeo-Marxist dominion.[78]

Who Volunteered for the Blue Division?

The key question of who volunteered for the Russian Front and why has often been addressed indirectly and its answer has usually been based on limited empirical evidence, except for some uneven work on specific provincial or local contexts. To date, however, the task of gathering a representative sample of volunteer biographies for all of Spain has proved impossible. Such a corpus would identify common characteristics of the volunteers, as well as their backgrounds, their social, political, and cultural origins, and their reasons for enlisting in the *first* Blue Division muster (June–July 1941) or any of the twenty-eight relief battalions dispatched to replace the fallen, the wounded, and the veterans.

The historiographic discussion about the motives and characteristics of Blue Division volunteers has oscillated roughly between two poles. At one extreme, the BD is seen as a primordially fascist and generally Francoist contingent who perceived the Russian campaign as a continuation of the Civil War and their anti-communist commitment of the 1930s. Though numbers began to decline in 1942, the Division maintained its strong Falangist flavour, which also contributed to the indoctrination of new soldiers in this ideal. In this line of thinking, the BD was a force composed mainly of Falangists, Catholics, and anti-communists.[79] At the other extreme, the BD has been considered as a punitive tool by which many or most of its members had been forced to serve in some way or recruited by coercive methods, especially where the army was involved. Most of the volunteers from 1941–3 would, in this view, not have been idealists but a mix of pseudo-mercenaries, conscripted soldiers who had been ordered to enlist, combatants with a leftist past seeking to clear their record, or peasants and workers attracted by the salary they would earn while they served. The poverty in Spain after the Civil War would have induced them to enlist.[80]

A third line of interpretation looks at the "first" Division volunteers of June–July 1941 as a mix of professional soldiers – ensigns, corporals, and sergeants mainly– who enlisted partly because they shared the ideals that had led them to fight in the Civil War, and partly out of the desire to make a career of the military. A very significant contingent of volunteers from the FET militias, most of whom were members of or sympathizers with the single party, had ideological motivations that included a generic desire to avenge personal or family sufferings at "Red" hands during the Civil War. They shared a conviction that the time had come to crush the communist enemy and ensure Spain's participation in the New European Order, with a view to strengthening the role of the Falange in the Francoist regime. Another group of volunteers would have enlisted mainly for economic reasons, or to flee from a disagreeable reality. Most replacement soldiers from March 1942 on came from the army, so the volunteer aspect of enlistment varied. Volunteers from the first recruitment campaign would have been attracted by the double salary, but some secretly sympathized with the left and were possibly looking for a chance to defect.[81]

The panorama is diverse, whether from the perspective of the volunteers' motives or of their prosopographic traits. The Spanish Division of Volunteers was certainly not so very *blue* in its composition. Though significant, the Falangists were always a minority, but they acquired clear symbolic hegemony. This coated the image and war culture of the Spanish Division with a fascist varnish. Ridruejo wrote in August 1941 that it was a "Noah's Ark with all the species," though the Falangists predominated.[82] The war against the common enemy also attracted numerous militant Catholics, some Carlists, and some "war Francoists," including NCOs and army officers. Volunteering for the Russian Front was for many a personal investment linked to a political gamble. For many others, there were practical advantages to being a war veteran in Francoist Spain.

The generational, political, and family experiences of many volunteers during the Spanish Civil War – whether they had participated or not as combatants, or had been in the fifth column, or had suffered as prisoners – played a decisive role in their decision to join the BD. War volunteering has scarcely been treated from a comparative perspective,[83] but it can be conceptualized as an individual decision taken in a context of limited rationality, reduced options, and imprecise information conditioned by propaganda. Volunteers' expectations were defined by a narrow range of predictions. The rationality of the decision to enlist in a war was also conditioned by other factors: group solidarity; nationalist, religious, or ideological indoctrination; an emotional landscape of war mobilization in a limited time frame; the connection between the cause and the defence of one's home or cherished local context; and the emphasis on values such as courage, adventure in exotic lands, and sacrifice for one's national community and/or religious faith. These classic attributes of masculinity were accentuated in interwar Europe and especially venerated on the Francoist side from 1936 on.[84]

These factors generated a *cumulative predisposition* to war in a social context marked by the mobilization of three years of civil conflict: an inherited war culture that conditioned individual motives.[85] Poverty, unemployment, restlessness, lack of social or work prospects, social pressure on families of leftist sympathizers or right-wing families who had not provided a son for the Civil War, socialization in values laden with vitalism and masculinity or assorted family, personal, or sentimental circumstances may have served as the immediate trigger for individual decisions. However, these motives overlapped with others that affected volunteers throughout their experience of the war, from setting out to shared combat experience to encountering the enemy. In their earliest days at Grafenwöhr, even soldiers from leftist family backgrounds expressed their eagerness to go into combat and "hammer the Russians [...] Up with Spain (*Arriba España*). Long live Franco."[86]

Reconstructing the reasons for volunteering constitutes a methodological challenge. Post-war testimonies are permeated with the self-justification of veterans looking back on their decisions in light of the outcomes and the dominant interpretations of the Second World War after 1945. Converting "life in combat" to war experience is a subjective process that partially depends on a veteran's desire to place the war years within his biography in a way that gives meaning to his subsequent development. Motivations expressed at that time in letters, personal diaries, or journalistic contributions always spoke of a desire to uphold a generalized opinion, creating a smokescreen behind which the majority went along with the vision rather than truly sharing it. Many war veteran testimonies ascribed the decision to go to youthful folly. In 1941, many thought the campaign would be short: "one doesn't go to war thinking he is going to die. One thinks he is going to see others die."[87] One ex-volunteer argued much later that really "most went out of inertia, the inertia acquired in our [Spanish civil] war was still going strong and drove us to it."[88] This inertia from an inherited war culture was activated by the emotional context of June–July 1941, which also conditioned individual enlistment. However, the impulse to volunteer was not only individual but collective in nature: the reference group was calling its members to arms, and backing out might expose one to stigmatism.[89] Other volunteers recognized having suffered from a transitory "madness" caught from their party comrades and friends.[90]

Enthusiasm was also promoted from above. In several provinces, the Falange leaders made substantial efforts to encourage enlistment. However, these pep talks did not always hit their mark. Results varied according to political families, generational groups, regions, and specific contexts, especially in areas where the degree of acceptance of the Franco regime had made no great progress since 1939.

Fig. 2.1. Spanish volunteers for Russia at the Madrid University campus, July 1941 (AGA)

The "Fever" of the Summer of 1941

After the first expedition had set out in August 1941, Pedro-Luis Fajardo – a decorated Falangist and mutilated veteran of the Spanish Foreign Legion – petitioned the Provincial Office of the FET in the southern province of Huelva to allow him to go to the front. He argued that

> It is not in my thoroughly Falangist spirit to be left behind in the heart-rending conflagration of the entire world, where our heroic Blue Shirts are fighting in cooperation with noble Italo-Germanic comrades for the destruction and extermination of the corrupted barbaric Asiatic hordes, who with their disastrous ideals bloodied our homeland leaving a terrifying trail of blood in their wake, and who with their fierce Bolshevik doctrine threaten Christian civilization and the resurgence of Europe.[91]

Along the same lines, when the request of Valencian FET leader Eduardo Aparisi was turned down in June 1941, he resolved to send a letter to the German embassy, asking to fight in the most difficult position possible to avenge comrades who had fallen in the "holy crusade" of 1936–9.[92] In Benavente (Zamora), theatre owner and disabled Falangist veteran Licinio de la Huerga made a similar plea to the provincial FET chief, asking "to be able to accompany you and the other comrades," driven by his "fervent Falangist ideal."[93] In similar terms, a provisional lieutenant from an Andalusian village requested the provincial FET chief to accept his application to become a volunteer: "now the time has come to sacrifice oneself for Spain."[94]

However, a provisional sergeant from Madrid had other motivations. When he was not called up by lottery from among those who had enlisted for Russia, he decided to write to General Franco himself. A "good Catholic," he revealed that "linked to this is my desire to polish up my service record with deeds on that front, and thereby qualify myself to at least obtain a post as full sergeant." He also needed additional income to compensate for the salary he would not be receiving as a specialist, in order to support his parents and save money to get married, "once the anti-communist campaign is finished."[95] Isabel Salado, an intern nurse at a hospital, petitioned in December 1941 to join the BD medical service because she could not help her family for lack of income.[96]

As has been explained, in the final task sharing between the Falange and the army, the party would assume responsibility for recruiting volunteer troops, while the army would provide leaders, officers, specialized personnel, and 75 per cent of the NCOs. In provinces where the enlistment quota was not met, volunteers would be recruited from among soldiers doing their military service. The response was quite positive among army officers and NCOs and FET members, especially in Madrid (which had supplied 2,304 volunteers as of 28 June). However, the social reaction to the call for volunteers was not uniform throughout Spanish territory. In areas where support for the insurgents in 1936–9 had been limited and where the FET had had difficulty establishing itself, precious few were drawn to the recruitment centres. According to British informants, the pressure on military commanders to recruit volunteers in the barracks was especially intense in Catalonia, and the quota was met with excess volunteers from neighbouring provinces Castellón and Valencia. In Girona, the entire garrison had been compelled to volunteer after a pep talk from the colonel left them with few alternatives. In Barcelona, almost all the officers had enlisted, but the barracks commanders had received the order first to avoid those volunteers who had fought for the Republic. Confronted with meagre results, the officer in command of the military district ordered everyone to enlist. The German consul noted that the numbers of ordinary soldiers who had enlisted had jumped from a few to several hundred within days, leading him to question the level of "volunteering" involved. Most civil volunteers were Falangists,

Fig. 2.2. Volunteers departing by train to Russia, Madrid, July 1941 (AGA)

many of them sons of middle-class or military families, along with peasants, day labourers, and a few others from the lower echelons of society.[97] Only unemployed or unqualified persons enlisted from the Catalan rural areas and the Carlist Requetés were excluded.[98] The commander of the 10th Expedition passed through Barcelona on 15 July and noted the coldness of the sending off at the station. Some mothers had even gone to demand that their sons be returned home. In his opinion, "Falange recruitment has been rather substandard or poorly organized."[99]

Similarly, recruitment was quite unsuccessful in the Basque provinces, Navarre, and other territories where Carlism constituted a dominant element within the FET. Though some Carlists were openly favourable to Germany, their leader-in-exile Manuel Fal Conde had ordered them to abstain from participation. According to the British embassy, only forty volunteers had come forward in Navarre. In Alava, the number of Carlists who enlisted was negligible.[100] In Teruel, Falange reports indicated scant warlike enthusiasm among its members, and compelled some of the provincial leaders to volunteer.[101]

In contrast, the fact that several provinces, including Madrid and Valencia, had remained under Republican control until the end of the Civil War had deprived numerous Francoist sympathizers – some of whom had collaborated in the fifth column and other clandestine groups in the Republican rearguard – of any real opportunity to fight under the flag of their choosing. In those territories, the Falange sought to galvanize regime sympathizers, taking advantage of the moment to gain adherents. In Madrid, the Falangist support base seemed ablaze with activity. A German informant confirmed that groups of young men, many of them Civil War veterans, were flowing into the militia headquarters to enlist.[102] The same enthusiasm could be felt in other territories but was limited to the Falangist support base and other social segments with Francoist-inclinations. In July 1941, the Falange in Murcia stated that more than two thousand affiliates or sympathizers had come to their offices to enlist, including some noteworthy "Old Shirts" (members before 18 July 1936, the date of the uprising against the Republic). The volunteer expedition had been able to leave a day before the draft period ended. In Albacete, the party worked hard holding meetings in several towns to encourage recruitment and reported a "magnificent spirit" that led 984 people to present themselves at the recruiting offices. Soon after, 329 of those – including five local leaders – left for Russia.[103] The party headquarters in the northern region of Asturias described a similar panorama in their monthly report of June 1941:

> The German declaration of war on Russia has been received with great enthusiasm ... in Oviedo alone ... more than 350 comrades have enlisted for all posts, and the impression is good in the towns. The departure of the first expedition of volunteers, without any kind of publicity, became a demonstration of authentically Falangist enthusiasm; the station platforms were overflowing with people deliriously applauding the first 140 Falangists who left for duty. [104]

Even some native people in Spanish Morocco showed interest in fighting in Russia, which the German consul in Tétouan saw as an interesting propagandistic element for attracting the Muslim population of the USSR. However, the military command vetoed enlistment of indigenous troops and, except for a few Moroccan sergeants in the first expedition, the contingent of nearly two thousand volunteers that left for the front was almost entirely composed of officers, NCOs, and European soldiers recruited in the barracks.[105]

Many volunteers also had personal scores to settle; they had lost brothers, fathers, and friends through repression in the Republican zone or had themselves suffered imprisonment or persecution. Numerous FET members and sympathizers had lived clandestinely in the Republican rearguard during the Civil War, had collaborated with the "Fifth Column" in Madrid and other cities, or had enlisted in the Republican Army to try to defect to the Francoist zone.[106] Now, they all saw the Eastern Front as an opportunity for their own personal shade of revenge. The British ambassador estimated in early July 1941 that this factor would motivate "thousands of Spaniards" to enlist.[107] Dozens of Falangist, Catholic, or simply "wartime Francoist" volunteers had suffered the loss of family and friends at the hands of diverse Republican militias, popular trials, or the Republican Information Service.[108] Even in 1943, a German officer wrote that many volunteers who arrived in Russia shared a "desire for revenge inherited from personal or family suffering during the Civil War."[109]

Generation also played a certain role. The social community of those who supported the Francoist regime influenced the youngest members, who desired to demonstrate their ability to take up arms in defence of the same ideals that had inspired the insurgents of July 1936. Those who had lived in Republican zones or had been too young to fight felt pressure from neighbours and fellow Francoists. The devout Catholic student Enrique Sánchez Fraile, whose Andalusian village had remained under Republican control until March 1939, felt the reproaches of right-wing neighbours against his parents: they had not been Spanish enough, nor had they provided even one son for the cause. Enrique, then a student in Almeria, resolved in March 1942 to enlist for Russia on the advice of his confessor.[110] Falangist leaders also felt this pressure, as even Dionisio Ridruejo wrote, "I don't want anyone saying I didn't fight because I didn't dare to."[111] The Falangist and law student Miguel Martínez-Mena stated that the BD presented an opportunity for those who had not fought in the Civil War to make their offering of heroism in a society where such military values had acquired great relevance:

> If it is true that some enlistments were a bit forced, by affairs of the heart and infatuation, while others set out to improve an uncertain personal fate, or to cross over to the Russian camp ... it is no less true that the vast majority of us thought that going to Russia was a manly action, a patriotic requirement, an inescapable decision for those of us who did not participate or who participated in the Crusade bearing arms but did not have the luck or lack of luck ... to suffer the anguish of captivity in the Red zone.[112]

War experience was prerequisite to demonstrating the values of the new national community, incarnated by the winners of the Civil War.

Fig. 2.3. Departure of Spanish volunteers, Madrid, July 1941 (AGA)

Many felt in the summer of 1941 that their time had come, that they could add their own war merits to those already acquired by comrades or relatives. For all the volunteers, idealists or not, one thing was certain: being an ex-combatant brought with it both social prestige within the Francoist community and a series of employment privileges. For those who had fought for the Republican side, willingly or otherwise, it was advisable to demonstrate merit in the cause of the winners. Ex-combatants, wounded veterans, and former prisoners had quotas reserved for posts in the state administration, which translated into better opportunities to be a concierge, a postal worker, or a schoolteacher.

For FET members, combat merit was a decisive criterion in the selection of political personnel.[113]

However, the "fever" of the summer of 1941 only affected the most mobilized portion of the winners of the Civil War. The FET militia recruiting offices found themselves unable to cover total troop requirements. About half of the soldiers – officers and NCOs included – came from recruitment in the barracks (9,699 civilians were enlisted in 1941, 9,802 in 1942, and 4,911 in 1943, adding up to 24,412 out of 47,200 total combatants).[114] Recruitment mechanisms were also rather opaque at times. Coercion was always present: whether directly from officers to subordinates or indirectly through the example of others, the desire to fit in, camaraderie, or the longing to prove one's masculinity. There were also some recruits in these barracks who shared the values of the winners of the Civil War and volunteered proactively. How many, then, were coerced, psychologically pressured in diverse ways, or motivated by the example of others? Such a question defies statistical quantification.

The Replacements of 1942–3: Mercenaries, Conscripts, or Volunteers?

As early as December 1941, both Agustín Aznar and Ridruejo were urging Serrano Suñer to begin partial troop replacements. The army minister, José E. Varela, embraced the idea of substituting the entire "first division" with units composed of volunteers recruited primarily or exclusively from the barracks or from among those who had exceeded the enlistment quota in 1941. He made no secret of his slight regard for the Falange volunteer recruits, whom he accused of lacking instruction and having "defects of a different order."[115] However, the chief of the Army General Staff, General Carlos Asensio, also reported to Franco that a complete replacement of the Division was required, but also stated that there were increasing difficulties in recruiting replacements in the military baracks, since soldiers returning from Russia spread news about the extremely tough conditions they had endured.[116] From mid-1942 on, the army acquired a dominant role in enlisting and assigning volunteers for the Russian Front, which diminished the influence of the Falange. They were losing posts within the regime as Serrano Suñer lost influence and was eventually removed in September 1942.[117] His successor was the Count of Jordana, a Catholic who favoured the Allies. Franco compensated his gradual turn from non-belligerence to neutrality with symbolic gestures towards the Axis.

By January 1942, several small relief expeditions of officers and soldiers had crossed the border from San Sebastian. In mid-March, they were named "March Battalions" and tasked with transporting replacement soldiers from Spain. In April, four battalions arrived at the front with almost four thousand soldiers. Twenty-three more battalions followed until October 1943. A total of 17,027 men were transported through February of that year and close to 10,000 more before the BD was dismantled. The traffic included soldiers on leave in Spain (almost a thousand enjoyed this opportunity), wounded and convalescent soldiers, officers urgently joining or leaving their units, groups of soldiers being repatriated for bad conduct or to complete sentences in military prisons, etc.[118]

Several testimonies from that time identified clear differences between the "first" BD of July 1941 and the "second" division, composed of later replacements.[119] However, the contrast in motives between the "first" batch of volunteers and the many that followed from 1942 on remains less clear. The dominant profile of the volunteers of 1941 carried over to the first replacements dispatched to the front in spring 1942. In part, this corresponded to the incorporation of the remnant of idealistic civilian volunteers who had not been admitted the year before and who desired to see combat. In May 1942, Dionisio Ridruejo, who was now back in Spain and remained a reference model for many Spanish fascists until 1945, was still receiving letters from Falangists requesting a referral for enlistment.[120] Until mid-1942, most of the civilian volunteers who enlisted in Madrid and Barcelona were Falangists. Many of them were "Old Guard" (party members before mid-March 1936, when the Falange was made illegal by the Republican government and its main leaders were imprisoned) and complained of the treatment they received from the military. For this reason, the rumour spread that the party was going to ban veteran Falangists from enlisting.[121] The "waiting list" gave several recruiting offices a reserve that would cover part of the 1942 quotas. In March of that year, the provincial headquarters of the FET militias of Albacete had 136 volunteers for Russia on their list.[122]

Other testimonies confirm this impression. José M. Blanch, who volunteered in 1942, described the social profile of his fellow combatants. There were some enlisted officers and NCOs who "were perhaps waiting for a promotion," but most of the soldiers "came from the Falange, students from Madrid or middle-class families, but also peasants and workers." The mechanic Joaquín Montaña also discovered that his mates "were university people" who "really felt the need to fight against ideas that ran contrary to their own." Manuel Tarín left for the front in April 1942; when his fiancée reproached him for having gone to Russia, he responded: "This separation is the work of Duty ... I have come to defend God, the Homeland and my dignity as a Spaniard."[123]

Manuel Tarín's tone did not change in the weeks that followed; he wrote in October 1942 that "seven months have already passed since I left all my loves and interests to come on this Holy Crusade to fight against the enemies of God, Spain and Civilization."[124] When his "war godmother" asked Corporal Antonio Herrero why he had enlisted in autumn of 1942, he answered: "My friend, my comrades and I have a monstrous and cruel enemy. Communism! This beastly and cruel enemy in earlier days – in our war in Spain – took cowardly advantage and with full fury maliciously damaged the lives of those we love most."[125]

Nonetheless, in the provinces where there had been excess militia volunteers in 1941, the number of new volunteers clearly began to diminish the following year. The stabilization of the Eastern Front led many to reconsider.[126] The head of FET militias, General José Moscardó, lamented the lack of recruitment propaganda in July 1942, in light of the "notable decrease that it has suffered lately."[127] The number of Falangist volunteers moved by ideological enthusiasm began to decline steadily in the second half of 1942. In July 1943, some provincial FET organizations acknowledged the lack of interest in volunteering among members. Recruits were thin on the ground from mid-1942 on, despite the insistence of the Military General Staff that "it is of great interest to obtain the largest possible contingent of troops." Not even officers came forward for the front. The situation, however, varied from one base to another; among new volunteers, there was more than one who had "re-enlisted." In March 1942, for example, the Moroccan native soldiers – the *Regulares* – of the Balearic garrison again showed greatest willingness to go to Russia.[128]

Accordingly, the number and proportion of volunteers who were more or less coerced, who came from the army ranks or, to a lesser degree, from the FET offices – persons who were advised to enlist to "clear" their record, for example – began to increase in mid-1942. On military bases, soldiers and NCOs doing compulsory military service in various garrisons on the Peninsula, the Islands, and in Northern Morocco were circuitously pressured by their superiors to volunteer for Russia. Habitual procedures included a lottery system or requiring all soldiers being trained on the premises to step forward when volunteers were requested. Such tactics were assisted by the fact that the "selected ones" feared being perceived as cowards. In some cases, if no one stepped forward, the officer would order all present to declare themselves volunteers.[129] In theory, the recruits could refuse, and if they were lucky a higher ranking officer would invalidate the enlistments.[130] However, if the officer directly involved insisted or was pressured by his superiors, very few could refuse.[131] For many others, volunteering for Russia presented an attractive opportunity in terms of adventure and pay, which was similar to that of the Legion. In theory, their German wages had to be spent in the rearguard or on the front, though this became more flexible from 1942 on.[132]

General Muñoz Grandes wrote in May 1942 that a quarter of the new volunteers had received no military training, though a considerable number of professional soldiers, especially legionnaires posted in the Spanish Protectorate of Morocco, had also been dispatched to Russia. Most of them had agreed to leave for the Russian Front, as they were already in fact mercenaries. In the Blue Division, they could earn war merit and double pay. Their biographies resembled those of the provisional ensigns and sergeants. Many had enlisted in the insurgent army in 1936–8 and had stayed on. In July 1942, the legionnaire Jaime de Assunçâo Graça was hand-picked and assigned to the front by a sergeant who was reviewing his company in Ceuta. He at least had anti-communist and pro-fascist sympathies, so his semi-forced enlistment would not require him to fight for a foreign cause.[133]

From mid-1942 on, the propaganda used to cover replacement quotas for the Division emphasized the economic advantages for those who returned. They would continue to earn wages from their regular job, maintain their rank in the administrative corps, or be granted certain privileges if they chose to take civil service exams.[134] One enlistment pamphlet published in Murcia entreated:

> Those who enlist will have fully guaranteed rights and privileges for themselves and their families. You will be paid the wages of a German soldier, and in Spain your families will receive a subsidy of 7.30 pesetas or the salary you received prior to your departure, your post and location will be held for you, and you will be given preference for them, [along with] free tuition, etc., which Spanish society reserves for its best.[135]

Propaganda was also broadcast on local radio stations, but not always well received. Openings for volunteer workers in Germany, facilitated by the August 1941 agreement between Spain and the Third Reich, were clearly not being filled either, with their lower salaries and dismal working conditions. Many workers wrote home expressing discontent over their working conditions in Germany, taking the shine off the information that was circulating about such opportunities. Beginning in March 1942, several Spanish workers in Germany even went to enlist at the BD office in Hof. They preferred combat to their harsh work in the Reich.[136]

It was no coincidence that in 1942 and 1943 there were considerably more volunteers for the Russian Front from the provinces of southern Spain with higher rates of seasonal agricultural work, high seasonal or permanent unemployment, and lower levels of social support for the Francoist regime, such as Badajoz and Huelva. In fact, the largest contingent of volunteers from Huelva departed from the first half of 1942 (22.8 per cent of enlistments) through mid-1943 (26.7 per cent of all volunteers from the province). In other regions, such as the Canary Islands, attracting volunteers in 1942–3 proved increasingly difficult. Most of those who joined the BD in this period seem to have been motivated by economic reasons.[137] However, it is impossible to provide a statistical estimate regarding percentages of volunteers who were motivated by any given incentive.

There are two nuances to consider concerning the "forced" or idealistic nature of the 1942–3 volunteers. First, many soldiers were drawn by the attractive if not decisive incentive of double pay and a reduction in their three years of compulsory military service. This may have been especially enticing to those who had fought on the Republican side in the Civil War and were required to repeat their military service. Every month of service in Russia counted for two in Spain, and full exemption was granted (upon return) after six months on the front. Their motives differed little from those of many young Europeans who joined the Waffen-SS in 1943–4. Recruits with scant political socialization enlisted for the pay, or because they wanted to see the world, or because they had inherited a fascination with the military from the 1936–9 war culture. Day labourer Angel Marchena from Cordoba enlisted in the Division in 1942, though his father had been imprisoned in 1936 by the rebels and died in captivity. He recalled why he volunteered: the pay was "seven and a half pesetas, [the wages of] a day and a half."[138] His story suggests that he never professed ideological motives, but valued loyalty to his comrades in arms. BD volunteer Joaquín Montaña from the county of El Bierzo (León) recounted decades later the reasons behind his decision to volunteer. The first was anti-communism, followed by the models of masculinity associated with military life, the influence of his mates, good pay, the possibility of reducing military service, and social prestige in his local reference context:

> There were other young men in the village who talked about joining up. And seven pesetas a day! With that kind of money, you could eat in the hotel and have some left over to treat your friends … I didn't know much about the Falange or communism. We dreamed about the uniform

[...] and we already saw ourselves as gallants in the cinema or in those documentaries you see about the war ... One day, when we returned, we would be hailed as heroes. Seven pesetas and thirty was a good salary and when we were incorporated into the German army, four marks, two for me and two that they sent home to my mother.[139]

Antonio Gómez, a seasonal labourer from Huelva who enlisted for the Russian Front in May 1942, summarized his decision to volunteer in similar terms:

I was a day labourer in the fields and unmarried. I enlisted above all because in the town they looked at me as if I were a highwayman or a dog, since my ideology was more to the left. This, added to the terrible economic situation of my family, forced me to find a way to earn a living.[140]

Secondly, even in the most difficult moments for recruitment, local Falange or Catholic Action groups told of young Falangists or Catholics – and more than one theological seminary student – who had enlisted collectively.[141] There were still cases of fervent anti-communist enthusiasm among the Falange recruits, NCOs, ensigns, and officers who volunteered from spring 1942 through autumn 1943.[142] Though in smaller proportion compared to 1941, they maintained a "blue," falangist line of continuity. These were members of new youth organizations (such as the FET-JONS and after 1942 the Falanges Juveniles of Franco), along with volunteers who had not been admitted in June 1941 and some who were willing to accept a lower rank to go to Russia as foot soldiers.[143] Several members of Catholic Action, including the presbyter, left the Catalan towns of Granollers or Ripoll for the Russian Front in late 1942 and 1943 as Catholic, anti-communist volunteers.[144] In 1943, some traditionalists also volunteered for Russia.[145]

Provisional lieutenant Benjamin Arenales was a Catholic Castilian, born 1917 in Burgos, and an "Old Shirt" Falangist, who, being a high-school student, had volunteered for the insurgent army during the Civil War. He left his post as an auxiliary military attorney in Cuenca to enlist in the first march battalion going to Russia. He wrote in his diary that he was joining a war "in which European civilization is at stake," to fight "for the same motives that drove me to fight the Spanish [civil] war." In addition to this idealism, he also noted a personal reason. He wanted to be "something in life" – to move up the ladders of military and social prestige to be able to wed his fiancée: "I have so little to offer her, that I have chosen all sacrifice to obtain greater security and offer it all to her." Captain Manuel de Cárdenas, a military surgeon and Catholic traditionalist, wrote in February 1942 that he felt part of a "great enterprise" for God and country. Other autobiographic accounts of the volunteers from 1942–3 demonstrate a spirit of disenchanted nihilism alongside ideological motives such as anti-communism, Spanish nationalism, or the defence of a Christian Europe.[146]

Several Falange leaders organized a great propaganda campaign in early 1943 to "re-Falangize" the march battalions that were leaving for Russia. They hoped to counteract the excessive influx from the army.[147] Pressure on local Falange chiefs combined with the appeal to manliness and individual valour, as seen in the letter that the local hierarchy in Huesca received in January 1943, signed by the provincial head Luis Julve. He reminded them that "the effort of our heroic comrades," who "cheerfully offer their blood in defence of our supreme ideals," had moved the party to establish periodical replacements in order to give an opportunity to participate in the campaign to "innumerable comrades, who repeatedly demonstrate their ardent desire to enlist in the Blue Division [...] Comrade, this letter should never be interpreted as a coercive invitation. Your own Falangist sentiment will dictate your duty."[148]

The initiative was abandoned by Foreign Minister Jordana, at Franco's order, as the latter had no interest in making the BD more Falangist in a moment of rapprochement with the Allies. Even so, the Falangists insisted, and several party leaders received authorization to enlist, partly to stir up enthusiasm in their territories. Several national leaders left for Russia, and there was an attempt to get a local and a provincial leader to join up from each province.[149] Warrior fervour had declined in the FET, and spontaneous enlistment of Falangists became less frequent. In some cases, the provincial leadership resolved again to encourage young members to go to the Russian Front by "setting an example." British reports indicated that in some provinces it had been almost impossible to persuade party members to volunteer. In Granada, only two of thirty-five provincial party leaders enlisted, along with a few lower-ranking leaders. The administrative personnel of the FET were also pressured to enlist, and more than one feared losing his post for refusing. The parish priest of the provincial jail worked to convince prisoners to go to Russia. A group of provincial FET leaders even promised freedom to prisoners serving sentences of less than thirty years and an economic incentive for enlisting.[150]

Local Falange leaders knew that both the quantity and the quality of the new volunteers fell short of expectations. As early as March 1942, the Falangist officer Guillermo Hernanz expressed disapprovingly that most of his expedition partners had a less-than-idealistic look about them. "And with these guys we are going to fight thousands of kilometres from our Homeland!" Several subsequent testimonies transmit a similar impression and refer to the frequent disputes that arose between Falangists and Legion volunteers in the march battalions.[151] In April 1942, the military governor of Guipúzcoa lamented that so many "undisciplined types and swaggering ones in particular" were to be found among the volunteers that came and went through San Sebastian.[152] Throughout 1943, various institutional complaints were made about the behaviour of the volunteers for Russia who were concentrated in Logroño. They were "feared by the civilian population" because they acted "with inappropriateness bordering on insolence" and were involved in "incidents and disputes" almost daily.[153] Another Falangist expressed disappointment at the atmosphere in the Logroño barracks, which reminded him of a prison yard: "it isn't as National Syndicalist as I had expected."[154]

General Emilio Esteban-Infantes complained repeatedly to the army minister, José Varela, regarding the arrival of politically unreliable soldiers. He adopted a more severe tone in March 1943 when he discovered that there were soldiers in a march battalion heading for Germany who had been given two years extra service for serious offences. He ordered their immediate repatriation and asked Madrid to "not send personnel of dubious conduct or with antecedents for misconduct." Two months later, the Division chief of staff insisted that the BD not be considered "a disciplinary corps."[155] Soon after, both the Spanish ambassador in Berlin and the Count of Jordana acknowledged the growing difficulty of recruiting volunteer troops, which had led to the use of coercive methods for conscripting the most recent replacements. This was recorded in the memorandum presented to the German foreign minister on 1 October 1943 as justification for the decision to withdraw the BD. The increasing difficulties in attracting volunteers might soon lead to a compulsory draft, which could not be kept secret and would put Spain in an even more difficult position with regard to the Allies.[156]

The Germans had made similar remarks, and Wehrmacht intelligence gave special attention to the political reliability of the BD volunteers that arrived from March 1942 on. In September, they warned that the soldiers arriving at the front were very different from those returning to Spain. While the latter were mostly Falangists and Germanophiles, the new volunteers were mainly legionnaires or "reserve soldiers, with Red elements among them," which explained the increase in desertions. Moreover, the new officers were much more monarchist than Falangist.[157] One SD report in November 1943 distinguished between the first Blue Division "composed principally of old Falangists who belonged to all the irreproachable social and political strata" and the second "Division of Spanish Volunteers," composed mainly of recruited and professional soldiers and NCOs, who were politically less trustworthy. However, the report indicated that the latter were under the command of a better-trained corps of officers and NCOs, most of whom had recently come out of military academies. Throughout 1943, the quality of the troops diminished as the "politically unreliable" elements increased. These could be expected to join the enemy without hesitation at the earliest opportunity.[158]

The career army officers who had been too young during the Civil War and had pursued military studies between 1939 and 1942 constituted a regular source of new volunteers. They relished the challenge of fighting alongside the idealized Wehrmacht in a demanding war scenario. As fervent supporters of the values of the "New Spain," these young men were no less anti-communist than those who had arrived in 1941. In fact, many had personal or family scores to settle with communism. According to the German liaison in August 1943, up to 30 per cent of the youngest officers in the Spanish Army had served several months on the Russian Front.[159] Many of them had been unable to accompany the first BD due to the excess of officers volunteering in 1941.[160] They sought referrals from friends and family members in hopes of being selected for the replacement contingents. Artillery Captain Fernando Muñoz Acera begged his uncle, General Muñoz Grandes, to accept his petition for enlistment, given his "true disappointment" at having been rejected earlier. Even in October 1943, many sergeants in Russia found themselves reunited with former mates from the academy where they had attended courses to acquire the rank of NCO during the Spanish Civil War.[161]

In their memoirs, some army officers adopted a professional focus and presented their enlistment as an important career step. Alfonso Armada, a Civil War volunteer who came out of the General Military Academy as a lieutenant in June 1941, summarized it this way years later:

> I went to the [Spanish] Civil War enthusiastically. I went to Russia as a professional to fight against communism ... I had just finished the Academy when they asked for volunteers ... And we all stepped forward, everyone, everyone. Then they selected seventeen captains ... after that they asked for volunteer officers to replace those already in Russia. We signed up and they chose four, and later they rejected one and I went, because there were three ahead of me ... Then I decided, and my father supported me, with great sadness, in going to Russia because he thought that since I had finished the Academy, I should demonstrate my abilities.[162]

Social and Prosopographic Profile of the Volunteers

What were the social origins of those who enlisted for the Russian Front? The Falangist press liked to emphasize the interclass nature of those who flowed into the recruitment centres. The Vice-Secretariat for Popular Education had instructed the newspapers to avoid publishing enlistment numbers, names, or information regarding "replacement due to enlistment of persons who occupy high State, Army or Party posts."[163] Occasionally, subtle references appeared: the Córdoba daily paper *Azul* indicated that several "workers and peasants" had gone to the provincial militia headquarters to present themselves as volunteers, but that there was also "a notable influx of students, technicians, craftsmen and urban workers, most of whom had permanent jobs," as well as "a young Falangist solicitor ... officers, sergeants, ex-combatants and even disabled veterans."[164]

The image was not far off the mark. Using data from several local monographs, which themselves are highly variable due to the irregular richness of sources, we can offer the following chart based on 4,770 cases (around 10 per cent of all BD volunteers, but representing a higher percentage of civilian volunteers) in thirteen provinces (Toledo, Santander, Huelva, Almeria, Córdoba, Badajoz, Murcia, the three Aragonese provinces of Zaragoza, Teruel, and Huesca, and the Basque provinces of Biscay, Guipúzcoa, and Alava) from June 1941 to October 1943. These data should be interpreted cautiously; these were volunteers, though 10–15 per cent of them did not make it to the front for diverse reasons (failing medical exams, repatriated for being useless or "undesirable," etc.). Moreover, the professional classifications, often based on what those who enlisted declared about themselves, also leave room for interpretative error. For example, several volunteers pretended to be drivers because this was a skill that military recruiters valued highly. However, some conclusions can be extracted from the data.

First, the inter-class profile of the volunteers roughly approximated the social profile of their provinces of origin, with greater relative weight on the middle- and lower-middle-class sections of the social pyramid. This was a nuanced interclassism with a preponderance of white-collar and qualified manual workers, artisans, employees, and low-ranking civil servants, along with significant student contingents where universities were present. Among the volunteers from Toledo with a known profession, the majority (26.12 per cent) were skilled workers and the same percentage were workers and day labourers, followed by civil servants, employees, and service sector workers (18 per cent), artisans and small-scale merchants (10.8 per cent), and peasants (9 per cent). Students, in a

Table 1. Social composition of civil volunteers of the Blue Division (%) 1941–3

	Toledo	Santander	Huelva	Badajoz	Aragon	Murcia	Álava	Guipúzcoa	Biscay	Córdoba	Almería
Farmers, agricultural labourers, sailors	9.0	5.9	44.44	41.14	28.38	9.04	14.38	11.4	18.03	28.88	9.38
Unskilled manual workers	26.12	35.0	14.5	12.6	13.96	3.75	30.93	19.6	20.31	19.16	13.78
Skilled manual workers, blue-collar workers	26.12	25.3	24.81	15.0	32.3	9.89	34.53	36.7	30.13	26.66	22.58
Artisans, shopkeepers	10.8	6.61	5.94	11.8	10.42	14.67	2.15	6.95	5.25	6.66	8.5
Clerks, civil servants (middle and lower strata)	18.0	18.43	9.2	10.45	11.30	27.98	7.91	15.65	18.94	6.66	28.44
University students	5.4	4.2	0.46	1.83	13.74	24.91	4.31	6.78	5.02	2.77	16.12
Liberal professionals, landlords, merchants, and industry owners	2.7	1.89	0.46	1.97	2.66	5.97	1.43	1.91	1.59	1.66	0.87
Others and unemployed	2.86	3.6	0.19	5.21	4	3.75	4.31	5	0.68	7.5	0.29
Total amount of the sample; 4,770	111	423	639	707	451	586	139	575	438	360	341

See Núñez Seixas, *Camarada invierno*, 92; for Álava, own elaboration from Archivo General Militar, Ávila, Cajas (C.) 5453–5 (courtesy by Dr. Virginia López de Maturana); for Guipúzcoa and Vizcaya: own elaboration from I. Fernández de Vicente, "El proyecto fascista en el País Vasco, 1933–1945" (PhD Thesis, Univ. of the Basque Country, 2019), pp. 520–63; for Córdoba: own elaboration from F. López Villatoro, *La Falange republicana en Andalucía. Guerra Civil, Movimiento y División Azul. Córdoba 1931–1945*, Córdoba: A. C. Cantamara, 2012, pp. 289–90, and for Almería, own elaboration from A. Viciana Martínez-Lage, *700. Los almerienses de la División Azul*, Almería: IEA, 2018, pp. 243–83.

province without a university but near Madrid, accounted for 5.4 per cent and were concentrated in the first expedition. The proportion of workers, day labourers, peasants, and soldiers from military bases increased between 1942 and 1943. In Santander, a province with a Falangist presence and where Republican repression had been strong until mid-1937, the social composition for the volunteers also corresponded mostly to the lower-middle and popular classes. The following results arise from analysis of the 423 volunteers with known professions: 35 per cent (148) were unskilled manual labourers, apprentices, or day labourers, and 25.3 per cent (107) were skilled labourers. Another 18.43 per cent were middle- or lower-ranking civil servants, employees, and service workers (who were over-represented among those who enlisted), 5.9 per cent (25) were peasants, fishermen, and sailors, and 4.2 per cent (18) were students. In 1941, at least 14.6 per cent of the volunteers were construction workers who were rebuilding Santander after the great fire that had devastated the city four months earlier. Predominant among the 451 civilian volunteers with known professions from the three Aragonese provinces were skilled and non-manual workers, artisans and small-scale merchants, civil servants and employees, along with a good number of university students. Manual and skilled workers accounted for almost two-thirds of the volunteers from Alava with known professions, followed by peasants and agricultural workers. Additionally, as many as 31 (or 22.3%) of those who enlisted were actually unemployed when they joined the BD.

The predominantly popular profile of lower and lower-middle classes, especially peasants and day labourers, was more acute in southern Spain. In Córdoba, more than 40 per cent of the volunteers were farmers, day labourers, and unskilled workers. In Badajoz, 41.1 per cent were farmers and day labourers, 15 per cent were artisans and skilled or semi-skilled manual labourers, 12.6 per cent were unskilled manual urban workers, and 11.8 per cent were artisans or small-scale merchants. A similar profile can be seen for the 639 volunteers from the province of Huelva with known professions: 40.06 per cent were farmers and day labourers, 14.5 per cent were unskilled manual labourers, and 31.81 per cent were skilled manual labourers. As in Badajoz, employees and low- to middle-ranking civil servants accounted for scarcely 11 per cent and the number of students was almost anecdotal, which is logical in a province without a university. In Badajoz and Huelva, a significant percentage of the volunteers were illiterate.[165] In contrast, the mostly agricultural province of Almeria presented a markedly urban and lower-middle-class profile, with farmers and day labourers barely surpassing 9 per cent of the volunteers. Murcia was an anomalous case. Falangist mobilization had been very prominent there and most recruits came from the FET militias. In that agricultural province also, scarcely 9 per cent of the civilian enlistments were peasants or agricultural workers; almost a quarter were students, and nearly half of the civilian volunteers were liberal professionals, landowners, and mid- to low-ranking civil servants.

Second, when these global samples are compared with the professions declared by the volunteers who enlisted in June–July 1941, the percentages vary. Though unskilled manual professions, peasants, and day labourers continued to dominate in absolute terms, in the first expedition there was greater participation from the middle classes, students, and white-collar professions. Among the 106 volunteers from Huelva with known professions, the percentage of students rose to 3.8 per cent, and that of shop assistants, civil servants, and employees increased to 15 per cent; skilled workers with a profession remained at 22.2 per cent, peasants and day labourers decreased to 36.8 per cent, and unskilled workers rose slightly to 16 per cent. Of the 258 civilian volunteers with known professions from Aragon in 1941, the percentage of students also increased (41, or 15.89 per cent), as did that of civil servants and employees (33, or 12.8 per cent), while the percentage of peasants, day labourers, and skilled and unskilled workers decreased slightly.[166] Students, clerks, and civil servants also accounted for 22.43 per cent and 23.96 per cent of Basque volunteers from Guipúzcoa and Biscay in 1941, respectively. Some authors also mention that 17 per cent of all volunteers from Madrid were students, and that 25 per cent of the volunteers had a university degree, which was an exceptional percentage vis-à-vis the Spanish population at that time.[167]

Third, in Madrid and other university district centres such as Seville, Valencia, Murcia, and Valladolid, Falangist students defined the character of the volunteer corps to a greater degree. Some later testimonies indicated that it was unusual to find peasant or working-class youth among the volunteers mustered in Madrid: most were "students, employees or shop assistants." According to one German diplomat, most of the Falangist students from the University of Barcelona had left for the Russian Front.[168]

An alternative way of constructing a meaningful sample of Blue Division volunteer biographies, which also reflects their diversity, follows the impact of Red Army bullets. It involves prosopographic analysis of the fallen, whose biographies were published in various newspapers. I have been able to reconstruct some of these from diverse sources. A sample of 625 fallen, which represents almost 13 per cent of total deaths (approx. 5,000), shows that as many as 225 (36 per cent) came from the ranks of the army: including officers, NCOs and soldiers who were completing their military service when they enlisted for the Division; 286 of the fallen (45.76 per cent) were FET members, 162 (25.92 per cent) of whom had joined the party prior to 18 July 1936. Most were civil servants, university students, and party employees. Another 105 fallen volunteers had belonged to the students' organization (Sindicato Español Universitario, SEU) of the FET-JONS (16.8 per cent of the total). Similarly, almost half (201, or 48.16 per cent) of those who died in Russia had fought or cooperated with the Francoist side in the Civil War. As many as 99 fallen volunteers (14.35 per cent) had suffered directly or indirectly (family) some form of repression in the Republican zone between 1936 and 1939. A total of 102 (16.32 per cent) had joined the Francoist Army during the Civil War and had been promoted by merit and training to ranks of ensign, lieutenant, or provisional sergeant. Thirty-one of the fallen (4.96 per cent) belonged to Catholic organizations; and 17 (2.72 per cent) had been Carlists.[169]

Again, the data should be interpreted cautiously. The published profiles of the fallen show a considerable number of Falangists, ex-captives, and ex-combatants, even during 1942 and 1943.[170] A systematic sampling of the complete alphabetical lists of the fallen indicates a much smaller number, from which it is possible to obtain a biographical profile. Of 158 fallen soldiers whose surnames began with the letters E and F, only 13.2 per cent (21) were members of the Falangist party; 7.54 per cent (12) were army officers, while 15.72 per cent (25) were corporals and sergeants. We know only the names of the remaining 69.18 per cent.[171] Some local studies suggest similar percentages. Of 590 volunteers who enlisted in the recruitment office of Santander, at least 81 (13.8 per cent) were affiliated with the Falange, and many of those were Old Shirts. Combined with the Carlist Requetés, the percentage increases to 17 per cent. Of the 1,216 BD volunteers identified from Aragon, at least 114 (9.37 per cent) were FET members and at least 361 (29.68 per cent) were Francoist ex-combatants. Falangists accounted for nearly 13 per cent of all volunteers from Almeria, and over a third of them were Old Shirts. The percentage of Falangists from among the volunteers who enlisted in Murcia was much greater, representing up to 62.5 per cent (429) of the volunteers with a known ideological profile (686, or 55.5 per cent of the total).[172] The number of Falangists among those from Alava was negligible (3, or 2.15 per cent), and even fewer were former traditionalist Requetés.

Ramón Serrano Suñer stated in July 1941 that the first expedition to the Russian Front had consisted of 75 per cent soldiers and 25 per cent devoted Falangists.[173] However, the proportion of Falangists who fell in the entire Russian adventure was smaller. Among the first twenty-three

Spanish prisoners taken by the Red Army through December 1941, eight (30.76 per cent) were "well-defined Falangists," two were army NCOs, six were "adventurers, rogues, commoners," six others were soldiers that had been more or less coerced to enlist, and four were "workers driven by misery and unemployment," according to a February 1942 Soviet report. Their professions: four students, two NCOs, one FET employee, seven *lumpen* (commoners), four artisans, four peasants, three workers, and one employee.[174]

Cross-referencing of the diverse qualitative sources tends to confirm this profile. Though militant Falangists did not constitute the majority of the Division volunteers, their numbers were by no means trifling: they ranged between 15 per cent and 20 per cent, with greater presence among the volunteers of 1941 and 1942. The fact that more than a fourth of the sample corresponds to soldiers who were fulfilling their military service does not necessarily shed light on the conditions of their enlistment. A portion of them demonstrated at least group willingness to volunteer. The same can be said of most of the army corporals, sergeants, and provisional ensigns. The common ground of anti-communism and a calculation of benefits (professional promotion, economic incentives, or prestige) were also significant factors. Even the Spanish communists in exile acknowledged that the backbone of the "first" Blue Division was composed of ardent anti-communists, especially Falangists (about half the contingent). Another 20–25 per cent were army officers, NCOs, adventurers, and *lumpen* individuals alongside a similar percentage of peasants and workers:

> The fact that there have been cases of coercive recruitment is not, however, sufficient motive to discredit the fact that most of the recruits are really volunteers, and that the core is composed of the militant Falangists (students from bourgeoisie or petit-bourgeoisie origins, sons of landowners, employees and bureaucrats of the Falange and the state apparatus, a few aristocrats, etc.).

The report detailed the differences by regions. In Madrid, Falangists were predominant among a volunteer corps composed of students, civil servants, and employees. Falangists and Francoist ex-combatants abounded in the north, north-west, and Castile, along with significant numbers of students and sons of prosperous peasants, civil servants, and some "peasants and Catholic workers." Among the recruits in the south were numerous *lumpen*: virtually illiterate workers and peasants, most of whom were ex-combatants.[175] Massive Falangist popular enlistment had only occurred in Valencia and Murcia.[176]

Falangists, Ex-combatants, and "Wartime Francoists"

What sort of Falangists volunteered? The FET statutes established an internal hierarchy based on number of years in the party: Old Guard, Old Shirts, and the rest. The great majority of the Old Shirts and Old Guard were also ex-combatants or ex-prisoners, many of whom held posts of local, provincial, or regional leadership in the single party structure or in the state administration. However, in 1941, the bulk of the membership corresponded to those who had been flowing into the Falange since the outbreak of the Civil War. The veterans often considered new Falangists to be mere opportunists, and even some camouflaged Reds.[177] The youth who enlisted after 1939 enhanced the heterogeneity of the FET. Many had come from the SEU and had not fought in the Civil War. One leader from Murcia indicated that the mobilization of volunteers for the BD had generated a new "unity" and strengthened ties among "comrades from different political origins" in a province that boasted 4,303 members and 11,309 affiliates at the time. In the province of León, the wave of enthusiasm helped to increase affiliation with the party. A sizeable percentage of FET members left for Russia, but not the majority. In Murcia, there were at least 429 Falangist volunteers, which accounted for 34.7 per cent of all volunteers and 10 per cent of the party members in the province: 148 of them (34.5 per cent) were Old Guard.[178]

Participation in the Civil War had converted many Spaniards into authentic "war Francoists" who were fascistized to some degree. There are some common features in the biographies of NCOs, provisional ensigns, sergeants, and provisional lieutenants who enlisted in the BD. Most came from Catholic, rural, or semi-urban social and family contexts. Frequently, their only political socialization prior to 1936 had been through religious organizations. During the Civil War they had joined the rebel side to defend their social standing and their traditional Catholic and Spanish nationalist values.[179] Some had become sergeants or provisional ensigns alongside those who had attended the General Military Academy (the *estampillados*, of "rubber-stamped"). Despite the scant technical training of the former, they were disciplined and shared the mystique of sacrifice. Some estimates raise the number of "provisional sergeants" within the total BD contingent to 4,500.[180] Many of them remained in active service after April 1939.[181]

For more than one provisional sergeant, the army became home and the military life they had learned during the Civil War warped the destiny of more than one promising son from the lower-middle classes. Leopoldo Mulet, son of a customs agent, described his life as one marked by the 1936–9 conflict, which interrupted a biography oriented towards a mercantile profession:

> I am a university graduate and teacher, I know French and English, I have travelled quite a lot ... Where have I been until now? The Civil War captured my interest while I was living at home, I have been an officer since March '37 and in the Legion since '38 ... When I get back to Spain, I will help my father with his work (customs agent).

Julio González, the son of a bourgeois family, had finished his baccalaureate studies prior to 1936 and was studying Maths in Madrid. The outbreak of the Civil War changed his fate, taking him first to the General Military Academy and then to the Russian Front:

> The war caught me on holiday and ... I traded in my equations for a rifle; after that I thought that my degree might serve to get me a month of leave and I went to a course for provisional artillery ensigns. I finished the war as a Lieutenant, and when faced with the dilemma of continuing my military career or living off my father ... I opted for the first ... I went to the Academy, finished and when I was beginning to enjoy garrison life away from home, it happened ... and here I am.[182]

Several officers in the sappers' corps had similar trajectories. They had gone through technical or scientific training before the Civil War and had volunteered for the insurgent army. After 1939, those with some military training stayed on in the Army Corps of Engineers.[183] All of them were simply Francoists without any further labels, who did not really care about military-Falangist-Catholic disputes. They shared the Catholic faith and a definition of the common enemy: communism, freemasonry, separatism, and "international Jewry." The borders were often blurred between civilians and soldiers, or between professional soldiers (or those who had enlisted while doing military service) and civilians who had enlisted through the militias. Many NCOs and provisional ensigns had enlisted through the Falange recruiting offices, while many soldiers had both professional objectives and ideological motives: anti-communism and a sense of patriotic duty were intertwined with the desire to pursue a career in the army or in the state administration.[184] A Falangist volunteer, Constantino Georgacopulos, wrote in 1942 that all his unit's corporals came from the lower social strata. Though all of them were "children from the orphanage," he liked the fact that they were all devoted Catholics.[185]

Though the Falange tried to ensure that among the officers who left in July 1941 there would be affinity with Falangist ideas, this did not entirely resolve an underlying tension between Falangist militiamen and professional soldiers in the Blue Division. Many of the former group were from middle-class families or were university students, while others had been decorated during the Civil War. It was difficult for the former to accept orders from illiterate sergeants who were frequently biased against them.[186] They also expressed mistrust of a military rather than militia venture, as a Falangist volunteer wrote:

> As I had predicted when we left Madrid, there was nothing "Blue Division" about it; instead of Falangists we are soldiers, but what kind of soldiers? In general, we are treated badly ... though the Falangist officers are really to blame, they treat us like conscripts.[187]

The friction began before they left. In the barracks of the university district of Madrid, the Falangists protested at being put together "with soldiers of no Falangist feeling whatsoever." During the training period, many grumbled at the "severe discipline, of a purely military type."[188] Many other soldiers were disgusted at the proliferation of Falangist symbols (such as the yoke and arrows) on the uniforms. Luis Aguilar noted one captain's displeasure at seeing his insignia: "'Don't think that you are coming here to steal like in Spain,' he shouts at us." A few days later, his comrades disregarded an ensign's command to stop singing the hymn "Cara al sol" (Facing the sun).[189]

Most of the FET hierarchy had become simple privates, but they held great influence over their comrades. In several units, a second political hierarchy ran parallel (informally) to the military command structure. The 2nd Anti-tank Company, for example, was composed of leaders such as Agustín Aznar, Enrique Sotomayor, Ridruejo, and "Old Guard Falangists from Madrid."[190] However, the Falangists wanted to be militiamen above all: Salvador Zanón, a student, wrote that "though the Militia has become part of the Army ... we must not lose our Falangist distinctivness."[191]

Clearing Your Military Record ... or Deserting

Many volunteers were motivated by material incentives. Misery and unemployment in post-war Spain drove them to enlist for Russia, especially in provinces with high rates of unemployment among agricultural or other workers. The double pay offered by the German and Spanish armies (7.30 pesetas and 4 marks per day, along with 1,000 pesetas for joining up) enticed them, along with a subsidy to the families of volunteers at the front. To sweeten the deal, they could also fulfil their military service requirement expediently: six months on the Russian Front were equivalent to two years of compulsory military service.[192]

Alongside these volunteers were others who had problems with military justice due to their political record or because they had fought – willingly or otherwise – with the Republican Army. Participating in the Russian campaign might serve to clear their record and was taken into consideration by military and civilian courts. The Falangists themselves knew of such people and at times protected them. One of them wrote of his childhood friend, a former Republican soldier:

> We have always been like brothers, but he went to the university … Then with the war, I was a Legion officer and he was an officer in the Republican Army … If I persuaded him to enlist to come to Russia with the Blue Division, it was because I believed and still believe that if he is lucky and returns to Spain, as an ex-combatant he will irreproachable in every way.[193]

In some cases, former leftists enlisted in the Division to find a way to get out of Spain and even cross over to the Red Army.[194] However, not everyone who enlisted was selected; volunteers were politically scrutinized at the beginning, during training in Germany, and as they arrived at the front. Vigilance became more intense in 1943, as recruitment became less selective in the military bases. The Blue Division Information Section (IIb) implemented tighter controls and compiled a dossier of "undesirables" that eventually amounted over the years 1941–3 to 2,271 names.[195] In late 1942, the BD General Staff had begun to show greater concern for the quality of the "human materiel" arriving in the replacement expeditions. The BD office in Madrid ordered the commander of the 18th March Battalion in December 1942 to organize "an information service, among persons they fully trust," in order to unmask soldiers "with turbid ideas and thinking, who might join the Red ranks."[196] The Germans also feared that among the march battalion officers there might be informants who were spying for the Allies.[197]

Certain British intelligence reports and Soviet propaganda spread an image that the Division was replete with soldiers looking for an opportunity to desert. Adversaries of the FET within the Francoist administration helped this impression along. Ambassador Samuel Hoare reported in August 1941, after a conversation with General Antonio Aranda, an Anglophile, that 750 volunteers had already gone over to the enemy.[198] However, the total number of politically motivated deserters remained low. During the first six months of the replacement system, scarcely 2 per cent of the soldiers from Russia were repatriated for political antecedents that would induce them to entertain the possibility of desertion or espionage.[199] Cases of self-mutilation (shooting oneself in the hand, doing guard duty barefoot to provoke frostbite in the feet, etc.) were equally scarce,[200] partly because of the volunteer screening that was in place. The Spanish Army and the FET itself were the first ones interested in sending reliable soldiers.

Some volunteers crossed over simply out of fear or desperation caused by the dire conditions on the front.[201] As of February 1942, there had only been six deserters (and one dubious case), who had declared to the Soviets that they had enlisted with the intent of crossing over. Most of them were Republican ex-combatants or former members of left-wing parties. According to Soviet reports, the total number of deserters may have been twelve.[202] In the two years of Division deployment on the Russian Front, as many as twenty-one soldiers were tried and sentenced to death for serious crimes (desertion, treason, etc.); fourteen of them were executed, along with two others in the Blue Legion.[203] The number may have been higher, but only slightly; from November 1941 to August 1942, twenty-four trials for desertion took place in the Blue Division.[204]

The BD intelligence services detected several cases of Republican ex-combatants who manifested sympathies for the Red Army and had tried to convince fellow soldiers to cross over with them.[205] From early 1943 on, a few more desertions occurred between Logroño and the border town of Irún, or between Hendaye and Germany: four soldiers of the 21st March Battalion defected before the unit arrived in Hof in April 1943. In October of the same year, four more volunteers deserted before reaching Irún and two others between Hendaye and Hof.[206] In total, eighty to one hundred soldiers – averaging scarcely two per thousand – deserted to the enemy. Numbers began to increase in the second half of 1942 and reached their highest point in mid-1943. The German 18th Army command informed in August 1942 that desertions had increased since the arrival of the first march battalions. The German military attaché in Madrid asked the minister of the army to postpone the departure of the three September relief expeditions in order to do background checks on the recruits.[207]

However, despite German worry, the number of desertions never really became significant. Though awareness of the risk of desertions was greater, it rarely gave cause for real concern in combat.[208] By comparison, the proportion of deserters in the International Brigades during the Spanish Civil War was at least eight times greater: between 1.7 per cent and 1.9 per cent.[209]

Elements unsympathetic to the Francoist regime could not always be purged in time, but not all of them had the opportunity to cross over to the Soviets. The fate that awaited those who managed to do so was very different to what the Red Army leaflets had promised them. Some collaborated with the NKVD propaganda services, but all were interned in prisoner camps. Though some captives decided to remain in the USSR after 1954, most returned to Spain when they had the opportunity.[210] Many of those who returned to Spain from Soviet captivity had been listed as deserters and faced interrogation. Some biographies were as picturesque as they were tragic. The day labourer Martín Ferrero, a communist during the Civil War, had enlisted in the BD in 1942 in hopes of crossing over to the enemy. Instead, he was treated as a prisoner by the Soviets. Alberto Moreno, an employee who had been an anarchist militiaman in the Civil War, enlisted in the BD in 1943. He crossed over to the Soviets, who sent him to prison camp. Sotero García had no political record but had been mobilized in the Francoist Army in 1937. After the war, he operated on the black market in Manresa (Barcelona) and spent some months in prison. Later, he killed two people and fled to Cádiz, where he enlisted for Russia under a false name, intending to defect. His efforts had the same outcome: ten years of harsh captivity in Soviet camps.[211]

Though few, the numbers of BD deserters surpassed the German average, even as early as January 1942. Unauthorized absences from the front (or defections towards the BD rearguard) were more abundant than in neighbouring divisions. This included intentional deserters as well as "disoriented" soldiers (*despistados*) who had been granted several days' leave but apparently had got lost while returning to duty: sometimes with the consent of their officers, sometimes for months.[212] Private José Luis Pascal drove a truck during the march of 1941. He was sent to Warsaw to acquire replacement parts, only to reappear in Vilnius in January 1942.[213] Secundino A. Cano volunteered in 1941 and spent the campaign in several hospitals. After re-enlisting in November 1942, he deserted in Germany and looked for work in Frankfurt am Main.[214] Others fled towards the rearguard and deserted out of fear, discontent, or desperation at being punished by an officer.[215]

"Spain on the Volkhov": Falangism in the Blue Division

Fervent Falangists never comprised a majority in the BD, even among the original contingent. However, they were a significant minority with a group conscience that permeated the dominant BD war culture. The Ourense Falange informed in October 1941 that 35 of its 97 volunteer militiamen were "Falangists," and 45 others were not.[216] Of the 89 volunteers from Santander in July 1941, 36 (40.44 per cent) were militant

Falangists and 16 of those (18 per cent of the total) had been members prior to 18 July 1936. As many as 9 (10.1 per cent) had suffered Republican violence personally or in their family. In Murcia, the percentage of Falangists reached 68.5 per cent (285 of 316 with known affiliation).[217] It is more difficult to ascertain how many had been members of the Falange prior to July 1936. Proportions varied from province to province and enthusiasm tended to intensify where there were more Falangists who had not been able to fight in 1936–9 on the side of their choosing.[218]

To boost volunteer enlistment, the FET secretariat suggested that provincial leaders enlist in the recruitment offices. Some of them would be permitted to leave for Russia. They also encouraged volunteering among those in local hierarchies with questionable commitment or records.[219] Eight of the provincial FET leaders who enlisted left for Russia in 1941. Among them were the party board members Dionisio Ridruejo, Mora-Figueroa, Agustín Aznar, Higinio París Eguilaz, Eduardo de Rojas, and José M. Gutiérrez del Castillo, along with youth leader José Miguel Guitarte and many second- and third-tier leaders, from village mayors to local councillors.

For many Falangists the adventure was initially a political investment. Enlistment was a temporary adventure that might yield personal and collective dividends. They would return home as victors, with the prestige of having defeated the "Great Enemy", which would enhance their possibilities of fostering the full fascistization of the Franco regime.[220] This vision of the campaign as a step towards national-syndicalist revolution was reinforced after the first combats: "Let them not forget that the volunteers, once the enemy is annihilated on the front, will return ready to die to prevent any postulate of our National-Syndicalist Revolution from not becoming a practical reality," wrote a volunteer. Similarly, Salvador López de la Torre noted that the fundamental motivation of his comrades, beyond their personal stories, was to fulfil the missional duty of the Falange. The letters of Falangist volunteers transmitted their self-perception of being the advance troops in the fight for the physical and "spiritual" reconstruction of Spain in distant lands.[221]

For the Falangists, the Russian campaign also represented an opportunity to restore Spain's "imperial destiny," by increasing its participation in the restructuring of Europe according to the Nazi New Order. Dionisio Ridruejo recalled that he had not gone to Russia for anti-communism alone, but because he believed in a "young, heroic and popular Europe that certain ingenious fascists have imagined." He and his comrades thought that "all the misfortunes and lowering of Spain – including poverty and social inequality – proceeded primarily from its submission to Anglo-French hegemony." With Axis victory, they expected "the constitution of a unified, independent and powerful Europe, in which Spain could play an important role." This would also make it possible to eliminate "the plutocratic and clerical complex that burdens the State."[222]

Like good fascists, however, the Falangist volunteers were proper nationalists. None of them was willing to serve explicitly as a battering ram for German influence. Though they hastened to the Third Reich to provide political support, they would never dare contemplate the overthrow of Franco by a pro-German puppet dictator. A memorandum arrived at the German embassy in July 1941, signed by "Crusaders against Russia," who requested support from Berlin to give the state and the army a decidedly Falangist agenda. They aspired to bolster the "imperial style of the Falange," but were careful to emphasize the "Christian character" of Spanish fascism and did not question Franco's leadership.[223]

Blue Division's Falangism is perhaps best expressed in the corpus of slogans that distilled the spirit of the first Falange. Adventuresome bellicosity also reflected a generational sentiment. Having been socialized since adolescence in an environment of political confrontation during the Republican period and war mobilization in 1936–9, more than one young Falangist felt himself a participant in a singular historical moment, in which great but mutually exclusive cosmovisions defended their existence in armed conflict. The Falangist writer Antonio Abad Ojuel expressed this in fiction: the BD would avenge the indecision of their elders, who had allowed the defeat of Cuba in 1898 ("you gave up without a fight") and trembled before the prodigious power of violence. The new fascist generation "had been born under the sign of the warrior," and war "met us as we took our first steps in baccalaureate, waited for us in the street brawls." This was not a time for theory; "we are in the pre-apocalyptic era, of fundamental values and firm decisions."[224] The volunteers were "new men" who prioritized "action." They rebelled against the nineteenth century and reason; they identified with the romantics, irrational values, and action for the sake of the nation as a "revolutionary synthesis" of virility and violence.[225]

This enthusiasm reached its highest levels in Falangist youth organizations such as the SEU, whose leaders enlisted together. As early as the winter of 1939, there were proposals to recruit volunteers for the Finnish Army in the Winter War. Some testimonies have indicated that as many as 10 per cent (or more in university cities) of the BD volunteers in 1941 were SEU affiliates. By May 1942, around two thousand SEU members were estimated to have departed for Russia.[226] The "wave" even reached students from anti-Francoist families. The later film-maker Luis García Berlanga, the son of a former Republican leader who was imprisoned at the time, declared years later that he had gone to Russia hoping to get his father released, but he did acknowledge that his Falangist friends at the University of Valencia had strongly influenced him.[227]

Anti-communism and radical Spanish nationalism provided a homogenizing varnish to the various ideological sensitivities of the winners of the Civil War, whether Falangists, conservative Catholics, or "war Francoists." Fifteen years later, one veteran wrote that though the BD had emerged from a Falangist initiative, volunteers from very diverse affiliations had fought on the basis of two common denominators: anti-communism and Catholicism. Thus, Menéndez Gundín indicated three intertwined motives in his diary: anti-communism, a sense of generational and patriotic duty, and avenging the death of his father at Republican hands. Others from the ranks of the Spanish Army expressed the conviction that they were fulfilling a patriotic mission.[228]

However, as some Falangists perceived it, the baptism by fire of October 1941 had given birth to a new political reality. The new community of combatants would be a revived Falange, a mix of Civil War veterans, Old Shirts, university students, sergeants who had come up through the ranks, and devoted Catholics: "the Division is and always will be Falangist, from the captain down," proclaimed Dionisio Ridruejo. This new Falange was also committed to Spain's destiny in Europe and incarnated a universal dimension.[229] One sign of this was the assimilation of Falangist symbols by volunteers from different provenances, first and foremost in the collective singing of the Falangist anthem "Cara al Sol" as the representation of the spirit of the whole Blue Division.[230]

This new Falange would be the epitome of the New Spain, grounded in the diverse social, regional, and political origins of the BD volunteers. The party newspaper *Arriba* insisted that solidarity with the Blue Division should help "reconstitute the moral and material architecture of Spain," restoring to it "the sense of solidarity" and "political unity." The joint participation of Falangists, Carlists, and the military would engender "an authentic synthesis of the forces representing the new political and social order of Spain." In Russia, "Carlists and Falangists, professors and students, engineers and workers had fought together," under the common banner of "loyalty to the principles of 18 July." The unity of destiny described by the mythified leader José Antonio Primo de Rivera had materialized in the Russian campaign: an enterprise that would bind all Spaniards in a missional sense of the nation, as preached by Falangism. The "Spain on the Volkhov" would endow the "national revolution" with real content.[231] This perception was also intimately shared by Falangists who enlisted in 1942.[232]

Many BD volunteers also cultivated a self-image of ethical integrity: they had neither been corrupted nor participated in Francoist post-war repression. Falangist volunteer José M. Castañón noted in his diary that, refusing to have anything to do with the "crimes of the rearguard ... I have come again to the front dreaming of a future ordering of Europe that will also order Spain." The British military attaché reported that Old Shirts claimed to have enlisted in the Division to "get away from Spain in its present state."[233] One Falangist from Santander even stated in a letter published after his death in Russia that his disenchantment over the deterioration of his ideals in Spain had moved him to enlist: "I do not conform to life at present; this 'black market' atmosphere asphyxiates me. Of undercover Reds, of 'lifelong right-wing men.'"[234]

Years later, the BD Falangist veterans sometimes named themselves the Generation of 1941.[235] However their *esprit de corps* was insufficient to influence the development of the FET in any decisive way or the regime upon their return. Their experience was one of a lost generation.

3 A Long March: From Central Europe to the Volkhov Front

In late July 1941, a group of Spanish officers left the Grafenwöhr camp for the Eastern Front. They had been assigned to German units in the Ukraine to familiarize themselves with Wehrmacht combat methods and returned several days later. Most of the Blue Division units, however, remained at the training camp for five to six weeks – half of the usual twelve-week training period for the German Army. On 20 August 1941, the first convoy of six trains with contingents of Spanish troops departed from the Grafenwöhr, Parkenstein-Ulten, and Wisek Stations. The 250th Division left in sixty-six trains over a five-day period. The motorized vehicles departed last, in a column of two hundred units. They were destined for Suwałki, on the border with occupied Poland, though some convoys went directly to Grodno in Eastern Poland.

Once they got off the train in occupied territory, the Spanish combatants encountered the first harsh reality of their new life. Like most of the German infantry units, they would have to make a good part of the journey on foot, assisted by some vehicles and hundreds of horses that carried impedimenta, munitions, artillery pieces, and heavy weaponry. The BD received 5,610 horses that had been requisitioned by the Wehrmacht in the Balkans and were in a lamentable state when they arrived in Grafenwöhr after such a long journey. Caring for the horses became a serious problem, made worse by the poor quality of the animals and the inexperience of many of their caretakers. In Spain, an excessive number of drivers had been recruited with the idea that the Division would be motorized. They had to be quickly retrained to tame horses.[1]

Thus began an interminable walk along the highways of Eastern Poland, Lithuania, Byelorussia, and Russia to the city of Vitebsk, where they again boarded a train for the sector of the front that had been assigned to the BD. The foot march was gruelling for most of the volunteers. Walking several dozen kilometres per day on poor, rocky, irregular highways in autumn weather that had turned unseasonably cold in September, with ever colder freezes at night, and under the constant weight of their kits was something that the short training period in Grafenwöhr had not prepared them for sufficiently. The hardships were especially unbearable for the middle-class urban volunteers, university students, and those without prior military experience. However, not even the most experienced veterans, the battle-worn Falange activists from the founding years or the sergeants and provisional ensigns, had suffered such hard and ongoing foot marches during the Civil War.

A total of 2,177 *aspeados* – the name given to soldiers who had virtually "walked their feet off" – developed severe blisters and had to be transported in cars to hospitals. As many as eighty-two soldiers and NCOs were repatriated in late September for improper conduct or lack of physical endurance. Many of the *aspeados*, according to military surgeon López Romero, arrived with a "rather relaxed" morale and attitude, corresponding to "those who would later be scabs on the Division, inseparable from the Field Hospital, who came to us full of complaints and laments, in a word, lack of spirit." This was reflected in their untidy appearance and bad behaviour:

> Many of them, a few days into the march, came in full of misery, with torn clothes, long hair, unshaven and lice-ridden. During the stay at this centre, they practiced their favourite pastimes, gambling and stealing. In places like Orsha, where we were quartered next to the town, they would even escape at night from their respective lodgings; to the point that we had to cordon off the Camp. In the Hearings for Disability in Grodno and Minsk, they came flooding in, demoralized, some trying to take advantage of the good faith of the Medical Tribunal with supposed ailments that would allow them to return to Spain.[2]

Discipline deteriorated rapidly in the march columns. The Spaniards distinguished themselves, as some had done in Grafenwöhr, for flouting the Wehrmacht norms of uniformity and organization. They scarcely concerned themselves with what they considered trifles, such as keeping their jacket buttoned, always carrying their weapons on their shoulder, or leaving clear space on the road. The resulting effect in the march columns was scarcely martial to German eyes and to those in occupied villages. Many soldiers tried to save themselves the effort of walking and climbed onto equipment vehicles whenever they could, overloading them further. The care and cleaning of their weapons and kits left much to be desired, and the state of their horses was worse. Many were lost to exhaustion, deficient care, and frequent overburdening.

Fig. 3.1. Spanish soldiers with *Soldatenbuch*, Grafenwöhr, July 1941 (AGA)

Added to this were minor incidents with the civilian population, beginning in the Masurian city of Treuburg (Olecko), where the German liaison wrote on 26 August of the "notable complaints" of the civilian population regarding the conduct of the BD volunteers. In a 6 September meeting with Field Marshall Günther von Kluge, commander in chief of the 4th German Army, the liaison officers described the situation in telegraphic terms:

> Confusing marching orders, lack of march discipline, scarce capacity of the youngest officers to impose authority, failure of the NCO corps, absolute lack of quartermasters, poor care of the already deficient Serbian horses, etc.

The only thing worth highlighting, according to the liaison officers, was the "good cheer and combative happiness of the Spaniards." There was the occasional case of desertion towards the rearguard from soldiers overcome by fatigue or those who desired to slip away.[3] However, in general their morale did not decline despite the harshness of the march, the increasing cold, and the visible signs of recent combat that became more and more frequent as the soldiers crossed the former Soviet border. Jesús Martínez Tessier, a Falangist journalist, penned in his diary on 8 September 1941:

> We pass destroyed towns and houses. In Lyda there is a large amount of war materiel destroyed by German air raids. There are enormous tanks and several military trains. On the highway, now and then, you find tombs of German soldiers.

Nine days later, the impression of getting closer to the scene of combat generated excitement among the troops: "gutted tanks, an occasional crashed Red plane and German tombs." The officers were sure that the combat would be harsh but short, and everyone expected a swift German victory.[4]

March discipline in the Blue Division improved after the second week of September and the unit increased its pace to almost thirty kilometres per day. Even so, when Muñoz Grandes and the German liaison commander visited the Army Group Centre headquarters to finalize the details of their incorporation on the front, the Germans were scandalized at what they saw when the Spaniards passed by. The panorama had not changed: units were walking on both sides of the motorway past Minsk and blocking traffic, and there were unwarlike scenes ("the march column was transporting livestock"), irregular clothing, and lack of agreement regarding how to carry their weapons. The Organization Todt drivers on the motorway were speechless at the spectacle that reinforced their biases regarding the southern "rascals."[5]

Von Bock appeared reticent to command Spaniards in Army Group Centre. Meanwhile, Army Group North needed reinforcements. After having sent part of its troops to the final Moscow offensive, it had been forced to repel heavy Soviet counter-attacks. In all probability, that was what motivated the German command – at Hitler's request – to assign the 250th Division to a new front. On 25 September, the OKH notified the 9th Army, who transmitted the order to the BD that they would be dispatched to the northern sector of the front. The Spaniards, thus, would participate in the operations for the siege of Leningrad and its adjacent scenarios.[6]

Despite their disappointment at not fighting in the next Moscow offensive, the *guripas* (what the BD soldiers called themselves) took the news with resignation and a touch of humour, as private Luis Aguilar recorded:

> They say that the General of the Army Corps we were assigned to doesn't want us, as in our marches we give the impression of being a useless force. Perhaps it is because we go unbuttoned, with our hats to one side and because some of our anti-tank pieces have names: Lola, Carmencita, etc., and the occasional chicken hanging from the tow.[7]

The Spanish columns had to turn around, return to Vitebsk, and board the train to Pleskau/Pskow, located in the rearguard of the Leningrad Front. On 1 October, Muñoz Grandes and liaison officer Günther Collatz arrived at Army Group North headquarters; two days later they were at the headquarters of the 16th Army, to which the Spanish Division had been assigned. The logistical problems continued: the horses and motorized vehicles were in poor conditions and the troops were scruffy and fed up at not having entered combat. The quartermaster of the liaison staff also observed that the BD's organizational deficiencies had become more acute during the foot march.[8]

On 10 October 1941, the Army Group North war diary indicated, with open mistrust, that it was not only dubious that the Spanish Division would be capable of going on the offensive, due to their slovenly appearance, but that "the troops create an unusual impression to German eyes. The state of the horses and vehicles is questionable."[9] The following day, the Blue Division was incorporated into the provisional army group under the command of General Franz von Roques, then commander in chief of the rearguard of Army Group

North. Instead of replacing the 126th German Infantry Division, the BD was deployed more to the south, between Novgorod and the Volkhov River, to the north of Lake Ilmen, to relieve the 18th Infantry Division in its defensive position. The German liaison command and the headquarters of the 250th Wehrmacht Division – the Spanischen Freiwilligen Division – were established in Grigorovo, on the outskirts of the destroyed, mostly abandoned city of Novgorod. The Spanish units began to occupy their positions on the front in the following days, just as the first snowfalls ushered in freezing weather – the prelude to a particularly harsh and early winter that would be decisive to the course of the war.[10]

The Wehrmacht and Spanish Soldiers

The Admired Wehrmacht: An Egalitarian Army?

The first thing that Spanish volunteers experienced in Germany was the Wehrmacht, regarded by all of them as a well-oiled machine. They were fascinated by its equipment, armaments, and organization, which made it possible for the Wehrmacht to fight a war which was, in their eyes, far more modern and brutal than that experienced in Spain five years before. In the process, many BD soldiers, or *divisionarios*, also implicitly juxtaposed the ostensible perfection of German logistics with the imperfect functioning of the Spanish Army. Bad supplies and the inefficiency of many Spanish officers and NCOs became particularly evident to them. Dionisio Ridruejo expressed an almost astonished admiration for the Wehrmacht as he wrote from the instruction camp of Grafenwöhr: "we are in the midst of a colossal army, almost painfully perfect ... an army which is like the people it serves." Even the cells in German military prisons were regarded as comfortable and clean compared to Spanish ones. This perception was also shared by the most professional Spanish military. Artillery Colonel Jesús Badillo wrote that the Germans as a "collective" were a "great people." Just a few months later, he admitted some nuances. Wehrmacht commanders were no longer demigods; they committed tactical mistakes, limited themselves to "obeying orders as robots," and lacked the ability to improvise when things went wrong.[11]

BD volunteers especially noticed the contrast between German military efficiency and the relatively careless organization of the Spanish military in areas of health care and food supply. Until at least mid-1942, it was clear to the *divisionarios* that their German comrades were better equipped and better fed, though in theory both groups

Fig. 3.2. German soldiers fraternize with Spanish volunteers, France, July 1941 (AA)

received a similar diet.[12] Contrasts in attention received at military hospitals were even more striking.[13] Convalescing Spanish soldiers usually pointed out the differences in treatment between German military hospitals (clean and well organized, with sympathetic staff) and Spanish ones. Such differences could also be observed in hospitals located in the German rearguard.[14] This perception was later reinforced by the Spanish soldiers' specific memories of German nurses, which oscillated between gratitude for their efficiency and idealization of their supposedly open-minded approach to sexual matters. Quite often, the *Krankenschwestern* became a sexual myth for Spanish war veterans.[15]

Moreover, many BD combatants, particularly Falangist volunteers, perceived the Wehrmacht as a socially egalitarian army, where harsh discipline coexisted with the recreation of a classless national community (*Volksgemeinschaft*) through comradeship and shared experiences at the front, and where many officers were deeply committed Nazis.[16] It was the true National Socialist army that many Falangists strove to create in Spain, and served as an uncomfortable reminder of the inadequacies of their own army. Many volunteers greatly appreciated the fact that German officers waited their turn in the daily communal meal queue, did not take extra portions of food and tobacco, sat among the soldiers on trains, and received the same treatment as the privates at the cantinas (*Soldatenheime*) in the rear.[17] Moreover, they also noted positively that German officers and NCOs did not inflict physical punishment on their subordinates, which was a common practice in the Spanish Army. The Blue Division was no exception to that rule, as many volunteers described in their war diaries.[18] This was consistent with the tradition of the Prussian Army and the Wehrmacht, where officers and NCOs were meant to reinforce the cohesion of primary groups. One Spanish veteran remembered years later how they acted as "the *mother* of his unit."[19]

Spanish and German Soldiers: Stereotypes, Coexistence, and Conflict

The German military welcomed the Spanish Blue Division and appreciated its contribution in ambivalent terms. From December 1941 on the Wehrmacht suffered too many casualties and the Spaniards were mostly regarded as useful for covering defensive positions. German commanders, whose views were conditioned by pre-existing stereotypes, were openly disdainful of Spanish military culture. They saw in their Spanish colleagues a blend of social elitism, professional ignorance, and laziness, and felt particularly angry upon observing the privileges enjoyed by BD officers in terms of food rations and accommodation.[20] Their remarks resembled those expressed by liaison officers in Romanian and Italian units, and they revealed the difficulties of cooperation amongst allies with diverse military cultures that all reflected the social hierarchies of their respective countries.[21]

Despite the rhetorical praising of Spanish "heroic deeds" at the front, most German commanders who had the BD under their responsibility disliked a foreign unit whose combatants were regarded as individually brave, but chaotic and led by untrained officers unable to understand modern warfare.[22] The views of Wehrmacht officers were influenced more by their professional arrogance than by racial doctrines. Nonetheless, there also were some exceptions. Oberzahlmeister Ludwig Schwab from the military garrison in Hof noted in 1944 that Spanish soldiers incorporated a conglomerate of different races, from Aryans who were "tall, blond and blue-eyed, descendants of the Goths" to the "*mestizos* of African descent, small, brown, with curly hair and Negroid traces." Despite being racially impure, he observed, Spaniards also were thought to be "proud" and extremely nationalist.[23]

The attitudes of German rank-and-file soldiers and NCOs towards their Spanish comrades were far more positive. Certainly, their image of the exotic Iberians rested heavily on pre-existing romantic stereotypes, spread by the press and cinema of the Third Reich.[24] These icons were also present amongst Nazi leaders: Hitler appreciated Spanish soldiers as undisciplined but reliable comrades.[25] German privates (*Landser*) particularly valued qualities related to virility, such as combat solidarity and individual bravery. In contrast to Romanian or Italian soldiers, Spaniards earned some respect in their allies' eyes. The positive references to Blue Division deeds in the daily *Wehrmachtsbericht*, which were thought to satisfy the Spanish government, undoubtedly contributed to this, as well as several press articles published by German, French, or Romanian newspapers.[26] Yet word of mouth communication amongst *Landsers* and their families was more decisive, as several examples from private letters suggest. From the Volkhov Front, Corporal Otto M. wrote in October 1941 that "a division of Spaniards has been deployed here and they fight quite well," while Captain Hermann Sch. stated that "our Spanish friends show themselves to be very courageous."[27] However, they also disliked the Iberian lack of concern for personal hygiene.[28] Not unsurprisingly, absurd rumours also circulated concerning the lack of discipline of the Spaniards: a German officer wrote in April 1942 that Spanish soldiers had shown up in Warsaw – a city they had never visited – with "almost no equipment and no weapons, because they had sold everything."[29]

Wehrmacht propaganda often exalted the spirit of comradeship between Spanish and German soldiers, which supposedly reincarnated the brothers-in-arms experience of the sixteenth century.[30] Yet, everyday relations displayed some ambivalence, reinforced by pre-existing stereotypes. Thus, the first impressions recorded in some Spanish war diaries after the *divisionarios* met their German comrades for the first time, once they had crossed the Pyrenees, pointed out a typical archetype, Prussian rigidity: "The Germans take over. I'm not sure what impression they make on me ... Anyway, what is sure is that I found them too cold and Prussian."[31] Though very few BD volunteers spoke German, many managed to scrape by and establish a solid camaraderie with German soldiers. Spanish and German officers resorted to French as their lingua franca and coexistence in forefront positions ran smoothly. In some sections, such as advanced artillery posts, platoons were often multinational and communicated using a mixed jargon of words from various languages.[32] Some Spanish and German soldiers even established real friendship ties, which often led the former to fully embrace identification with Third Reich war aims.[33]

Most contemporary accounts communicated a friendly, relatively positive image of German combatants, which endured despite differences in military culture. While Spaniards saw Germans collectively as cool and distant, when approached individually the Iberians found the latter to be honest, hard-working, and respectful people, who of course were incredibly clean and kept their equipment in good order. However, after dealing with Iberians, some Germans became "more down-to-earth and behave more and more like *gypsies*. They were on the fiddle, smuggling and trading everything imaginable."[34] The Blue Division trench journal insisted that shared front-line experience gave a fraternal tone to everyday relations between Germans and Spaniards.[35]

However, transnational comradeship was not always so idyllic in the rear. In September 1941, before the Blue Division arrived at the front, there were quarrels between Spanish and German soldiers. A Soviet report based on prisoner statements mentioned that the relationship between BD volunteers and their allies tended to be tense: "in Novgorod some clashes between Spaniards and Germans arose again."[36] Skirmishes between Axis soldiers in the villages in the rear of the Leningrad Front were also frequent. These were often related to competition for supplies of food and petrol, or to the scarcity of resources in a territory that had been systematically plundered.[37] On occasion, the consequences of such clashes were significant. In November 1943, six Spanish soldiers were at the core of various scandals in the taverns of Königsberg. When confronted by German combatants who reproached them for their conduct, the Spaniards opened fire on their brothers in arms. It left one *divisionario* dead and several wounded.[38]

However, the most common motive for dispute between Iberians and Germans was related to masculinity and the competition for Baltic, Russian, or even German women in the rearguard. Russian eyewitness accounts highlighted frequent clashes between Spanish and German occupants in the villages at the rear the Leningrad Front. In January 1943, for example, Spanish soldiers unleashed a wave of violence against the Germans to avenge the mistreatment of a Russian woman by a *Landser*.[39]

The disdain of Wehrmacht commanders was especially hard for the Germanophile Falangist volunteers to accept. As early as December 1941, Ridruejo wrote that "we may have felt ourselves abandoned by the Germans." Muñoz-Grandes acknowledged too that Germans "appreciate us, but [...] as a nation, I think they don't take us seriously."[40] However, most Spanish volunteers came to terms with such attitudes. Rank-and-file soldiers barely changed their positive view of Germans, and returnees

Fig. 3.3. The march to the front, Eastern Poland, September 1941 (AGA)

brought home positive memories of their treatment by the Wehrmacht. German diplomats and spies in Spain observed that most returned soldiers from the Eastern Front became sincere supporters of the Third Reich.[41]

On the German Home Front

The "Achievements" of the Third Reich: Spanish Impressions

The Spanish volunteers barely reflected at length on the theoretical principles of National Socialism in their diaries, letters, and memoirs. Many of their writings referred to the vague pro-European rhetoric of the "New Order" and the defence of Christian civilization that Nazi propaganda proclaimed as the common goal of all "crusaders." However, the Europe that the Spanish volunteers experienced was a continent dominated by the Third Reich. First and foremost was Germany, which they experienced during basic training at camps in Grafenwöhr (Upper Palatinate) and Hof

(Upper Franconia), during their occasional leaves, or on their trip back to Spain. For many Spanish volunteers, war tourism essentially involved visits to Germany and sometimes Latvia. What was their impression of the German home front, then, and what impression did it leave on them?

Most accounts left by *divisionarios* express sincere admiration for what they perceived to be the great social achievements of the Third Reich: the construction of a pseudo-welfare state that particularly benefited the working class and the peasantry. This perception was oblivious to, or else wilfully ignored, the racial costs of that peculiar welfare state, shaped by the concept of *Volksgemeinschaft*. Segments of the German population had been excluded and killed for biogenetic reasons, and their possessions had been appropriated by the state. Germany's slave labour and economic exploitation of occupied territories were also omitted from the BD accounts.[42]

Spaniards focused mainly on what they saw and how it contrasted with their country. The prevailing order and discipline as well as the external appearance of villages and farms shaped their initial positive impressions upon entering German territory. The military surgeon Manuel de Cárdenas penned in his diary as he crossed the Reich's border "in Germany no poor houses can be seen." The apparent well-being surrounding them also impressed convalescing Spanish soldiers on their walks through Königsberg. Even those who were not staunch fascists marvelled at German order and cleanness.[43] Daniel Torra was struck in October 1941 by the collective harmony he perceived all around him: "Germany will undoubtedly win the war ... It is an immense gearbox and its pieces work with chronometric precision."[44]

Once in German territory, every volunteer seemed to see what he wanted to see. Falangists regarded in the Third Reich a perfect model of a state that had achieved a high degree of social justice and national solidarity: a combination of nationalism and socialism that stayed loyal to the revolutionary principles of fascism without concessions to the Church, landowners, or bourgeoisie. This was what they felt still had to be done in Spain, where the Franco dictatorship was in their eyes more Catholic than truly fascist. Private José Luis Morales affirmed on his return to Spain that Germans loved a regime that "had given them their national dignity back."[45] Others considered that it was particularly Hitler who had enabled this new German well-being, after "breaking the chains of the Versailles Treaty."[46] Another Falangist summed up this perception:

> Within a few years, Hitler had managed to reconcile in a true social synergy the workers' forces and other national forces ... Seen from Spain, younger people really admired that ... What was particularly fascinating

in the new Germany, was to see millions of satisfied workers, who felt that their work had been endorsed. It was a strong, beautiful German youth, full of ideas, projecting themselves forward. It was like touching the creation of a new world and a new way of life.[47]

Many aspects of everyday life were also interpreted within this frame of meaning. In February 1942, the Falangist José M. Castañón admired the correct functioning of the food rationing system in Berlin and was astonished by the fact that no black market seemed to exist. He attributed this to the deep sense of national community that helped social justice to prevail, as was reflected in the lack of beggars in the streets:

> For Germans, justice is more rooted than charity ... Certainly, a *Gauleiter* must be better off than a common citizen. But there is no beggary. The basic necessities of living are well-covered for every German, and much more for those who work manually. The working class is privileged – although internal hierarchies are admitted – within the State.[48]

This also led to wishful thinking. Until 1943, many volunteers considered Berlin to be a city that "looks like anything but the capital of a nation in wartime."[49] In August 1941, only a handful of astute observers noted the increasing sacrifices that war required on the home front. Nevertheless, the perception of the German rearguard as a paradise began to change in 1942, as the massive air raids modified the image of German well-being. Soldiers convalescing or on leave could notice increasing shortages of food, clothing, and other basic goods. Some even noted, when they visited Berlin, the mounds of debris; they were heavily impressed by the sight of the victims' corpses left behind by bombardments.[50]

However, material welfare was not the aspect of Nazi Germany that impressed Spanish soldiers the most. Many of them appreciated what they saw as the patriotic stoicism of civilians on the home front and their commitment to the war effort of the Reich as well as their austerity. In their eyes, life was mostly harmonious on the German home front despite all the hardships. Citizens made sacrifices for a higher principle and understood that their future required "the joint effort of all, regardless of gender, age and class." Such stoicism was seen as the key factor behind the German "rebirth." A convalescent Spanish soldier noted that not even the defeat of Stalingrad had broken the link between the home front and the army.[51] Another volunteer was fascinated by what he regarded as the example of a strong community united by a common principle of national resurgence and social equality:

It is among the highest prizes and an indescribable honour to fight side by side with the Great German People and their commander Adolf Hitler; here there are no wealthy people, just a nation ready to put an end to all existing injustice in the world; they all eat the same; rationing is similar for the tall guy and the little guy ... here there are no beggars, they all earn their salary, and the work-disabled have the support of institutions that see to their education ... This is a paradise, something we would desire for our own nation.[52]

In short, the Third Reich was the sum of many qualities that Spanish fascists envied. It was a self-disciplined, hard-working nation that did not deserve defeat: "I would even like to fight just to help a people so united and convinced of its ideas"; another Falangist student wrote that "if God keeps me alive, I would like to apply to Spain the German method for greatness."[53]

Iberians and Bavarians

Despite the admiration of many ordinary Spaniards for the victories and shared anti-communism of the Wehrmacht, the Spanish volunteers with deep Catholic convictions continued to perceive one major obstacle in Nazi Germany: its pagan, anti-religious character. Many admirers of the Third Reich and the German people lamented that Luther's seed had germinated in that soil. To counteract these sceptical voices, some other *divisionarios* emphasized the fact that there were also many Germans who prayed to the true God. To them, this meant that good Germans were above all good Catholics, particularly Bavarians from the Upper Palatinate (Grafenwöhr) and Upper Franconians from Hof. Although Franconians and residents of the city of Hof in particular were mostly Protestants and did not particularly fit the Bavarian stereotype, they were sometimes portrayed as "very Catholic people," or "not very Germanic."[54] This fit very well with the stereotypes of German character and culture that the BD soldiers had acquired prior to their arrival to the country. One volunteer, for example, saw Hof as a "typically Tyrolean village [sic]" where "beer, coffee and potatoes" were abundant. Another Spaniard wrote that Bavaria was synonymous with "bright churches, simple affections and silent breweries," and particularly appreciated the many wooden carvings of Christ at the crossroads. Luis Riudavets recalled from his time spent in Hof how he had found some humble churches in a bucolic landscape, which gave him some hope for the future of National Socialism: "in spite of it all, not even the Germans have forgotten God."[55]

The German people were, in essence, a community as well organized as the Wehrmacht. Yet, individually Germans lacked sophistication. According to Ridruejo, a great cleavage existed between the "immense intelligence that such perfect mechanization and such detailed foresight reveals" in the Wehrmacht and the "awkward elementary character of each individual." This aroused some doubts in him when imagining Germany ruling its empire: "It just makes one uncomfortable with the idea of having this people ... sending around governors and drill sergeants all over Europe." Guillermo Hernanz and Captain Carlos Figuerola arrived at similar conclusions: the Germans were coarse, but well organized.[56] Not all volunteers had the chance to meet the civilians who lived near their training camps. In their accounts and letters to Spain, however, they painted a positive picture of the inhabitants of Hof and Grafenwöhr/Auerbach. When convalescent or on leave, Spanish soldiers were often greeted by civilians during their walks: "These Germans are extremely nice," wrote Manuel Tarín. Lieutenant Arenales wrote in similar terms about his short stay in Nuremberg: "I greet everyone. Everybody looks at us and says Hispanis [sic] as we pass by."[57]

Among the locals of Upper Palatinate and Upper Franconia, the impression left by Spanish volunteers on local memory seems to have been positive and was marked by dozens of funny anecdotes and stories.[58] In Grafenwöhr, the relative idealization of the Spaniards seems to have acted as a counterweight to the impression left behind by the many Waffen-SS soldiers stationed there later on. However, internal reports from the BD Information Section pointed out that Spanish soldiers were responsible for "disgusting scenes relating to women" and "incidents of a moral character" involving the civilian population. On occasion, divisionarios tried to flatter local girls, "making obscene gestures and addressing them in a very improper way." The locals had therefore adopted a distant attitude towards the Iberians, and the NS-DAP branches prevented their female members from having any contact with them. Complaints also arrived from the regional authorities in Bayreuth regarding the "unworthy behaviour" of some Spanish soldiers in the local taverns. As Private Joaquín Ros reached Grafenwöhr in September 1941, he noted, "Germans like us, despite the fact that our predecessors have also done some damage."[59]

A similar pattern was noticed in Hof, the Upper Franconian town where the relief expeditions from Spain arrived from early 1942 on, and which also served as Blue Division depot barracks in the German rear. Local shopkeepers benefited from the regular presence of Spanish soldiers in the town, who were eager to acquire consumer goods and even souvenirs. However, Iberian volunteers triggered several incidents in bars and restaurants. They also encouraged the growth of the black market for coffee, liquor, and tobacco.[60] The prostitutes of Hof, according to several accounts, also counted the Spaniards amongst their most regular clients. A well-known local sex worker was even put on trial and condemned to nine months in prison by the Bayreuth *Sondergericht* in May 1944, for seriously offending Wehrmacht honour by affirming that she preferred Spanish lovers to German "bastards."[61]

Small incidents were also common among the reserve soldiers who stopped over in Hof throughout 1942 and 1943, on their way to the Russian Front. A BD report in mid-1942 complained of how the officers and soldiers of the 14th March Battalion were getting drunk, starting public quarrels, and displaying "intolerable behaviour" towards the locals.[62] Complaints abounded at their lack of hygiene and their tendency to create public scandals that were shocking to the inhabitants of a small town in wartime.[63] Until mid-1942, indiscipline reigned amongst convalescents in the hospitals, who liked German nurses but were reluctant to obey the orders of Wehrmacht officers. The latter often complained about the Spaniards' disdain for basic standards of behaviour and dress. They also grumbled frequently about the inappropriate conduct of convalescents and soldiers on leave from the front.[64]

German Girls: "A Taste of Paganism and Nature"

German society welcomed the first expedition of Spanish volunteers with a mixture of wonder and curiosity. These feelings were shared by representatives of the Nazi Party and the civilian population, particularly young women. Internal reports from the commanders of the Spanish expeditions pointed out the great enthusiasm with which they were welcomed in Strasburg, and especially in Karlsruhe.[65] Some soldiers' letters referred to the "cheers and abundant tobacco" that volunteers encountered in the railway stations of the Reich; others explicitly highlighted the "kind reception" of the Germans.[66] Though less effusive, this positive reception in German territory continued to characterize the passage of Spanish convoys in the ensuing years.[67]

At the beginning, Spaniards seemed to encounter an endless supply of smiling female faces in Germany: the *Krankenschwestern* who handed out cigarettes and coffee, "blond, rosy and sweet girls" or "*Froilan*," apparently eager to be flattered by the moody Iberians.[68] A Falangist volunteer wrote that German women were "chatty, very easy-going in their behaviour, I would say they like to show off their charm."[69] Certainly, the transit of Spanish soldiers aroused the curiosity of the German girls. Lisa Mees remembered in 1943 the exchanges of letters and gifts that emerged from the brief encounters at Karlsruhe train station between BD volunteers and local girls two years before:

> When the Spaniards passed through Karlsruhe, we, German girls, felt very happy and wanted to see the Spanish volunteers. We found them all very nice, yet unfortunately we could not understand each other properly ... I gave over my address with a picture of mine to a Spanish comrade. Some weeks later I received a kind letter from him.[70]

The Nazi regime had certainly created a secular society, which seemed much more liberal in public and private than prudish, Francoist Spain. Some female leaders of the Spanish Falange had already perceived this as a potential danger in 1937–40; they considered their German counterparts to be excessively liberal in sexual and religious matters. However, Nazis held contradictory views concerning the social role of Aryan women. Though they attempted to pitch themselves as the defenders of traditional values, sexual mores were quite liberated in the Third Reich. This process had been accelerated by the exceptional circumstances of war and the shortage of young men on the home front.[71]

Therefore, Germany seemed to many *divisionarios* a kind of gift-wrapped sexual paradise: "a garden of unanimously blond girls."[72] But it was an earthly paradise presided over by order and modernity, where some scenes fascinated the Spanish volunteers, such as the vision of a broad road "sprinkled with blond girls wearing jeans, riding a bike," certainly a rare sight in Spain at that time.[73] This was accompanied by the abundance of German girls in uniform, who took up typically male tasks.[74] The volunteers observed in German girls a mood that was very different from Spanish women. It vaguely evoked what many of them had watched in Leni Riefenstahl's films and considered to be the sum of virtues ascribed to women by fascism: "the fragrance of paganism, of nature, of fresh air, of sun and stadium that emanates from these blond, tanned girls."[75] German women openly approached social intercourse, in stark contrast with the stiff morality imposed by Spanish national-Catholicism in public life. This also led some returnees from the front to believe that German *Froilan* lacked any notion of morality.[76] Whether false or true, Spanish volunteers often found an idealized love in their first German "war godmothers," which helped them to better resist the loneliness on the front, and which they missed long after their return to Spain.[77]

Many Spanish soldiers were devout Catholics and considered German "paganism" to be a problem. This was not only for political reasons, like many Italian fascist visitors,[78] but also due to sincere religious conviction. To counteract these sceptical voices, some other *divisionarios* emphasized the fact that there were also many Germans who prayed to the true God. This meant that, to them, good Germans were above all good Catholics, particularly Bavarians. Yet, those volunteers who had been socialized within strict Catholic milieus found themselves at odds with the liberty of sexual mores in the Third Reich.[79] While such short-lived romances were problematic in the rural and Catholic region surrounding Grafenwöhr, they were commonplace in the bigger towns such as Nuremberg and Berlin or even in smaller cities like Hof. Military surgeon Manuel de Cárdenas wrote in his war diary after having visited some cafés there:

> After work, coffee shops get full of *Mädchen*, Spanish guys and German ladies devote themselves in a joyful and open way to teaching each other their respective languages. We are accustomed to our beauteous Spanish morality, and are shocked by some of the liberties that German girls take with the Spaniards in the most natural way ... Almost every Spaniard has got a German girlfriend. The boys say this is to learn German properly.

A couple of days later, he noticed too that in a Berlin cabaret there was "quite a lot of freedom in the love expressions of the clients." In fact, the Oberzahlmeister Schwab noted that, on the eve of the arrival of the first Spanish soldiers to Hof, both state and party authorities had recommended that local women remain loyal to the principle of racial purity. However, there were soon quite a number of exceptions. By mid-1943, approximately sixty newborn illegitimate children had been registered at the town registry office, purportedly sired by Spanish soldiers. Many of these children were later adopted by German fathers.[80] On the road going east, Sergeant Jesús Martínez-Tessier also noted in August 1941 the great success of Spanish volunteers when they approached German girls in East Prussia. Thus, he noted in Treuburg/Olecko that "the locals welcome us with great sympathy, and we often see our soldiers accompanying young German girls." Another volunteer wrote that the *Froilan* were "eager to *do favours*" and that almost all comrades of his platoon went out with girls at night. In doing so, however, many *divisionarios* experienced some of the darker aspects of the Nazi regime. Martínez Tessier described how the "boys belonging to the Hitler Youth wrote down the names of the girls who stay with Spaniards after sunset."[81]

The NSDAP warnings certainly did not prevent German girls from close contact with Spanish convalescent soldiers at the hospitals of Königsberg and Berlin, which sometimes featured elements of male picaresque. Minor incidents involving BD soldiers led the Spanish high command to issue detailed instructions in early 1942 on how to behave correctly in Germany. Such orders included refraining from spending the night with local women.[82] For their part, German soldiers who passed through Hof during their *Fronturlaub* (temporary leave) were instructed to treat their Spanish comrades with respect. Leaflets distributed to them insisted on the brotherhood of arms formed during the previous years, as the Condor Legion had been deployed in Spain.[83]

During their stay at the training camp in Grafenwöhr, the Spanish volunteers found alternative ways to satisfy their sexual appetite. They soon learned of the existence of a camp of female Polish and Russian forced workers in the nearby village of Auerbach and began making regular visits. Some were seeking romance, others wanted sex in exchange for food and clothing. The flow of Spanish soldiers late at night scandalized German sentinels, who were unable to prevent them from approaching the girls. The frequency of such romantic encounters came to the attention of the BD General Staff, which feared for the prestige of the Spanish Army and the "sanitary danger" of "carnal contact with the girls." Thus, the guard was reinforced, and the night outings to the female *Lager* came to an end.[84]

These were not the only love affairs that occurred between Spanish volunteers and forced workers. A Spanish soldier returning from the front insisted on travelling to Zwickau (Saxony) to visit a former Russian girlfriend from the Leningrad Front who had been deported to Germany as a forced worker. The trip ended in his arrest and repatriation to Spain. Similar incidents took place in Hof throughout 1942 and 1943, where Spaniards soon became aware of a camp of female French and Russian conscripts close to their barracks. These were among the many who were forced to work at the armaments factories and the railways. One *divisionario* even killed the guard of a spinning mill, who had caught him trying to enter the factory at night to visit a French girl who worked there.[85]

Occupied Populations on the March to the Front: Spaniards, Poles, and Baltic Peoples

The *divisionarios* began their march on foot into occupied territory in August 1941. Eastern Poland and its peasants played a prominent role in the BD experience and memory. Diverse testimonies described the attitude of the local people to the passing of a division of brown-skinned soldiers – the Polish peasants sometimes called them the *czarna Dywizja* (black division) – as one of expectation and curiosity. The German liaison officers stated that throughout the march the food supplies of Polish, Lithuanian, and Byelorussian peasants were constantly being pillaged.[86] Other testimonies point in the same direction: when Leib Reizer passed through the Byelorussian village of Radun in September 1941, he asked a peasant woman if the Spaniards had been in the village. She replied expressively:

> "Yes, they were here," she answered more boldly. They had gestured with their hands in sign language and asked for "greasy stuff" – butter – as well as "cock-a doodle-doo" and "oink-oink" – that is chickens and pigs – in exchange for shirts, scarves, socks and the like.[87]

Trading with the peasants continued throughout the march. The Spaniards ignored the warnings of the German commanders regarding dealing with the locals in the occupied countries, where numerous Wehrmacht soldiers had been sabotaged and poisoned. However, the less hierarchical *guripas* enjoyed communicating with the civilian population in occupied territories. Early on in Treuburg/Olecko, a Spanish soldier noted how "there are many Poles working as cooks and servants; the Germans consider them to be an inferior race, but as a Christian for me they are all equal."[88] The BD combatants often traded parts of their equipment, such as boots, clothes, or lighters, for chickens, eggs and pigs. The more astute ones perceived that the peasants perhaps needed food more than money, but they smiled in resignation before soldiers dressed in the uniform of the occupier. Though the Poles were considered to be a hospitable people, not all exchanges were voluntary. The Russian interpreter Vladimir Kovalevskii described how the Spaniards looted Polish peasants and how such actions temporarily ceased after the BD command executed one of the plunderers.[89] Another letter by a Spanish private confirmed this impression:

> We did not behave like angels either. While shouting *Spanisch alles katholik* [sic] they took everything from the poor Poles, eating all their stores; and when a more audacious one added *Deutschland nicht katolisch, laput* [sic] accompanied by a meaningful gesture around the neck, the Poles gave them everything.[90]

While many German soldiers in 1939–41 described the Poles as foreigners to European culture,[91] Spanish impressions were more nuanced, partly because the Catholicism of the losers made them more familiar. Polish peasants frequently attended the open-air Masses organized by the BD.[92] Sergeant Carlos Ródenas highlighted the "infinite fervour of the Polish people as they knelt before the religious images." Catholic volunteer Sanz Jarque expressed pleasant surprise at the mystic devotion to the Blessed Virgin Mary that he encountered among Poles and Lithuanians; it reminded him of his own village.[93]

Because of their Catholicism, Spaniards represented Poles as fully European. The apparent talent of the Polish middle class for foreign languages made them privileged interpreters. Polish and/or Byelorussian women – Spaniards seldom distinguished between them – were also considered to be "the most similar to our women in kindness and self-sacrifice." The contrast of the Orthodox, "oriental" Slavs – the Russians – drove this perception even deeper into their memory.[94] José-Luis Gómez-Tello described a Polish peasant wedding party in 1945:

> Among these young peasants – who still belong to the civilized world – with their fair beards, their shirts buttoned at the neck, their Bohemian velvet jackets, and their shiny patent-leather boots; between this and what I have seen wandering back from the Soviet hell, there is an entire world of difference.[95]

However, the inverse process surfaces in the diaries that followed the rhythm of the foot march. Unlike later memoirs, in 1941 BD combatants compared occupied Poland with what they had observed in Germany. On the heels of their admiration for German well-being came the first brutal encounter with the East, and the effects of the war. As they passed through Poland, and before they had witnessed the even greater misery of the rural Soviet population, many Spaniards perceived the striking difference in the standard of living between Poland and the Reich. They also noted how contemptuously the Poles were treated by ethnic Germans.[96] Thus, in Treuburg/Olecko Corporal Martínez-Tessier noted that the Poles suffered various forms of discrimination. "The Polish inhabitants are required to wear the letter P embroidered in dark brown on a cloth diamond placed over their breast ... The German population despises them tremendously." Upon entering Eastern Poland some days later, the contrast between German well-being and the poverty of the Polish villages was very evident: "the clean, happy towns disappear and grey wooden houses appear, dirty and miserable, dusty roads through pine forests ... the people are poor and dirty." In Suwałki, a city in ruins, the only inhabitants were children, women, and the elderly, "dirty and ragged, full of misery and hunger."[97] Luis Aguilar described a similar panorama:

> The houses are virtual hovels and the inhabitants covered in rags and barefoot despite the mud caused by the persistent rain. The abundant flies do not respond to swatting. We notice how this misery and filth contrasts with what we saw in Germany.[98]

The social origins of the BD combatants also influenced the perception of this abysmal difference in living conditions between Polish peasants and prosperous Germans. For volunteers who were familiar with the situation of the peasantry in many areas of Spain, the contrast diminished. Jacinto Santamaría wrote years later, as he remembered the Polish villages, that "those poor, humble, simple, and self-sacrificing peasants" were similar to "our poor farm workers" in Castile.[99] Many BD volunteers had the opportunity to gain first-hand information about the experience of the civilian population in occupied Poland. Some DGS reports in April 1942 related information from repatriated soldiers of how the Germans carried out "singularly in Poland, Lithuania and Russia" a "bloody work of repression." It included shooting people down in the streets and incarcerating Poles and Russians in "isolated camps."[100] BD volunteer Antonio Herrero corresponded in German with Ursula, a middle-class Polish girl from Poznań (Posen). She described in explicit detail the living conditions in that region annexed to the Reich:

As Poles, we are treated terribly. We live horribly, we have nothing decent to wear, we are given ridiculously small food rations, we are not allowed to have radios, gramophones, bicycles, or photo cameras. We are forbidden to enter all the shops, cinemas, and theatres. They do not allow us to walk in parks and gardens, and everywhere we go we see signs saying, "No Poles allowed." Right at the beginning of the war we were expelled from our home, we could not take furniture, clothes, or sheets, and now we must squeeze four people into a very small bedroom ... The churches are closed and many of our friends and relatives are dead.[101]

Through Spanish eyes, the Polish people represented the tragic destiny of an idealistic nation – one with a religious fatalism that equipped it for martyrdom – that as early as the 1930s had been seen as a bastion of anti-communism and anti-Semitism.[102] The Spaniards perceived them as victims of the one and the other, as was reflected in their encounters with Polish peasants who had lost children at the hands of both occupiers. The anti-communism of the civilian population surprised the BD soldiers, who felt their moral stance doubly justified as they witnessed the effects of Soviet repression on the inhabitants of the region. Martínez Tessier had an instructive encounter with a "Polish peasant who spoke Spanish, as he had worked four years in Argentina. The Reds destroyed him. He had a son who had studied engineering, who was taken by the Russians and nothing more has been heard of him." Many BD combatants felt empathy for that purportedly heroic eople, victims of historic fate. In 1943, an ex-combatant symbolized this admiration by evoking the "Catholic mothers who offer water for our thirst as we walk and speak to us of the son who broke his sabre on a German armoured car or another who was taken prisoner by the Russians." The Polish civilians were amazed to find soldiers wearing German uniforms in their Catholic churches. BD combatants sometimes came to blows with Germans who refused to pay in the Polish cafés,[103] and who frequented Polish women. Their gallantries were often successful thanks to the rather unromantic motivators of hunger and fear. All in all, Polish women still seemed attractive to the BD volunteers; their perception of Russian female peasants would be quite different.[104]

After the discovery of the mass graves of Katyn in April 1943, the Francoist press made great efforts to declare its solidarity with Catholic Poland as the victim of geopolitics, caught between two powerful neighbours. While avoiding blaming Germany, they pointed out the continuity between the Republican killings in 1936–9 and the mass execution of Polish officers.[105] The BD press later emphasized the "conflicting emotions" of the *divisionarios* as they passed through "foolish, wretched, martyred Poland." Despite the fear on the faces of the locals, "the sweet talk and shouts of the soldiers" eventually convinced them that "Spaniards did not eat people." Manuel Bars recalled the relief of the Poles: "Ah, Spain! Land of God. We are also of God."[106]

The civilian populations of the Baltic countries, especially in Vilnius and Riga, deserve an entire chapter of their own. Many Spanish soldiers had occasion to experience both cities while on leave or during convalescence. The initial impression of the volunteers upon entering Lithuania during the foot march of 1941 resembled that of Poland. Some diaries describe their disgust at the poverty in the villages. On 8 September 1941, on entering the country, Jesús Martínez Tessier noted the desolation that reigned there: "Women with scarves on their heads, barefoot and carrying their shoes in their hands. Long carts with four small wheels, and ponies with long manes."[107] A few months later, in March 1942, Manuel de Cárdenas expressed a similar impression after crossing the Lithuanian border at Virbalis:

The sensation upon entering this first Lithuanian town is truly disagreeable because everything around us seems miserable and filthy. The station is bad, poor, and dirty, and long lines of rubbish are piled up on top of the snow between the rails ... The women are fat, but dirty.[108]

Lithuania, like Poland, also enjoyed a benign assessment due to the deep Catholicism of many of its inhabitants. Martínez Tessier indicated his satisfaction with Vilnius, "a great city." The beauty of its temples was even more noteworthy: "Its monumental churches are the main feature. The Catholic faith is very big in this city. In almost every church there are images of our Saint Theresa. Our Lady of Vilnius is venerated to the extreme."[109] Occasionally, Vilnius was remembered as a place with a civilized and European feel. The city, where most of the population spoke Polish, became for many convalescents in the Spanish hospital there a kind of pseudo-paradise. This was partly due to the friendly treatment they received from the local inhabitants: "formal and genteel. And Catholic like us."[110]

Finally, Latvia represented worldly pleasure for the Spaniards. Its cosmopolitan capital, Riga, was idealized as the "last European city" before reaching the front. "There, we thought, the shops would have everything, the food was exquisite and the women fair." A multicultural swarm of soldiers frequented restaurants and courted Latvian women. Signs in Castilian Spanish were even hung from some downtown shops and cafés, which served as meeting places for *divisionarios* on leave or convalescing. To Menéndez-Gundín, Riga was a "city of lovely legs." Upon returning from the front, Alfonso de Urquijo noticed in Latvia "something familiar, in common with our civilization; I thought I was back in Western Europe."[111] Spaniards had such intimate contact with Latvian women that the German command acquiesced to allow some to marry them and take their spouses to Spain.[112]

The BD volunteers saw the Latvians also as victims of communism who deserved their solidarity. Some drew a parallel between the fate of that country invaded by the USSR, and what would have happened in Spain if Franco had not prevailed. Though there were cases of stealing from Latvian civilians, the Spanish soldiers remembered the gallantries above all, which more than once took place in brothels organized and run by the Wehrmacht.[113] The Falangist volunteer José Luis Gómez Tello wrote that "Europe – its lands and souls – extends only a little beyond Riga." What came after that? The "Jews and ... Eastern ghettos."[114]

4 The Blue Division on the Front

Tasks were assigned for Operation Barbarossa: Army Group North, composed of the 16th and 18th Armies and the 4th Panzer Group, would advance through the Baltic region to take Leningrad on about 20 August. It would then wait for the arrival of Army Group Centre, and they would advance together towards Moscow. The OKH, and Supreme Commander Franz Halder in particular, would have preferred to concentrate their efforts on the Soviet capital. However, the symbolic interest of Leningrad as the cradle of the Bolshevik Revolution and the strategic interest in clearing out maritime traffic in the Baltic provided Hitler with sufficient motives to take that city. After gaining control of the essential campaign objectives – the industrial area of Leningrad, the oil wells of the Caucasus, and the farmlands of the Ukraine – they would deal a final blow to Moscow. However, the slowness of the German advance made it necessary to modify the plan, and the Leningrad Front became a secondary war theatre. The OKH knew that taking a Soviet city would involve a bloody battle in which the superiority of armoured vehicles lost value. So, instead, the German command decided to lay siege to the cities and starve them to the point of surrender.

What was the real motive behind the decision to besiege Leningrad? Some authors attribute it to Hitler's personal obsession with the cradle of the October Revolution. Others argue that the evolution of the autumn 1941 campaign and the desire to avoid a costly urban battle conditioned the decision. Still others maintain that the decision was coherent with plans for a war of extermination that determined military priorities. The most plausible interpretation is that the OKH made the decision in July 1941, not so much for tactical reasons as from the conviction that the campaign would in the mid-range become a war of positions. Thus, they had to decrease the number of objectives and concentrate their strength on a final attack of Moscow. Letting the population of

Fig. 4.1. General Agustín Muñoz Grandes (left) at BD headquarters, 1942 (AA)

Leningrad starve solved a considerable logistical problem for Army Group North and was coherent with mid- and long-range aims of conquering *Lebensraum* for economic use. The nearly thirty million Soviet citizens inhabiting the region were considered superfluous to that endeavour, so the decision was taken to physically eliminate most of them. Around Leningrad, this involved extermination, slavery for the survivors, and the Germanization of the region.[1] The directives of the colonization projects for the outer "Marches" of the German Reich were developed between 1939 and 1941 and best expressed in the Master Plan for the East (the Generalplan Ost, or GPO) of May 1942, written under Himmler's supervision. It indicated that Leningrad should be progressively emptied of the Slavic population.[2] Recovering its historic Swedish name of Ingermanland, the region would be colonized by Germans and other Germanic people groups brought in from the Reich, the Americas, and Eastern Europe. Thus, the decision to starve Leningrad resulted from the intersection of a mid-range ideological project to Germanize the region and the short-range project that served the immediate logistical and tactical needs of the Wehrmacht.

In early September 1941, German troops reached the outskirts of Leningrad and cut it off from outside communication. Finnish divisions attacked from the north and reconquered the Karelian Isthmus. Except for a few strategic points, however, they did not cross the border that existed prior to the Winter War or occupy the east bank of Lake Ladoga.[3] Field Marshall Ritter von Leeb, commander in chief of Army Group North, wanted to attack and seize Leningrad, but on 6 September the OKW diverted the 4th Panzer Group from the Northern Front to participate in the Moscow offensive. The city would not be taken by assault. They closed in and on 6 November conquered Tikhvin, the railway hub to the east of Lake Ladoga, cutting off the train lines between Leningrad and the Soviet rearguard. Fourteen Wehrmacht divisions faced at least thirty Red Army divisions.[4]

After the German conquest of Tikhvin, the objectives seemed to be met, but the Soviets launched a counter-offensive in early December 1941 and reconquered the town. This meant that Leningrad could again be provisioned by rail convoys from Lake Ladoga. From that point on, the 16th and 18th Armies became enmeshed in a lengthy war of attrition. Trench lines extended from Lake Ilmen to Leningrad, forming a rather stable front until January 1944. The Leningrad Front became a secondary concern for Stalin. The Red Army tried and failed to break the siege in several offensives throughout November-December 1941 and the spring and summer of 1942. To the south of Novgorod, the Soviet attack formed part of the operations intended to benefit from the success of the Moscow counter-offensive. Six German divisions – the Demyansk Pocket – resisted in a prolonged siege that lasted until March 1942.

In early 1943, the Soviet command again tried to break the Leningrad siege. The main offensive, Operation Iskra, began in mid-January with coordinated attacks from the Volkhov Front and Leningrad. After gruelling combat, the Red Army pushed the Germans back from their positions on the south side of Ladoga. On 18 January 1943, they opened a narrow land corridor on which they constructed a rail line that brought provisions and reinforcements, slowly but steadily stabilizing supply to Leningrad. The siege continued and in February 1943, the troops that were amassed to the south-east of the siege perimeter attacked in an attempt to advance along the Leningrad-Moscow rail line. Despite initial success, the exhausted Soviet troops eventually had to fall back. Two other local offensives in the summer of 1943 also yielded unfavourable outcomes for the Red Army.[5] In fact, compared to Stalingrad, the Don region, and Kursk, the Army Group North was not involved in large-scale military operations after December 1941. Though war proved difficult in the Volkhov swamps and some combats were notoriously harsh, conditions were less brutalized than on other sectors of the Eastern Front.

From September 1941 on, the German Army worked harder to intensify the siege. Though it refused to feed the civilian population,[6] the logistical needs of the 16th and 18th Armies in the harsh winter of 1941–2 made it advisable to begin adopting pragmatic attitudes towards civilians in the rearguard. Most peasants in the occupied area were elderly, women, or children; many had been deported there from other areas.[7] Soon, however, they were fulfilling auxiliary functions: they sheltered and partially fed the occupiers, cleared roads and train tracks, and provided manual labour for the Reich. A degree of acquiescence from the locals would minimize peasant support for the partisans.[8] Thus, depending on the decision-making margin of the Wehrmacht lower command and regular soldiers, subtle differences appeared on the Northern Front when it came to enforcing OKW directives for occupation.[9] Each week, the rearguard security forces (*Sicherungstruppen*) – composed of more mature soldiers, anti-partisan units, and later of auxiliary Baltic and Soviet troops recruited from among the prisoners – detained hundreds of civilians and shot dozens of them for collaborating with the partisans. All this transpired in the midst of an everyday reality defined by pervasive hunger and abject misery.

The 2.9 million inhabitants of Leningrad went through hell. The Stalinist regime required enormous sacrifice: civilians worked in the factories, built fortifications, and constructed roads going east for trucks to bring provisions. In the most intense months of the blockade, more than five thousand people died daily from hunger, cold, and harsh work. From Christmas 1941 on, rations gradually improved, but until February 1943, they did not reach nutritional minimums required for survival. By January 1944, the population of Leningrad had fallen to 630,000.[10] Meanwhile, Stalin's terror machinery insisted on keeping the population productive and combat ready. Those who failed to reach the recommended objectives were suspected of sabotage or defeatism. Non-Russian minorities in the region (both German- and Finnish-speaking) were suspected of being sympathetic towards the enemy and deported.[11]

The liberation of Leningrad was not a priority for the Red Army. Soviet forces did not attack German lines until 14 January 1944, forcing the Wehrmacht 18th Army to retreat in order to avoid a disaster. On 10 June 1944, the Red Army also attacked the Finnish troops, forcing the Helsinki government under Marshal Mannerheim to sign an armistice treaty three months later. Official data published in 1945 stated that 632,253 civilians had died in the siege of Leningrad. During the

Khrushchev years, the figures were raised to 800,000 deaths. Since then, other calculations have situated the total between 1 and 1.3 million persons, almost half the population of the city.[12]

Lost Victories: The Volkhov Front (October 1941–August 1942)

On 1 October 1941, Muñoz Grandes was informed that the Blue Division would be incorporated into the 16th Army under the command of General Ernst Busch. Two days later, he flew over the front where the Spanish volunteers would eventually be assigned to relieve troops of the 126th Division, led by General Paul Laux, and the neighbouring 18th Division.[13] By late September, both divisions – but especially the 18th – had lost more than a third of their combatants and had requested reinforcements upon confirming that fresh Siberian troops had arrived on the other side of the Volkhov River and Lake Ilmen.[14] The BD was briefly assigned to a provisional army corps under the command of General Franz von Roques, who was responsible for Rearguard Zone 101 of Army Group North.[15]

The Spaniards assumed their posts between 7 and 17 October. The BD occupied a section extending 40 kilometres between Novgorod and Lake Ilmen to the south, and to Udarnik – afterwards Borissovo – to the north. They occupied the west or right bank of the broad Volkhov River, with an average width of two hundred metres. The terrain was largely wooded and marshy, with scattered villages and a highway leading to Leningrad, along with a railway connecting that city with Moscow. The Spaniards arrived to rapidly falling temperatures, the first snowfalls, and heavy frosts. Opposite them, on the east bank of the Volkhov, stood the 267th and 305th Soviet Infantry Divisions.[16]

The southern third of the section was covered by two battalions of the Spanish 262nd Regiment, the centre third by the 263rd Regiment, and the north and most active third by the 269th Regiment. Artillery was divided among the three sections, and the remaining units (one artillery group, one battalion from the 262nd Regiment, one sapper battalion, an anti-tank group, and the mobile reserve battalion) were placed in the reserves. Across the river, the sector controlled by the Red Army seemed ill provisioned with scant artillery and no armoured vehicles. However, Soviet aviation dominated the skies. Though numerically modest, this was a constant problem because the Spaniards lacked adequate anti-air defence.

Horses were also in short supply after the march from Poland. By early October, 1,205 horses had been lost and only 414 replaced. When the time came to launch an offensive, this created delays and difficulties in organizing the provision of food, medical supplies, weapons, and ammunition to the troops on the front lines. The BD had several damaged cannons and more than a hundred broken-down vehicles. The anti-tank vehicles had received little care from inexperienced drivers, and 30 per cent of the bicycles could not be used. The soldiers had not practised shooting since Grafenwöhr, and the officers and NCOs barely managed to impose discipline in their heterogeneous ranks.[17]

All this caused the Germans to question the performance they could expect from the Spaniards, before they ever became active on the front. Prejudice aside, they had some reasons for it. A report from the liaison officer of the I Army Corps indicated that the over-abundant Blue Division officers lacked authority and resolve, the NCOs lacked technical training, the soldiers tended to be undisciplined, weapons were not properly cared for, treatment of horses was "especially rough (kicking, etc.)," motorcycles were systematically overloaded, and so on. The troops might be "willing" and the "personal bravery of all the Spaniards gives no room for doubt," but in the absence of systematic training, their combat capabilities remained a mystery.[18]

The initial design of the Volkhov offensive gave no decisive role in the vanguard to the Spanish division. The Soviet plans were intended to complement the offensive that would be launched more to the north: to conquer Tikhvin, connect with the Finnish troops north of Lake Ladoga, and tighten the siege of Leningrad. Only after the enemy's resistance had been worn down would they advance east and south-east of the German units that had initially opened the breach. The scepticism of the German command regarding Spanish combat capabilities was mainly due to the Division's lack of mobility.[19] However, the German plans would eventually change, giving the BD an opportunity to establish bridgeheads in the vanguard of the attack.

After a few tentative and failed strikes, they prepared to take the island between the "little Volkhov" and the Volkhov, coordinating with the advance of the 126th German Division. This offensive move to cross the river and reach the Valdai Hills complemented the German offensive to take Tikhvin more to the north. The first attempt failed, but on 19 October a section of thirty-six men consolidated a bridgehead on the left bank near Udarnik. The 2nd Battalion of the 269th Regiment and other units joined them the following day. A few days of relative calm transpired before the Soviets reacted on 27 October. Sitno became the scene of harsh combat: in the bloody clashes that ensued, the Spanish combatants attacked towards the south and took the villages of Tigoda, Dubrovka, and Nikitkino. Freezing temperatures made the fighting harsher for the poorly equipped combatants and complicated

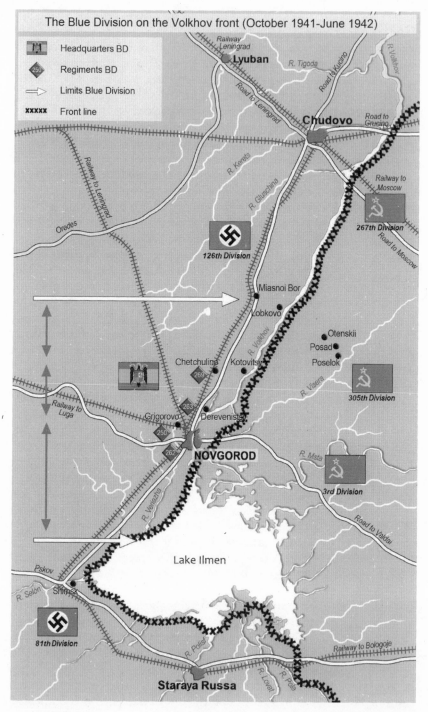

Map 1. The Blue Division on the Volkhov Front (October 1941–June 1942)

communications with the bridgehead. Soviet resistance was also stronger than expected. The 23 October log entry for Army Group North noted that "the valour of the Spaniards in combat is reassuring, they have repelled a Russian attack today, resulting in three hundred deaths and three hundred enemy prisoners."[20]

The commanders decided to focus their efforts on taking Tikhvin and ordered the BD to relieve the Germans in the monastery of Otenskii and the villages of Posad and Poselok. As temperatures dropped to -20°C, on 9 November a reinforced Spanish battalion replaced the Germans a few kilometres to the east in Posad, to cover the sector of the Vishera River. Fearing Leningrad would be cut off, the Soviets launched fierce counter-attacks with air and artillery support, causing heavy losses to the Spaniards stationed at Posad. There, they resisted infantry attacks and light artillery fire for almost a month. Connections were precarious between the Otenskii monastery, Sitno, and Posad. The road ran through a dense snowy forest where visibility was almost nil. The Soviet soldiers knew how to move in the thick brush and set several ambushes. However, many Spanish troopers were accustomed to this type of combat. More than one soldier noted proudly in his diary how the Spaniards engaged in "fantastic heroic deeds."[21]

In early December, the Red Army intensified its counter-offensive to retake Tikhvin. East of the Volkhov, the Soviets redoubled their attacks on Nikitkino, Lake Ilmen, Posad, and Otenskii. The German command began to dread that both positions would fall into enemy hands. Muñoz Grandes reported to the XXXVIII Army Corps that only thirty-eight men remained capable of combat in Posad. The Germans feared that Red Army reinforcements would cross the river, wipe out the Spaniards, and conquer Novgorod. Such a significant blow on the front would also strain Hispano-German diplomatic relations. The impact of the cold had also been brutal on the German and Spanish units, who were barely surviving.[22] Finally, on the night of 7 December, the Spaniards abandoned their positions in Posad for fear of being besieged by the enemy, with their well-equipped Siberian reinforcements. The following day, they evacuated Sitno, Dubrovka, and other positions near the east bank of the Volkhov. Without waiting for German orders, they left light cannons, equipment, and weapons behind. According to the German Army Corps command, the Spaniards were not systematic in laying mines at the abandoned positions, nor did they destroy the artillery and mortars that they could not carry.[23] On the afternoon of 9 December, the last Spanish units crossed the Volkhov and fell back to their positions on the western shore. The retreat concluded eleven days later. The Soviets found many dead in Posad and *Pravda* published reports about the "bleeding out" of the "Fascist Blue Division."[24]

At this point, it became urgent to reinforce the line of defence, while maintaining a few outposts of resistance on the east bank of the Volkhov. The commander of the XXXVIII Army Corps feared a Soviet attack on an overly wide section of the front (150 km) protected by a debilitated 126th German Division and the "rather unreliable" Spanish units. The latter had shown themselves unprepared for combat in extreme weather conditions and were described as a "hole in the front line." The German command did not trust the Spaniards with building shelters or barbed-wire fences, so German sapper units were sent to do the job.[25] The Germans also worried that the Soviets would now counter-attack on the west bank of the river, concentrating on the weakened left flank of the BD and right flank of the 126th Division.[26] They did not know that Soviet reports highlighted how the Spaniards, though demoralized by the cold, had solidly resisted the Red Army attacks. Based on prisoner interrogations and enemy war diaries, the Soviet command perceived the BD as a highly motivated volunteer corps full of fanatic fascists.[27]

After several strikes, on 24 December the Soviets began trying to penetrate the Spanish positions. Three days later, they crossed the river and attacked the BD support points, including the "hermitage position" and the reinforced "intermediate position" that linked Udarnik and Lobkovo. The Soviets wiped out the squadron that was defending the latter. When the Spaniards counter-attacked and finally recovered the position, they found forty cadavers mutilated and staked to the ground. They also reconquered the hermitage position, where they found a similar spectacle. Then, after a desperate fight in which no prisoners were taken, they forced the Soviets back to the west bank of the Volkhov. The fallen soldiers of the intermediate and hermitage positions, who had been ordered to be literally nailed to the ground in their places, became the subject of poetic praise and were mythicized in BD propaganda and literature.[28]

The front stabilized. By 7 December, the Soviets had reconquered Tikhvin and Leningrad could receive provisions via Lake Ladoga. From then on, the 16th and 18th Armies were engaged in a war of positions along a line extending between Lake Ilmen and Leningrad. They maintained a stable front there until the final Soviet offensive of January 1944. Further south, Army Group Centre had also failed in their attempt to take Moscow, so the war went on longer than expected.

BD losses in the bridgehead combat of the Volkhov included a harsh toll in bloodshed, but the death reports present striking disparities. The often inaccurate computations of Army Group North reported nearly 500 fallen Spanish volunteers in late 1941.[29] However, a BD medical report dated 18 January 1942 listed 793 dead, 1,883 wounded, 899 frostbitten, and 1,365 infirm, collectively representing 27.4 per cent of the BD total.[30] The 126th German Division suffered similar losses, with 3,405 casualties from October to December.[31] Another report a month later indicated that the BD had incurred 1,032 deaths, 800 severely wounded, 1,400 with minor injuries, 160 missing, and 300 frozen to death.[32] As of 25 July of the same year, BD casualties numbered 1,247 deaths (including 61 officers), 3,263 wounded (including 123 officers), and 127 missing (including 3 officers).[33] In most German divisions, only a third of the initial troops remained fit for combat by mid-December, including soldiers who had recovered sufficiently from their wounds.[34] However, the Spaniards had also taken at least 800 prisoners by November 1941, captured a sizable amount of Soviet war materiel, and inflicted heavy losses on the enemy.[35] Even so, the Spanish command and soldiers were disappointed at the fact that their baptism by fire had ended in retreat from the positions they had conquered at such great cost. Soldiers in the 269th Regiment were also discontented with Colonel Esparza's tyrannical treatment of subordinates. He had even ordered his men to attack without adequate artillery cover, causing many unnecessary casualties.[36]

Still, there was the solace of glory. From 11 November 1941 to 31 March 1942, the Spaniards were awarded 159 Iron Crosses, Second Class, compared to 161 awarded to the German soldiers of the XXX-VIII Army Corps. Another 325 Spanish soldiers received the War Merit Cross, Second Class, compared to 210 Germans. Some Wehrmacht commanders explained this asymmetric treatment as sheer political deference towards their allies.[37] Though there were no great victories to sing about, episodes such as the defence of Posad and Otenskii were soon mythicized.[38] The same occurred with the Tigoda combats and the frontal assault on the fortified headquarters near Dubrovka, which ended in the senseless massacre of dozens of soldiers and the removal of their incompetent commander.[39]

Partly for political reasons, the official Wehrmacht reports broadcast far and wide the valiant deeds of the 2nd Battalion of the BD 269th Regiment, with its strong Falangist component.[40] Prominent Falangists and members of the Falangist youth figured among the fallen, such as SEU leader Enrique Sotomayor, José Antonio's former adjutant Vicente Gaceo, and several illustrious Old Shirts. These combined with German propaganda to create a romanticized image of the Spanish combatants among the German infantries. Spanish officers perceived admiration from their German colleagues, "in contrast with the Italians, Romanians, Finnish, etc.," due to the enormous effort the BD had made. Meanwhile, doubts arose regarding the supposed invincibility of the Wehrmacht on this especially difficult front. By November, Colonel Badillo had already concluded that the material resources of this campaign were no better than those of the Spanish Civil War; the troops had to make do with scarce provisions, insufficient artillery, and a very long front line.[41]

In contrast, the commanders of the divisions that fought alongside the BD, and the high command of the 16th and 18th Armies, were rather unimpressed with BD combat performance, which worsened under the effects of the harsh climate, poor training, logistical deficiencies, and the lack of horses and vehicles. Friedrich-Wilhelm von Chappuis, commander general of the XXXVIII Army Corps, predicted in mid-November that the "250th Spanish Division would not last long." This led him to propose the deployment of a third of the 61st German Division and return the BD to its starting position in the west bank of the Volkhov, where it would remain in a "relatively calm" place. General Busch commented that, despite taking Tikhvin, the offensive had not completed its second objective, which was to wear down the Soviet troops and shorten the front line to the north. He thought that the Spaniards had failed in this due to their lack of mobility, heavy losses, and the effects of the cold. He advised deploying them only defensively in calm sections of the front. The Red Army had mobilized reserves from the East, which threatened to destroy the troops on the front north of Ilmen. Two days later, Marshal Georg von Küchler was informed that the "fighting courage" of the Spaniards was "slowly but surely" waning and asked the OKW to replace the Blue Division with a German division.[42] Von Chappuis concurred after meeting with Muñoz Grandes, who acknowledged heavy losses and low morale due to the cold but refused to withdraw.[43]

However, the command of Army Group North realized that replacing the Spanish division with a German one (the 81st) north of Novgorod and amassing the Iberians to defend the Ilmen sector or the city of Novgorod as a "sort of Spanish enclave" involved "questions of foreign policy" and did not depend entirely on the army. The head of the 16th Army sent the request to Hitler himself, but it was not approved. The fact that the Soviets did not focus their strikes on Novgorod and the north Ilmen area calmed von Küchler for a while and allayed his fear of a breach in the front at the sector protected by the BD.[44]

The lack of interest in fortifying positions in the calm sections of the front occupied by Spanish units led to disproportionately heavy BD losses from Soviet artillery fire. Outbreaks of mange also threatened to decimate the horse reserves.[45] The Germans doubted that the Iberians could hold the positions during the winter on a front extending more

Fig. 4.2. Spanish soldiers in Russia, Winter 1941–2 (EFE Archive, Madrid)

than forty kilometres along the banks of the Volkhov and twenty-one kilometres along the Ilmen.[46] Their slow reaction capability favoured the activity of Soviet patrols, who could now cross frozen Lake Ilmen to strike.[47]

However, the diminished human reserves and materiel of the Wehrmacht made it impossible to replace the BD with sufficient personnel to ensure the positions. The new German division that had been requested to reinforce the area between the BD and the 126th Division never arrived. The German 422nd Regiment – with combatants averaging thirty-five years of age – that relieved the exhausted 269th Spanish Regiment was less able to resist the climate and combat conditions than the reviled southerners.[48] Since early October 1941, Army Group North had been receiving lower-quality relief troops with less combat experience. Having endured four months more of intense combat, the horses, the morale, and the living conditions of the German troops in the sector were not so different from those of the Spaniards. The units that had participated in the bridgehead combats were in no better physical or psychological condition, either.[49] In January, the Dutch Niederlande Regiment was deemed apt for defensive tasks and placed between the Spaniards and the 126th Division. Hitler had sent it to ensure that the Spanish Division not end up besieged by the Soviets, as this would create serious problems in his diplomatic relations with Franco's regime.[50]

In Madrid, there was increasing concern regarding the new situation in the East by the end of 1941. At Christmas, Franco ordered the Spanish ambassador in Berlin, José M. Finat, to transmit to the Reich authorities his desire that the Blue Division enjoy a respite. This temporary withdrawal was unthinkable for a German command that lacked reserves. Although Finat and Serrano Suñer insisted during the first months of 1942, the answer from the OKW remained unchanged. They argued that the BD protected a relatively calmer front, with fortified positions and a city (Novgorod) that offered additional possibilities for shelter. Withdrawal of personnel would only be possible if Spain guaranteed replacements. Also, acquiescing to such petitions from Madrid would create a comparative grievance among the other Wehrmacht divisions.[51]

The Spanish government had been working on the issue of replacements since December 1941, given the failed German offensive on Moscow and the realization that the war would consume more time and lives than originally foreseen. Agustín Aznar and Dionisio Ridruejo insisted that Foreign Minister Serrano Suñer address the need to find partial replacements. While the many Falangist deaths had provided martyrs for the single party in its drive to recover spheres of power in Spain, it had also deprived the organization of some of its most prestigious leaders and decimated the influential Old Shirts, who were needed in Spain. General Varela worked with the idea of substituting the entire "first Division" in block. He would send soldiers recruited exclusively from the military barracks and those who had enlisted in 1941 but had not been dispatched to Russia because the quotas had been met.[52] The first relief expeditions, modest in numbers, began to cross the Pyrenean border in January 1942. In mid-March, they were officially recognized as march battalions involved in transporting replacement soldiers. This helped to maintain the supply of BD combat personnel and gave the Spaniards considerable logistical value for the German command. Their combat capability might be questionable, but at least they did not have to replace fallen combatants with older ones, as other Wehrmacht divisions did.

Meanwhile, the enemy gave no respite. In January 1942, some BD units engaged in heavy defensive combat against Soviet counter-attacks on their northern flank at Teremets, while the 126th Division and some

SS companies had to repel Soviet attacks in the south at Lake Ilmen. In the north of that sector, the Soviets launched a powerful offensive to alleviate the situation in Leningrad. On 13 January, the Soviet 2nd Assault Army crossed the river and took Miasnoi Bor, on the western shore of the Volkhov. At the end of January, the Soviets directed the attack to the north-west, towards the rail lines. This reduced the possibility that the Spaniards would be surrounded. A few days later, the 2nd Battalion of the 269th Regiment and a company of the 263rd were again attached to the 126th German Division. After many hours of harsh fighting and marching through snow, they entered Maloe Zamosh'e, broke the siege, and rescued 140 German soldiers. Several other Spanish units fought alongside the German forces to eliminate the pocket at Miasnoi Bor.[53]

Added to the harsh combat, significant casualties, and the cruel temperatures – the thermometer did not climb above zero for even a few hours until 10 March 1942 – were the strikes on the eastern shore of the Volkhov. The most notorious action was that of the "ski company," led by Captain Ordás. On 11 January 1942, the company left its Spanish positions to cross frozen Lake Ilmen in an attempt to rescue a German unit that had been surrounded in the village of Vzvad. The crossing was so difficult that 102 men froze to death in the first two days. Those who survived were attended on the opposite shore by groups of German and Latvian soldiers. Ten days later, after several combats, the remainder of the company joined those under siege. Only twelve men returned uninjured to the starting point; eighteen of the wounded had to endure amputation of both legs. Though the high human cost placed the modest results in question, the "Feat of Lake Ilmen" became an indisputable Blue Division propaganda success and was mythicized as one of its most "heroic deeds."[54]

Operation Raubtier (Predator) began on 15 March 1942, with the objective of cutting off the Soviet forces that had crossed the river. The Soviet attack had failed, and they now faced the possibility of finding themselves under siege between the German rearguard and the Volkhov. On 19 March, the Spaniards and Germans again took Miasnoi Bor and closed the Volkhov pocket, trapping almost 130,000 Red Army soldiers. Aided by T-34 tanks, the Red Army broke the siege temporarily on 29 March. The Germans again closed them off, leaving them to endure slow attrition. The German command feared that counter-attacks by an enemy with almost endless reserves would definitively compromise the positions protected by replacement troops, who were older and ill prepared for offensive tasks; by other units, exhausted from combat and the winter; and by foreign troops (Dutch, Spanish, and some Flemish), whom they saw as rather unreliable.[55] In the second week of April

1942, bellicose activity began to decline drastically. The thawing river facilitated a few strikes on the east bank of the Volkhov or to capture prisoners in the Pocket.[56]

The first significant replacement of Spanish troops took place in May, when 290 officers, 88 NCOs, and 1,121 soldiers left for Germany.[57] In June, the 1,435 men of the 2nd Battalion were repatriated. The final battles to liquidate the Volkhov Pocket took place from late May to the end of June, around Bol'shoe Zamosh'e. Several Spanish units participated (3rd Battalion of the 262nd Regiment under Major Ramírez de Cartagena, a company of sappers, an anti-tank section, and an exploration group), led by Colonel Harry Hoppe (126th Division), along with the Flemish Legion and other German units, under the joint command of the SS *Standartenführer* Burk. Amidst swarms of mosquitoes, the Spaniards fought against a desperate enemy for several days in forests and bogs. Despite fierce Soviet resistance, the operations were successful.[58]

The German officers praised the BD in public but qualified their combat performance, especially during the fighting of 21–2 June, as another fiasco. The Spanish officers and NCOs had little experience in forest combat. They had been surprised by several enemy attacks and forced to retreat, leaving ammunition and heavier weapons behind. Added to this was deficient preparation for the attack by the Spanish commander, the lack of coordination with German and Flemish units, and the incomprehensible pauses in the fighting. At four in the afternoon, the officers ordered a one-hour break for "cognac, ham, and tea biscuits." Though BD volunteers possessed individual valour, the German opinion of Spanish fighting capability had not changed. Compared to "Nordic style" combatants, the Spaniards demonstrated greater impetus at the beginning of an attack, but less discipline when it came to repelling counter-attacks. The main problem was that they lacked "adequate guidance" from reliable NCOs on the ground. Spanish officers also neglected provision and ammunition duties, which often rendered the heavy weapons useless for want of projectiles.[59] The Germans were equally displeased when the BD underperformed in isolated actions to capture Soviet prisoners, due to the "failure of leadership and lack of preparation of the troops."[60] However, the XXXVIII Army Corps command had no reserves with which to substitute the Spanish battalion. For months now, the German replacement troops had fallen far below Wehrmacht standards. Around the same time, Army Group North received reports indicating that the recruits arriving on the front lacked capabilities, technical training, and combat morale.[61]

The Volkhov Pocket was liquidated on 28 June 1942. The Germans paid a high price in fallen soldiers, especially those of the 58th and 126th

Divisions, who were relieved in order to give them rest. Some of those positions were occupied by the Blue Division. General Andrej Vlasov, the commander of the encircled troops, was captured on 12 July. More than thirty-two thousand Soviet soldiers were taken prisoner with him, and sixty-five thousand more died in combat.[62] Meanwhile, the Red Army soldiers who had fled from the Volkhov Pocket increased guerrilla activity in the rearguard, creating new difficulties for the XXXVIII Army Corps.[63]

In early July, the German command still feared that the enemy would counter-attack from their positions on the west bank of the Volkhov and focus on the north of the Spanish sector. Neighbouring German units were instructed to come and support the Iberian troops in case of a Soviet attack. Some reserves, mainly an SS anti-aircraft section, were placed in the immediate rearguard to intervene if the Spaniards yielded. In late July, their fears were partly dispelled: the Spaniards engaged in fierce hand-to-hand combat but managed to repel a Soviet attempt to strike at Zapol'e.[64]

It was dangerous to expect the BD to cover such a long section of the front. The XXXVIII Army Corps command communicated its increasing apprehension to the 16th Army and the Supreme Command of Army Group North, which led them to place the BD on another front. Even Muñoz Grandes doubted their chances of holding the positions on the west bank of the Volkhov once the river froze over for the winter and facilitated the movement of enemy troops. Added to this was the desire to participate in the upcoming Northern Light offensive, initially planned for September 1942, that Hitler had entrusted to Army Group North.[65] On 14 July, Muñoz Grandes notified his chiefs of staff about the change of front and the news travelled quickly. He claimed that he had informed the troops of the imminent move to avoid rampant defeatism, as his officers had been expressing an increasing desire to return to Spain and growing discontent with the role they had played so far. The German command, however, feared that the news would relax their fighting spirit, which was already ebbing with the arrival of the replacements.

The Spaniards were finally replaced in phases by units of the 20th and 212th Divisions from 8 August until 10 September 1942, when the 2nd Battalion of the 269th Regiment was relieved from its positions. The XXXVIII Army Corps command realized that 50 per cent fewer German soldiers would be covering the sixty kilometres of front, as the BD had been replacing its fallen with new troops from Spain. However, they hoped that this decrease would be compensated by the greater experience and military capability of the German soldiers, and fewer operative inconveniences derived from collaborating with foreign combatants.[66]

War of Positions in the Siege of Leningrad
(September 1942–November 1943)

In early September 1942, the BD took over new positions on the Leningrad Front. They set up headquarters in the Pokrovskoe estate, relieved the 121st German Division, and joined the LIV Corps of the 18th Army, commanded by General Erik Hansen. A Waffen-SS brigade was posted next to the BD on the north, and an SS police division on the south. The BD was to cover twenty kilometres of front from Pushkin to Krasnyi Bor: an area traversed by the Leningrad-Moscow road and the Ishora, a tributary of the Neva River. In terms of density, or soldiers per kilometre covered, they were now the second-most-numerous Division of the 18th Army.[67] The terrain was fairly flat, with peripheral towns boasting parks and sumptuous palaces, such as that of Catherine the Great in Pushkin and that of Tsar Paul I in Pavlovsk. The occupying forces used these as barracks, storehouses, and artillery lookout posts; they also made war cemeteries in the gardens. The climate was somewhat less severe. Though the peasants of the area appeared to live better than those of the Volkhov region, improvements in provisions to the civilian population beginning in spring 1942 could not hide the devastation caused by the famine of the previous winter. Most of the inhabitants had been deported to labour camps in the Reich, while those who remained were forced to work for the occupying forces.[68]

The BD now participated in the siege of Leningrad, in a phase characterized by a static war of attrition. The general monotony was only interrupted by sporadic strikes, efforts to repel Soviet attacks, and occasional artillery exchanges.[69] The troops were better equipped for the cold, and BD mobility had improved. The horses were also in better condition, though inferior to those assigned to the neighbouring German divisions.[70] During their first months on this new sector of the front, the priority was to consolidate defensive positions. The Blue Division had plenty of soldiers (unlike most German divisions, beginning with the neighbouring 170th Division and the SS Police Division), which gave the German commanders more confidence in the Spaniards' capacity to resist Soviet attacks.[71] They also valued the goodwill and enthusiasm of the troops, but lamented that the constant replacement of officers and NCOs prevented them from accumulating experience. They still thought of the Spanish Division as not very mobile and therefore inadequate for offensive actions. The BD would never be able to withstand a strong enemy counter-attack, and never passed above level three of the four categories used by the German command.[72]

German biases continued to condition these periodic evaluations. They held to their conviction that the Spaniards were good guerrilla fighters but rather inept at modern warfare. True to their "fighting style," they preferred hand-to-hand combat.[73] They also lacked grand offensives in which to participate. In theory, they would have been included in Operation Northern Light to take Leningrad, meet up with the Finnish troops, and advance on Soviet ports in the Arctic. However, Field Marshal Erich von Manstein communicated to Muñoz Grandes that the attack had been postponed indefinitely due to renewed Soviet activity on the Ladoga Front. Personnel had to be diverted to stop the offensive, so the BD would be deployed as reserves for the 121st Division in and around Pushkin/Slutzk. Due to the combined pressure on the entire Eastern Front from Soviet activity in the Don and Stalingrad, Operation Northern Light was never launched. The course of the war in the East was slowly and definitively changing.[74]

After four months of delays by the German command, Muñoz Grandes was officially relieved in December by order of the OKW and Hitler himself. The new commander-in-chief of the Division was Minister Varela's trusted man, General Emilio Esteban-Infantes. After several weeks of waiting for Hitler's approval in Berlin, he arrived at the Grigorovo headquarters in August, but as second in command until the Führer saw fit to heed Franco's urging to let Muñoz Grandes return to Spain. Esteban-Infantes had been a part of the Spanish Army General Staff and was less concerned with cultivating his good image amongst the troops than Muñoz Grandes. He was cold, not given to being seen on the front lines, and not particularly inclined towards fascism. However, he was more methodical, and his German interlocutors thought him a good professional.[75] Muñoz Grandes made a stop on his return journey to visit Hitler at the Wolf's Lair, where he was awarded the Knight's Cross of the Iron Cross, complete with the oak leaves. The Führer transmitted his concern that Spain maintain its neutrality but not fall in with the Allies. He also promised German military protection in the case of Anglo-American attacks on Spanish territories.[76]

Parallel to operations on the Don Front, which eventually led to the crumbling of the Italian sector and the surrender of the 6th Army in Stalingrad, on 12 January 1943 the Red Army started the first phase to lift the siege of Leningrad: the Iskra offensive. They launched twenty-one divisions at the southern flank, east of the city and south of Lake Ladoga, in an attempt to apply a pincer movement to the German XXVI Army Corps. The 2nd Battalion of the Spanish 269th Regiment was again required to reinforce the German positions held by the 61st Division near Poselok. The Spaniards also had to cover a longer section of the front when the SS Police Division posted south of the BD was withdrawn to contain a Soviet offensive. On 22 January, the Soviets attacked Poselok and cut off a company. The Román Battalion fought back despite numerous fallen, counter-attacking and then containing a new enemy offensive. They lost 124 soldiers in two days, while the wounded, frozen, sick, and missing came close to almost four hundred.[77] Meanwhile, the BD fell under the command of General Philipp Kleffel and the I Army Corps. On 28 January 1943, the remainder of the Román Battalion returned to its former positions.

In early February, it became clear that the Red Army was concentrating light and heavy artillery, along with tanks and infantry, on the Krasnyi Bor sector of the plain, which was protected by the Spanish 262nd Regiment. The only thing left to ascertain was the date of the attack. Esteban-Infantes pre-emptively organized three defensive lines. At 6:45 on the morning of 10 February 1943, a devastating attack began with very intense artillery bombardment that gave way to a frontal assault by four infantry divisions – very superior in numbers – supported by airplanes, a hundred tanks, motorized units, skiers, and anti-tank cannons. The objective of the offensive, as part of Operation Polar Star, was to turn towards the east and break the siege of Leningrad, closing off the enemy units that protected the Ishora sector. This was planned to coincide with an attack on the Pogost'e sector to the south-east, in order to take the Lubań rail hub. In the mid-range, along with the Don offensive and the destruction of the Stalingrad pocket in the south, the operation sought to bring about the collapse of the German 18th Army and a general retreat of Army Group North, thanks to coordinated attacks from the Demyansk Pocket to the south of Lake Ilmen. However, this parallel offensive, which was intended to reach Narva and cut off Army Group North, did not take place because the German 16th Army had retreated from there as a precaution weeks before.

The Spanish units in the first line of the front were overwhelmed by the enemy's firepower and superior numbers. However, the survivors tenaciously resisted the Soviet advance and established several defence nuclei that slowed enemy progress. German aviation in the early afternoon of 10 February helped stop the offensive, as did the arrival of German reinforcements along with some Estonian and Norwegian units, which consolidated a new line of defence to the south of Krasnyi Bor. Soviet reserves of men and ammunition were dwindling; the attacking troops, exhausted and unaccustomed to offensive operations, failed to penetrate quickly in the breach that had been opened in the enemy lines. When the front was finally stabilized on 15 February, the Wehrmacht had to assume the loss of three to six kilometres. The time gained had come at great cost to the Blue Division, but they were no longer in danger of being surrounded by the Soviets. There were 1,100 fallen

Blue Division Operations, siege of Leningrad
(September 1942 / October 1943)

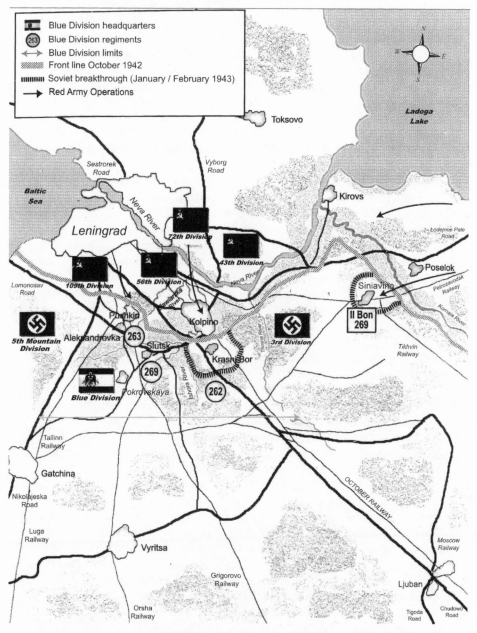

Map 2. The Blue Division Operations, siege of Leningrad
(September 1942–October 1943)

soldiers, including 46 officers; around 200 prisoners; over a hundred missing, and 1,500 wounded and sick. The Battle of Krasnyi Bor accounted for 20 per cent of total BD deaths on the Russian Front, claiming nearly half of the Spanish captains and a quarter of the lieutenants and second lieutenants who died in Russia.[78]

Once more, the German command thought the defensive capacity of the Spanish Division contemptible. On 11 February, they concluded that the Spaniards must have "cut and run from the artillery fire," and tried to replace the BD with German troops: "for our combat operations they are nothing but trouble." However, the only available option was one inexperienced division and one Luftwaffe field division. In the following days, Spaniards and Germans engaged in several counter-attacks, recovering part of the territory that had been lost. To avoid compromising the positions now occupied by the decimated BD troops, the German command placed a reserve intervention unit behind their lines. This made it possible to salvage the situation of the Spaniards, "who believe to have fought heroically."[79] The commander of the 18th Army, General Georg Lindemann, even proposed replacing the Spaniards in the mid-range and dispatching them back to the Volkhov. However, Hitler considered the Novgorod flank to be more vulnerable and refused the proposal.[80] Sporadic combats of diminishing intensity occurred in the Ishora sector through mid-March. When a new Soviet offensive attempt on 19 March proved unsuccessful, the Red Army considered the front stabilized.

Krasnyi Bor is to date the last big battle involving a regular unit of the Spanish Army. It also marked a new high point in the love-hate relationship between the Blue Division and the German command. For the Spanish General Staff, the disaster could have been avoided had the Germans intervened earlier on 10 February and given them sufficient heavy armament. The high commands of the L Army Corps, the 18th Army, and Army Group North wanted to avoid creating diplomatic friction between Berlin and Madrid. They had to allocate ever-scarcer resources among divisions whose combat efficacy was measured in inverse proportion to their Germanness. Thus, they could not permit the BD to receive better resources than their own divisions.[81]

Despite their need for personnel to defend a broad sector of the front, General Kleffel, General Lindemann, and other staff officers remained distrustful of the Spanish capacity to resist an attack preceded by intense artillery fire.[82] A German regiment was kept in the BD rearguard with orders to assume control of the Spanish Division in an emergency. They required Esteban-Infantes to withdraw a regiment from the front every four weeks for training in offensive operations, and they planned to reduce the length of the portion of the front assigned to the Spaniards. Similarly, the BD concentrated on regrouping its personnel – thanks to the arrival of a march battalion with replacements in March – and on fortifying positions against new armoured attacks.[83] In May, Kleffel requested that the most vulnerable section of the front line, which included the Ishora River, be entrusted to German soldiers and that the Spaniards be deployed in safer areas. In the following weeks, the 401st German Regiment was placed in reserve behind the BD and the Spaniards were given more anti-tank weapons and artillery.[84]

The German command was concerned about the possibility of another Soviet attack on Spanish lines, which materialized in mid-May with a small-scale assault on the positions of the BD and the 170th Division. For half an hour the Germans feared that a significant breach had been opened in the front, but the situation stabilized.[85] During the following month, the high command of the L Army Corps remained apprehensive of another big attack on the Spanish positions, as a prelude to an expected offensive to break the siege of Leningrad.[86] Their fears were intensified by the precision artillery attack on the BD headquarters in Pokrosvkoe on 18 July 1943, during a banquet to which several German officers had been invited.[87]

The German commanders continued trusting the Spaniards to carry out strikes, such as the attack of August 1943 against several Soviet bunkers. Though they were considered masters of guerrilla warfare for good reason, the results generally proved unsatisfactory to the Germans. The Spaniards captured too few prisoners, took too long to prepare actions, and tended to suffer too many casualties.[88] During the summer of 1943, the Germans' opinion on the offensive capacity of the BD remained invariably severe. Though mobility had increased, their combat capability was considered inferior to that of the 170th or 215th German Divisions, due to their lack of training and insufficient anti-tank weapons and artillery. The occasional replacement of their more experienced combatants was now regarded as a disadvantage: when they left, the new ones had to be trained. It was said that while the Spaniards excelled at small-scale warfare, they could not withstand frontal attacks with artillery and tank support. The Iberian combatants waged war in their own way: they neglected provisioning and took little care of their trenches, and their pride made them reluctant to accept advice.[89]

The morale of the Spanish Division declined throughout the spring and summer of 1943, according to German reports. Discontent with the command of Esteban-Infantes had grown among the officers and troops; the quality of the recruits had diminished; and the quality and

technical training of the NCOs was still very low by German standards. Therefore, the combat capability of the BD did not substantially
improve. Despite eventually being considered close to fully armed, including some anti-tank weapons, the German command never contem-
plated the Spanish Division capable of more than defensive warfare,
and then only if the enemy attack did not involve much in the way of
tanks or artillery.[90]

In early October, after several days of rumours at Army Group North
headquarters and the Reich Chancellery in Berlin, Esteban-Infantes
endured the humiliation of hearing from General Lindemann – before
hearing it directly from Madrid – that the Spanish government was
buckling under Allied pressure and had ordered the withdrawal of
the Blue Division from the Eastern Front. The Council of Ministers had
agreed on 23 September that one legion would remain, with a maximum of three battalions.[91] Though Hitler initially rejected the idea, he
changed his mind and allowed an exclusively volunteer force to remain on the front. Progressively, personnel decreased from an initial
proposal of two regiments comprising 7,200 combatants to barely one
regiment.[92]

In mid-September, Esteban-Infantes was received in the Wolf's Lair.
There, Hitler awarded him the same medal as his predecessor. After
spending some time in Berlin, Esteban-Infantes returned to the front
in November. There, he oversaw the withdrawal of the last BD units,
which had gathered in the Volosovo-Nikolaevka region, and he organized the Spanish Legion of Volunteers – the "Blue Legion." One of his
final acts was to propose 491 soldiers for the Iron Cross Second Class,
for merits including unusual valour "on numerous occasions in the
vanguard, always volunteering for the places of greatest risk," for participating "in numerous strikes, distinguished for great valour and se-
renity," or for demonstrating "always a fighting spirit, discipline, and
leadership." He also requested the War Merit Cross Second Class for
509 officers, NCOs, and privates sometimes for such modest deeds as
"excellent care of weaponry," demonstrating "great love for work" in
handling communications, or giving "great attention to the cattle of his
unit." The list of those proposed for distinction in infantry assault was
restricted to ninety-seven soldiers and officers of the 263rd Regiment.
This gives an idea of the decreasing combat intensity to which the Spaniards were exposed during their final six months on the Eastern Front.[93]

The Blue Division was officially dissolved on 16 November 1943.
Meanwhile, the Francoist regime struggled along the road from
non-belligerence to strict neutrality amidst the reticence of Franco and
many of his ministers to leave the Eastern Front entirely.

The Short-Lived Blue Legion (December 1943–March 1944)

According to the agreement between General Carlos Asensio, the new Spanish minister of the army, and General Rafael García Valiño (Army General Staff), the Spanish Legion of Volunteers would be organized as an infantry unit without an initial limit on the number of soldiers. However, *General Instruction L.V.1* provided for a guaranteed minimum number through compulsory enlistment of all BD combatants who had served less than ten months on the front.[94] After an exchange of views between the Division commander and Franco himself, a mixed system was implemented in the end. The new Legion was largely constituted of personnel from the last march battalion that had arrived in October 1943. The BD General Staff requested that the officers of several units ask around among the soldiers who had arrived in the 8th to the 21st March Battalions, to determine how many would be willing to re-enlist in the new unit. The offer excluded "all those who have demonstrated unsatisfactory conduct or have poor records." Their responses were generally rather deflating.[95]

Implementation of the order depended substantially on the individual inclination of the unit commanders. Some officers yearned to return to Spain and did little to encourage recruitment of volunteers to continue on the front. Others chose to remain and pressured their men to do the same. After several contradictory orders reflecting the political competition between the Ministry of Foreign Affairs and the Ministry of the Army, the Blue Legion comprised a broader set of combatants than was initially foreseen by Esteban-Infantes: 2,269 men divided into three battalions or *banderas*: two grenadier battalions and one mixed battalion. There was a General Staff as well as exploration units, logistics, vehicle repair, and police sections, along with rearguard services in Riga.[96] All types filled the ranks, from idealists to those who re-enlisted because they could not adapt to civilian life after their return from Russia. One of them recalled, "I missed my comrades, and I had nothing to do in Madrid."[97] Though some units had significant numbers of re-enlisted soldiers, altogether they accounted for less than 6 per cent of the total combatants.[98]

Colonel Antonio García-Navarro became the supreme commander of the Legion. Until 11 December, the unit received technical and theoretical instruction in Kingisepp/Jamburg, to the east of Narva – some fifty kilometres away from the rest of the BD, who were being repatriated in phases. The 18th Army command planned to keep one Spanish battalion on the front and another in the reserves. After the retraining period, however, there was no decision about where to deploy them. They still wanted to send the Legion to cover relatively calm positions, such as the coast, thereby liberating German personnel to serve in the more active areas on the Leningrad Front.[99] Before training finished, one Legion battalion had to be deployed along the road from Kingisepp to Narva and participated in anti-partisan action to empty several hamlets. With almost 60 per cent of the new unit composed of army and Legion personnel, behaviour in the rearguard was no better than before. The training period in Kingisepp was sprinkled with complaints from the local population and German soldiers, who reported the Spaniards for robbery, assault, and other minor incidents. One legionnaire wrote that the place had a great inconvenience: "there are no *pañenkas* [girls]."[100]

During their brief deployment on the Russian Front, the Blue Legion suffered fourteen desertions and as many as six cases of self-mutilation. Alcoholism was rampant, and seventy-five soldiers were repatriated as "undesirables."[101] German liaison reports described how the human resources that had arrived at the front since the summer of 1943 were politically and militarily unreliable. Some of the BD returnees communicated their negative impression of the composition of the most recently arrived march battalion to comrades who were still on the Russian Front.[102] The Spaniards could be useful on a static front, so long as they only had to hold their positions, resist strikes and attacks without much tank or artillery support, and occasionally raid the enemy camp to take prisoners and obtain information regarding the situation on the enemy side. However, their performance in reconnaissance, attack, and strike missions remained limited, partly due to their lack of technical training. The Germans saw that a full-scale attack on the Spanish positions would quickly destroy their resistance capabilities.[103]

In mid-December, the entire Blue Legion was moved to the southeast of Leningrad, in the Bogoslovo-Schapi-Kstovo sector. They were attached to the 121st Division, to protect a marshy, eleven kilometre section of the front. The legionnaires were constantly harassed by partisans and Soviet ski units; they disliked the area, which was impassable for armoured vehicles. There at least, the Legion would not be overrun by tanks, which was a concern for the German command. The Spanish troops had a relatively calm month; the monotony of winter was only interrupted by a few strikes and typhoid fever.

At the onset of the Soviet offensive on 14 January 1944, the German positions flanking the Spaniards were hit especially hard. At risk of being surrounded, the Legion retreated west to Lyuban, under mortar fire and partisan attack. When they arrived, they entered fierce combat in a context of general retreat. On 26 January, García Navarro received the order to retreat by train to Luga, 140 kilometres to the south-west.

However, the train lines had been cut by the partisans, so the Spaniards began a miserable march with their scant vehicles along a road strewn with tree trunks, amidst growing chaos, skirmishes with partisans, and signs of rebellion in the ranks.[104]

In early February 1944, General Anton Grasser, who had recently assumed his post as general commander of the XXVI Army Corps, observed the deplorable condition of the Spaniards who arrived at Luga. The German command had originally intended to assign them to prevent partisan attacks along the rail lines between Luga and Pskov/Pleskau. However, the senior German liaison officer communicated to his superiors that the legionnaires were exhausted, demoralized, and showing signs of disintegration. Desertions were foreseeable in stressful situations. For that reason, he recommended that the Spanish troops spend time retraining in Estonia. Grasser managed to get his petition approved and ten days later the legionnaires boarded a train for the Estonian town of Tapa/Taps, located eighty kilometres south-east of Tallinn.[105]

The move to Estonia did not put an end to the problems that the Spanish soldiers, with their growing discontent, created for the German command. On 5 February, the commander general of rearguard security forces of Army Group North communicated his apprehension at the imminent arrival of the legionnaires. The conduct of the Spaniards in the rearguard had in the past been characterized by "looting, theft, sexual crimes, etc." Thus, it was foreseeable that they would generate ill will towards the Wehrmacht among the local population. He requested that the Legion stay be as short as possible,[106] and was relieved when it happened that way.

Developments in the front, with pressure from the British, and German awareness that ensuring the continuity of the wolfram supply from Spain as well as German espionage in Spanish territory, outweighed the scarce military contribution of the Legion. This led the Madrid government to suggest that Hitler authorize the repatriation of the Blue Squadron and the Blue Legion. The Führer acquiesced on 20 February, and on 6 March 1944, the order from Spain for definitive withdrawal arrived at Legion headquarters.[107] The Blue Legion surrendered arms ten days later and returned in phases to the barracks at Stablack Süd (Königsberg). There, Wehrmacht officers identified soldiers who wanted to continue fighting. Some legionnaires resolved to stay in the Third Reich as civilian workers; the rest returned to Spain. On 12 April, the last battalion of the Blue Legion crossed the border from France into Spain.[108]

The Spanish Division of Volunteers and its short-lived successor thus ceased to exist as units integrated within the Wehrmacht. They left behind almost five thousand dead in Russian territory. Though the total number of deaths is not exact, a 1960 report by the Spanish War Ministry estimated 4,800 fallen and some 200 more missing, increasing the total to 5,000. Added to these were 115 soldiers who died in Soviet prisoner camps, almost 2,200 who were disabled, and many more who were injured.

Life on the Front: The Daily Experience of Spanish Combatants

Internally, the Blue Division was socially and politically heterogeneous, but the first expedition in the summer of 1941 had an atmosphere of increasing cohesion and comradeship as they travelled to Germany, trained at the Grafenwöhr camp, and left for the front. Though militia life had hardened the volunteers, and despite discontent about the food, the hours, the climate, or the friction between Falangist volunteers and army officers, the dominant spirit was one of genuine camaraderie. Ridruejo described his impression of the collective BD mood in mid-August:

> There is also singing and drinking and underneath – though perhaps in a rather rudimentary and barbarian way – there is happiness and enthusiasm. Sometimes you hear "if I had known I would not have come," but never "I want to leave" or anything that contradicts the general "let's get started because we'll be fine there once the action begins."[109]

As in the Wehrmacht, this comradeship certainly had its limits, the first of which were social: despite the idealization of interclassism and later recreations of community in the trenches, coexistence was not always easy between students and peasants or workers and middle-class lads.[110] There were also political limits. In some units, leftist volunteers might be protected by their Falangist companions. In others, they might be watched or even reported. Luis Aguilar noted during his stay in Grafenwöhr that "this morning they detained three 'volunteers' of the Company for being Reds, among them Corporal Dionisio Rubio ... as he had belonged to the red SIM [Intelligence Service]. Quite the specimens!"[111]

During the march, many BD volunteers envisioned a war of rapid manoeuvres followed by tank divisions in the vanguard, which would have them parading through Moscow's Red Square in a few weeks' time. In September 1941, Dionisio Ridruejo still assumed that "the army in which I will march on Moscow is innumerable, futuristic. It will be a splendid spectacle worth a life to see." Within a few weeks, they slammed up against an altogether different reality.[112] Like many Wehrmacht divisions, after the advance came stabilization of the front, the return to a war of positions, and combat conditions that rivalled

Fig. 4.3. Spanish *Feldpost*, 1942 (AGA)

the First World War in brutality. The Volkhov offensive and subsequent withdrawal gave way to a war of attrition and positions.

Cold, Filth, Boredom … and Peril

Daily life in the trenches and the fortified vanguard positions imposed some inglorious realities. Many soldiers felt the need to write, partly to recover a shred of dignity or an illusion of routine and the normality that belonged to civilian life. Their diaries and testimonies reflected this in real time. The day-to-day of the war became an idealized construction in their narratives, based on emotional compensation mechanisms: writing about their hardships was as important as recording the prosaic details that reminded the soldiers of their former life.[113]

A stable front made for a miserable life. Squalor invaded the living spaces of the vanguard troops and the second-line artillery positions. It was not infrequent to find human waste in them; unlike their more systematic German comrades, the BD combatants did not always dig holes in some discreet patch of ground that might serve as latrines. In spring and summer, rodents flourished. Artillery officer Guillermo Hernanz awoke on more than one occasion in the unexpected company of rats. However, "we got used to it, we have masses of spiders, bedbugs, rats that even eat our tobacco." Some soldiers saw the rodents as allies: "if the sentinel saw them running towards him, he knew that the Russians were coming to strike that night."[114]

The filthy surroundings accompanied a rapid decline in personal hygiene, especially in the trenches and the *chabolas* – the shanty-like living spaces that provided shelter for the section, with bunks, basic furniture, a stove, and a sort of sod-and-timber roof. These were common to all combatants on the Eastern Front, as they had been in the trenches of the First World War. The Spanish soldiers, however, tended to be even more unkempt than their German comrades, due to negligence and lack of insistence on the part of their commanders. This was not only about laxity in the care and cleanliness of their uniforms, or how rapidly their clothes wore out, or the diverse accessories – from Soviet balaclavas to clothing bought or confiscated from the locals – that they wore over their German kit. The lack of hygiene implied a greater risk of disease. Teeth were rarely brushed and opportunities for washing were scarce indeed. Motorized liaison Martin Velasco wrote on 2 November 1941: "Today is a great day for my diary, I had a shower ... the first I have had in at least three months."[115]

Inevitably, the lack of washing also led to the proliferation of lice – those bothersome companions that even the winter cold could not eliminate. Salvador Zanón wrote from his shanty in the Nikitkino forest: "Mostly I scratch myself. I feel life teeming under my arms, at my waist, on my back, around my ankles."[116] Killing lice in the evenings became a frequent pastime for the soldiers. Eczemas proliferated, and pustules from scratching. Using blankets on which the parasites formed "a crust that hides the colour of the cloth,"[117] the troops could not sleep well for itching and suffered from lack of sleep and nervousness.

Added to these typical inconveniences of life on the front was the unbearable climate that aggravated everything. The extreme temperatures of the Russian winter were the most common subject transmitted in BD memoirs. The omnipresent snow, the ice, the freezing wind became the icons associated with the Russian Front and transmitted in multiple narratives, cinematographic reproductions, and coetaneous reports. For many of them, it was an entirely new experience.

This was a problem for the invaders in general. The Wehrmacht had not adequately foreseen the need to equip its troops with appropriate gear for a war of positions in conditions of intense cold. Moreover, winter weather came especially early in 1941–2. The poorly equipped combatants suffered through many days of temperatures below -30° C. The *Ostheer* lacked sufficient balaclavas, gloves, fur coats, and felted wool boots to equip all its troops. Supplies arrived too late: by Christmas almost 133,000 cases of frostbite in varying degrees had been registered on the Eastern Front, resulting in numerous partial amputations of limbs or digits. In some German units, more than 5 per cent of the soldiers had injuries from partial freezing. Weapons also jammed frequently at such low temperatures, creating insecurity.

The great actors on the Russian Front were undoubtedly the cold, the snow, and their effects. These new experiences had begun to surface during the foot march, when the Spanish soldiers found that the Russian autumn was short and harsh. On 3 October 1941, before the first snows, liaison Martín Velasco noted in his diary how bothersome the cold was to the BD volunteers, but stated haughtily, "we hide it better than the Russians … we walk uncovered and they with their old fur coats and heads completely covered." In the following weeks, such quixotic postures proved insufficient for sub-zero temperatures; only stoicism and discipline would get them through.[118] In March 1942, the Wehrmacht had only provided 15 per cent of the Spanish combatants with felted boots; another 5.5 per cent had sheepskin footwear and 15.5 per cent had boots made of straw and reeds. Despite the efforts of the FET Women's Section to send warm clothes to the soldiers, scarcely 30 per cent of them had received a jumper for the cold and only 20.4 per cent had overcoats.[119] Packages received from Spain, beginning with the Christmas box that arrived in late January 1942, contained knit wool sweaters, socks, sweets, glasses and tobacco, and liquor. None of that effectively counteracted the cold, and the situation was no better in the German units. In some of them, records indicate that 12.9 per cent of the troops were affected by frostbite.[120]

The extra difficulty caused by the cold, the snow, and the ice created additional problems for the transportation network, which affected the distribution of food and victuals in the rearguard and on the front. Frequently, the mess arrived at the trenches completely frozen, 80 per cent of the bottled water, and a good portion of the liquor, froze, and bottles broke. The motor oil also froze, affecting the autonomy and manoeuvring of the trucks and armoured vehicles; the pasty mess that formed when the snow melted and mixed with the mud made transit extremely cumbersome. Urinating or defecating outdoors became torturous. Ditches, shelters, or graves could scarcely be dug in the frozen earth.[121] The low temperatures were an unfamiliar experience for most of the Spanish volunteers, and the cold also affected their minds. "If it continues as it seems we can expect it to, it can do us much harm and even threaten our morale," wrote Ridruejo.[122] The cold made the combatants hazy; it slowed their reflexes and reaction time to unexpected events. Daniel Torra expressed accurately his physical sensations in the days prior to Christmas 1941:

> I think I have lost some of my faculties since I have been here. I don't see well, I can't remember things or express myself clearly, or express myself rapidly, or understand or describe things quickly. I am growing physically weaker and weaker. This is so very hard![123]

A first effect of the cold was frostbite in the extremities, especially the feet. By April 1942, this had affected up to 6.5 per cent of the Spanish troops and accounted for 30 per cent of the casualties. To avoid freezing, the night guards had to be relieved every hour or every half hour at temperatures lower than -25°C. Guard duty was torturous for the soldiers, as fighting against the cold distracted them from vigilance and every shadow became a false alarm.[124] The snow that accumulated during the long winter infused the surroundings with a false sense of calm that might be interrupted at any moment by gunfire, explosions, or enemy strikes. Clearing paths through snow that sometimes came up to their knees, with a heavy pack on their back, in dense pine and birch forests that resounded with the echo of their movements became a physical and psychological torture for the combatants.

The trenches and huts in the advance positions were often full of water and little better than open exposure to the elements. The troops' feet were always wet, which sometimes led to a form of gangrene known as trench foot. In the vanguard listening posts the soldiers had to take shelter day and night in underground refuges that were damp and cold, with no more than a camp stove. Often, it was too dangerous to go out during the day, so the troops could only move at night. This included moving the wounded, who would sometimes bleed to death.[125] Private Ramón Farré recalled such moments:

> A trench about three metres long, sloping down, and at the end a hole of scarcely four metres, with the ground covered in straw mixed with snow that the wind constantly blew in and at one end a stove built from an empty can. [My comrade] "Ramper" is in charge of lighting the fire, but this damned hole never warms up ... Six o' clock. Private Polón has begun his guard duty. Private Valentí has sat on a log near the fire and the rest try to find a way to sleep, but the space is so tight that it isn't likely to happen

Fig. 4.4. Spanish soldiers in the rearguard, 1942–3 (AGA)

... Our postures allow for not the slightest movement and the munitions and machete in our belts dig into our bodies relentlessly, the lice make us itch desperately but it is impossible to scratch.[126]

The lice-ridden soldiers did not get regular rest. They were thin, though they did not actually go hungry. They suffered from general exhaustion, respiratory and intestinal maladies, chilblains from the cold, calluses, and much more. Many combatants suffered from colds, throat infections, rheumatic maladies, kidney and gastric infections, and diarrhoea. On the Russian Front, as many as 3.5 per cent of the combatants in some *Ostheer* units suffered from respiratory ailments. Lack of sleep kept soldiers in the vanguard in a permanent state of drowsiness. The snow also provoked eye ailments. The panoply of maladies that the Spanish Division described resembled what was recorded in the medical reports of nearby German units.[127]

Spring and the abating cold did not improve conditions as much as might be expected. The thaw was accompanied by the *rasputitsa*, or "time without roads," which turned the world into an impassable mud puddle. Vast areas turned to marshes and the mud impeded the transit of provisions, trucks, troops, and virtually all traffic. The soldiers' problems did not end there: human remains also thawed and floated down the Volkhov. As they decomposed, they filled the air around the battle sites with a sickening sweet stench. In the midst of it all, soldiers kept fighting and dying. The worst of many war actions was having to move on foot, sometimes for many kilometres in rain or intense cold, with heavy packs, struggling through the snow and the mud.[128] Patrols in flooded forests meant hours of walking in mud up to the knees; the combatants ended the day drenched in mud that soaked through their underclothes. The water filled the trenches and underground positions, so that the soldiers had to spend entire days half-soaking in it.[129] They were also terrified of the dense, immense forests, where it was easy to get lost for hours, and where sounds echoed deceptively in the distance.

After the spring thaw came the intense heat of the brief but suffocating summer and the persistent clouds of mosquitos, which were especially fierce on the Volkhov Front. The combatants used netting over their helmets for protection, which did not provide a long-term solution. The resistant, aggressive insects "bite right through jackets and trousers." They drove artillery officer Guillermo Hernanz to distraction: he returned from commanding a patrol with his face and hands swollen, bleeding from so much scratching.[130]

Combatting the punishing climate and environment was often a greater concern than enemy fire. As Gutiérrez del Castillo put it, "fighting in Russia is ... something mystical and fanstastic that fills you with strange terrors; it feels unfocused, as if you were in a giant vastness ... it is like immersing the spirit in frightening darkness."[131] Though the inconveniences affected both sides equally, the Soviets were better equipped for the cold. Despite numerous cases of frostbite and freezing, they were more resistant to the hardships and survived on scarce rations. They were content to stay alive, despite brutal treatment from their superiors.[132] The Germans recognized that the *frontoviki* – the Soviet rank-and-file soldiers – seemed to be "less vulnerable than our soldiers" to the cold and the snow.[133] This demoralized the invaders. In December 1941, the XXXVIII Army Corps reported that the troops were in poor condition due to the cold and high casualties. Worse than that, however, was the apathy that affected some commanders and the predominant anxiety among the troops.[134]

Such deprivations and physical sensations were typical rites of passage in military experience, especially in life on the front. They were not so new for Civil War veterans, many of whom had participated in harsh combat and were familiar with hunger, cold, filth, lice, and boredom sprinkled with moments of danger.[135] They were novel, however, for

students and volunteers from urban environments, who were less accustomed to physical work and a life exposed to the elements. The radical intensity and accumulation of these experiences combined with the
gruelling foot marches and the uncertainty that accompanied such an
exotic location were incomparable to anything in their prior experience.

Not everything that was seen, heard, and suffered on the Russian
Front was transmitted in the same manner. The combatants – conditioned as they were by their rank, their unit, or their destination – registered different impressions of the cold or contact with the enemy, and to
different degrees. It follows, then, that they did not selectively transform
their impressions into similar experiences. Their assorted formative,
ideological, and social background led them to express authentic war
experiences in diverse ways, according to their pre-existing cognitive
frames.[136] The officers and many NCOs, even in the vanguard positions,
lived through the war in better conditions than the regular soldiers.
They had relatively comfortable shelters, they were not always exposed
on the front line, and Spanish officers were allowed one or even two
assistants and their own cook.[137] Soldiers in the rearguard, in logistical
services, in the General Staff, or intelligence also had different experiences than those on the front lines. The sappers and pioneers, as well as
the artillerymen, communications technicians, and anti-tank soldiers,
constituted specific clusters. The first group endured greater exposure
to danger and sometimes spent hours and days laying in the snow, suffering heavily from extreme winter conditions while performing their
risky duties.[138] The second followed just behind the vanguard. The li-
aisons seldom engaged in combat but were often exposed to sniper, artillery, and aviation fire. Medical personnel scarcely experienced trench
warfare but dealt with its consequences and the psychological fatigue it
entailed. The soldiers belonging to the radio sections spent most of the
time in comfortable posts behind the front line but were required go out
and repair communication lines among front units.[139]

Liaison driver Martín Velasco was able to shower with somewhat
more regularity from November 1941 on. His services (mostly taking messages to troops far away from headquarters) were not always
needed and every day he enjoyed a relatively calm breakfast of coffee
and toast with butter. Sometimes he visited comrades who were "frying
up some beef fillets, and mashed potatoes with milk and butter," and
went to bed early. Danger came in the form of sporadic bombardment
from Soviet artillery. Also, the bad conditions of the terrain sometimes
made it necessary for him to ask for help from the peasants to pull his
motorcycle from the mud. He had to spend the night of 24–5 October
1941 in a Russian hamlet, and the following day required help from

the inhabitants of another locality. "I politely asked some Russians in a house to hitch a horse to a cart and come with me; we reached my machine, put it in the cart, and they took me to the entrance of Novgorod." Indeed, the real danger came from the partisans.[140]

Private Farré Palaus was in an advance position of the section around Lake Ilmen. He had to spend the nights in a hut, taking turns at guard duty in the perilous cold. During the day, he had to do innumerable tasks that lacked warrior glory but ensured the habitability of the shelter:

> When there isn't guard duty in Babki, there is wood to collect, or supplies, or snow to shovel, munitions to fetch, mines to place in the lake, a thousand necessary errands, and when they are done there is barely time left to sleep a couple of hours and spend the night on alert again.[141]

Since 1945, BD memoirs began to focus on recreating the actions on the Volkhov and in Krasnyi Bor – epic images of ferocious combat on bloody snow. However, considering that Spanish soldiers stayed an average of ten months on the front, moments of inactivity were much more abundant than those of combat. Testimonies coincide regarding the unbearable monotony of life on the front, which was a classic feature of modern warfare that could lead to a "calm desperation" and an obsession with the miseries of everyday life.[142] The most common subject after December 1941 was lament over the paralysing routine of days in the trenches. That month, Daniel Torra wrote how "not being able to escape the monotony of the hours is the worst thing." Joaquín Ros noted months later that "life is very monotonous." Boredom accompanied lack of hygiene, cold, and a diffuse sense of insecurity that increased at night.[143]

This was a war of positions, but it never became a "calm front" as many had known during the Spanish Civil War. It was taking place in a hostile geography, against an enemy only a few dozen metres away. There were occasional armed encounters, but the adversary lurked in the forests of the rearguard like some menacing, ghostly presence whose unpredictability made it all the more dangerous. The tedium was deceptive: a few hundred metres away there might be a camouflaged partisan, a sniper, an ace gunner. The hours of night watch tried the soldiers' nerves: "The worst is sensing something out there, feeling a confused, inexplicable apprehension, not knowing what is happening or what is coming upon you."[144] The routine was occasionally interrupted by strikes, reinforced patrols, and moments of brief but intense combat.[145]

The most terrible experience was holding the positions during enemy artillery fire or occasional air bombardment. The Spanish troops had no adequate protection from the latter; Soviet planes could interrupt improvised "war tourism outings" to neighbouring villages on the front.[146] In an artillery or air attack, the anguish of not knowing what to expect dominated the minds of those who sought refuge underground or risked going out. Ridruejo wrote: "What was a safe place? We had to invent a specific conviction that it would not fall 'there,' wherever 'there' was at any given moment, and live naturally." Inside the hovels, the sensation of security was only illusory:

> If you are inside, everything shakes, you are deafened and resigned to what must happen at any moment. If you go outside the air is filled with shrapnel, the houses that remain are on fire, shelters are caving in, people are scurrying, passing, and falling.[147]

The arrival of spring somewhat alleviated the cold-related hardships and allowed for better personal hygiene: "We began to wash ourselves more and not go so heavily dressed and we all talked to each other more, because in winter we were like coal miners," wrote Joaquín Ros.[148] This did little to alter the monotony of the days, however. Lieutenant Arenales wrote on arriving at his position on the Volkhov Front on 12 June 1942 that "here there is absolutely nothing, it is an extremely calm sector," which reminded him of his experiences in the Civil War. Daily life was filled with routine tasks: guard duty, cleaning weapons, card games, letter writing, meeting up with comrades, and once in a while a visit to the rearguard. Arenales wrote again two days later that his shelter had a "bedroom in the style of the quaternary period."[149]

Artillery Lieutenant Guillermo Hernanz had the same impression of the front when he arrived on 2 May of the same year; it bore absolutely no resemblance to the heroic environment he had imagined before. "I have suffered a small disappointment; we are on the front, it has been several hours, and we have not heard a single cannon." The worst for him was to see the low morale of many veterans. "They all speak critically of … how they are treated by the commanders, by the Germans, and no one is content or thinks of anything else but to leave."[150] In fact, rumours about imminent replacements had been circulating in the BD since December 1941. At the end of that month, Daniel Torra heard "various stories about the future of the Division." This generated anxiety among the soldiers, who were already tired after the first series of hard combats. By mid-January 1942, optimism was fading: "[hope] of replacements, not much."[151]

Even during times of inactivity, things were not so comfortable for Arenales. Worse than the inescapable mosquitoes were the monotony, the homesickness for his family, and the inclement weather. On 1 June he noted that he had not left the shelter all day and had done nothing more than write letters home. He had to give signs of life, though "I don't know what more to tell them." On 20 June, he was cheered at the expectation that he might be selected to participate in a strike and "catch a Russian," which might earn him an Iron Cross if successful. However, his captain did not select him. When the strike group returned on 26 June, he was shaken by the death of a friend who had fallen in the raid. This was accompanied by a contradictory sense of relief: if Arenales had gone instead, he would have died and never been able to fulfil his greatest desire: to return to his girlfriend. "I will console my spirit and try not to be a coward, to return to her side as I left." Even so, he also envied those who had taken part in the strike and were now being recommended for medals.[152]

Lieutenant Hernanz, who was assigned to the headquarters at Grigorovo, experienced an equally contradictory sensation. Though he longed to be sent to a battery on the front, he could not avoid the fear of being gravely injured or killed on the front line and never see his beloved girlfriend Maruja again.[153] Daniel Torra mourned the death of two comrades in a strike in late March 1942 and bitterly mused at the meaning of this loss: "Why did it happen? They were so worthy, and their death was not purchased at its value."[154] On 28 June 1942, Arenales was consumed by nostalgia and anguished over the absence of letters from his girlfriend: "I don't know what to think, everything makes me bitter, it's been so long that I don't know what to believe about Sagrario." His mood turned depressive some days later:

> It is the maximum, utmost boredom to know that we will spend all winter here, this is not a war, it is a summer but ... the mosquitoes make life impossible, I can't sleep; I blame them, but it's really because I haven't had any letters from home or from Sagrario.[155]

Hernanz was not faring much better in his position, in a "war too idiotic and dull to even want to write about in a diary." A few days later, the lack of activity made him apathetic, "disgusted with Russia and ... sick of the BD." He scarcely moved beyond a radius of two hundred metres from his post. The interminable daylight of the arctic summer made sleep more irregular, and fatigue accumulated despite the inactivity.[156] Daniel Torra wrote in May 1942 that "I am losing my interest in observing and taking notes," overcome as he was by a sense of "complete abandonment to fate."[157]

Arenales was dejected until 16 July, when at last he received a letter from his girlfriend and his diary again overflowed with enthusiasm. In that he was no different from most other soldiers. Hernanz counted the hours until mail delivery and was deeply disappointed when there were no letters for him. The inactivity led him to become obsessed with the idea that his girlfriend had abandoned him. However, these depressive states gave way to euphoria when the courier brought new letters from his beloved.[158] A few lines from his girlfriend gave Arenales fresh inspiration to survive, to "earn the privilege of calling her my wife ... for her I will fight and endure anything fate throws at me."[159]

However, the mail from home did not only bring good news. It also reminded the soldiers of ongoing family, sentimental, or social conflicts, which were intensified by questions such as how to allocate the combatant's salary. These things worried the soldiers deeply and became entangled with their hardships on the front. The distance made them feel helpless. Arenales' parents and sisters demanded the part of his earnings that he had stipulated should go to his girlfriend. This was a frequent concern in the correspondence of Spanish volunteers with their families.[160] To make matters worse, another letter from his beloved Sagrario expressed to him her jealousy of Arenales's "war godmother." Wives and girlfriends considered "war godmothers" and nurses real competition in a world they imagined to be an exotic Gomorrah.

When there were no letters from home, the days passed in a strange calm. On 26 July, Arenales wrote that "this does not seem like a war; once in a while there is an exchange of gunshots, but it goes no further." On 4 August, an alarm was recorded at his post, but afterwards everything was "as boring as ever." Outings to the rearguard towns and villages were the sole distraction. On 15 August, he wrote that he and his companions had danced with "some really ugly *panienkas*."[161] The improvised fetes with the locals did not always have a romantic aura. Hernanz could not comprehend how other artillery officers had the "stomach" to dance with "fat and smelly" females in a rank, almost dark room "smelling of humanity."[162]

Circumstances did not change much when the section of Lieutenant Arenales was relieved, and he was moved to the Kolpino sector. On 12 October, he was transferred and put in charge of a machine gun in Pavlovsk, where he remained until 22 December. The days resumed their monotonous course. Here, his entries come to an end; within six weeks, by mid-February 1943, he had fallen in combat. Some months later, Arenales's family received his written diary and some photos – including one of his grave – from a returned comrade.[163]

The war diaries of Hernanz and Arenales illustrate the daily perception of danger many soldiers experienced. The monotony of tedious weeks, physical hardships, and filth might be interrupted brusquely by an enemy strike, a snipers' bullet, or well-placed artillery fire. Death hounded

Fig. 4.5. Tomb of Benjamín Arenales, 1943 (private archive of Carmelo de las Heras, Madrid)

every moment and frequently came in the most absurd manner. After almost a month of stupefying boredom, Hernanz resisted several hours of artillery attack, which claimed the lives of numerous companions at his position. After that experience, he felt he had been reborn. Weeks later, Soviet artillery hit three of his comrades, leaving them disfigured. Emotional tribute to the fallen could not mask the sensation that death lurked nearby. The late arrival of mail from Spain for those who had just fallen became a superstitious premonition.[164] Captain Figuerola wrote in his diary about the monotony of the days at the front, his encounters with other officers, and the ever-increasing demoralization of his comrades in arms. However, occasional artillery impacts caused sudden casualties. On 14 July 1943 he was also hit by a shell.[165]

Fear of dying in a strike, from a stray bullet, or from enemy mortar fire became doubly anguishing. However, the prospect of being awarded a medal for taking part at an action could appeal to the pride of even the least idealistic soldier. Angel Marchena expressed his delight at receiving a distinction from his captain after participating in an isolated strike. In contrast, Sergeant Valeriano Ruiz lamented that he had been denied a medal for the only armed action in which he had participated during his ten months in the trench.[166]

Jünger or Remarque?

The Spaniards had few opportunities to go on the offensive during their time on the Eastern Front. When they did, not all units participated in equal measure. In most of them, periods of tense calm and waiting outnumbered those of offensive. The sensations experienced during moments of intense combat were rarely reflected upon in BD testimonies, partly because such impressions and experiences could not easily be transmitted after the fact. At most, Dionisio Ridruejo observed (his impressions clearly evoking those written by Ernst Jünger years before), offensive actions were recognized as a moment of liberation from all the fears accumulated during times of waiting and passivity. Attack, even with a bayonet in an open field, became a chaotic but cathartic experience because of the adrenalin surge that accompanied it: "attacking strengthens, lifts the spirits: it releases your tensions, you get a thrill when the anti-tanks hit their mark. Danger seems to elude you personally and doesn't seek you out like some anonymous and passive mouse. But waiting in the cold is almost terrifying."[167] In the words of Falangist Andrés Gaytan, "running forward warms up your feet."[168]

Some exceptions offered an equally classic example of how comradeship was strengthened through blood bonds forged by killing, participating in the spectacle of violence and death, and surviving. The act of killing, as in all war experience, was shielded by collective responsibility. Private Sánchez Diana remembered the effect of an action on him and his comrades during the Volkhov offensive as a baptism by fire. It reinforced a brotherhood created from shared experiences that could not be transmitted:

> I climb into a haystack to rest and put my thoughts in order. My comrades are different now. They have a different personality. The blind instinct to fight has changed the spirit born in the camp, in the marches, and in the

days on the train and at the post. We are like workers of death. We bear the ancient mark of destruction. We are warriors, life has a different sign.[169]

Individual and collective combat experience, the emotional impact of killing and seeing close comrades die, marked the soldiers for life, more than any rite of passage in the barracks or during the march to the front. It was a sort of inner journey to the deepest survival instincts, which Sánchez Diana captured in idealized but very expressive terms:

> The change of mentality that we have all suffered and that will mark us if we survive ... The terrible hours on the front, and the disappearance of good friends and comrades has this positive aspect. It surrounds this place with bitter, intensely lyrical dregs ... we kill, and we die simply because. It is a hidden instinct in humankind that we like to dress up with pretty words. The significance of war is that it reveals the end reason of man. War is the mother of everything ... The more we disregard life and the less we desire it, the more intensely we live it. Our animal fury blossoms in a gigantic display of unique vitalities. Faith in oneself increases with death. The spirit becomes rough, prickly, hard. It is something higher than barbarism.[170]

With less literary acumen, another veteran recalled the state of excitation that had come over him during combat: "You don't hear what they say to you, you don't hear yourself, nothing! Your blood begins to boil, and you don't even know where you are, no? You can easily die without noticing it."[171]

For many soldiers, in the quiet after the battle, the warrior's immediate repose brought with it reflection on what had been experienced. Often, the appearance of the exhausted combatants returning from armed actions clearly expressed how their lives had changed. After watching several combatants return from Posad, Ridruejo described two at length: two Falangists who had distinguished themselves in battle and whom he now saw transfigured by exhaustion and suffering:

> Those two and all the others who "have been there" now look like sleep-walkers. Their conversation is incoherent and missing half the words. They have a sunken, lost look, without vigour, with a feverish sheen and veiled. They have become horribly thin and are black from gunpowder ... One might say the shadow of death, which was so close to them and has repeated its deed so many times before them, still hangs over them.[172]

Was the war an inner journey, an orgy of blood and violence that liberated unsuspected vital energies in the soldiers, like the "storms of steel" that Ernst Jünger idealized in 1920? The monotony led many to conclude that the war was no more than their everyday experience: dirtiness, hardships, the satisfying of basic needs, nostalgia, danger of death ... Others, the Falangists in particular, had a more idealistic reading. Ridruejo refused to think like Erich M. Remarque – author of the pacifist novel *All Quiet on the Western Front* (1929), which denounced the brutality of trench warfare during the First World War – that a soldier's life was reduced to "the pure experience of the human animal without illusion or belief, without encouragement or happiness and without value." He conceded that Remarque might be right about "the anecdotes," but not in the deep meaning of the war experience.[173] Despite the cold, the harsh environment, and the numerical superiority of the enemy, the combat experience was an almost mystical initiation into comradeship and the purification of their ideals:

> Do we Spaniards live well through this difficult campaign or not? If you put living well into a bourgeois or material category, I will tell you that here we live badly; if, to the contrary, you put it on a moral plane, of what is exemplary or satisfying to the conscience, I can tell you that we live very well, better than we will ever live again.[174]

Life on the front was a source of permanent pride for the most idealistic soldiers. They fought for what they considered a moral and just cause. This feeling was encouraged from a distance by family members, girlfriends, and wives who shared their world view. Dolores Gancedo, the fiancée of BD volunteer and FET provincial leader Alberto Martín Gamero, wrote how she felt proud of "this true Falange that you all are" and that she suffered with uncertainty in the absence of her spouse. The suffering of war served to *purify* ideals and give meaning to an otherwise dull and anonymous life:

> The sorrows of war are the kind that fill us with pride, and after the hard moments have passed it is at least for me the only thing in the world that fills me with satisfaction, it is the highest, most noble thing in this world to elevate oneself from the vulgarity of life and purify our weaknesses in life with the purity of our suffering for the best ideals.[175]

The letters received from Spain gave encouragement and revealed concern. This did not stop other Falangists from describing the same war experience as an accumulation of penuries and risks, of constant fatigue heightened by snow and cold, steeped in permanent nostalgia for home. However, this longing for Spain gave strength and inspired courage in co-religionists who awaited the return of the Blue Division volunteers.[176]

Fig. 4.6. Spanish soldiers take Soviet prisoner, 1942 (private archive of M.X. Nogueira, Santiago de Compostela)

Comradeship and the Cult of the Fallen

One way of combatting fear of death was to cultivate bonds of camaraderie. Even as the Division first entered combat, Ridruejo wrote: "The visible presence of death cannot be seen impassively. But this death makes so much noise, the spectacle of watching others gives courage and passion." Training had contributed to this. Ridruejo noted "the collective discarding of certain habits of delicacy, sentiment, moral sweetness, and intellectual elegance," as "everything becomes more robust but smaller. The men confine themselves to an elemental layer, that of primary necessities." Getting up early every day, the harsh training, the frugal meals made every soldier close himself within a "rather blissful and sedating detachment."[177]

However, military life was for many Falangists too mechanical and different from their own ideal of political comradeship. Ridruejo complained also of the "puerile collective climate that muffles spiritual life." He felt comforted by a compact, interclass community that generated a "collective pride," when "seeing one's column going around a curve, you join it as a man, visible in its harmonious unity ... and single objective." The example of others and shared fear led them to demean "anything in life that required no effort." The adventure was also an inner experience.[178]

A strong sense of cohesion marked the Blue Division, especially in the first expedition. It was mainly composed of volunteers from relatively small political and student primary groups. This made the Division a "little world"; in other units or field hospitals one might encounter relatives, acquaintances from the same city, or brothers in arms from 1936–9. Many old friends and comrades found each other at boot camp in Grafenwöhr. One correspondent wrote: "it is frequent to see the scene of one soldier embracing another soldier and slapping him on the back. 'Hi, man ... I didn't know you were here.'" However, such encounters could also be unpleasant, when acquaintances and hometown friends showed up in the cemeteries. Santiago Muñoz Césaro found the crosses of a childhood friend and two Civil War comrades in the Mestelevo cemetery.[179]

The BD serves as a good example of cohesion based on the strength of its primary groups, which were easily reproduced in the many moments of relaxation that accompanied a war of positions. At least until mid-1942, this cohesion could be explained as the fusion of "primary groups" of origin, defined by political or hometown bonds, and new groups whose camaraderie was solidly cemented in their common experience on the front. Time and combat made the contours of the diverse pre-existing political cultures and affinity groups of the soldiers soften and meld into a new identity tied to the Division itself. To a degree, the same occurred in the Wehrmacht.[180]

Conversation circles played an important role in consolidating old and new groups of reference. More prestigious Falangists could talk about politics for hours in their shelters, while playing cards and sharing drinks and food.[181] Politics went hand in glove with hometown origins. Volunteers from the same town tried to meet up often; together with comrades and friends, they would celebrate birthdays and patron saint days.[182] "I met a friend and neighbour who is the son of Mr. Luciano who lives next to the Civil Guard headquarters, and we celebrated with a drinking binge," wrote Alfredo Rodríguez to his mother in December 1941.[183]

There were also several cases of brothers from the same family assigned to different units, who tried to see each other when they could. Several of them were of Old Guard pedigree – such as the Ruiz Vernacci brothers, the García Noblejas brothers, etc. Similarly, the BD volunteers from Catholic Action Youth, though dispersed among several units, tried to meet up on Sundays to pray the rosary or hear Mass together.[184] The BD trench newspaper often printed requests of individuals or groups of soldiers from the same place who were interested in discovering the unit or whereabouts of a friend, relative, or hometown acquaintance.

The hometown or political collective, whether the group itself or the company, served as a refuge from sorrows, fear, and loneliness in a strange land. Falangist volunteers, who were often university students from middle- or upper-middle-class homes, lived alongside half-illiterate peasants, manual labourers, and sergeants who had come up through the ranks. On the front, tensions from the training period softened, and soldiers learned to function together in the same units. Sharing quarters also led to some homosexual relations, which were silenced in almost all testimonies but sometimes insinuated in the diaries. The Russian interpreter Vladimir Kovalevskii referred in his memoirs to a case involving two sergeants.[185] One logistics driver wrote of an ensign who was "really close" to his assistant: "they even sleep in the same bed."[186] BD internal sources indicate as many as seventy cases of homosexuality among officers, NCOs, and soldiers by the end of 1941.[187]

Comradeship added new ties to the old ones, and existing friendships were reconfigured by the war. Ridruejo expressed this when he referred to the evenings spent in conversation with his comrades: "We talked a lot. In my house there are always fellow conversationalists, some permanent, others variable." Luis Aguilar noted that in his shack other Falangists often met to talk "about politics in Spain and in the Falange."[188] Talking about transcendental themes, girls, or their own little problems created a fictitious but necessary illusion of normality for the members of the fighting community. "In this atmosphere, I feel as if everything is alright; all my companions have their own little problems," just as if he were among friends at university, wrote Salvador Zanón. However, another reality met them when they left the *izba*; the war changed people: "friends I went to secondary school with or played with in the park as children, I see they have changed."[189]

For many Falangists, the camaraderie also had a political reading. Ridruejo surmised that the shared effort had bonded Falangists and non-Falangists within his company. He thought he was witnessing the birth of a new community of true believers.[190] In his view, a new Falange had emerged from the blood of the fallen, one that combined Civil War veterans, university students, NCOs, and Catholics: "The Division is now and forever Falangist, from the captain down." Enrique Errando captured something similar in a conversation with a traditionalist volunteer: in Russia "we stop dividing ourselves up ... because of our labels."[191] However, political affinity was not always the main thing. Private José Linares, recruited in 1942, recalled some years later the behaviour of his comrades. Among them were "anti-communists like me, many opportunists who hoped for advantageous positions when they returned, some who were indifferent, Falangists, religious ones on an anti-Bolshevik crusade, melancholy ones, non-conformists," but they all fought "most arduously for something of little concern." Why? Group solidarity and survival.[192]

Comradeship also extended to the fallen. The Spanish cult to the fallen on the front differed little from what had been reinvented in the trenches of the First World War – new adaptations of a traditional rite – or from the standard practice of the German Army.[193] Each Wehrmacht division or regiment established a cemetery in its rearguard. The simple burial rites were observed with care and involved a concise religious ceremony. In contrast with the Red Army's negligence of its own fallen,[194] the Wehrmacht worked to locate its fallen soldiers. Honouring fallen comrades kept them alive in the heart of the "fighting community" and motivated the living to avenge their deaths. It was also a psychological coping mechanism for surviving the experience of mass destruction. Such rites reaffirmed blood bonds and exorcized the fear of death. War cemeteries in conquered territory thus became a symbolic occupation and land bathed in the blood of *heroes* a perennial reminder of past victories as well as a permanent warning for those who returned: their comrades buried in Russia served as moral examples for the future tasks of the Falange.[195]

The Blue Division rapidly assumed this modus operandi. They had their own cemeteries, but also shared space with the German dead. The abundance of fallen Falangists in the winter of 1941–2 also gave rise to an improvised campaign ritual. After the chaplain spoke, the comrades sang the Falangist hymn, put birch poles around the tomb, and placed a Latin cross with asymmetric arms, along with the flags (or symbols) of the Falange and other religious elements.[196] Comrades tended the graves, prayed, and placed flowers at them, thereby integrating the absent ones into the combat fellowship. Those who returned to Spain felt the moral duty to visit the families and deliver the personal effects of the fallen as a final tribute to those who would not return.

5 Occupation Practices of the Blue Division in Northwest Russia

According to the BD narrative after 1945, the Spanish Blue Division constituted an exception in the Wehrmacht for its extraordinarily benign treatment of Russian civilians and Soviet prisoners. This had to do with seeing the presence of the BD in Russia as an anti-communist enterprise, devoid of any Nazi sympathies. However, beyond this self-complacent image, there is room to ask the same historiographic questions that would apply to other occupying forces. To what point were the Spaniards *different* from the rest of the Wehrmacht? Was the Blue Division a sort of oasis in Army Group North with respect to the treatment of civilians and Red Army prisoners? Was there a Hispanic variant of the war of extermination? A sociocultural focus on the war experience of BD combatants that explores their vision of the enemy, of Russia, and of the Jews may provide some answers. This should be accompanied by empirical analysis of their behaviour towards civilians, prisoners, and Jews in context and as it occurred, using a combination of sources rather than an acritical accumulation of later testimonies from the combatants themselves.

As indicated above, Nazi Germany had planned a war to exterminate large portions of the Soviet population. Fundamental aspects of the project to create an empire under the continental hegemony of the Third Reich included denying Soviet combatants the right to civilized treatment, eliminating political commissars, collaborating in tasks to annihilate the Jewish population, expanding military justice to assimilate treatment of the civilian population, and neglecting to provide them with food. Some of these premises are recorded in "Instructions for the Conduct of Troops in Russia" of 19 May 1941, including the "Commissar Order" (6 June 1941), the "Decree on the Exercise of War Jurisdiction" (13 May 1941), and "Guidelines for the Treatment of Prisoners of War" (16 June 1941).

A Spanish version of the "Instructions" was distributed to the BD, translated as "Directives for Troop Conduct in Russia." As in the original German, it identified Bolshevism as "the moral enemy of the new Europe." Accordingly, the present conflict was directed "against its disintegrating ideas and those who represent them." Thus, "this fight requires energetic, unwavering action against all Bolshevik, agitator, sniper, saboteur, or Jewish elements and complete elimination of all active or passive resistance." Furthermore, "all components of the Red Army, including prisoners" should be treated with "an extremely severe attitude and maximum precaution, as treacherous methods of combat can be expected." Particularly dangerous were the "Asiatic soldiers of the Red Army," who were "inscrutable, unpredictable, insidious, and unfeeling." Upon capturing entire units, "the leaders should be immediately separated from the troops." As for the civilian population, the guidelines indicated that most of them were anti-communists, very ethnically diverse, liable to express rejection for the Soviet regime through religious observance, and should not be interfered with. However, "maximum precaution" should be exercised "in conversations with the population and behaviour towards women." Pillaging was forbidden, but "all kinds of merchandise and military requisitions, especially food and fodder, fuel and clothing, should be preserved and confiscated."[1] In fact, political commissars were stigmatized by the Spanish Falangist press and presented as the direct instruments of Soviet tyranny and Judaism.[2] These ordinances were softened somewhat by General Directive 3.005, published by the BD General Staff on 4 August 1941, which was as generic or more so than the former ones. The inhabitants of occupied territories, their person and possessions, should be respected; requisitions had to be compensated; the prisoners were to be treated well and enemy wounded would receive medical attention. Spies and snipers should not be summarily executed but handed over to superiors for internment in prisoner camps.[3]

There is no empirical evidence that the Spanish officers were notified of the "Commissar Order." Hitler ratified it just prior to the BD arrival at the front but specified that it should only be transmitted orally to the troops.[4] Comparatively, war brutality on the Northern Front was certainly less severe than in other sectors. Of the 2,253 documented executions of commissars in the first twelve months of the war (a minimum estimate), only 17.32 per cent (405) corresponded to Army Group North. From October through December 1941, the total number was 101 (15.2 per cent of the total on the Eastern Front), and the numbers decreased quickly in the first months of 1942.[5]

Most likely, the Spanish combatants simply followed orders, separating out the political commissars and shooting them on site. However, we cannot rule out that, as in some German units, Spanish officers spared the troops such actions by ordering the transfer of the *politruks* to Division Command, where they would be handed over to the Germans. Indirect data suggests that the BD command and officers knew about the order; it was explicitly countermanded in specific operations through orders transmitted by the corresponding Army Corps. To encourage the surrender of the units under siege in the Volkhov Pocket, Directive 2.018 of 12 May 1942 established that propaganda leaflets be distributed. They promised good treatment to those who laid down their weapons: "Troops will be instructed immediately that it is forbidden to shoot captured political commissars or those who willingly join our ranks. The commissars will receive the same treatment as the other prisoners."[6] It would make no sense to forbid the execution of commissars unless the practice was habitual. Likewise, in May 1943 the BD General Staff received notice from the L Army Corps indicating that captured political commissars had been ordered to "present themselves voluntarily for work in the German legions," since "the Russian command has noticed the fact that we no longer shoot captured Russian commissars on principle."[7]

Another Image of the Enemy

To what degree did the Spanish volunteers share the intent of German soldiers during the war of extermination? How did they perceive the enemy, particularly Soviet civilians? To what degree did the better behaviour of Spanish occupying forces towards the civilian population reflect a different view of the enemy? Was it merely a result of the more static nature of the northern sector of the Eastern Front, which had less partisan activity than in the Ukraine or White Russia and less (or less significant) radicalized and brutalized fighting conditions, as occurred in other German divisions?[8] In other words, if the Blue Division's treatment of the civilian population constituted an exception, to what degree was this caused by, or to what degree did it create, a different image of the enemy – one inherited from the Spanish Civil War but not radicalized by a biological world view?

Setting aside for a moment the monumental suffering and the thousands of dead among the besieged civilian population in the city of Leningrad, the war in the northern sector of the Eastern Front from September 1941 was (in relative terms) far more static and somewhat less radical and brutal than in the centre and south, and with less partisan presence. The Volkhov offensive (October – December 1941), the battles of the Demyansk (February – April 1942) and the Volkhov forest pocket (February – June 1942), the engagements at Lake Ladoga, and others were certainly bloody battles, yet not all German divisions were affected to the same degree by the intensity of the combat. Like the other divisions of the 16th and 18th Armies of Army Group North, the Spanish soldiers preferred to make camp in Russian villages near the rearguard. On the Volkhov Front, where peasant poverty was extreme in 1941, cohabitation between peasants and occupying forces became especially tight. Several soldiers would accommodate themselves in the miserable three- or four-space dwellings where a family also lived.[9]

The Spanish officers observed that the famished civilian population, subjected to German requisitioning, was much more concerned with survival than patriotic resistance. For this reason, most peasants were quick to collaborate with these invaders. Peasant women would wash the soldiers' clothes, and older people taught them how to build wooden shanties. In such close quarters, many *divisionarios* were practically adopted by these peasant families and came to see the *mamuskas* and their *izbas* as a "real extension of their own home."[10] There were even cases of unauthorized weddings between Spanish soldiers and Russian women. Generally, though, the tight living quarters and especially the food scarcity led to daily quarrels, as the peasants hid their meagre reserves from the preying invaders.[11]

The relationships between Spanish soldiers and the peasant population in occupied villages – comprising mostly women, children, and the elderly – were cast in a very favourable and idealized light in post-1945 testimonies. They unanimously spoke of harmonious cohabitation, full respect, appreciation, and mutual solidarity.[12] The Blue Division trench journal *Hoja de Campaña* introduced this imagery as early as 1943: the Russian villages had been peacefully occupied by soldiers, "who were part missionary, part bohemian artist, and another part globetrotter."[13] However, this representation should be duly contrasted with testimonies published and written by BD combatants prior to 1945 – particularly in their letters and diaries – and with news articles from that time. The image found there conveys greater nuance and resembles that of the German soldiers in some aspects. The Spaniards, however, had not been subjected to racial indoctrination. They lacked any prior contact with the Slavic East and filtered their perception of "Russia" and the Russians through their Catholic convictions. Many Spanish volunteers described the peasants' poverty in literary style, thereby crafting a singular image of the enemy.[14]

From "the Horde" to "the Ruski"

In the testimonies published after 1945, BD veterans established a clear difference between their behaviour and that of the Germans with regard to their appreciation of individual Soviet combatants and their (good) treatment of prisoners. This was recommended in the first instructions of the BD General Staff.[15] The enemy would not be regarded as a racially inferior being, but as a military adversary with human characteristics, a victim of the neglect that the Red Army and the Communist regime displayed concerning the dignity of their soldiers.[16]

The Red Army, as a collective entity, was for many Spanish volunteers a formless and anonymous mass, devoid of all respect for spiritual concerns and the individual. Soldiers with Asian features, drunk on vodka, who advanced to the whistle of their officers in great waves: "beastly masses prepared by Timoshenko for the invasion of Europe," thrown together "from all the provinces of Asia ... in the animal panic of a stampede."[17] Such an image accurately reflected the dreaded Communist and *Asian* invasion of Western civilization that had been evoked by European fascist imaginary since the early 1920s. The attacking hordes would not be an example of romantic heroism, but symbols of the spiritual *degeneration* to which Bolshevism subjected the individual, without the transcendental dimension of existence.[18] A "meek and motley mass" of "dirty, tattered [men] tyrannized by Stalin"; or rather, "stupefied cannon fodder, forced to fight by murderous commissars."[19] Colonel Jesús Badillo believed that the Soviet combatant, like the Republican of the Spanish Civil War, had little internal motivation; only the whip of the political commissars pushed him forward, "with a fatalism bordering upon suicide."[20]

The enemy soldiers were deserving of some individual commiseration – this collection of "hungry and betrayed sons of the Russian people, sacrificed by the madness, pride, and evil of their Judaeo-Masonic leaders."[21] Once shot down, however, thoughts regarding the defeated did not always evoke compassion among Spanish soldiers. Stylized descriptions of dead adversaries abound, with the implicit dehumanization and derogatory treatment of the enemy's body so habitually found in modern warfare. The Falangist José Martialay described the "great carpet of Russian bodies" that had been left by a Spanish attack as a heap of "spectres."[22]

The Soviet soldier was a ferocious adversary but lacked initiative. He could fight until exhausted but lacked ideals. Good proof of this was his submissiveness once captured: Sergeant Martínez-Tessier wrote that Russian combatants were "Poor devils, whose eyes and mouths open wide with admiration at the humane treatment they receive."[23] In this regard, the Spanish Division members were no different than the Germans, who looked upon the Soviet soldiers as examples of untamed fanaticism.

In fact, several authors concur in detecting a mixture of fatalism in the Soviet *frontoviki*, combined with a sense of collective sacrifice and subjection to the repressive Stalinist apparatus, all enveloped in a simple but effective patriotism.[24] The Division members also acknowledged some warlike qualities in the enemy: a "dark friendliness" recalling the contradictory feelings towards the flesh-and-blood adversary that First World War combatants also experienced.[25] Several repatriated BD combatants asserted that "the Russians fight well. They lack technicians, but they did not lack convictions," while "The young Russian generations are Marxists." Guillermo Alonso del Real admitted later that "the Russian soldier ... was disciplined, brave, and magnificently trained." And General Esteban-Infantes added that the *Ivan* was persistent, but slave to a secular "mass instinct," lacking initiative. This appraisal, expressing admiration for the austerity and resistance of the *frontoviki*, was repeated in the testimonies of ex-BD members.[26]

Praising the enemy forms part of the military codes for recreating the myth of a gentlemen's war. Some accounts sent by Division members emphasized this sense of combat in the East as a classic duel: the fight against the inhospitable climate and the difficulties of the front became a new test of Latin virility.[27] Although some testimonies expressed that the fighting in the East pitched European soldiers against masses of slant-eyed, yellow-faced combatants from "the extreme Far East,"[28] dehumanized descriptions of Soviet combatants such as those found in letters sent by German soldiers were rare amongst the BD. Amongst many *Landser* (Flemish and Norwegian SS volunteers also, and many Italians as well), the prevalent image of the enemy as subhuman had been constructed over years of constant indoctrination.[29] In contrast, visual representations of the Russian soldier that appear in the BD trench press were often more benign than those appearing in the Wehrmacht and Italian trench newspapers. Many of them were signed by "Kin," the cartoonist for the Falangist newspaper *Arriba* and BD volunteer Joaquín de Alba. They were also less biting than those drawn *a posteriori* by "Kin" himself for the exhibition *That's What the Reds Were Like! Aspects of the Red Rearguard*, which opened in Madrid in May 1943. There, the Soviet soldier was distinguished by his Asian features, which seemed to fit with expectations from higher up.[30]

Similarly, the images of the Soviet soldier from the BD trench journal were less aggressive than those published by Francoist magazines

Fig. 5.1. Watercolour by Joaquín de Alba (*Kin*): *They bring us a new culture for Europe* (AGA)

Fig. 5.2. Watercolour by *Kin, The Soviets built their palaces over the people's misery* (AGA)

during the Spanish Civil War and even reproduced by comic book artists in Spain during late Francoism.[31] There were no deformed and bloody monsters, but these more contemporary images tended to portray the enemy as bearded, tattered soldiers with naive expressions. This reflects an interesting transposition of images of Russian civilians onto soldiers: the *frontoviki* tended to be clean-shaven and their hair was often close-cropped, whilst peasants of a certain age were known for their long beards.[32] This icon varied little in representations of the future of Spain in Soviet hands, if the war were lost. However, the aversion towards "Anglo-American" imperialism was often more cutting than the image of the Soviet soldier.[33]

The BD soldiers saw the *Ruski* as a victim of communism and a spawn of atheist and materialist ideology. Their servile nature only confirmed how low individual self-esteem had fallen in an inhumane regime.[34] The Soviet combatant might be a worthy enemy and awaken compassion and human feelings once a prisoner. However, the Spanish and German soldiers concluded, he would never be a better combatant than a European.[35] The BD would uphold the "civilized" and "moral" values that made them champions of an ideal. Their sense of religious transcendence would give the Spaniards an advantage over their adversaries: a "fanatic enthusiasm" to find God in the frozen trenches.[36] This conviction helped them resist the "avalanches" of the Red Army and turned the BD's modest military performance into a victory. The Iberian talent for defensive warfare sprang from an ancient source, inherited from their resistance against the Romans and Napoleon.[37] Their military merit now consisted of containing the new threat to their homeland within Soviet territory.[38]

The Soviet soldiers who surrendered could not always rely on immediate good treatment from their enemies, whether Spanish or German. In the clamour of combat, and to facilitate the freedom of movement of their own forces, it was common practice amongst Spanish units not to take prisoners. Shooting those who surrendered on the spot was a habit many officers had acquired in the Moroccan War. It it was also used by armies in the Second World War, particularly in the Pacific and in the fighting following the Normandy landings. The excitement of combat influenced this behaviour: the basic desire to avenge dead comrades, the inconvenience of dealing with prisoners, and even envy among the captors because the war was over for the captives. Thus, the conventions relating to the treatment of prisoners were not always respected.[39]

What to do with prisoners led to frequent disputes amongst the BD soldiers. Isolated executions of those who laid down their weapons were not unusual and were justified on the conviction that the Soviets would do the same to their prisoners. Captives who refused to cooperate during interrogations could be shot as a warning to the rest.[40] This practice was customary during the Volkhov offensive. A soldier who crossed the river to take supplies to the troops noted with displeasure that wounded prisoners were liquidated ruthlessly:

> Shortly afterwards, they began to bring wounded Spaniards because there were no wounded Russians. Well, they catch them and we kill them, and it's very unpleasant to see wounded Russian prisoners asking for mercy

and we grab a machine gun and mow them all down, I'd never seen more dead together in that way, and it's not a pretty sight.[41]

Acts of this kind, also common in the German divisions, have been acknowledged in timely accounts published since the 1990s.[42] They capture the violence of hand-to-hand fighting, also the enjoyment of risk and danger, and the "terrifying beauty" of combat, in the manner of Ernst Jünger. José M. Sánchez Diana, described it thus:

> We reach the very edge of the enemy trench … We are possessed of a firm madness, swearing and shouting "*Viva España.*" I knock against a body into which I've stuck the bayonet. Blood slipped through my fingers … The Russian figures with their brick-coloured capes shake like a moving stage without limits or end … We enter the houses in the town, which is a really long street. We search them. If there is an enemy soldier inside, he's killed. Some surrender but some of the company, excited, shoot them on the spot without listening to them … People drunk on blood don't behave well with some prisoners, which makes me sick. Running off gives the prisoner a certain sense of freedom, as he figures that he has some freedom for a few seconds … The worst is the savagery of the act which at the same time is terrifyingly beautiful.

The blood binge, adrenalin, and violence continued the next day: "Private Heredia shoots endlessly, eliminating several Reds who were approaching with their arms held up to surrender … You take a prisoner, you dispatch a prisoner. There's no time to gather them all together." Other captives, after being relieved of their weapons and belongings, were sent to the rearguard. But that didn't always guarantee them life:

> I take a prisoner, an ugly and dirty bloke with a shady expression who is hugging my boots. *Ne spanki, ne, neruski liubet, ne obide.* In his haversack I find a little bread and a handful of rice grains, which I eat like almonds. I deliver him to the sergeants, but one of them cries out:
> "What are we going to do with him? Take that, you son of a bitch …!"
> And he puts a bullet in the back of his head.

A similar scene took place a few days later, during the Posad fighting: "We took three prisoners. They had the communist star on their caps. Morillo took them away, stomped on them, and then bam bam bam! He shot them down."[43]

There were days of merciless combat, such as those of the "intermediate position" at the end of December 1941, partly motivated by the Spaniards' desire for revenge after finding their own comrades nailed to the ground. Some sources state that the Soviets sometimes nicknamed the Spaniards "headhunters," perhaps because some of them cut ears and noses from bodies and even from prisoners before returning them to their lines.[44] Nevertheless, apart from some offensive actions and surprise attacks, after 1941 there were few opportunities to live up to that reputation, whether true or false. During fighting in the Volkhov pocket, Private Raigán Abellán wrote in his diary that "several prisoners have been taken. There is an order to kill them all," which he justified because the besieged often fired from trees. Surprise attacks could also be settled without prisoners: "There was a real bloodbath; since the enemy were in their hideouts and didn't want to come out, they were all blown up," wrote sergeant Alonso in April 1943.[45]

Many BD members rejected the German treatment of captives. Their first encounter with columns of Soviet prisoners in easterE Poland being led by German guards towards probable death created open contempt in some Spanish officers. It would be easy to defeat such an enemy. Most Spaniards reacted, however, with a mix of fascination and compassion: "Of course they deserve that and a bit more, but as I am a Christian, it saddens me."[46] Repatriated soldiers provided similar accounts of the unmerciful, "truly criminal" attitude of the Wehrmacht towards Soviet prisoners.[47] Private Menéndez Gundín wrote in August 1941: "I see Russian prisoners, it's a right mess ... we feel sorry for them, they're a martyred people and dragged into the fight by their executioners."[48] This curiosity and even pity also appeared in the report written in late October by the Spanish military attaché in Berlin, following his visit to the Eastern Front:

> There are contingents and enormous columns of Russian prisoners everywhere, starving and impoverished: some are carried on stretchers, others march, laboriously resting on their friends, and finally others fall physically by the roadside, and are often seen collapsing from exhaustion, never to get up again. However, the ones you see are in the best condition ... the ones who are in the prison camps out in the open and with hardly any food for days and weeks would be in an even worse state.[49]

The first autobiographies published by BD veterans in the 1940s highlighted the dehumanized appearance of the columns of prisoners: "Soulless bodies," reduced by communism to the subhuman abyss: a mix of races, including "the Mongols, the worst scum of Asia"; or rather "monstrous and filthy ghosts who throw themselves to the floor like beasts to fight, biting and punching, for a fruit peel or a bare bone."

The impression of the members of the BD Information Section who attended prisoner interrogations in late August, at the invitation of the Germans, was no different: illiterate soldiers from central Asia, dehumanized and with no sense of religion, commanded by Jewish commissars.[50] Others qualified this image years later to emphasize compassion for the defeated and described encountering the columns of captives as a genuine emotional shock.[51]

The situation changed in October 1941, when Division members themselves began to capture prisoners and keep them in custody for weeks, until they were delivered to German units. Private Fernando Torres recalled how good treatment could turn captives into comrades and even supporters of the BD cause.[52] Another volunteer reminded the Division members that they should treat those victims of Soviet barbarism humanely, whether they deserved it or not, because they had been so brutalized: "We were fighting for civilization and love amongst all men on earth and they are engulfed in barbarism."[53]

A classic motif of BD commemorative prose is to evoke the quasi-camaraderie between Division members and their prisoners. Numerous anecdotes reflected this: from the sentry who left his weapons while he slept in the care of a *Ruski*, to the soldier who evaded an ambush thanks to a warning from his prisoners. On one occasion, a Soviet parachutist surrendered to "a chauffeur who was driving alone, surrendering his firearm to him." The driver then handed over the prisoner "to a sergeant and a chauffeur who were going by in another car." However, "none of these three soldiers had a firearm on them." BD Headquarters therefore reiterated that soldiers were prohibited from wandering about the rearguard unarmed.[54]

The submissive, rough prisoners were an object of curiosity for BD members, who enjoyed writing down their impressions. Huddled together like "a wretched herd of animals," the captives quickly became collaborators who were "as loyal and devoted as dogs." They even celebrated Easter with their captors. One account also described how the Russian auxiliary nurses in the Spanish hospitals, grateful for the good treatment they had received, learned some Castilian and complained about the Soviets. Some captives were very young, and like so many orphaned children they deserved compassion because they had been brought up on Soviet values. One article in the *Hoja de Campaña* featured a kind, commiserating image of the good *Ruski* prisoner who would have seen the Spaniard as his liberator.[55]

Why were the *ruskis* so docile? BD soldiers were not always aware of the Red Army rule to shoot or intern in concentration camps any of its soldiers who were taken prisoner, and accused them of cowardice and treason. Moreover, the winter of 1941–2 was characterized by low morale and cases of desertion amongst Soviet troops from Leningrad and the Volkhov front.[56] Gaining the trust of captors who treated them humanely often became the only rational option for survival in the short term, before they were handed over to the Germans. For the Ukrainians and other peoples, the Spaniards were "liberating" them from communist and/or Russian servitude. Some fought on the side of the invaders.[57] A few Russian prisoners or deserters were even taken to Spain with the knowledge of division officers.[58]

The Spanish soldiers who arrived in the successive replacement units were surprised, when reaching the front, to see "prisoners who were wandering around freely everywhere," mixing with the Russian civilians who did their bidding, and who received coffee, cigarettes, and food from the Spanish soldiers.[59] In some sections, considerable numbers of captives were used in auxiliary tasks.[60] Many units had a prisoner in their service, which was tolerated by their command. A captain of the sappers' battalion, Guillermo Díaz del Río, recalled that his own Spanish assistant had a Russian assistant and a boy for everything.[61] Such situations led the German high command to order in July 1942 that the soldiers keep their distance from captives and treat them correctly, but firmly. They also pointed out that prisoners "are additional workforce; their employment by the troops must not lead them to stop working." Excessive fraternization, such as sharing tobacco, was forbidden.[62] However, as late as November 1942 the SD post in Pushkin received reports indicating that some Russians in German uniform had been seen wandering around and working for the Spaniards, who were "extremely reckless" in this respect.[63]

These situations also occurred in hospitals, particularly those located near the front. Russian male nurses cared for the wounded by night, and the Spanish female nurses had various Russian women in their service. Unlike the hierarchical treatment tinged with racial contempt that often characterized the attitude of many *Krankenschwestern* towards their Slavic assistants,[64] the relationships between Spanish and Russian nurses were in general quite friendly. In Porkhov hospital, a Spanish-Russian Christmas festival was improvised in 1941, with *flamenco* performances, popular Russian songs, and gymnastic displays.[65]

German treatment of Soviet prisoners softened considerably from mid-1942 on, owing to the revocation of the "Commissar Order" and the need to employ the captives as a workforce in the Reich. Accordingly, the BD was also ordered in May 1943 to give preferential treatment to deserters, providing them with medical and nutritional care.[66] These measures were followed by specific BD orders that additional food rations be provided to prisoners of war who were "sick in and out of hospitals," and that Soviet deserters not be robbed of their belongings.[67] All prisoners, including those serving the BD, had to be transferred to the nearest *Durchganglager*, or provisional German prisoner camp, to be sent to the "Reich for their respective tasks."[68] In May 1943, the Division had to hand over one hundred additional prisoners, replacing them in their duties with "Russian or Finnish civilians."[69]

Victims, Exotics, and Noble Savages: Russian Civilians

A "Stinking and Depraved Poverty"

The Falangist journalist Jacinto Miquelarena was the first Spanish correspondent to visit the Russian Front, in August 1941. He enjoyed describing the poverty of the "Smolensk Hotel" and how communism had "created tattered beggars and scallywags."[70] To the Iberian volunteers who arrived a month later, and many others after, Russians – including the people of what was then Eastern Poland – represented a kind of step backwards in human history. One Falangist wrote:

> We see here "equality" and "paradise." Every person is barefoot, scarcely clad, and unaware of the most basic personal hygiene. The "people," as they call the workers, live in wooden huts in the most miserable way imaginable, while the Commissars inhabit lavish palaces.[71]

As with German and Italian soldiers, the first Spanish volunteers to set foot on Soviet soil concurred in reporting the most basic element: filthy poverty. It was captured in watercolour by cartoonist and Blue Division volunteer Joaquín de Alba (*Kin*) upon his return to Spain in 1943.[72] Captain Ángel Muñoz described life in Russia as "a pendulum swinging between work and misery," in "sordid" towns where the rooms were "more fit for animals than people."[73] Dionisio Ridruejo condensed into a few sentences all the meaning he attributed to the misery he saw:

> Terrible, this life I see. Terrible misery, infrahumanity, and desolation. This is a landscape of nothingness, and only the cities reveal that Europe was here, and then a Revolution with a dictatorship of the proletariat. The villages recall Ivan the Terrible if anything ...[74]

The tales told obviated the fact that this desolate panorama partially corresponded to the effects of war. It was all presented as an example of what communism would have brought to Spain, had it triumphed in 1936 and throughout all of Europe and had the Third Reich not *pre-emptively* invaded the USSR. In other words, the Bolshevik destruction of property, order, and social values had condemned the Soviet peasants to an existence that could not be called living, which would be nourished by transcendent belief, but was instead a vegetative state concerned only with immediate survival.[75] José Luis Gómez Tello described a "Russian village": Soviet materialism had turned the churches into warehouses and schools; the administrative headquarters consisted of a "cuboid form the colour of blood," accompanied by a group of "ramshackle, dark, and miserable" *kolkhoz* buildings. The peasants had stepped several centuries back in time and lived in an "infrahuman zone" next to the Communist Party millionaires.[76]

Newly arrived volunteers after 1942 expressed similar impressions in their letters. They described the Russians as a people lacking hygiene, whose saunas seemed a "savage, primitive system." A corporal wrote how the Russians "are unacquainted with lights, electricity, European-style clothing, plumbing; their huts are poorly constructed of wood and full of misery, in short, words cannot describe what they call the 'Soviet Paradise.'"[77] Personal diaries tended to be even more acerbic. Ensign Juan Romero wrote that the villages were "made of several wooden houses that looked more like stables."[78] Corporal Jesús Martínez Tessier described his first impressions of the Russian peasants as "dirty and impoverished ... The Russians were all beards and tall boots. The dirty houses must surely be full of parasites."[79] A few months later, upon arriving at the village where he would reside on the front, Benjamín Arenales also remarked on the contrast between the Soviet myth propagated by the left and the panorama he saw:

> The village couldn't possibly be constructed any worse. The houses are all made of wood, filled with a foul stench that I would not recommend, as the stables are in fact a room in the house. This is the Russian Paradise the Reds dreamed of![80]

All testimonies until 1945 concur regarding these images. Gómez-Tello considered the misery he saw in the Polish villages a luxury compared to the "infrahuman life of the Soviet peasantry," permeated by a "beastly stigma" upon their faces.[81] José M. Castañón expressed the same views:

> The houses look like large wooden barracks, formed by one room in which the people and livestock and farming instruments live all stacked together.

There are piles of hay that serve as beds ... around the stove, which they built themselves out of tins that often cause intoxication; 90 per cent of Russian villagers have never known any other sort of bed.[82]

Many of these descriptions were intended to convince any remaining USSR sympathizers of the error of their ways. Corporal Adolfo Fernández-Velasco wrote to those "blinded by Marxist propaganda," telling how what he saw proved that communism "had turned people into beasts, filled with inhuman materialism." A repatriated soldier also told his fellow villagers of the "miserable way in which millions and millions of Russians lived."[83]

The common terms in the descriptions of these BD volunteers referred mainly to overcrowding, bad smells, dampness... Unlike Germans, Spanish soldiers tended to contrast dirty/clean more than wet/dry.[84] The most prominent words for describing Russia were undoubtedly *dirty* and *foul-smelling*. Montserrat Romeu, a nurse, described in her diary the unpleasant impression upon entering an *izba*: "the stench is like a slap to the face, as with all Russian homes." Gómez Tello vividly described it as a smell of the Orient, accentuating humidity and putrefaction: "It smells Russian: rotten potatoes, *kapuska*, human misery, manure, and all manner of fermentation in an atmosphere that has not been ventilated for ten months."[85]

Vaguely Asian phenotypes occasionally accompanied the despictions, as Falangist Antonio Aragonés expressed in his impressions regarding the grimy inhabitants – with supposedly Asian features – of the Novgorod area:

From afar, they all look the same. If placed on the horizon at night, they would all have the same profile: tough riding boots, usually large and always dirty, breeches of different colours and fabrics fallen around the knees, a wool-lined tunic or long pelisse, up to the neck, and a black or khaki cap. Everything is grimy and broken. Their faces are all the same; round with olive complexion, brown or sometimes blond hair, a strong beard rounded at the chin, a dirty moustache yellowed from tobacco, sunken blue eyes, and prominent cheekbones, tinting their faces with a sadly oriental air ... All of them, young and old, look like Siberian Eskimos.

"Animalization" was another characteristic the Spanish occupiers often perceived in the peasants. Russian homes were putrid inside, with animals and people living together in a "human pigsty." Antonio Aragonés spoke of how he won the trust of a "human cub" with chocolate. Months later he described how the Russian women deloused each other, killing the insects with the same knives they used to cut bread. Jaime Farré ascribed to the peasants almost ape-like traits, describing the "hovels" where they "slept around the stove, all together; the parents hunted in their children's hair for lice at the same table where they would eat."[86]

The astonishment of the Iberian volunteers at witnessing the misery of Soviet peasant life stems in part from the fact that many of these soldiers had urban origins and were unfamiliar with the rural context. The contrast did not seem quite as stark to those from relatively underdeveloped areas of Spain. This was the case for Joaquín Montaña, who compared the living conditions of the Russians with those of the peasants in his home county. Although the wooden *izbas* of the Russians were indeed less comfortable than the peasant homes with which he was familiar, he also understood that good stone houses could not be built in a land where stones were scarce. For this reason, he felt closer to the Russian peasants than many of the more urban volunteers.[87] Military engineer Alfredo Bellod and Major Joaquín de la Cruz also appreciated the rational structure of the wooden Russian homes, built to efficiently maintain a warm interior.[88]

However, through Spanish lenses, the spiritual indigence of the peasantry was even more disturbing than the material misery. The lack of religious values was starkly apparent – especially in the generations educated under Soviet rule – alongside the lack of progress and well-being. Sargeant Sánchez Aladro wrote how the Bolshevik "materialist barbarians" had isolated Russia from the civilized world by supressing all aesthetic expression. "There is no philosophy here, only exact math and a compass; and absolutely no consideration for individualism." Maths, but no notion of God. The socialist architectural style seemed materialistic and impersonal: "On the inside men neither feel nor live, they are like machines ejecting warped ideas."[89]

There was indeed a culprit for the desolate, materialistic, inhuman panorama the Spanish volunteers found in the Soviet Union: communism had preyed upon "these poor, dirty, bearded *Ruskis*!" Tricked by the regime, something even more painful than material misery was added: "wretchedness of the soul."[90] The Russian people could not even compensate their material deficiencies with a sense of transcendence. The Russian soul seemed "sheep-like, almost unfeeling." Stripped of their religion, "their beast-like instincts run rampant."[91]

Atheism and the return to a state of nature was correlated with lack of sexual morality, which many BD members attributed to the influence of communism rather than the habitual permissiveness of rural life. Private Salvador Zanón expressed his surprise upon meeting a

Russian student for whom love was merely "a sexual need to be satisfied like any other." The "Russian way" of love implied "carnal relations from the very beginning."[92] Ridruejo was scandalized by Russian weddings, which he described as a "carnal zoology."[93] Recalling a night in which a peasant couple shamelessly made love next to the Spanish soldiers sleeping in their *izba*, he concluded that in sexual matters the Russian people had degenerated to "a beastly sexual impulse." Spiritual misery and atheism had led to "the most appalling moral depravation," that even erased "a mother's affection for her children." Soviet communism sought "free love … women as production instruments serving the proletariat."[94]

The Karamazov Revived?

Were these new images? Did the volunteers find, or think they had found, confirmation of the preconceived icons and stereotypes needed to consolidate the image of the enemy?[95] Russia, as its own nineteenth-century writers had depicted it, was as present in the Spanish mind as anti-communist indoctrination and the identification of Russia with the Antichrist. More than one "cultured" volunteer believed he had found affirmation of the exotic and mystical images distilled from Russian literature, from Fyodor Dostoevsky to Lev Tolstoy. This somehow provided a line of continuity from Dostoevsky's pan-Slavic expansionism to that of the Bolsheviks.[96] Ridruejo wrote how "the people here seem like the characters in the novels we all so avidly read with eager sympathy, but without an adequate understanding of tragedy."[97] Gómez-Tello was far more eloquent: "I became familiarized with the black and mossy environment of these people of lost humanity in the pages of Dostoevsky and Tolstoy." He found the substance of these literary characters in the mystical, "disorganized, wild exaltation" of a people who had brought the Soviets to power, with "a soul burning with the wind of Genghis Khan."[98] Alvaro de Laiglesia evoked similar images when describing the *izba* in which he slept; where a skeletal, paralytic old man lived assisted by "an old lady with a chickpea face and high boots made of grey felt." Not even Dostoevsky's "exciting misery" or Tolstoy's "rascals and rogues" could match this Soviet reality.[99]

The people and the scenes felt like they belonged to a literary déjà vu. The military surgeon Juan Pablo D'Ors wrote how "many of the events, characters, and landscapes that are now a part of my life I had already lived in Gorki's pages, under the vivid light of reality." Enrique Errando found many parallels between the peasants he often met and those in Dostoevsky's *The Brothers Karamazov* (1880). Other veterans voiced similar views years later; what they saw in Russia helped them understand the characters they were already familiar with through Russian literature: "Kindness, oriental fatalism ... Respect bordering on servility."[100]

These images were often used in Spanish anti-communist media, blending literary icons with political propaganda, and had already been embedded in the minds of many volunteers. They could even be reinforced by their families back home. In October 1941, Dolores Gancedo wrote from Toledo to her fiancé, the Falangist Alberto Martín-Gamero, describing what she imagined the Russian people to be like, reflecting a mix of literary images and icons formed by anti-communist propaganda:

> I liked it when you were in mainland Europe, but I don't think you will enjoy Russia much. I have read some Russian novels, and I liked them, but ever since I read Chekhov's *Room number 5* [sic], I feel terribly repulsed by Russia. I imagine it to be filthy and cold, how should I say, like the sticky, smelly cold of a dirty, greasy suit; or a butcher's cloak after unloading meat; that's the environment I imagine. I have also heard about the characters there, and that's how I imagine the peasants to be: incapable of becoming anything else, for serving as vassals won't sharpen the mind ... Rasputin, Stalin, Lenin, I imagine them all with [the former president of Second Spanish Republic] Alcalá Zamora's face.[101]

Captain Manuel de Cárdenas described the atmosphere of the civilian population of Luga in a similar fashion, mingling poverty and stereotypes formed by images from Russian literature. To him, old *muzhiks* looked like "Christ's apostles," as if they had "escaped from Tolstoy or Andreyev novels."[102] Yet these scenes certainly seemed worthy of pity and curiosity rather than hatred and disdain, and the peasants' misery reinforced the most negative aspects of older stereotypes. Menéndez Gundín felt sympathy for Soviet citizens, rather than repulsion: "Honestly, I thought the stories told in Spain about the Russian people were merely propaganda, but they fall short of reality. These people are dirty, poorly dressed ... they evoke more pity than hatred."[103]

In this way, a contradictory relationship formed between the Spanish volunteers, or at least those most identified with the anti-Bolshevik crusade, and Russian civilians. It was marked by certain disdain and a sense of superiority, but also by compassion and growing familiarity with the peasants. Moreover, the common people with whom the BD interacted were politically rather passive. As one wrote, "communism has not triumphed in the Russian countryside because ... though somewhat degenerate, it still has a spark of spirituality in its being, it is still the corner where the last essences of the old traditions are preserved."[104] Sergeant Manuel Martínez pointed out how the locals he met also hated Stalin's tyranny; he subconsciously identified the term *Russian* with *communist*, thereby perpetuating stereotypes inherited from the Spanish Civil War:

> The neighbours who did not evacuate want nothing to do with the Russians [*sic*], and if you ask them about Stalin, they will invariably reply that he should be hung from a tree, for these people have been severely grieved by the communist regime ... They are good people for the most part, and communism has condemned them to remain extremely backwards.[105]

Falangist volunteer Eusebio Donaire declared similar opinions in January 1942. The "Russians" (communists) were "beasts" for subjecting "those poor people" to a "slavery" that was the reality of the "Soviet Paradise": "cold, dirty, loveless villages."[106] Communism was perceived as a form of modern absolutism that had turned the once prosperous peasantry into the vassals of a totalitarian state.[107] This caused many volunteers to feel sorry for the population victimized by Stalin, "and lament a horribly oppressed people who must be liberated."[108] The rather naive drawings for the *Hoja de Campaña* often depicted quaint old men, jovial women, and scenes from daily life, such as soldiers playing games with Russian children and fraternizing with the peasants.[109] Guillermo Hernanz concluded that "the people I've met since arriving here are not nearly as bad as I was led to believe, they are simply unfortunate wretches condemned their entire lives (first by the Tsars and then by communism) to being horribly and truly oppressed."[110]

A Pseudo-Asiatic People?

The Spanish reading of the Russian countryside went beyond scenes of an innocent people victimized within a triad of material misery, communism, and historical fatalism. For many volunteers, especially the Falangists, communism had prevailed in Russia because of the tormented Russian soul: it was the outcome of an extreme climate, hostile landscapes, and barren fields – a "godforsaken land, heat, mosquitos ... this is a living hell."[111] The Russian people were both deprived of civilization and made spiritually lethargic by the harsh physical environment. This was a "primitive land," with only shanties "built simply as shelter from the terrifying winter, not intended as homes." Those living there could be no more than "slaves to the harsh environment," incapable of establishing an architectural style in stone. Indeed, the absence of stone construction reflected the Slavic "lack of traditional spirit" or sense of "historical continuity and effort." The land seemed to require a dictator capable of ruling the immense steppe.[112]

As in German accounts, hardship as part of Russian nature became a common feature in BD perceptions. Since the nineteenth century, the theory of social hygiene had postulated cleanliness as a mark of civilization and bourgeois culture. Accordingly, a dirty, wretched people were so by nature and not by accident. Dirty, crude, primitive and, uncivilized people, or simply physically unattractive people, were not in the same league with European invaders. Many German and Italian soldiers expressed in their letters from Russia how the border between cleanliness and order – which they associated with the Western world and masculinity – and dirtiness and disorder now constituted the border between civilization and barbarianism.[113] The Spaniards were not substantially different in this respect. In fact, many officers of the Blue Division had experienced similar sensations among the Berber population during their years in Africa.[114]

Similarly, Spanish combatants saw "the river of resignation, the conformity of those poor people" as the outcome of centuries of subjection to a despotism that was foreign to European tradition. Their adaptation to despotism had forged an indifference towards death – the end of an inane existence – which for Soviet soldiers translated into an obstinate determination to fight to the end:

> The Russian peasant is unlike any other man. One must take into account that until the last century slavery existed in Russia; perhaps this is one of the causes of the complete bestiality of Russian peasants. Also, the absolute misery of the countryside, the infrahuman life they are accustomed to and have been for centuries, the despotism of all tsars, red or white, have created a special type of man, the most perfect undoubtedly for suffering the experience of Communist collectivization. They fight because they don't care, since death is ultimately for them the complete liberation from a life that has given them nothing.[115]

Antonio Aragonés expressed sadness for the "misfortune of these people," but also asserted that they deserved their fate: the "Russian slaves" had a "psychology of resigned servility."[116] Similar thoughts were expressed by Luis Riudavets de Montes, who was responsible for the custody of the Soviet prisoners. He described the Russian people as "indifferent, fatalistic, fervent believers" who, due to the influence of climate or customs, were resigned to tyranny: "for this very reason, they have borne the Revolution well. Another people would have grown weary of it years ago."[117]

In other words, this people with "oriental" cultural, spiritual, and sometimes even physical features, accompanied by an instinct for subservience, lived in a state of barbarism, poverty, and brutality. The ingrained servility of these Russians, with their "prominent cheekbones [and] small, slightly slanted eyes," was attributed to centuries of tyranny by tsars and overlords. Such fertile ground had been ripe for manipulation by the Bolsheviks.[118] It convinced the Spanish volunteers that they were fighting for a just cause. In fact, the same notion reverberated in the letters and testimonies of their German counterparts. They were engaged in a quasi-apocalyptic struggle against a ferocious enemy with essentially subhuman (according to some Germans) features.[119] More than one combatant expressed the conviction that he was serving Spain and Europe "in this breach of Civilization."[120]

Centuries of "Asian" despotism and an inhospitable physical environment could only result in a boorish, indifferent, and submissive people. Many Spanish accounts described Russians as lethargic, indifferent, and lazy. Sometimes they hinted at identification with Jewish stereotypes.[121] For Martínez-Tessier, the characteristically "lazy movements" of the Russians gave an impression of being "eternally fatigued." He also observed that "the locals are dressed in rags and in everything appear to belong to an inferior race."[122] And José Otero-de Arce described Russian peasants as "indifferent towards everything that means progress and simply novelty," victims of a "collective stupor."[123] This comment carried more cultural than biological meaning. The cultural racism apparent in many testimonies echoed a historical and geographical determinism that recalls the attitudes of German and Austrian soldiers towards Russia and the Slavic East during the First World War – the reservoir from which new racist attitudes developed after 1920.[124]

Among the Russian people, however, more than one Spanish volunteer was able to appreciate human, even modern features. For a start, most peasants were literate, especially the younger generations. Some were surprised by the abundant community libraries, with plenty of popular literature but no pornography.[125] Ridruejo described Russians as a medieval people who were blinded "by progress, machines, Darwin ... and the pedantry of the many schoolteachers provided by the regime." Though communism had taught them to read, it had deprived them of their "last spiritual resources," beginning with religious rites.[126]

After literacy, some volunteers noted two other anecdotal features: "They never strike their horses and they make wooden nests for birds; but they mistreat men [other humans]."[127] These more minute aspects spoke of the Russians as strange, treating animals with greater respect than humans. This coarse, pitiable people had endearing aspects but were indecipherable to the Spaniards. The mix of exoticism, apathy, and fatalism defined them as truly savage and incapable of self-governance; according to Errando, Russians had an "infantile temperament. Like children, they are naive and cruel." Even their sad popular music expressed the contradictory characteristics of the Russian psyche.[128]

The Noble Savage: An Opportunity for Redemption

According to German propaganda, the ultimate objective of the *European crusade* against Bolshevism was to banish the threat of *Russia* to Europe. However, Spaniards seldom gave thought to what the destiny of the Soviet people would be once "liberated," albeit with a few interesting exceptions.

Thus, the Falangist Manuel Bendala acknowledged the unassailable legal basis on which the Third Reich could justify the appropriation of Soviet wealth. He observed that in Russia there were no "intangible individual rights." There were only "virgin elements that in the hour of peace would be handed over to those who thanks to their weapons had carried the breath of Europe to the place where hatred had flourished."[129] Russia, however, should not only be "subjected but also divided": the danger lay in communist appropriation of "Slavic messianism."[130] The Soviet regime had brought its people out of centuries of lethargy and had advanced "by resuscitating all the atavisms and promising that the hardy, combative peoples of the steppes could bathe in Western blood." However, the peaceful coexistence of Russian civilians and Spanish soldiers led Bendala to conclude that it was possible to incorporate the Russian people into European civilization. How? By economic subjection, tutelage, and control of their natural environment through a much more benign combination of colonization and protectorate than what the German occupying authorities had planned. This seemed to match some of the tenets of Alfred Rosenberg:

> The interposition or establishment of strong European colonizing nuclei – as is occurring with the Dutch, Germans, and Romanians – the political independence of the Baltic states, of Ukraine and White Russia, disarmament and abolition of war industries ... intensification of agriculture, which would need little more than the re-establishment of private

property, direct European intervention in the industries to be preserved, and perpetual concession of the oil wells to Europe.[131]

This more or less friendly colonization rested on an appraisal of the Slavs as a people not yet come of age, located on the lower rung of civilization. Europe should offer them tutelage and guidance – something akin to the colonized peoples of Asia and Africa – with no clear indication of when emancipation would occur. The narratives of BD soldiers were amplified back in Spain. Domingo Lagunilla indicated in the Falangist journal *El Español* that the history of the Slavic peoples had always been fraught with "ignorance and fanaticism." Slavs were seen as culturally inferior because they acted on "intuition, routine, and submission," they believed in "occult powers" and "visionary messianic religions."[132]

An article published in the BD trench journal went so far as to construct arguments similar to the biological-genetic tenets of National Socialism. The "Russian masses" had lived immersed in alcoholism, crime, and sexual degeneration prior to the Bolshevik Revolution. According to "all scientific laws of inheritance," alcoholic parents could only engender "deficient children with abnormal tendencies." Communism easily took root in this fertile ground but further aggravated the degenerative state of the Russian people "by spreading pornographic novels and ... the theory of free love." The malignant tumour, "the Marxist canon that threatened to place Europe in the hands of a congenitally defective race," had to be extirpated "through a moralizing and sanitary labour."[133] Some even rhetorically called for extermination; letters from Spain spoke of "the extinction of the faecal race of humanity ... the nation of hatred and carefully organized against God." In ironic analogy to the conquering of Jerusalem by the crusaders (1099), one volunteer wrote in September of 1941 that they hoped to make an offering to the memory of Falangist leaders killed by the Republicans by "passing two hundred thousand women, children and elderly under the knife" as soon as Moscow fell.[134]

However, this extermination rhetoric was not the dominant tone in the Falangist propaganda regarding the Eastern Front. The Blue Division's mouthpiece recalled on 12 October 1943 that race expressed "a homeland based first on blood," but "also on mixed blood." These defined the Hispanic race in terms of culture, faith, and external projection. Lenin and the Jews had erased "whatever is noble in mankind" from the Russian people, but the youth of the *New Europe* would re-educate them and return them to Christian faith. They envisioned Spaniards treating the Russians as the sixteenth-century conquistadors had treated American natives: offering them bread and carrying God into their homes.[135] This was for them Spain's real duty in Russia, which transcended the more insipid images of colonial mission held by some German officials.[136] Few noticed that the Soviet regime relied on patriotism to mobilize the population against the invaders, opportunistically invoking the very principles that the Iberians sought to restore.[137]

Many Spanish soldiers reacted to the Russian people in a manner resembling that of their fellow countrymen in Africa. Like the indigenous peoples of Guinea or Northern Morocco, Russians were good-natured and indolent, but with customs inappropriate for civilization. They therefore required tutelage in order to access it.[138] This attitude represented an adaptation of the traditionalist concept of Hispanidad that had been coined in the early 1920s and ideologically codified by the Catholic writer Ramiro de Maeztu in 1934. He had projected Spain as a civilizing empire that had extended the Catholic faith, by which the subjects of any race could access salvation. In theory, all men were equal; in practice, the Catholic order divided classes and races into those it considered culturally advanced or backward. The black Africans, the "masses of the Orient," and the Jews were among the permanently backward races. European treatment of such groups should be based on "charity and piety."[139]

According to most Spanish volunteers, Russians could be *converted*, as a key to their collective salvation. This marked a significant departure from the racial world view of the Nazis but was less distant from the individual perspectives of many German Catholic combatants.[140] They subscribed to the mission that several Falangist journals had imagined for the "armies of Europe" on Soviet soil. In this, the dominant tone in Catholicism resonated with the German conservatives of the 1920s and the view of certain Nazis such as Rosenberg, who distinguished between the Russian people and its regime.[141] Restoring the Russians to civilization also meant restoring them to Christ, as was frequently expressed by the BD military chaplains.[142]

In fact, during their time in Russia Spanish soldiers participated in local religious ceremonies, from infant baptisms to funerals. Iberian fascists did not consider the Russian people as a biologically inferior race. In contrast with many Wehrmacht combatants, the Spaniards did not consider regeneration impossible. The Russian people were susceptible to *spiritual* redemption, mainly through the re-establishment of religion as a substantive aspect of the tradition of the country.[143]

An Idyllic Relationship? The Occupiers and the Occupied

As mentioned above, the image of the Blue Division soldiers as "good occupiers" has rarely been subjected to critical enquiry or historical questions similar to those addressed in the vast historiography concerning the conduct of Axis troops on the Eastern Front. Were the Spaniards an exception or just a variation in the war of extermination? Was their collective behaviour determined by the combat environment, or was it related to prior indoctrination?[144]

Nazi Germany embarked on a War of Extermination aimed at several segments of the Soviet population. Many of the guidelines for the German soldiers were soon adapted to the Spanish troops as *Directivas para la conducta de la tropa en Rusia*, which identified Bolshevism as "the moral enemy of the new Europe." The battle targeted their "corrosive ideas and representatives," and "the fight requires robust, impartial action against all Bolshevik elements, such as agitators, snipers, saboteurs, or Jews; and complete elimination of all resistance, whether active or passive." Similarly, a "most severe attitude and utmost care should be observed" towards "all members of the Red Army, including the prisoners." They branded the "Asian soldiers of the Red Army" as "inscrutable, insidious, and insensitive," and particularly dangerous. When entire units were captured, "the commanders should be immediately separated from the rest of the troops." Though much of the civilian population was reportedly anti-communist, "the utmost caution should be employed when speaking to the population and when addressing women." Looting was forbidden, but "merchandise of all types ... should be preserved and impounded."[145] These orders were softened by the *Instrucción General 3.005*, issued by the BD General Staff in August 1941, which stipulated that the inhabitants of occupied territories were to be respected, requisitions had to be compensated, prisoners were to be treated well, and injured enemies were to receive care. Spies and snipers should not be executed on sight but delivered alive to higher authorities for internment in prisoner camps.[146]

The war was certainly more static and less vicious in the area covered by Army Group North. They were responsible for only 17.32 per cent (405) of the 2,253 (minimum estimate) documented executions of commissars in the first year of war. Between October and December 1941, the total figure was 101. The numbers rapidly declined in the first months of 1942.[147] There is no empirical evidence to date that the "Commissar Order" was ever communicated to the Spanish officers. It is likely that orders were followed, and political commissars were summarily taken aside and shot. It is also possible that Spanish officers would spare their troops from such an act – as occurred in certain German units – by ordering the transfer of the commissars to the BD high command, where they would be handed over to the Germans. However, some data suggests that the Spanish command and officers were aware of these instructions, because the German Army Corps – under which the BD served – sent orders to repeal them in specific operations. For instance, to encourage the surrender of the Soviet units surrounded in the Volkhov pocket (March–June 1942), Instruction 2018 from 12 May 1942 ordered the use of propaganda promising good treatment to whoever surrendered arms. "The troops shall promptly be made aware of the fact that it is forbidden to shoot political commissars, or those who voluntarily join our ranks. These commissars shall be subjected to the same treatment as the rest of the prisoners."[148] Clearly, it would be senseless to forbid the execution of commissars unless this was the usual practice. Similarly, in May 1943 the Spanish General Staff received notification from Army Corps L, stating that political commissar prisoners were ordered to "voluntarily offer themselves for employment in German legions," as "it was evident to the Russian Command that we recently stopped shooting Russian commissars when they are captured."[149]

To what extent can we empirically corroborate the benign image of the Spanish occupation policies on the Eastern Front? To begin, the Germans did not always behave so differently from the Spaniards.[150] Moreover, the relationship between a civilian population and an occupying army is always complex, even when the locals do not sympathize with the regime the invading force seeks to topple. The need to survive in a brutalized environment motivated many civilians to find common ground and avoid open confrontation with the invaders. This created a distinction between the impersonal *occupying force* and the individual occupiers with whom amicable relations were often formed. Eventually, social conventions began to crumble; flirting with the occupiers carried the inherent risk of developing a sense of closeness.[151]

Moreover, a delicate balance existed between the Russian peasants and the occupying army in the area encompassing Army Group North. With a more static war than in Army Group Centre and Army Group South, the peasants provided the invading soldiers with food and housing. Post-war accounts suggest that the peasants on the Volkhov and Leningrad Fronts hated the Germans less than the Russian collaborators, Latvians, and Estonian auxiliary troops. Willingly or otherwise, the village mayors (*stárosta*, elders) and local families often cooperated with the occupiers. Peasants would even report the partisans who seized their possessions without a second thought.[152]

Colourful and Undisciplined Occupiers

The Spanish soldiers were already implicated in a series of minor incidents involving the peasantry during their first march on foot from Eastern Poland to the Russian Front (August–September 1941). In response to first complaints from the German liaison officers, Muñoz-Grandes issued an edict reminding the soldiers that "any attack to people, property, or unauthorized requisitions could be considered an infraction of the rights of the people against devastation or looting" and punishable by the Spanish Military Code.[153]

However, the behaviour of the BD volunteers did not change upon entering Russian territory. In late September, a German unit reported that a passing "division of Spanish soldiers" had requisitioned livestock and chickens from local peasants in the village of Izifovo.[154] BD troops arrived at the rearguard station in Novosokol'niki between 29 September and 13 October. The local German military police was ineffective in keeping the Spanish soldiers from engaging in looting and intimidation. They destroyed the station to obtain firewood, looted warehouses, and requisitioned livestock and grain from peasant households.[155]

The arrival of the Spaniards to the Volkhov Front certainly began chaotically. They lodged with the local residents in nearby villages, disrupting the routines the peasant families had become accustomed to under German rule. The BD General Staff ordered that behaviour towards the locals be "prudent and proper," avoiding "coercion and violence ... as well as familiarity, which could invite espionage."[156] However, Germans soon began receiving complaints from peasants that the Spaniards were plundering food, livestock, and warm clothing.[157] They also looted "exotic souvenirs," especially Orthodox icons. It is difficult to discern how much of what the soldiers took corresponded to larceny, requisitions, or other forms of acquisition or bartering. In November 1942, a Spanish volunteer described his personal booty: "I found a little Russian suitcase, in which I plan to take four books and icons if possible ... It's not much, and certainly not 'pretty' – there was quite the icon hunt around these houses for the first few days – but enough to stir a memory."[158]

The Germans attributed such behaviour to relaxed discipline, mismanagement by ill-trained NCOs, the indifference of the BD high command, and especially the hierarchical position of the Division quartermaster, who distributed much to the officers and little to the soldiers.[159] This inefficient provisioning system had been a feature of the Spanish Army since the colonial wars of 1895–8, and it became evident during the foot march to Russia. By November 1941, Army Group North was seriously considering replacing the BD quartermaster with an annexed department under German command.[160] The situation may have led the discontented Spanish soldiers to provision themselves from the civilian population, as their German comrades had been doing for weeks and months.[161] However, violence was not always necessary. Upon arriving at the front, Sergeant Ramón Abadía described how easy it was to obtain food from the villagers, whom he regarded as good savages: "with a little chocolate and some sweets we can trick them into giving us milk and potatoes ... probably using the same methods as Columbus did when he discovered the Americas."[162]

There was not much to requisition. The local food situation in the rearguard of the Volkhov Front was critical from October 1941 on. Subjected to Wehrmacht demands, the peasants had already sold most of their livestock and almost everything of value they owned, including coats and boots. It was a poor region to begin with; there was very little mechanized agriculture, and only half of the fertile lands could be farmed in that area. In October 1941, many women, children, and elderly people began to withdraw to the rearguard from areas close to the front. On 24 October, Army Group North command drily noted that "sooner or later these people will all die of starvation."[163]

The unruly conduct of the BD towards the peasants had already alarmed the German liaison staff by late October 1941. They had caught wind of the pervasive lack of discipline in the relations between the Spanish volunteers and the civilian population as well as the indiscriminate and sometimes coercive plundering of food and livestock. The Russian peasants themselves even complained to the Spanish command.[164] Worst of all, the Spanish soldiers' "lack of control with women" generated "distasteful scenes" and the threat of propagating venereal diseases.[165] Adding to the continual requisitions, "rapes and other nuisances to the civilian population" made the exasperated locals less cooperative in the anti-partisan fight.[166] Though the BD General Staff recorded few cases against soldiers for "dishonest abuse,"[167] the complaints even reached General Franco and the Spanish army minister in December 1941. Confidential reports described the "unsavoury characters in the Division, who rob, murder, and burn whatever they wish" as well as the fact that officers "had to watch the troops, to avoid them requisitioning everything they found in the neighbouring villages, as these were frequent, embarrassing cases."[168] The lack of appropriate equipment for surviving the winter aggravated the situation. When necessary, the Spaniards – and others – took felt boots, hats, and coats from the peasants, leaving them defenceless against the winter cold.[169] The delay of the Christmas bonus dispatched from Spain, and its scarcity compared to what was promised, generated additional discontent among the troops in late December 1941.[170]

Aside from their prejudice against the Spanish, the German high command concluded that the structural cause of BD conduct stemmed from the hierarchic culture of the Spanish military. The chief commander of the XXXVIII Army Corps attributed the "brutal conduct of the Spanish soldiers" to the lack of discipline in the BD, pointing out how "the best food is unabashedly eaten by the officers as extra rations." In December 1941, the commander of the 16th Army demanded from Berlin that the BD volunteers be relieved of their duties, to keep their lack of discipline from spreading to the German soldiers.[171] Not only were the troublesome soldiers jeopardizing the Wehrmacht's *honour*, but their anarchic actions could also lead the civilian population to support the partisans. Of course, German soldiers also created disturbances, but these were subject to Wehrmacht discipline. Systematic exploitation and more or less organized plundering was different to uncontrolled requisitions.[172]

The BD enjoyed the privilege of not being subject to Wehrmacht military justice. This troubled the Germans, as they could not always impose their discipline on their allies. In November 1941, when two Spanish soldiers killed the town elder of Novgorod, the culprits were only sanctioned by BD command after significant pressure from the Germans.[173] In December 1941, the XXXVIII Army Corps began to fear that incessant BD pillaging would make the peasants unwilling to collaborate in reporting sightings of Soviet incursions.[174] Three months later, the Army Corps Martial Court explicitly indicated that the Blue Division was responsible for all major discipline issues within their jurisdiction. At that point, the Germans decided to arrest Spaniards caught pillaging or stealing, and to incarcerate them for several days before handing them over to BD military justice. The conduct of the volunteers also led to relaxed discipline in the German 126th Infantry Division.[175] However, other German divisions that had little or no contact with their Spanish comrades were also involved in aggression and the mistreatment of civilians.[176]

The relief battalions arriving from Spain from March 1942 onwards were no better behaved than their predecessors. Food theft was common during train stops in Polish, Baltic, or Russian territory. From December 1942 on, the troops began to receive better food rations and winter clothing under the command of General Esteban-Infantes, and thanks to increased supplies from Spain.[177] A better quartermaster and German insistence also helped to improve daily relations between the Spanish volunteers and the civilian population.

Sleeping with the Enemy

The Volkhov and Leningrad Fronts were panoramas of hunger and desolation. Some records show that the Spaniards were aware of the terrible living conditions in the besieged city, thanks to the stories of Soviet prisoners.[178] Misery was the status quo in the rearguard of the occupied area as well. In the village of Vyritsa, for example, the civilian mortality rate increased elevenfold in April 1942. Captain Serafín Pardo described months later how children and women would fight over the scraps the volunteers gave them.[179] When Manuel de Cárdenas passed through the town of Gatchina, he described the malnourishment with clinical precision in his war diary:

> There are lots of people on the streets ... old, bearded *muzhiks*, dirty and ragged; shabby old women with faces yellowed from many months of hunger. Pretty young women nonetheless poor and dirty; not as thin as the old women as they can work some and are better suited to finding food thanks to their youth. Barefoot urchins with hats on their heads but so horribly thin their legs look like they belong to skeletons ... The hunger among these civilians is honestly frightening. They may not even survive the next winter. I often see men with juvenile features but who look so horribly aged, paled by avitaminosis and their legs swollen from hunger. And these half-men are the lucky ones, they are not in the prisoner camp.[180]

The civilians were so underfed that malnutrition weakened their immune systems. Spanish military surgeons in the immediate rearguard often helped the civilian population, but their good intentions were not always enough.[181] In June 1942, Cárdenas visited a hospital for civilians and Soviet prisoners in Kolmovo, and what he saw horrified him: "The civilian population ... survived this winter and now suffer from the most awful hunger and misery." The hospital environment was frighteningly gruesome: "Each body is more emaciated than the last; their faces, hands, and feet look like anatomical illustrations, where even the smallest tendon can be seen."[182]

Despite their plundering, from the beginning of 1942 on the Spanish soldiers were generally amicable with the civilian population. In May 1943, General Esteban-Infantes instructed the Division officers to be wary of soldiers or officers living with women or Russian families, but their responses showed little concern for this issue.[183] Soviet citizens who worked for the Spaniards often presented their chaotic occupiers from a positive angle in their memoirs: the Spanish were less predictable and disciplined than the Germans, but also less heartless. The testimony of Soviet collaborators portrayed BD soldiers as devoted Catholics, for the most part friendly, who shared their rations with peasant families and were hostile towards the Germans.[184]

For many Russian women, children, and elderly people, having an officer and his assistants or a squadron of soldiers in the house could be a lifeline for ensuring survival, by giving their family access to extra rations and clothing. Two months after their arrival at the front, the Spaniards were generally more welcome than the Germans, as they did not force the elderly to clear roads and let the peasants use their livestock for ploughing when the ground thawed. The Iberians often found in Russian peasant women "the family we lacked because it was far away," while Spanish lodgers were seen as protection against the greater rigours of German occupation.[185] However, Spaniards also became aware of the misery their "adoptive" families suffered. Salvador Zanón acknowledged that the hungry family of the *izba* where his platoon lived also had to feed them:

Craba lives with her small, dirty, crying baby, two very ugly women, and two other lads of eight or ten, who teach us Russian and eat the candy and chocolate we supply. These poor people live a sad, harsh life, but where else can they go? Here at least they have a few potatoes, well-hidden so that we do not take them.[186]

Ochapkina A. Dimitrieva remembered the Spanish soldiers' good behaviour towards the peasant families taking refuge in the Otenskii monastery: "they were more human than the Germans."[187] Spanish officers were particularly welcome, as they brought with them better supplies. Vasíly P., a thirteen-year-old boy at the time, was lucky enough to have a Spanish lieutenant living with him and his mother. The officer shared his additional food supplies with his host family, as did many BD volunteers.[188]

According to the local collaborator Lidia Ósipova, in Pavlovsk the locals' first impression of the exotic occupiers was ambivalent: instead of being "proud, noble, beautiful," the Spaniards were very kind, but "unruly like monkeys; dirty swindlers like gypsies." The success of the Iberian volunteers was not entirely due to their southern charm. From mid-1942 on, they often received packages from Spain containing products impossible to find in Russia – everything from chickpeas to liquor – and would distribute their surplus among the local people. Naturally, this endeared them to the civilians, who "had never been fond of the Germans." On 17 September, Lidia recorded that a Spanish captain had risked his life to save a homeless child during a bombardment. On the downside, the organizational chaos that reigned in the BD rearguard created uncertainty as to what was and was not allowed. Compared to the Germans, the Spanish occupiers were rather unpredictable, but clearly preferred by the local population.[189] The *starosta* of Antropchina village reported to the German information services in November 1942 that the Spaniards treated civilians fairly well, and that under their surveillance the locals were not required to do as much forced labour. He added that the "mood of the Russian population shifts more and more in favour of the Spanish occupation."[190]

The requisitions did not end when the Division was transferred to the southern flank of the siege of Leningrad. The peasants occasionally reported these events to Spanish officers, and the forceful occupation and ransacking of homes by soldiers led to several court martials.[191] The Iberians were particularly unsystematic in pillaging. This caused trouble for the German command, as the peasants also pillaged everything they could find.[192] The adverse effects of requisitions on the image of the Blue Division among the Russian peasants were not always compensated by equivalent acts of kindness from other soldiers and officers. As with other Wehrmacht divisions, experiences varied greatly among units and villages. When Captain de Andrés's detachment passed through Vyritsa, they found a group of famished elderly persons and children whose chickens had been stolen by another Spanish unit. To repair this deed, de Andrés sacrificed a horse and distributed it among them. Similarly, when Captain Serafín Pardo arrived at his new post on the Leningrad Front, he took in a starving Russian family to work as auxiliaries in exchange for ample rations.[193]

Ugly Panienkas, *Idealized* Katiushas, *and the Children*

From the very beginning of the Spanish occupation, plenty of romances occurred between *divisionarios* and *panienkas* – the Polish word for "girls" that the Iberian volunteers also applied to Russian women. Numerous orders were issued from the BD General Staff prohibiting close relationships between Russian civilians and soldiers. This extended to dancing, walking arm-in-arm with "Soviet women," and accepting their invitations.[194] The reiteration of these instructions speaks of their ineffectiveness.[195] Many a Spanish volunteer maintained virtually platonic relations with young women they could barely communicate with through gestures. Soldier Roberto Rivera described in August 1942 how "My dear little friend Tatiana (19 years old) tries to teach me to speak Russian ... I have only learned to say *jorasó* = pretty and *lin-blin* = I love you."[196] Spanish soldiers portrayed themselves as surrounded by doting women who washed their clothes "because I give them sweets in exchange."

Fig. 5.3. Spanish soldiers reading sports illustrated press, 1943 (AGA)

Though gallantry with Russian women was more intense on the Leningrad Front than the Volkhov Front,[197] matches between the occupying soldiers and Russian women were plausible in the shared living conditions that prevailed in both areas. This was not limited to the Spaniards either; even the supposedly cold Germans fancied Russian girls.[198] Spanish romances with local women sometimes ended up in unauthorized weddings, and by mid-1942 the situation was scandalizing the OKH. The BD command decided not to officially recognize any marriages between its soldiers and Russian women, forbidding them from accompanying returning soldiers to Spain.[199] However, some of these marriages served to hide a different type of relationship. For example, Colonel Robles Pazos ordered his Russian lover to marry one of the Division's Russian interpreters so he could bring her back to Spain.[200]

Though some marriages occurred, it seems that very few sincere relationships emerged out of these circumstances. For a start, the Russian women were quite removed from the feminine ideal held by the

Spaniards, especially those from middle-class backgrounds. Even when they could find Russian women with urban habits, similar feelings surfaced.[201] Letters and diaries portrayed Russian country girls as dirty, unkempt females who lacked social graces, were aged by work and hunger, dressed in rags, and did not always respect traditional morals.[202] Sergeant Martínez Tessier noted the want of silk stockings and delicacy in form and dress among the first Russian peasant girls he saw. He remarked that they had "no femininity" and "manly" manners.[203] Another volunteer even wrote that "the woman, in Russia ... lacks the most exquisite sense: femininity. She is a bear who works the fields."[204]

The distance between Russian peasant women and aesthetic ideals concerning Spanish women was also interpreted as one more example of Soviet barbarism, which had supposedly stripped women of all feminine and moral content in order to facilitate the destruction of traditional family ties. Their lack of hygiene also fit with the purported dirtiness of the Russian context. Arenales noted that only schoolmistresses "seem to wash, which is uncommon." The pseudo-Asian physical features he saw in them did not contribute to their beauty: "slanted eyes that seem sunken due to exaggerated cheekbones."[205]

Not everything qualified as the innocent love that was later published in the memoirs of Spanish veterans.[206] Often, the objective was mere sexual entertainment with peasant women, who were seen as primitives that might lack morals and welcome promiscuity. In October 1941, several Spanish soldiers entered a house in Podberez'e, looking for a sergeant and a corporal who were missing from their unit. There they saw their comrades having intercourse with (raping?) some local girls with purportedly Asian features in a dirty environment:

> There were two rooms ... and they smelled disgusting; in one were the "parents" and the "children" of the *femmes fatales*, not at all concerned with the shrieks or with what their daughters or sisters were doing ... and in the other, unbelievably, none other than the sergeant and the corporal, talking little and doing much, with two Spaniards and two Germans sitting there drinking and singing and "admiring" the Russian beauties. You should have seen them! And especially – what a fright – two of them were short, stout, with slanted eyes, mongoloid lips, and repugnant arms ... one was missing half a nose and half of her face was burned, and the other kept farting so much that it turned my stomach ...[207]

Blatant prostitution also occurred. One teacher from Samokhvalovo, finding she could no longer give lessons, supported herself and the children by "selling herself as a prostitute to the Spaniards who occupied the school complex."[208] Some diaries suggest that other *panienkas* offered their charms in exchange for food, and relationships could also blossom from such encounters, which were even promoted by peasant mothers for the sake of their daughters, who now were "protected" and fed by Spanish soldiers.[209] Near Sitno, a soldier visited "some *panienkas* that I was told were quite nice looking. They laughed and 'we had fun.'" He visited one of them several more days. When his unit was forced to withdraw, she asked in vain that he take her with him.[210]

Antonio Herrero wrote in April 1943 that after attending a Catholic Mass, he took part in a "magnificent banquet followed by a fun dance with the local girls." Evening parties were common in spring and summer, often in front of an Orthodox church that had been reopened.[211] However, some testimonies suggest that many of these fetes were organized by the German *Kommandaturen*, which recruited local women with food. One Russian interpreter revealed that his main duties involved travelling in the rearguard seeking girls for the officers' parties.[212] Relations with Russian women implied a mix of seduction and distrust, as they might be collaborating as decoys for a partisan ambush at the party.[213] The daily disputes between German and Spanish soldiers often revolved around women. Antonina Davychenko wrote of a fist fight that occurred when Spanish soldiers protected a Russian woman from the harassments of German soldiers. Lidia Ósipova indicated that when the *divisionarios* arrived in Pavlovsk, "all the loose women who were with the Germans immediately went to be with the Spaniards," attracted by their Latin nature... and better food rations.[214] However, Evdokiia Bogacheva-Baskakova, a female surgeon from the same area, wrote down in her unpublished war memoirs that "a Spanish soldier is just the same rapist like a German one, with the difference that when a victim puts even the slightest resistance, a Spaniard would abandon her without hurting her." On the contrary, the German soldier "is a dyed-in-the-wool rapist – if he caught his prey, he would never let her go, and ater the deed he would simply shoot her." What was the explanation for such behaviour? According to her, it was not a matter of "Latin" versus "Germanic" character, but the consequence of military discipline. While the German soldier was afraid of the military court and preferred to leave no traces of his rape, "the Spanish army is very dissolute, and the Spanish soldier has no fear of the people above him."[215]

In fact, the Spanish Division also court-martialled some of its members on charges of looting and rape. Nevertheless, some examples suggest that they rarely ended in harsh convictions. On 7 April 1942, a court martial was conducted against Sergei Ponomariov, a Russian interpreter for the BD and a former White Russian exile, for "an alleged crime against international law" that had occurred in January 1942. According to the judicial record, the interpreter organized "the provision of food and supplies" for his regiment in the village of Chechulino. Vera Korichava, wife of the former local head of the Communist Party, was "suspected of hiding weapons." The house was searched and Ponomariov was charged with having sexually abused her and stolen objects and money, according to the statements of several Russian witnesses. However, the defendant was acquitted because the soldiers and the local *starosta* – recently appointed by Ponomariov himself – who were with him testified that they had not witnessed any rape, theft, or abuse. Moreover, they alleged that the testimonies came from "Russian civilians whose family members are enlisted in the Red Army," and the charges were undoubtedly intended to "discredit the occupation." Ponomariov was sentenced to three months in the penal battalion for having exceeded orders, "needlessly harassing the civilian population, which they threatened."[216] Ultimately, Russian civilians did not benefit from the military law imposed by the occupiers, which included the Spaniards.

Children constitute a very different chapter in the BD narrative, as their innocence could easily symbolize and reinforce the re-Christianizing mission Spaniards attributed to themselves.[217] Many volunteers saw themselves as protectors of children and gave them treats and food. Young ones were sometimes taught to pray or speak a few words in Spanish.[218] Compassion for the children in their misery showed up in war diaries. Martín Velasco wrote of the hunger in Vitebsk:

> Four Russian children near me are holding in their little hands a greasy paper with lamb bones from our mess, which the cooks gave them. It is pitiful and sad to see how these children gnaw at bones with almost no meat on them and look at me with small sad eyes, saying *gout* [sic], which in German means "good."[219]

Many Spanish veterans described having nourished and protected native children as their best memory of Russia. Later accounts of elderly peasants from the Novgorod area corroborate this. Unlike the Germans, the Spanish soldiers were often surrounded by children.[220] Many of these *malenkis* were war orphans who sometimes formed bands that wandered about the rearguard, searching for food or shelter, begging or engaging in petty theft.[221] BD soldiers and officers frequently supported orphans or the children of widows, although sexual favours from the mothers sometimes were implicitly acknowledged as the price for such protection.[222] Despite the Franco regime's zeal to avoid infiltration by Soviet spies, several documented cases tell of Russian children and adolescents hiding in wagons or dressing as Spanish soldiers and being taken to Spain by BD soldiers and officers, who then incorporated them into their families.[223] This also constituted a clear divergence from the attitudes of most German soldiers.

Dealing with Partisans: Benevolence or Inefficacy?

Anti-guerrilla operations are among the thorniest issues in the memoirs of BD veterans. Though partisans were responsible for numerous BD casualties, burnt Russian villages and hanged peasants are generally recalled as the work of their German allies in the memoirs.[224] During the march through occupied territories, members of the first Spanish expedition witnessed German reprisals against partisans or suspects. In their diaries, several BD members wrote of seeing partisans – and civilians accused of collaborating with them – being shot.[225] They also saw plenty of partisans hung in town squares. Some equated them with Jews, based on a characteristic slogan of Wehrmacht propaganda.[226] These scenes multiplied proportionally when Spanish volunteers reached the Volkhov Front. Víctor J. Jiménez described how his literary alter ego was ordered by the Germans to execute two partisan commanders the very day he arrived at the front line.[227] The BD Information Section interrogated dozens of prisoners to identify political commissars and possible partisans. They were then taken to the German Army Corps headquarters and most likely shot.[228]

The Spanish Division had very few *Feldgendarmen* who could take charge of counter-insurgency. The territory covered by the Spaniards on the Volkhov Front was simply too broad to be effectively watched, and the lack of spatial penetration in the BD occupation meant that vast forest areas and remote villages were not effectively controlled by the invaders. The Spanish soldiers perceived partisan danger as a diffuse, omnipresent threat, like "ghosts" who populated the dense forests: "We hear news of betrayals, ambushes, and then reprisals. It is common to see someone from the towns on the banks of the Volkhov hanging from a beam or telephone post."[229] By early 1942 nearly twenty thousand Soviet partisans operated in the rearguard of Army Group North and were particularly abundant in the Novgorod region. However, the level of partisan activity was moderate, compared to White Russia or Ukraine.[230] The command of the Army Group North rearguard applied less aggressive measures to combat partisans and used propaganda to encourage peasant cooperation or the surrender of guerrilla members.

Reprisals and firing squads intensified after mid-1942, but the bulk of partisan activity occurred in the far rearguard, where no Spanish soldiers were deployed.[231]

In October 1941, instructions from the BD High Command recommended that if "any individuals of the opposing army, in isolation or in groups," were caught "carrying out acts of sabotage such as blowing up bridges, assaulting vehicles or lodgings, or carrying out guerrilla warfare dressed as civilians," the officers in charge were authorized to do "whatever needs to be done with these individuals, depending on the tactical situation." Eleven days later, new instructions indicated that in light of the increasing intensity of guerrilla activity, sector chiefs and officers who caught partisans should assume guilt and not seek conclusive evidence, which might have been destroyed with the "complicity of the locals." Officers must not be "lenient given the ensuing threat to the security of the area entrusted to us." Suspicious individuals should be handed over to the closest German command and "snipers" should be interrogated, then hanged in a public place and left there for several days as a warning.[232]

The guidelines were softened in mid-1942, with instructions that partisans who surrendered be given the same treatment as Red Army deserters. In theory, Spaniards were to transfer all punishable cases, and summary procedures against prisoners of war were to be carried out by the closest German military authorities. The few testimonies that mention retaliatory operations indicate that locals were always handed over to the Germans, who also carried out massive reprisals in towns where sentries had been murdered. There is evidence that Spanish soldiers ceded escaped prisoners to the competent authorities in the 16th and 18th Armies.[233] However, on some occasions Spanish *Feldgendarmen* undertook their own reprisals, such as when a Spanish anti-partisan unit led by Captain Martínez de Tudela located and murdered several Soviet soldiers as they attempted to return to their territory in late 1941.[234]

In early 1942, the German command decided to relieve the Blue Division of all sentry duties in the near rearguard, partly because the Spaniards had to cover a very broad section of the front.[235] Where they were responsible for these duties, evidence suggests that control of the civilian population was less severe than with the German "security divisions" and "protection teams" (*Sicherungsdivisionen* and *Schutzmann-schaften*) that operated in the rear. The Iberian practices were reminiscent of those used in the former colonial wars, rather than the brutalized "totalitarian counter-insurgence" methods of the Wehrmacht.[236] As in the German-occupied areas, the Russian villagers were generally willing to collaborate; many peasants thought that collectivization had ended and expected to recover their land. Former Tsarist officials also denounced Communist Party members who had not yet fled to "Red" territory.[237] Spanish efficacy in the anti-partisan fight was also dubious; their evacuations of the civilian population from towns were often chaotic, without "any military supervision whatsoever." This might facilitate Soviet espionage and favour the partisans. In July 1943, cases of Spanish soldiers losing their weapons to Russian civilians prompted the L Army Corps command to recommend that the Spaniards exercise stricter control over the population.[238]

In May 1943, increased partisan activity led the XXXVIII Army Corps command to involve the divisions on the front in the persecution of partisans operating in their respective rearguards. Thus, the Spaniards were required to work with detachments of auxiliary Russian and Baltic troops. Some testimonies corroborate that the BD command had given orders to their units to execute any captured partisans on site. In October, L Army Corps instructed that reprisals be carried out against local civilians wherever Wehrmacht soldiers had been attacked. However, Spanish efficacy in controlling partisans and civilians acting as informants did not improve. On 18 July 1943, the Blue Division headquarters in Pokrovskoe suffered a precise Soviet artillery attack due to information provided by spies infiltrated among Russian assistants to the BD.[239] Four months later, the German command learned of the presence of a group of partisans to the south of Nikolawja and requested the assistance of two hundred BD soldiers to "cleanse" the area. However, the operation failed for lack of efficiency among the Spaniards. German officers blamed the botched operation on their allies' indiscretions with their Russian aides, who then passed on the information to partisans.[240]

Few BD internal reports mention explicit anti-partisan actions, but the exceptions show that they did occur.[241] Spanish testimonies do not always clarify who shot the partisans and provide few details regarding reprisals. Several BD deserters interrogated by the Red Army at the end of 1942 admitted hearing stories of reprisals against partisans from their German comrades but said they had never actually seen any.[242] Other testimonies allude to German soldiers "finishing off" injured partisans and prisoners. However, the Germans did not act alone: some BD members stated that they were ordered to execute those who had been arrested and summarily tried.[243]

The perspective of the Russian civilians suggests something similar. Spanish soldiers occasionally carried out reprisals against civilians when blinded by a desire to avenge the death of a comrade. Lidia Nikolaévna was eleven when her village of Rogavka, located in the rearguard, became the residence of several detachments of Spanish soldiers

Fig. 5.4. Convalescent Spanish soldiers, Königsberg, 1942 (AA)

who were resting from combat in early December 1941. Partisan activity immediately increased, involving several Spanish victims.[244] The Russian girl witnessed how some angry Spaniards rounded up all the inhabitants from the town and surrounding area to take revenge and hang a partisan fighter. It was the local German commander who intervened to stop greater reprisals, as the Wehrmacht needed the civilians for labour.[245] The BD rearguard was no blissful Arcadia. However, it was never characterized by collective reprisals and ruthless brutality.

The Spanish Division and the "Jewish Question"

As they marched on foot through Eastern Poland, the first contingent of Spanish volunteers saw what the Jewish inhabitants of the area were experiencing. Spanish military hospitals were operating in Vilnius and Riga when the local Jewish communities were deported and their ghettos filled with Jewish families from Germany, through mid-1942. Spanish soldiers in the rearguard of the Reich also had opportunity to witness the effects of Nazi anti-Semitic policies. Letters and war diaries of Blue Division members reflected this reality to a certain extent, though persecution of the Jews remained a taboo topic and was rarely referred to openly in the written testimonies of their German comrades from that time.[246] What was the reaction of Spanish volunteers to the German persecution, discrimination, deportation, and extermination of Jews? What did the BD volunteers see, and how did they interpret it in light of their world view, prejudices, and past experiences?

Anti-Semitism without Jews

Spanish fascism shared to some extent the generic, anti-Semitic propaganda objectives of other European interwar fascist movements. These aims were also latent in Spanish traditionalist thought and fed by new images that appeared during the first third of the twentieth century. A discursive *topos* was being created at that time, which suggested an association between international Jewry, Freemasonry, and communism. It was deployed in the propaganda with greater or lesser intensity depending on the ideologue or group involved. Though anti-Semitism had been a constant feature of rebel propaganda and iconography during the Spanish Civil War, it could hardly function as a mobilizing myth due to the obvious fact that there was no significant Jewish population on Iberian soil. Curiously, a trace of philo-Semitism appears in aesthetic Falangism, as expressed by Ernesto Giménez Caballero, who considered members of Sephardic communities in the Balkans and Asia Minor to be Spaniards.[247] The few Jews in Spanish territory, specifically in the Protectorate of Morocco and the North African cities of Ceuta and Melilla, suffered some discriminatory measures from 1936 on. Anti-Semitism certainly existed, but virtually no traces of biological racism can be found.

There were two aspects to the Jewish question. One was the Judaism anathemized in Francoist propaganda and often cast as an outside force dedicated to weaving conspiracies against Christian nations. The other aspect was much less clear and had to do with how Jewish people and Jews were perceived as a differentiated collective. During the early 1940s, Francoist propaganda kept the flame of anti-Semitic rhetoric burning. The hundreds of Jews living in Spain were under pressure by the authorities and some synagogues were closed. The Francoist police compiled a Jewish dossier, but they were not subjected to purges or discriminatory measures with regard to their civil rights. Positions on the Jews and the Sephardic contribution to Spanish culture past and present were often contradictory, as was the admission policy for Jews fleeing Nazi persecution. They were generally allowed to pass through Spanish territory, on the condition that they left as soon as possible. There were also cases of refugees being returned to the border. However, the individual actions of diplomats such as Ángel Sanz-Briz in Budapest saved the lives of dozens of Jewish citizens, who were given Spanish passports.[248]

Racial postulates of a scientific nature were generally absent from the public sphere. Ambassador Eberhard von Stohrer reported in February 1941 that the Jewish question in Spain did not represent "any real political problem" because most Jews had converted to Catholicism long ago. What the Nazi diplomat considered a "modern conception of the Jewish question" had very meagre support in Spain. Some months later, von Stohrer reiterated that despite the recent increase in anti-Semitic propaganda in Spain, the general attitude of the Spanish population towards the Jewish question had changed little because there had been virtually no Jews in their country since 1492.[249]

Public support and exaltation of the Spanish volunteers as they left in the summer of 1941 echoed with earlier tones of anti-Semitic propaganda. Allusions to the Jews were often semantically associated with Soviet communism. Some of the brochures published in July 1941 to honour the volunteers who were dispatched to Russia also expressed that rhetoric. Arturo Cuartero wrote that the Blue Division should serve as a patriotic lesson for a "minority of Freemasons and Jews who still loiter around the greatness of the [national] idea" and that the "Jewish segment of Spain" represented by "capitalist, industrial and commercial elements" would be reduced to "a pile of slag" once the Blue Division returned. Desiderio Carrión, a pharmacist from a Toledo village, invoked the BD soldiers: "as a knight swear / to tie your banner / to the eagles of the Reich" in order to defeat Soviet communism, whose weapons were supposedly controlled by the Jews and "the Godless."[250] The 1942 documentary film *La División Azul*, directed by Joaquín Reig and Víctor de la Serna, reproduced the association between communism and Jews intent on destroying Christian culture:

> The Comintern order is a standing order of the damned race: to destroy everything that evokes the presence, remembrance, or pride of Christian culture. Spain must be [considered by them as] the wick by which the communist torch will set fire to the venerable Europe. It is the order of Zion launched from Moscow.[251]

This type of rhetoric was persistent in the Blue Division trench press. The conspiracy theory was consistently – though not constantly –

presented in op-eds and inserted in propaganda banners picturing Judaism in bed with international Marxism, plutocracy, and liberalism, which were responsible for the outbreak of the Spanish Civil War and the Second World War.[252] Some articles stated that communists in Russia were a tiny percentage, "two per thousand of the total population," but well-organized to serve a despotic tyranny, composed largely of Jews and Freemasons. Most of Lenin's and Stalin's counsellors were labelled as Jews, who were said to have inspired Soviet communism and its obstinate de-Christianizing ambition.[253] However, these expressions were still framed within the same discursive patterns inherited from Catholic anti-Semitism. In the pages of *Hoja de Campaña*, on the occasion of the "Day of our Race," 12 October 1943, the author wrote that race was "the homeland built first on the foundation of blood." It went on to say: "Even mixed blood. Often unity resides in mixing. From intense effusions of very diverse elements, Spain created perennial racial bases," a race manifest in a distinctive culture, the Catholic faith, and external projection.[254]

Even the most Germanophile Falangist in the Blue Division did not embrace biological racism. Yet they did demonstrate conspicuous generic cultural and religious racism against Jews. At times it manifested itself openly, but on other occasions it was expressed subliminally. The Andalusian temperament and flamenco dancing, for example, were declared free from "cowardly" Jewish influence.[255] Certain discursive elements sporadically appeared, displaying clear anti-Semitic tones in descriptions of Russia as "the land of Jews," comments about enemies that "looked like Jews," a desire to "shave the beard off that Jew Stalin," etc.[256]

Encountering the Eastern European Jews, 1941–3

The Soviet-German War was planned and executed by the Third Reich as a war of extermination. This became clear to the Spanish soldiers, even in the rearguard, but especially as they observed the Germans mistreating Soviet war prisoners and civilians during their march towards the Rront. The Polish embassy in Madrid, which was not closed until January 1942, and Spanish diplomats in the former Polish territory informed the Franco cabinet of the sufferings of the civilian population under occupation, including the persecution of the Jews.[257] This contrasted with the sugar-coated descriptions of some war correspondents. Luis Sánchez-Maspons portrayed the Krakow ghetto in October 1941 as an "enclosed space, with wide streets and clean houses," much more hygienic than the old Jewish quarter. He emphasized how the Jewish police were in charge of maintaining order, "wearing caps reminiscent

of our porters" under the Council of Elders, the autonomous government of the neighbourhood."[258]

According to a 1942 report from the Spanish political police, the first
returnees from the Eastern Front informed that German occupation
troops were carrying out a "bloody repression campaign" in Poland,
Lithuania, and Russia. It was directed against Poles and Russians in
general, who were executed in the streets and sent to "remote prison
camps."[259] Towards the end of 1941, Spanish diplomats had many opportunities to hear about the mistreatment of Jews in the occupied territories. Serrano Suñer himself had already been informed about the
situation of Jews in occupied Poland by press correspondent Ramón
Garriga. Though specific details might not have been available, from
mid-1942 on Spanish leaders knew that the Jews of East-Central Europe
were being deported in large numbers, and in July 1943 they knew full
well that Jews were being murdered. In August 1944, Ambassador Ángel Sanz Briz reported to Madrid that Jews were being deported and
exterminated. It was not until April of 1945 that the censors allowed the
Spanish press to publish anything about the existence of the concentration and extermination camps of Buchenwald, Bergen-Belsen, and
Auschwitz. They were presented as a mere consequence of the final
chaotic stages of the conflict.[260]

Spanish soldiers encountered almost no Jews in the northern sector
of the Russian Front. There was no significant concentration of Russian
Jews on the Volkhov Front or the southern flank of the siege of Leningrad. Einsatzgruppe A had already "cleaned up" the Volkhov region
before the Spaniards arrived there, including villages such as Staraia
Russa and rearguard areas such as Pskov/Pleskau, where there were
still some five hundred Jews in August 1941 – they were annihilated by
German troops in a nearby forest from late December 1941 to February
1942. In Staraia Russa, about two thousand Jews were arrested, locked
in a prison and a monastery near the city, and shot a few days later. After that, the likelihood of Spanish soldiers encountering Jewish civilians
in the rear of their front sector was small. By then, Einsatzgruppe A considered it *judenfrei* – free of Jews – apart from isolated individuals who
had managed to escape extermination. This partly explains why collaboration of Army Group North units, including the 281st Rearguard
Division, with Einsatzgruppen tasks was much more limited than in
other areas of the Eastern Front.[261] As a result, the possibility of Spanish
soldiers seeing anything or anyone Jewish among the civilians of occupied areas near the front was extremely low.

The general instructions for the Spanish Division were the same as
those transmitted to the German Army Corps to which they belonged.

From October 1941 on, the word was that the Jews were the "main up-
holders" of Bolshevism, and "any collaboration" of the army with the
Jewish population was forbidden. This included the BD. There would
be no more "employing Jews for auxiliary services to the Army," except
in "special columns of workers ... under German surveillance."[262] This
instruction, however, was a translation of generic German orders and
not a reference to the presence of Jews on the front line. It was more
likely that the *divisionarios* had heard some tale of the killing of the Jewish population from Russian locals or German soldiers. Some of the latter had looked on while the Einsatzgruppen and the Sicherheitspolizei
committed these acts, which helped to spread news regarding the fate
of the Jews.[263] Around a hundred Jews had been killed a year earlier
in positions held by the Spanish from August 1942 on. In the palace
gardens of Catherine the Great in Pushkin, 250 Jews had been shot and
buried. Similar incidents had occurred in Pavlovsk or Vyritsa.[264] Private
José-Luis Pinillos declared later he had become aware of the fate of the
Jews through conversations with German officers.[265] However, the vast
majority of the Spanish soldiers were ignorant of the end logic of this
persecution, which, after the Wannsee Conference of January 1942, was
one of systematic extermination.

The Spaniards thus would scarcely have encountered Jews on the
front. In late August and early September of 1941, however, the first
BD volunteers had the opportunity to contemplate the situation of
Jews under Nazi dominion as they came across significant Jewish
communities in the Białystok-Grodno district. This preceded the Final
Solution, in which the Jews were first confined to ghettos and later
deported to extermination camps. In the Baltic cities of Vilnius and
Riga as well as in Germany, Spanish soldiers also encountered Jewish
civilians. Accordingly, some post-war testimonies refer to incidental
encounters of replacement contingents with Jewish civilians who were
cleaning the train stations and tracks in occupied territory in Poland
or the USSR. The astonished Spanish soldiers threw them tobacco and
food from the train.[266]

Grodno, Oshmiany, Vilnius, and Riga

Prominent among all the cities with important Jewish communities that
the Blue Division passed through was Grodno (today Hrodna) in Eastern Poland. On this ethnic frontier, Poles, Byelorussians, Lithuanians,
and Yiddish-speaking Jews lived in precarious harmony. The Jewish
community in Grodno numbered around sixty thousand people and
was solidly positioned in society. There were educational institutions

in Hebrew and Polish, a flourishing cultural life in Yiddish, and active social democrat, conservative, and Zionist organizations. The Jewish middle class tended to be culturally Polishized and had been rather Russophile since the Tsarist empire. They coexisted with their Orthodox and Catholic neighbours, but not always smoothly: the Polish nationalist and conservative elements instigated pogroms in 1935, 1937, and again in September 1939, as war broke out.

In late September 1939, Grodno and its surrounding area were incorporated into the USSR. Though the Jewish community suffered economically from the collectivization imposed by the occupiers, they considered the Soviets a lesser evil, as the communist regime guaranteed them equal opportunities and access to education, public services, and the state administration. This attitude reinforced the conspiracy theory of connivance between Jews and Bolsheviks in the eyes of Catholic Poles.[267]

As in other cities in Byelorussia and the new occupied region known as Ostland, the Grodno Jews began to feel the consequences of Nazi racial policies shortly after the Germans occupied the city in June 1941. During July and August, they endured diverse discriminatory measures by the occupiers, and a good portion of their professional and cultural elites disappeared. At first, they were required to wear an armband with a six-point star, then two Stars of David had to be sewn onto the breast and back of their clothing. Soon after, they were forbidden to walk on the pavement and required to uncover their heads and salute passing German soldiers. Jewish men were put to forced labour. Finally, on 1 November 1941, the Jewish community in Grodno was confined to two ghettos: a "productive" ghetto in the historic centre of the city and an "unproductive" one on the outskirts. Both ghettos were eliminated between November 1942 and March 1943; only three hundred Jews managed to survive.[268]

On the road to the front, the Spaniards camped near Grodno for several days in late August and early September 1941. There, they had occasion to establish contact with Jewish men, women, and children doing heavy labour under the supervision of German troops. What did the BD volunteers see and feel when they first witnessed signs of the Nazi racial segregation policy? Their testimonies from the time described the Jews in an apparently neutral way as dirty, ragged, hungry individuals who approached the columns of soldiers to beg food scraps and looked at them with frightened eyes. However, they were also wary lest the Jewish civilians kill careless soldiers, support the partisans, or poison their water and food. Andrés Gaytan described the days of the trek in March 1942, when they marvelled at the fear of the

Jews and their flighty behaviour, as if discriminatory measures had not been the cause:

> Of course, the Jews are absolutely forbidden to go near the military. When there were Jews in one of the towns where we rested, the difference between their race and the others was obvious. They frighten easily, like whipped dogs, and lower their eyes when they move to let soldiers pass. They are forbidden to enter the canteens or cafés frequented by German soldiers and threatened with the most severe punishment. They meet in certain hovels where you don't hear a single voice. Only the breath of repressed lament steams up their windows.[269]

The same year, Errando Vilar wrote laconically of the Grodno Jews and the warnings of the German command:

> The Jews, with their unmistakable racial features, represent 35 per cent of the inhabitants. You have to defend yourself from them. They wear a yellow star with five points [sic] on their suits. You also have to know where they live. In the cities they have established a neighbourhood, a true Getho [sic], and in the towns there are signs everywhere saying "Hier whonen [sic] Juden" (Jews live here) in the houses where an Israelite family makes its home.[270]

A chronicle published several months later by Private Manuel Nofuentes alluded to his encounter with "multitudinous Jews that the Germans had put white armbands on to identify them" in Poland. The autobiographical notes of Salvador Zanón told how the Spanish volunteers ignored the order to distrust the Jews, while Jiménez Malo de Molina described the multi-ethnic panorama of Grodno and the discriminatory measures applied to the Jewish population, without expressing any value judgement. Despite the snipers, the time in the city had generally been very pleasant for the Spanish volunteers. They openly fraternized with the local girls, whether Jews or Catholics. In the village of Lyda, Guillermo González de Canales observed that Jews were "more refined, but therefore more dangerous."[271] Some mentioned ghettos (real or supposed) as another element in the urban landscape.[272]

The Spanish volunteers could not ignore the persecution of the Jews, but normative judgements are generally absent from their testimonies. Most of them either silenced the issue or accepted it as something relatively normal that the Jewish population had to wear a yellow star on their clothing, or that they could not walk on the pavements. Such silence was not exclusive to the Spaniards, however; it is also typical of the diaries of the Polish Catholic population from that time, who often witnessed with indifference the segregation, deportation, and murder of their fellow citizens.[273]

Descriptions from those moments expressed no explicit sympathy for or even compassion towards the Jews. One soldier noted upon arriving in Grodno that the Jews had "bad intentions, at night they try to shoot the German or Spanish soldiers." Two days later, he acknowledged them as "poor people" who were content to work for the Spaniards in return for food scraps. Occasionally, they were even seen as picturesque humans in a degenerate environment: Ridruejo described his visit to a "filthy, ramshackle photo studio" run by a "fantastic Jewish photographer." More frequently, the image was implicitly negative: the Jews were anti-Polish oriented and allied with the communists; only hostility could be expected from them. Ramón Abadía pointed out the intrinsic danger that motivated the prohibition of dealing with Jews: "they all live badly; when the soldiers show them a mark, they want to take them to sleep or eat." Menéndez Gundín wrote how the Grodno Jews "look at us with all the hatred that the Israelite race holds towards fascism." In May 1942, Revuelta Imaz justified the discriminatory measures of the Germans: the Spaniards themselves were in no position to judge, as they had already "solved" the Jewish question in 1492.[274] Only some insightful observers pointed out that if the Bolsheviks had assigned many local political positions to Jews, it was not because they specially appreciated them, but because they were alien to the Polish ethnic majority and, therefore, more reliable.[275] This was the case in other areas occupied by the USSR, such as the Baltic countries.[276]

Similar scenes were reproduced in Vilnius a few days later. There, however, the Nazi terror machine had progressed further in its spiral of extermination. The German occupiers had killed thirty-seven hundred Jewish men, women, and children in a reprisal in early September 1941. They had established two ghettos on 6 and 7 September, crowding forty-six thousand people into them.[277] Only those with work permits could leave the ghetto, and there were rumours that the inhabitants would be moved to another place. The rumour reached the BD, as Martínez Tessier reveals:

> The Jews are forbidden access to shops and public spaces. They cannot walk on the pavements and they live closed up in the "ghetto" from where they only leave to work if their work has been authorized. They receive a scant food ration and sleep without beds. Most will be evacuated.[278]

Other Spanish combatants heard more precise stories. Ramón Abadía wrote that "the Germans have hundreds of Jewish prisoners whom it is rumoured they plan to shoot the next day."[279]

Some stood out for their explicit, highly articulated anti-Semitism. José Luis Gómez Tello, on his way to the Russian Front, wrote harsh words about the Jews he observed in Riga. He stated that Jewish barbers were happy to "continue skinning Christians." The Jews of Grodno had been "the police and executioners of the G.P.U. [Stalinist political police]," always wearing "large greasy coats" and living in filth, which the Falangist felt must implicitly correspond to some internal spiritual foulness.[280] Having never actually seen a Jewish community before, Gómez Tello sought to satisfy his anti-Semitic curiosity by observing the small Jewish community of Oshmiany, where the BD passed through a few days after leaving the outskirts of Vilnius behind. It was then a small Polish-Byelorussian city of eighty-five hundred inhabitants, almost half of them Jews. The Oshmiany ghetto was eliminated in phases from October 1942 to May 1943, when the remaining 2,830 Jews were deported.[281]

Gómez Tello's descriptions of the ghetto in Oshmiany reveal his contempt for the Jewish "race", and his firm belief in the link between Judaism and communism. The local Jews were "most fabulously rich in their wretchedness," their opulence surpassing even the French Jews. In the ghetto were "streets that were canals of filthiness," occupied for the last three hundred years by the same misery-trafficking Jewish families. The Falangist volunteer saw misery and fear in the homes, but this led him neither to compassion nor to rejection of the anti-Semitic policies that had reduced the Jews to these terrible conditions. Rather, he asserted that the Jews "are so burdened by their sins" that they deserved what they were getting. In fact, "there are some things that I would only tell in a whisper." At some point the Jews would again wander, and then a "storm" from heaven would come upon them. He stated that those who had sparked the Bolshevik Revolution had come from apparently poor places like Oshmiany:

The "ghetto" of Oshmiany, lost on the steppe, would be of no consequence if it weren't for the fact that it is the spearhead of Israel. From here and other such places have come the great figures that caused the revolution and directed the politics of the Kremlin. Everyone knows that Trotsky and Clara Zetkin were Jewish millionaires, and that Lenin's wife was a Jew ... Why not mention the fact that the Jews organized the Societies of "the Godless," and the sacrilegious processions, and the destruction of churches, and the relentless and unending fight of the Communist State against Religion? Is it worth mentioning that the Jews followed as executioners and police when the Soviet regiments marched into Vilnius and Riga and Poland in 1939?

All this led to one conclusion: the USSR had become the preferred instrument of the Jews in their centuries-old desire for expansion and vengeance on Rome and Christianity. "Moscow is Israel's great camp, and Oshmiany is one of its outposts."[282]

However, it was one thing to harbour an anti-Semitic prejudice towards Jews in general, and quite a different matter to see how they were systematically persecuted, even if one was ignorant of the end awaiting the Jews confined to ghettos, where they were visibly mistreated. This gave rise to heated reactions from even the most devout Falangists. In his war diary, Dionisio Ridruejo stated openly that the Jews he had encountered in Poland were "repulsive" to him, and that the measures adopted by the Third Reich were justifiable. Still, he recognized that Spaniards were "offended in our sensibilities" by the Germans, who were exercising a "cold, methodical, impersonal cruelty," according to a predefined plan "that was not a reaction to anything on the ground." In other words, anti-Jewish prejudice was understandable, but not the systematic version of anti-Semitism. Ridruejo showed understanding for spontaneous reprisals, such as "looting with fire and blood," but not the confinement and marking of elements to be excluded from society. Even though Spaniards would feel repulsed by Jews as a collective, "we can feel nothing but solidarity with the individuals." What Ridruejo had observed seemed excessive to him. In fact, as they sought to "associate fully with Germany, the hope of Europe today," the Spanish volunteers found that the greatest obstacles to overcome were their experiences with anti-Semitic measures.[283] Castañón had a similar reaction in Vilnius:

> I see the poor Jewish people walking about with the discriminating stigma of a star. This poor race, which has preached love and now we see them like this, so that we don't mix with them. I do not understand, I do not understand such discrimination and, as a Spaniard, I cannot have any racial complex, I observe them with tenderness though I cannot say anything to them.[284]

Nonetheless, these obstacles were in no way an insurmountable barrier for Spanish fascists. In fact, the traditional anti-Semitism of the volunteers was enhanced by the anti-Jewish feelings of many Poles and Byelorussians who lived in the territories occupied by the Germans. Some Spaniards equated Jews to partisans and saboteurs.[285] Many members of the Polish resistance, from national democrats to left-wing groups, were also ambiguous about Nazi racial politics.[286] Ridruejo wrote that the local Poles hated the Grodno Jews were more than the

Germans did, and with a hatred that "grinds audibly." This would help explain the anti-Semitic measures implemented by the new occupiers.[287]

Some evidence suggests that, during the march towards the front, Spanish volunteers were not averse to contact and dealings with the Jewish population, ignoring the official prohibition. Since the Grodno ghetto was not set up until November 1941, the Spaniards had many chances to meet Jews on the city streets, despite the several restrictions that were imposed on the latter by the Germans since June 1941, including their use as forced labour. Thus, Spaniards could observe for themselves the effects of the segregation measures, though they may not have been aware of the sporadic raids that ended in the random killing of groups of Jews.[288]

The BD soldiers were also surprised that some Jews could make themselves understood in Spanish, as they were immigrants who had returned from Argentina in the prior decade. Some survivors confirmed this impression.[289] Generally, this contact did not involve solidarity or explicitly fraternal motives. Rather, it mainly involved small commercial exchanges: bartering for goods, animals, or tools, and hiring Jews for auxiliary jobs, from shoeshine to cook's aid. Jews preferred to do forced labour for the Spaniards because they were less brutal than the Germans and Lithuanians. Survivor Daniel Klovsky recalled that relations with the Spaniards were particularly warm and friendly. Bronka Klibanski also remembered that the Spanish volunteers "allowed us to eat as much as we wanted and to take food home, so we did not need to steal anything."[290]

Concluding the list would be the demand for sexual favours from Jewish women in exchange for money or food, or the occasional courtship. Apparently, Spanish soldiers demonstrated no prejudice on this matter. Jewish and Catholic women looked attractive to Spaniards, and numerous love affairs were recorded.[291] In fact, German officers in Grodno complained about the Spanish behaviour of fraternizing with the "indigenous" women in general.[292] Even the commander in chief of the German Army Group Centre, Marshal Fedor von Bock, noted in his diary that the Spaniards had "orgies" with Jewish women.[293] Ridruejo wrote that some Spanish soldiers made love with Jewish women in the middle of the Vilnius streets.[294] Manuel Bars recalled years later that "we devoted ourselves to 'playing the bullfighter' with the Jewish girls – the Germans couldn't prevent us from doing that." And Sergeant Manuel Grande stated that he had only been with Jewish women as he travelled through Poland and Byelorussia, and during his stay in Riga.[295] Other testimonies suggest cases of sexual harassment in Grodno by groups of Spanish soldiers.[296]

What did the inhabitants of Grodno think of the Spanish soldiers? Only a few Jewish survivors mention the Spaniards in their memoirs. Alexandre Blumstein (born 1930) wrote that the newcomers "were very strange 'Germans,' outgoing and sociable, visiting civilian homes, walking casually, laughing ... one could see these soldiers joking with Polish and Jewish girls, singing Spanish songs, playing the mandolin. Some appeared to be embarrassed by the bowing and the armbands worn by the Jews." Blumstein considered the presence of the Spanish soldiers as a "refreshing interlude." And their departure left behind "good impressions and a few broken hearts."[297] To Leib Reizer, the Spaniards were not so different to Jews: "All of them were dark and sunburned, had curly hair and Semitic noses, and gesticulated with their hands – just like Jews. There was no trace of the pure Germanic race. The only thing German about them was their uniform."[298] And Felix Zandman stated that the Spaniards showed the Grodno Jews the difference between German anti-Semitism and traditional anti-Judaism:

> As if to illustrate how different the Germans were, one day a Spanish brigade came through the city, sent by Franco to fight against the Soviets. They were in Grodno for about two weeks, and while they were there, the atmosphere changed entirely. They associated with the Jewish men without a sign of dislike or hatred. They went out with the Jewish girls. And when they left, it was even harder to face the barbarians who had taken control of our lives.[299]

Other sources confirm this impression. Moshe Berkowitz, a Jew from Voronovo, a little village on the road between Vilnius and Lyda, wrote that the arrival of the Spanish soldiers meant for the local Jewish community a brief interlude of joy and relax. The *divisionarios* behaved correctly, protected them from mistreatment by the collaborationist police, and shared their food supplies with the Voronovo Jews. Spaniards even had "typically Jewish features."[300] The clandestine organ of the Polish right-wing resistance group *Szaniec* informed in September 1941 of several incidents in Grodno between Spanish volunteers and German soldiers who were guarding Soviet prisoners, as well as friendly contact between Spaniards and the Jewish population.[301] While this does not necessarily mean that the Spanish troops protected the Jews in any systematic way, playing cards with an old Jewish man or walking about with a Jewish girl on your arm was certainly a gesture that communicated humanity, implicit acknowledgment that Jews deserved the same treatment as any other civilian, and veiled defiance of the rules of the occupying German power.

Amazingly, there are no photographs left of these encounters between Spanish soldiers and Jews in Grodno, and only a few Spaniards visited the Warsaw ghetto. BD nurse Montserrat Romeu spent some days there with her expedition companions in September 1941. The tram line took them through the ghetto, where they found a "nightmarish scene." She saw "classic rabbis with their beards and hooked noses, dirty and decrepit," along with well-dressed women who "strolled nonchalantly among that riffraff."[302]

The probability of encounters between Spaniards and Jews was highest in the Baltic countries or Spanish military hospitals in the rear. Spanish sections were opened in the German military hospitals of Königsberg, Riga, and Vilnius. There, Spanish surgeons and nurses employed the local Jewish personnel as auxiliaries, nurses, and translators.[303] They cared for Spanish convalescents and were highly appreciated, as they were usually fluent in several languages, including Spanish.

The Spanish medical personnel seem to have heard about the fate of the Jews, but barely reflected on it in their war diaries. Alfonso Urquijo witnessed "brigades of Jews" in Riga, who shovelled snow and walked "on the road, like beasts." Jewish employees at the Spanish hospital in Vilnius came and went from the ghetto, where they slept, and were escorted by convalescent soldiers who occasionally looked after work detachments of ghetto Jews being subjected to forced labour. Menéndez Gundín, who was posted in the Lithuanian city in May 1942, wrote that the Jews were mistreated and wore "the classic patch on their breast and back." Another Spanish volunteer who spent several weeks in hospital stated years later that on one occasion the Jewish employees were declared indispensable personnel to prevent them being deported in reprisal for an act of resistance. Through the windows, the convalescents could see the "gorgeous" Jewish women who "cleared the snow from the garden paths and flower beds." Many ignored the prohibition of speaking with them. Juan-Eugenio Blanco stated that the Spaniards became "friendly visitors to the ghetto" to court Jewish girls.[304] Other Spanish convalescent soldiers were eyewitnesses to collective reprisals against inmates in the Jewish ghettos, particularly in Vilnius, as expressed in the war diary of private Benigno Cabo in April 1943. Five months later, a group of Spaniards saw another slaughter in the ghetto.[305] Some autobiographical accounts pointed out that in Vilnius, during November–December of 1942, convalescent Spanish soldiers were sometimes ordered by the German command to guard groups of Jews working outside the ghetto.[306]

The same thing occurred in other rearguard towns where there were field hospitals. One convalescent in Porkhov confirmed the presence of "Jewish women cleaning the streets," who were easily distinguished by the "yellow star they wore on their clothes." He limited himself to expressing his displeasure at seeing "those girls, some very young, working like labourers at an endless task."[307]

Protectors or Bystanders?

The attitudes of Blue Division soldiers must be linked to the historiographic debate regarding the role of bystanders: those who did not proactively collaborate with the Nazis but witnessed what was happening and did not intervene to prevent it.[308] Certainly, some testimonies mention isolated but explicit initiatives of Spanish soldiers to *protect* Jewish civilians. These can be understood as unselfish acts that involved risk for the BD volunteers, and went beyond a spontaneous reaction of solidarity or gallantry to obtain sexual favours. According to the Israeli historian Bobe Mendel, a Spanish officer helped a group of Jews to flee from the Riga ghetto and got them to the French-Spanish border. However, they were discovered by the Germans and required to get off the train.[309] Similarly, Swedish-Israeli writer Cordelia Edvarson, who was born in Munich in 1929 as the illegitimate daughter of a Jewish father and Christian mother, received help from a convalescing BD officer in 1943. He agreed to a marriage of convenience so that she might opt for Spanish citizenship and avoid deportation. The plan failed because Cordelia was underage, and the officer was himself too young to legally adopt her. He contacted two Spanish servants who agreed to adopt her, but this also failed. Cordelia ended up in Auschwitz but managed to survive.[310]

The post-1945 idealization of the attitudes of BD volunteers towards the Jews in Eastern Europe has been accepted, with a degree of methodological simple-mindedness, as a recreation of what really happened. The volunteers have even been cast as conscientious *protectors* of the Jews, through the reproduction of diverse anecdotes reflecting occasional defence of Jewish men and women in the face of German abuse.[311] Such generalization is debatable. The volunteers lacked opportunities for cumulative radicalization of attitudes towards the Jews and had scarce occasion to make contact with Jews after October 1941. This meant that Spaniards did not participate in killings or raids, nor were they ordered to do so. Thus, the Spanish volunteers were never involved in the systematic annihilation of the Jewish population, unlike their Romanian counterparts in Bessarabia and the Ukraine, or some Hungarian troops.[312] However, instances of BD members incurring risk and working selflessly and conscientiously over a significant span of time to *protect* Jewish civilians are very infrequent and – unlike the Italians in the Ukraine or in the Balkans – did not provoke any serious confrontation with the Germans.[313]

Apart from sporadic altercations, the Spanish soldiers generally behaved like archetypical bystanders – mere observers – though perhaps rather confused ones at first. "We perceived something abnormal in them; they walked about fearful, flighty, pale, and gaunt."[314] Their more conflicted personal reactions might include incomprehension at the extremity of the measures they were contemplating or Christian compassion for the victims, but no empathy for the Jewish collective.

There is room to ask if the Spanish soldiers had any real possibility of reacting differently. Their conduct resembled that of many other German, Polish, or Baltic citizens.[315] In the brutalizing life and combat conditions of war, German soldiers generally assimilated predisposed patterns of behaviour that were congruent with years of National Socialist indoctrination to accept the tenets of the Nazi war of extermination. This did not correspond so much to fear of their commanders as to a gradual absorption of those ideological patterns in their ethical positions and their decisions. Examples of "protectors of the Jews" within the Wehrmacht are few.[316] In the Blue Division subtle but significant differences can be detected with regard to the Germans. Historiographically, in the current debate between intentionalists and functionalists regarding the interpretation of the Holocaust,[317] the Spanish fascists did not harbour an ideology that favoured systematic segregation or extermination of the Jews. They had no clear sense of what the Jews as a collective entity actually were: a religious faith, an ethnic or cultural group, or a "race." There was even a Hispano-German BD officer with Jewish ancestry: Lieutenant Erich Rose, who died in action in 1943. Part of his family had perished in the Shoah.[318] Moreover, brutalization from life and combat conditions on the front would not have led BD soldiers to adopt genocidal attitudes towards the Jews, as they were virtually non-existent in the areas where the Spaniards were deployed.

However, this does not mean that the Spanish position went much beyond that of typical bystanders. They passed through scenes where the Holocaust was gestating or already under way, though few had the opportunity to witness mass executions. They showed no ill will in word or action to the Jews they encountered, but traditional anti-Jewish prejudice surfaced in their diaries or later reflections. They perceived that something unusual was happening to the Jews, and some reacted spontaneously in favour of the persecuted, though this does not necessarily imply any ongoing protection. In the rearguard hospitals, the Spanish commanders adopted limited measures that qualify as protective. There may have been a BD volunteer somewhere who stood up and risked his life, but most remained silent or spoke only obliquely of what they witnessed.[319]

One example illustrates this attitude. Sergeant Martínez Tessier narrated years later that in Grodno he was overseeing a disciplinary

Fig. 5.5. Members of BD General Staff, among them General Esteban-Infantes, taking part at a Catholic ceremony, headquarters in Pokrovskoe, 1943 (AGA)

platoon of soldiers who had been assigned to do physical labour. A German sergeant appeared with a group of Jews to do the work instead. Martínez Tessier took charge of them and ordered they be given food. A girl told him in broken French of their misery and asked the Spanish corporal to petition the BD command to have a group of Jews assigned to him regularly, to ensure better treatment. He did not. It was one thing to show spontaneous humanity towards the Jews, and quite another to commit oneself to protecting them.[320] Surely, most volunteers could not imagine where such segregation would lead. When they arrived at the front, they were still frivolous about what they had seen in Poland. *Kin*, the cartoonist for the *Hoja de Campaña*, narrated in a humorous column how the Russians, having never tasted green beans, were perplexed by their Castilian name, *judía*, which also means a female Jew. "Too bad: we'll have to put a yellow star on each one, so they'll believe us!"[321]

6 The Last Crusaders of the Nazi New Order (1944–5)

After the dissolution of the Blue Legion in March 1944, Spaniards who wished to continue to fight in the German Army lost their Spanish citizenship. Many veterans of the Blue Division admired the Wehrmacht and believed that the Third Reich represented an authentic example of revolutionary fascism. It could be transplanted to Spain, overcoming the constraints imposed on Falangist influence by monarchists, Catholic traditionalists, and the army. They also felt that the international war against communism that had begun on Spanish soil in 1936 was not yet finished. Altogether, between six hundred and one thousand Spanish volunteers – adventurers, opportunists, fascist fanatics, survivors – chose to remain and joined the German Army after March 1944. Some of them went into regular army units, others joined the Waffen-SS. They were scattered throughout different units and deployed on various fronts. More than half of them died; some of those who returned faced military trials, but they were usually acquitted.

Spaniards in the Wehrmacht and the Waffen-SS (1944–5)

As early as December 1943, more than one hundred Spanish officers and soldiers expressed to the German liaison unit of the Blue Legion that they wished to join the Waffen-SS as volunteers. They also hoped to recruit further volunteers in Spain and were counting on Falange support.[1] Some German diplomats believed that Blue Division veterans could form a collaborationist force in case of a German or Allied invasion of the Iberian Peninsula. The German ambassador in Madrid firmly disapproved of any attempt at conspiring with radical Falangists to set up new units of volunteers for the Eastern Front. However, members of the German embassy in the service of the Abwehr and the Sicherheitsdienst (SD) frequently went their own way.[2]

From early 1944, dozens of Spaniards crossed the Pyrenees on their own initiative. Many of them contacted the German embassy in Madrid. They were given no explicit support, but SD members and consuls usually advised them on how to reach the German recruiting stations close to the French-Spanish border.[3] In mid-January, Hitler was informed about the new volunteers. He enthusiastically outlined the project of forming a "Foreign Legion" composed of Spaniards and other "appropriate human material" from any country. He gave the green light for accepting Spanish volunteers into German Army units.[4] The SD attempted to trigger a clandestine campaign for recruiting Spanish volunteers within Spain and contacted some radical Falangists. British intelligence reports even mentioned that "it is rumoured that plans are afoot to organize a 'Black SS Formation.' These thugs are also to be recruited from returning members of the Blue Division, are to be paid 50 pesetas a day and work closely with the Germans."[5] In early August 1944 the project was abandoned. German diplomats feared a reaction from the Spanish government; they also had no way of preventing sheer adventurers, mercenaries, and particularly British spies from joining. For the German embassy, it was more important to keep Spain neutral than to attract a few hundred volunteers.[6]

In the meantime, several German officers began competing to attract volunteers. On their own initiative or with some help from the Deutsche Arbeitsfront (German Labour Front) office in Madrid, along with Abwehr and SD agents, a number of Spaniards crossed the Pyrenees, often by bribing border policemen or smugglers. Once in France, they were brought to a meeting point close to Lourdes, the "F (Fritz) Special Staff" (*Sonderstab F*), where former members of the German liaison unit with the Blue Division awaited the newcomers. The influx of volunteers was modest: about 150 Spaniards, most of them fanatic fascists, were reported to have reached the F Section between June and July 1944.[7]

Other recruits came from German territory. Deserters from the Blue Legion jumped off the trains taking them back to Spain, sometimes with the help of their officers, and stayed at the Stablack-Süd barracks in Königsberg. Besides these, there were still more than three thousand Spanish foreign workers (*Fremdarbeiter*) in German territory in mid-1944, the last of the civil workers' contingent that Francoist Spain had begun dispatching to Germany in the summer of 1941. Last but not least, at least three thousand Spanish Republican refugees in France had been taken to Germany as forced labourers (*Zwangsarbeiter*). Some of them were active at the Organization Todt, and Hitler himself considered them as potentially reliable allies for shaping a new Spanish fascism.[8] Foreign and conscripted workers joined Wehrmacht and

Fig. 6.1. Two Spanish soldiers take a studio shot before returning to Spain, September 1942 (AA)

Waffen-SS units, often motivated by the desire for better salaries and food rations, especially after Allied bombing raids had deteriorated their working conditions. Others hoped to reach areas that were closer to Spain (Italy or Switzerland), while a handful seem to have sincerely embraced Nazi ideology.[9]

In late February 1944, the OKW concentrated the Spanish clandestine volunteers from the Pyrenees in the La Reine barracks, in Versailles. They were then taken to Königsberg to join their compatriots. The Germans soon realized that the new volunteers were too few in number to set up more than a couple of companies, or at best a battalion. The German high command also hesitated about how to use the volunteers. Since 1941, they had been convinced that Iberians were better guerrilla fighters than disciplined soldiers. The Spaniards were eager to fight the Red Army on the Eastern Front, yet the *Abwehr* preferred to recruit some of them, including the former Blue Division officers Luis García-Valdajos and Miguel Ezquerra, for anti-partisan "special units" deployed in France.[10] Their objective would be to infiltrate French resistance groups, which might include Spanish Republicans in exile. Some volunteers were sent to Southern France, while others joined special operations units facing the US troops in Northern France.

In early September 1944, two companies of Spanish soldiers left Königsberg for the Hollabrunn and Stockerau barracks, near Vienna. Shortly afterwards they were grouped at the Solbad Hall instruction camp (Innsbruck), for training as mountain troops. They were called the Spanish Volunteer Companies (Spanische-Freiwilligen Kompanien) 101 and 102 and given German officers. Coexistence was not easy: regardless of their previous ranks and merits, all Blue Division veterans were reduced to the grade of private. In late August 1944, the 102nd Company was dispatched to German-occupied Slovenia and incorporated alongside French and Italian soldiers into the Brandenburg Division, to fight the Yugoslav partisans. Although partisan sources seem to have overestimated the size of the Spanish units, they were deployed in the north-eastern Zagorje region to protect railway lines and patrol the villages in search of partisans. Some village representatives protested to the Germans and accused the Spaniards of stealing from the civilian population. Meanwhile, the 101st was dispatched to Bukovina to support the German withdrawal from Romania.[11]

In early December 1944, the survivors of both companies returned to Hollabrunn and Stockerau. With some Spanish newcomers, their units were reframed as the Spanish Volunteer Reserve Battalion (Freiwilligen-Ersatz-Bataillon) and the Spanish Training Battalion (Freiwilligen-Ausbildungs-Bataillon) and adhered to a Croatian SS unit. Several Spaniards deserted and there were frequent quarrels with German officers. Apparently, in December 1944 both units were dissolved and placed under the command of the Waffen-SS.[12] Then, as the new year began, the Spanish soldiers were ascribed to the 357th Infantry Division and deployed against the Soviet Army in Northern Hungary and Southern Slovakia. Only a few survived those weeks of intense combat. These were released from their oath to the German Army and given false personal documents that identified them as foreign workers, in hopes they might be able to return to Spain.

A parallel initiative, perhaps triggered by the Abwehr, was undertaken by two Walloon officers, Alphonse Van Horembeke and Paul Kehren, who had fought on the Francoist side in the Spanish Civil War and had also served in the Walloon Legion. Along with García-Valdajos, they turned to Léon Degrelle, who enthusiastically approved their plan. In collaboration with some supervisors of Spanish foreign workers, it was possible for them to recruit 150–200 Spaniards in Germany from among foreign workers, conscripted workers (*Zwangsarbeiter*), and soldiers from the companies stationed in Austria. All of them formed a company of the 28th Walloon Division of the Waffen-SS.[13] However, not all the Spaniards enlisted in the SS went into Degrelle's division. Some were given the option of accompanying several dozen Italians to Northern Italy, where they joined some veterans of the Brandenburg Division who had remained there. One of them was the officer José Ortiz-Fernández, a BD veteran who worked in Berlin as a translator until he was recruited by the *Abwehr* to fight the French resistance. His mixed French-Spanish-Italian unit was later renamed as Einsatzgruppe Pyrenäen, and from July 1944 placed under the command of the SD, as part of Jagdverband Südwest, led by the charismatic SS colonel Otto Skorzeny. However, Ortiz went back to Italy, recruited a hundred Spaniards from among the Spanish workers interned in camps (some of them had been fired due to lack of discipline) near Vienna, and formed a group that also included former Walloons and Brandenburg veterans. By mid-December 1944, this company was incorporated to the *59. Gebirgsjäger-Regiment* of the 24 SS Mountain Division. Until its dissolution in May 1945, these Spanish SS soldiers fought Italian partisans and the advancing US Army.[14]

The Spanish members of the Walloon division took part in the fierce fightings against the Red Army in Pomerania. In March 1945, the surviving Spaniards gathered in Potsdam, where they were ordered to join a new SS unit commanded by Miguel Ezquerra. It relied on the logistic support of the Iberoamerican Institute of Berlin, directed by Wilhelm Faupel. Captain Ezquerra regrouped Spanish veterans from different units, and recruited other volunteers from among Spanish workers and even some Spanish students in Berlin. The Einheit Ezquerra barely amounted to two companies. Many members deserted, devoted themselves to plundering, or attempted to return to Spain with help of the Spanish consulate, which consistently boycotted Ezquerra's activity. Others departed for the Alps, where, instead of joining the "Alpine fortress," they fled into Italy and waited there for a chance to return to Spain. Meanwhile, a few dozen Spaniards remained in Berlin and fought alongside French, Latvian, and Scandinavian volunteers in the Nordland Division until the final collapse of the Reich.

In the final battles of the war, some Spanish survivors were captured by the Soviets, others by the Americans and British. A handful managed to flee disguised as civil workers and reached Paris, Switzerland, and Rome, where they were helped by the Spanish consulates, which provided them passports and return tickets to Spain.[15] When the bulk of the surviving prisoners of war from the Blue Division were released from Soviet captivity in April 1954, there were twenty-one former members of the Waffen-SS among them. More SS veterans returned to Spain in the following years,[16] but most of the Spanish SS soldiers perished in combat, were killed by partisans, or died in Soviet captivity.[17] Others were scattered among German field hospitals, where they suffered from their wounds and the inability to communicate with surgeons and nurses.[18]

Nazis, Radical Falangists, and Survivors

As the Blue Division and the Blue Legion retreated from the Eastern Front, many local and provincial leaders of Falange expressed their disagreement. Some ultra-Falangist intellectuals even sought German support, unsuccessfully. One of them was the historian from the University of Madrid, Santiago Montero Díaz, who upheld the "revolutionary essence" of Spanish fascism. Until February 1945, he made public speeches calling on Francoist Spain to endorse German resistance against the Soviet invasion of Europe to the last. He was confined by the Francoist security forces until the end of the war. However, the Falangist mainstream party remained loyal to Franco, adopted a Catholic and anti-communist profile, and sought to distance itself from European fascisms.[19]

The ideological program for the Spanish volunteers of the Nazi "New Order" was crafted outside Spain by a German, Wilhelm Faupel, and the defrocked Basque priest Martín de Arrizubieta. The latter had been close to the Basque nationalist movement until 1937, then became a Republican refugee in France, joined the French Foreign Legion, and was captured by the Wehrmacht in 1940. Arrizubieta spent four years doing forced labour in different parts of Germany until he was released from captivity August/September 1944, thanks to Faupel's influence. He was taken to Berlin and charged with editing *Enlace* (Liaison), formerly the mouthpiece of the Falange in Germany. It had been purchased by Faupel and given a new, radically anti-Francoist and ultra-Falangist stance. After his time in Spain in 1936–7 as first Hitler's envoy to Franco's headquarters, Faupel was convinced that an authentically "revolutionary" fascist regime in Spain could only be achieved if Falangists were also endorsed by the defeated Republicans and Reds, thereby nationalizing the left. When he again assumed leadership of the Iberoamerican Institute, he also developed a clientelist network among Spaniards and Latin Americans living in Germany. He protected Spanish foreign workers, including Blue Division veterans and *Rotspanier* (Spanish Republican prisoners or conscripted workers).

The "National-Socialist Falangism" developed by Arrizubieta and Faupel, helped by some more radical Falangists and Blue Division veterans, mostly consisted of a radicalized version of the founding tenets of Spanish fascism, seen through the mirror of Nazi "Europeanism," an expression coined in the propaganda of the "European crusade against Bolshevism."[20] Similar affirmations had also been reproduced in the *Hoja de Campaña*, and in the written contributions to the Spanish edition of *Das Junge Europa* by veterans of the Russian Front.[21] The new *Enlace*, however, presented clear distinctions on some points. The first of these was its insistence on something close to biological racism, to endorse a more radical anti-Semitism.[22] Second, it advocated nationalization of the left: the national fracture caused by the Civil War in Spain had to be overcome by a new national revolution that should be secular, abandoning the role of Catholicism. Finally, its radical "socialist" rhetoric was aimed at attracting *Rotspanier* to the new national cause.[23] All these tenets would lead to the overthrow of General Franco once the Third Reich had won the war and should be attained within the framework of the European New Order.[24] To what extent did the last men to fight under the German flag share the Nazi creed? *Enlace* was undoubtedly the most ambitious attempt to shape a kind of "Spanish National Socialism," independent of the Falangist party and of the Franco regime.[25] The last Spanish soldiers to serve the Third Reich may be considered a marginal phenomenon, a band of adventurers, thieves, murderers, and a few desperate war veterans unable to shift back to civilian life. Some authors regard them as the tip of the iceberg, the seeds of collaborationist Nazism within the ranks of Spanish fascism, which could fit the Quisling model. However, there is no reason to suppose that their motivations were essentially different from those that drove other West European volunteers to join the Waffen-SS units, beginning in 1943.[26]

A view from below, centred on letters and accounts from Spanish SS and Wehrmacht volunteers in 1944–5, shows a mixture of motivations. Many of them were fascist adventurers imbued with a zeitgeist of fight against communism. Others were youth hungry for adventure. Many others were simply trying to survive. The members of what is sometimes called the "Ghost Battalion" left few traces of their experiences and even fewer written memoirs, which were usually full of fantasy.

However, there is enough evidence to allow an attempt at creating a collective portrait. Miguel Ezquerra and other veterans who published their memoirs after returning from Soviet captivity depicted their decision to join the final war effort of the Third Reich as simply an extension of the motives that had led them to take up arms in July 1936. They were motivated by anti-communism, the defence of Christian and Western civilization, and loyalty to the original principles of Spanish fascism. All this was also shrouded in a thin layer of generational non-conformism. Many appeared as angry young Falangists, but on returning to Spain several were labelled as "complete gangsters."[27]

A sample of the letters sent by Spanish volunteers in the Wehrmacht and the Waffen-SS between November 1944 and March 1945 may provide some insight as to the motivation of these last combatants. Most of them saw little difference between the Falangist and anti-communist creed they had embraced in 1936 and 1941 and what had motivated their final resolve to fight to the death in German military units. The final-hour volunteers presented themselves as "true" Falangists: loyal keepers of the traditions of early Spanish fascism before it "surrendered" to the power of the Catholic Church and the army. This belief was cloaked in a general appeal to the "destiny of Europe," but they gave no sign of having adopted any National Socialist creed that could be considered mimetic of the German model. Juan M. Pons stated in October 1944 that "we are now within the ranks of the German Army, and ... continue the fight we began for the sake of Spain on the 18th of July 1936," though forced to wage war far from Spain and "under another flag."[28] Wehrmacht soldier José-Luis Ibáñez wrote that the Spaniards loyal to the Falangist legacy were fighting alongside rather than for Germany. Blue Division veteran Manuel Díaz-Tella, when enlisted in the Waffen-SS, stated that he was fighting for all that he had defended in 1936, but also for the sake of "European civilization."[29] Six Spanish guest workers in Vienna manifested their desire to join the Waffen-SS, to carry on "the great task that we initiated in our country on the 18th of July [1936], and that we have not yet given up, which we began in arms and later continued with our work."[30] The Falangist surgeon José-Ignacio Imaz, at that time a medical volunteer at a hospital in Braunschweig, said in December 1944 that while "raising my arm" in a Fascist salute," he saw in the pages of *Enlace* that "there are still true Falangists: long live the Old Guard!"[31]

There were even some isolated cases of former Spanish Republican Army soldiers who, after experiencing French labour camps during 1939–40 and years of forced labour in Germany, expressed that they had become convinced of the "social revolutionary orientation" of National

Socialism. Thus, Adolfo González-Almenara wrote in January 1945 that he saw the Third Reich as the "real Fatherland" of all workers, comparing it with the disappointment he felt upon entering France in 1939.[32]

Faith in the "Europeanist" propaganda of the Third Reich, and a belief in the project of a New Order for the Continent, seemed to be more than just slogans for many Spanish volunteers. This was surely the case for David Gómez, who crossed France with two BD veterans after leaving Spain on 15 August 1944. They managed to reach German territory and were working in a factory in Chemnitz, but also expressed their eagerness to "again wear the grey uniform and take part in the new European order."[33] Similarly, worker Antonio Lucena saluted the editors of *Enlace* with the slogan "Arriba España" and wrote that "the victory of the Great Reich must be a victory for all of us."[34] He was fascinated by "this great German country," along with many other unknown Spaniards who were also members of the Waffen-SS and would fight to the end.[35] Galician volunteer Pedro Portela defined himself as a "young warrior for the new Europe," and signed with "Heil Hitler! Up with Spain! Long Live Germany!"[36]

In other letters, anti-communism appeared to be the main motive for joining the German Army.[37] Lorenzo Ocañas, an ensign who took part in the defence of Berlin and was captured by the Soviets in May 1945, identified images of bombed German towns with "memories of my country," imagining "what Spain would have been like if the Moscow monster had managed to root itself in our soil ... I closed my eyes and saw my own village in flames." Ocañas, who had been a volunteer in the insurgent army of 1936, firmly believed that the cause of 1936–9 on Spanish soil was being defended in a different scenario until 1945. Even after returning from Soviet captivity, he wrote that the war was not over yet.[38]

All these examples suggest that even the most fanatic Spanish soldiers, who fought as volunteers in the Wehrmacht and Waffen-SS during the final desperate months of the war, did it for the same principles that had motivated many of them to fight for Franco eight years earlier. In fact, some of the volunteers who were subscribers to *Enlace* disagreed with its editor, Martín de Arrizubieta, because they found the anti-Catholic and "National Socialist" articles published in the journal too removed from the key element of authentic Spanish tradition, which they felt should permeate any purely Spanish fascism.[39] Beyond adopting a "Europeanist" rhetoric, involvement in the German Army and even the Waffen-SS clearly did not lead these volunteers to embrace a new world view. Their ideological motivations remained true to a few simple but fairly effective key tenets: the fight was between Good and Evil, between God and the Godless, between "civilized Europe" and "Asiatic barbarism." Apart from anti-Semitic rhetoric of religious extraction, there was no biological racism. But the social potential for "National Socialist Falangism" was extremely limited in its final hour. It only reached a few hundred Falangist adventurers, Spanish guest workers in Germany, and some second-rank Falange leaders and intellectuals in Spain. The last Spanish fascists disliked the conservative general who was now chief of state, but their own political survival was tied to Franco's. In the end, this was their main contradiction.

7 War Veterans and Memories from the Eastern Front in Franco's Spain (1942–75)

In November 1941, Spanish officers and soldiers who had served on the Russian Front began returning home: some on leave, some wounded or mutilated, some repatriated as undesirables. The haphazard treatment they received at the Irún train station, after crossing the French border, sparked protest among the returnees.[1] Though many of these difficulties were sorted out, the first great wave of some five hundred returnees in April 1942 received a cold, ill-prepared homecoming from the civil and military authorities.[2] The War Ministry was moved to organize a better welcome for returning soldiers after complaints were heard from German consuls and Falangist leaders. Accordingly, the thirteen hundred men in the second wave of returnees, who stopped in Irún on 24 May, were regaled with military honours before continuing on to a triumphal welcome in Madrid.[3] Throughout the year, discharged, wounded, or disabled veterans received all manner of homage in their hometowns. The National Delegation of Ex-combatants (Delegación Nacional de Excombatientes, DNE), the state organization in charge of war veterans from the Francoist Army, assumed the task of providing for the most pressing needs of those who returned from Russia in a situation of indigence.[4]

German diplomats felt that many returnees were simply abandoned to their fate at the other end of the homecoming parade. The sight of BD veterans, Iron Crosses on their lapels, unemployed or even reduced to begging, moved German consuls to act decisively. In July 1942, the consul in Bilbao interceded with the local authorities to find work for returnees from Russia.[5] However, local employers were not always eager to hire these veterans, knowing that it might stir up resentment in other workers, who were hostile to the Franco regime. The German ambassador, concerned that the honour of the Wehrmacht was being tarnished, insisted to Serrano Suñer that he send BD veterans preferentially to

Germany as civil workers.[6] The Foreign Ministry sent the proposal to the competent authorities, but got no reply. Even so, many, many veterans managed to return to the Third Reich as civil workers.

Beginning in July 1942, the newly established General Office for the Blue Division within the DNE, directed by the Falangist war veteran Luis Nieto, became more actively involved in meeting the needs of those who returned from Russia. The post of BD provincial inspector was created, and Labour Minister José Antonio Girón announced in March 1943 that state companies would assume "tutelage" of workers who had served on the Eastern Front. The German consulates also received instructions to expedite the administrative work involved for BD veterans or their families to receive their wages and pensions. Similarly, they interceded with local businesses and institutions to secure work for unemployed veterans.[7] After 1944, job placement was often channelled through DNE recommendations based on individual petitions. Returnees from Russia were more insistent, as they claimed the benefits associated with being a Francoist ex-combatant later than others, who had already applied for them in 1939–41.[8]

This administrative support proved especially effective for prisoners of war who were repatriated from the USSR in April 1954. Of the 286 who returned, 192 were awarded the title of ex-combatant for having served in the BD, the Blue Legion, or successor units, and for having conducted themselves "respectably" during their years of captivity. On that point, military justice enquiries often became quagmires of uncertainty, beginning with conflicting accusations of collaboration with the Soviets among the prisoners themselves, charges of desertion, or the fact that some of those who had joined German units in 1944–5 had left Spain illegally, or had court martials pending. A pragmatic solution was adopted: almost all BD soldiers were granted the condition of ex-combatant; and fifty-four of the returnees were eligible to receive the title if their officers during captivity could certify their good behaviour. Through the intervention of the DNE and civil governors, almost all those repatriated were given employment.

However, the returned prisoners of war were inconvenient heroes in the Cold War era. They complained that Franco had not welcomed them back in person. Though the War Ministry pushed to award all returnees military distinctions and medals created *ad hoc*, Captain Teodoro Palacios and Captain Gerardo Oroquieta, the two highest-ranking officers among the Spanish captives, waited ten years to be awarded their medals. Palacios was treated as a hero by the regime and was given some control over seven later expeditions to repatriate "war children" from the Soviet Union, until 1959.[9]

Prosopography of the Trajectories of BD Returnees

The Falangist journals hoped that incorporating the returnees from Russia into civilian life would help revitalize Spanish fascism from below, while also serving as a "Europeanizing" and modernizing element in its political culture.[10] The single party found them to be a source of local and provincial leadership; they could reinvigorate its structure in the provinces where ex-combatants were thin on the ground, such as south-east Spain. However, the BD veterans never became an articulated generation that left a uniform impression on the Francoist regime. "Those from Russia" had hoped to become the vanguard of the Falangist creed,[11] and sometimes declared themselves eager to take up arms again to keep Spain from becoming a "socialist" republic. This was an issue in 1946, when external pressure from the Allies threatened to overthrow the Franco regime. A BD veteran from Almadén (Ciudad Real) wrote then that "again we hear the voice of alarm and it orders us to take up combat positions."[12] However, the dictatorship managed to survive without the help of the BD veterans.

After returning from the Russian Front, diversity marked the trajectories of the BD veterans, accurately reflecting the social heterogeneity of the volunteers of 1941–3. Thirty years later, the writer Tomás Salvador observed that any myth the Division had created around itself owed to the internal diversity that had allowed its memory to filter into broad sectors of Spanish post-war society:

> Many men from the Division, who were lieutenants or captains then, are high officers in the Armed Forces today. And not a few of their men have been either ministers or leaders in Spanish politics. A handful of them are writers. But most of them ... belong to the ordinary people. Part of their legend owes to this circumstance.[13]

Returned officers and many NCOs continued their military career, but most soldiers returned to civilian life. Their life trajectories were indeed varied.

Being recognized as an ex-combatant from Russia had advantages when it came to accessing civil service posts. A quota was reserved for BD soldiers – along with Civil War veterans, disabled soldiers, and ex-prisoners in the Republican zone during the Civil War (*excautivos*) – in state civil service exams at all levels. Those who chose to pursue university studies were exempted from tuition and exam fees. In February 1942, the condition of ex-combatant, as described in Law of 25 August 1939, was extended to anyone who had served four months on the Russian Front or had been wounded there.[14] These modest advantages gave BD veterans and other ex-combatants access to low- and medium-skill posts ranging from schoolteachers to chauffeurs. Veterans were also given priority for obtaining petrol station concessions and jobs in public companies.[15]

Within this generally favourable framework for integrating Francoist ex-combatants into the civil service work force, each veteran had to make the best of his own skills and relational networks to reinsert himself into the labour market. Even those who did not benefit directly from these comparative advantages had brought something back from Russia: they had "seen the world." This prepared them for emigration to Latin America and Europe. In fact, several BD veterans returned to Germany as guest workers after 1955.

The prosopographic data available on the political and social provenance of the ruling elite in early Francoism does not corroborate the idea that serving in the Blue Division and the associated prestige of being a veteran of the Eastern Front had any immediate or intrinsic "trampoline" effect on the political careers of the returnees. The BD veterans received some symbolic distinction until 1944, but always as a group within a larger collective of ex-combatants or Old Guard Falangists. However, their presence in these groups tended to be noteworthy. To be a veteran from the Eastern Front was no isolated distinction: it often correlated to a career that began with Falangist membership in the 1930s and had involved imprisonment, combat, a "provisional ensign" post, and duties in some branch of the single party. In addition to loyalty to the Falange, being an Old Guard Falangist, an ex-combatant, an ex-captive, or a member of a FET mass organization were among the accrued "merits" that qualified one for town council membership during the 1940s and 1950s. Former BD volunteers were included in the quota for ex-combatants. BD veterans were not numerically significant in the state political power structures, but they were more relevant in those provinces where there had not been mobilization or recruitment of Francoist combatants until 1938–9.

Returnees from Russia did not even constitute a specifically defined political faction, though those who were organized in associations tended to be aligned with the more fascist sectors of the FET after 1944. Only two ministers in the Franco cabinets were BD veterans: the former commander-in-chief of the Division, General Muñoz Grandes, who became Minister of the Army (1951–7) and Vice-President of the Government (1962–7); and Fernando M. Castiella, professor of international law at Madrid University, who served as an ambassador and Minister of Foreign Affairs (1957–69). In 1968, 11 of the 109 members of the FET National Council (approximately 10 per cent) were former *divisionarios*, and 22 BD veterans were members of the Francoist Cortes or legislative chamber (4 per cent of its 530 members). These were small proportions, but larger than the generational cohort of BD veterans in Spanish society, which amounted to less than 2 per cent, or even the collective of Francoist ex-combatants of the Civil War.[16] When General Franco died in November 1975, there were two BD veterans – General Carlos Fernández Vallespín and General Ángel Salas Larrazábal – among the sixteen members of the Council of the Realm (Consejo del Reino), the group tasked with selecting the candidates for head of government and proposing them to King Juan Carlos I.

BD veterans were more plentiful at the second level of state administration. They were especially over-represented among the directors of the Falangist Vertical Syndicate, where Old Shirts abounded. From 1942 to 1951, 10.5 per cent (19 of 181) of the provincial syndicate bosses were BD veterans.[17] Percentages were similarly higher for provincial leading figures of the FET and other intermediate posts in the administrative apparatus of the regime. The relative youth of the veterans from Russia, in relation to Civil War veterans, made their presence less notable at first in the municipal administrations of the provincial capitals, provincial councils, or among the Falangists who eventually held posts as civil governors.[18] In the 1950s, the participation of former BD members became more visible: at least twenty BD veterans became mayors in small and mid-sized towns. Though present throughout Spain, these veterans were more abundant in the southeastern provinces. Significantly more veterans from Russia were elected as town council members during Francoism, but the exact numbers are difficult to ascertain.[19]

There is a separate chapter in the story for the generation of army officers who finished their training at the General Military Academy between 1939 and 1942 and served in the BD. The Eastern Front was one of their first assignments, and many chose it as a way of acquiring war merits. Some 166 high-ranking officers passed through the BD, all of them career military men. Many had begun their trajectory in the colonial wars in Morocco, others in the Civil War. Additionally, 2,030 lower-ranking officers and as many as 4,083 NCOs had been assigned to the Russian Front, and many acquired a certain prestige among their colleagues for having served in the Wehrmacht. Medals were earned, at least 21 officers, 34 non-commissioned officers, and 2 soldiers were promoted to a higher rank, and at least 218 officers were promoted on the field.[20] This enabled them to climb the military ladder and ascend to positions of high command relatively more quickly than cohorts that had remained in Spain.

Yet, the *esprit de corps* of the veterans from the Russian Front and their generational solidarity within the Spanish Army did not reach the degree of cohesion that had characterized the "Africanists" two decades earlier, those who had fought at the colonial war in Morocco. Their time in Russia had left a meaningful but thin lustre on their service records, affording them promotions, medals, and experiences. According to the late general Alfonso Armada, "it was as though we had completed a doctorate." This informal criterion barely found room in the army for creating specific associations or even for cultivating lasting group bonds.[21] A few officers collaborated with veterans' associations, which were mainly promoted by BD veterans returned to civilian life.

Thanks to the accumulated promotions for war merits, during the years of the Spanish transition to democracy (1975–82) a significant percentage of division and brigade generals in the Spanish Army had formerly served in Russia. Between 1962 and 1983, seven commanders-in-chief of the Civil Guard – the militarized rural police corps – along with six generals and eight colonels were former BD officers. At least 300 generals in diverse branches of the Armed Forces (2 captain generals, 66 lieutenant generals, 62 division generals, 170 brigade generals) had also fought on the Eastern front.[22] However, this did not necessarily determine political alignments. While BD veterans were plentiful among the military top brass, which mainly identified with maintaining Francoist values, not all of them were hardliners. In fact, the military commanders who played central roles in the failed coup d'état on 23 February 1981, including the perpetrators – General Jaime Miláns del Bosch and General Alfonso Armada – and those who remained loyal to King Juan Carlos I and democracy – Generals Aramburu Topete, José Gabeiras, and Quintana Lacaci – had one thing in common: the Iron Cross, awarded for service on the Russian Front. Generals Luis Álvarez Rodríguez and Federico Gómez de Salazar, who presided at the court martial of the conspirators, were also veterans from Russia. They had all shared a common past experience but were on very different roads four decades later.

Agents of Memory: Blue Division Veterans' Associations

Compared to veterans' brotherhoods of the German Army and its allies,[23] or even those of Francoist ex-combatants, the origin of BD veterans' associations was closely linked to the cult to the fallen. In January 1942, the German embassy proposed a project to organize an association for returnees from the Russian Front.[24] However, the suggestion failed due to lack of interest on the part of the Spanish government.

The army feared that the veterans might promote radical Falangism and complicate diplomatic relations with the Allies, or that they could serve as a Trojan horse for the Third Reich. However, the Spanish police attributed much more relevance to these groups than was warranted.[25]

In late 1942, the German embassy became sensitive to the petitions of the families of Spaniards fallen in Russia. The consuls often awarded Iron Crosses to family members of the dead, and even sought German pensions for them.[26] In 1943, the Franco regime began to make it complicated for families of the fallen and BD veterans to receive individualized attention from German diplomats; in June 1944, Ambassador Hans-Heinrich Dieckhoff lamented that he was unable to send propaganda to the returnees, as he had no access to their mailing lists.[27]

Decisive impetus initially came through the coordination of wives and daughters of the volunteers, especially those linked to the Falange, in the summer of 1941. Solidarity increased as news of the first battles arrived in mid-October and BD soldiers began to send greetings via Radio Berlin. The fiancée of a Falangist combatant described these gatherings, which took place after Mass and Rosaries:

> Here there are veritable circles for listening to Radio Berlin, and groups of mothers and sisters form in homes with radio reception … we discuss it, comment on it, sometimes we are envied and other times envious, depending on if we have received a letter or not.[28]

Girlfriends, sisters, and relatives wrote to encourage the combatants in far-off Russia, their anxiety increasing when the radio reported on the Volkhov battles or when there were delays in receiving letters from the volunteers.[29] The mothers, girlfriends, and relatives of those who died in Russia often met after Masses for the volunteers in four Madrid churches. In June 1942, the idea arose to create a brotherhood of ex-combatants to coordinate administrative work related to pensions and subsidies for veterans and their families.[30] Spanish Army reticence explains why the families of the fallen again took the initiative. In 1943, the Brotherhood of Families of the Fallen of the Blue Division (Hermandad de Familiares de Caídos de la División Azul) was formed, with a chapel in a FET headquarter where a replica of a sculpture by Víctor de los Ríos, a religious carver, was installed. There, relatives could attend daily Mass for the fallen, and for BD prisoners of war in the Soviet Union later on. Gradually, symbolic dates were established in memory of the BD, such as All Saints' Day (2 November) and 13 July, the anniversary of the 1941 departure of the largest volunteer expedition. The initiative soon spread to other cities. In late 1942, an analogous

Fig. 7.1. Home of the Blue Division, Madrid, 1943 (AGA)

brotherhood requested the patronage of a local patron saint from the Bishop of Málaga. In June 1943, the foundation for the Pious Memory of the Fallen in the Glorious Blue Division was established in Valencia.[31]

In late 1944, the Spanish government ordered the closure of the Blue Division Home, but the chapel was moved to the headquarters of the Provincial Delegation of Ex-Combatants. Two years later, it became the Brotherhood of the Families of the Fallen of the Blue Division (Hermandad de Familiares de Caídos de la División Azul), with activities limited to periodical religious acts and the celebration of Mother's Day on 8 December. In 1953, it became the Brotherhood of the Families of the Fallen, Prisoners, and Ex-Combatants of the Blue Division, and began negotiations that ultimately led to the repatriation of most prisoners from Soviet camps in April 1954, thanks to the mediation of the Red Cross. Hundreds of veterans welcomed home the released prisoners at the port of Barcelona, giving the act high emotional impact and increasing the visibility of the collective memory of the Blue Division.[32]

The authentic "transmission agents" of the official memory of the victors of 1939, the ex-combatant associations from the Civil War (National Ex-Combatants Brotherhood, National Brotherhood of Provisional Ensigns), worked in coordination with the DNE. The burgeoning BD brotherhoods fit within this structure, but with some singularities. First, many of them formed on the spontaneous initiatives of groups of BD veterans. Second, the necessity of adapting to the Cold War context required the regime to downplay its attention to a unit that had fought in the Wehrmacht. Therefore, the dictatorship gave scant official support to the BD brotherhoods.[33] This became evident in May of 1959, when BD veterans held a reception for a delegation of the Condor Legion Veterans' Association, which had been founded three years earlier. During a religious offering in Barcelona, some shouted pro-Nazi slogans, which proved awkward for the West German embassy.[34] However, support for commemorative acts of the brotherhoods in some provinces revealed complicity with provincial leaders of the FET, civil and military governors, and even town mayors. Thus, the Alicante brotherhood received donations from the provincial government and several municipalities.

Some ex-BD members maintained strong informal links with former comrades and met occasionally to commemorate specific dates.[35] This also found expression in the spontaneous foundation of brotherhoods in several cities, sometimes with no organic link to the DNE or the Falange. In Alava, a provincial brotherhood was already organized by February of 1954. Subsequently, the Alava group proposed the creation of brotherhoods in all the provinces to the National Delegate of Ex-Combatants and BD veteran Tomás García Rebull. In 1954–5, 26 more brotherhoods sprang up in Madrid, Barcelona, and other provincial capitals. Apart from the exceptionally large Asturian brotherhood, membership ranged from 45 to 150 members spread mainly throughout Castile, Andalusia, and the south-east.

In June 1956, 250 BD veterans representing 29 local groups converged in Valencia for the first National Conference of Blue Division Brotherhoods, presided by García Rebull.[36] One of its primary objectives was to create a National Federation of BD brotherhoods. Conference speakers exuded anti-communism, Catholicism, and loyalty to the founding tenets of Francoism. They also called for fulfilment of the "revolutionary" tenets of the Falange, which included a "fair redistribution of national income" as well as a "socio-economic policy that avoided excessive differences among workers," the gradual dismantling of "pressure groups, cartels, trusts, and monopolies," and the vague goal of "transforming the entrepreneurial structure and concept of property." Achieving these objectives while avoiding poverty in the lower classes – which might

LA CRUZ DE HIERRO A LA MADRE DE UN HEROICO CAIDO DE LA DIVISION AZUL

La Cruz de Hierro, la condecoración alemana representativa de la abnegación; la cinta y el diploma, concedidos a su hijo por el Führer Canciller de Alemania, le ha sido impuesta, en una emocionante ceremonia, a doña Aurora Vega Lozano, madre del heroico caído de la División Azul, cabo Nemesio García Vega, muerto gloriosamente en el frente ruso luchando por las grandes ideas de la civilización occidental y por el espíritu de España.   Foto Contreras.

Fig. 7.2. Mother of Corporal Nemesio García Vega, decorated with the Iron Cross awarded posthumously to her son (*Informaciones*, 24 March 1942)

open the door to communism – required a vague "reform" of the dictatorship, revitalization of the Falange, and allowing some kind of "orderly" freedom of speech. They also petitioned to establish quotas for BD veterans to access civil service posts and subsidized housing.[37]

The number of brotherhoods continued to increase after the first conference. The first National Council of BD Brotherhoods held in Sobrón (Álava) in October of 1958 hosted forty-two delegates from twenty-three local and provincial brotherhoods. The geographical distribution loosely coincided with provinces under Republican control until March

Fig. 7.3. BD veterans' lunch in Calella (Barcelona), early 1950s (Calella City Archive)

1939; there, BD veterans were more visible in the absence of other Francoist ex-combatants of the Civil War.[38] The corporative and mutualistic nature of the organization was reinforced and they agreed to invite the Ministry of Foreign Affairs to oversee dealings with the Federal Republic of Germany, to procure German war pensions for mutilated veterans or families of the fallen.[39] Yet, the National Brotherhood of the Blue Division was not officially established until the Second National Council, which took place in Alicante in June 1959. Even with a national structure and its monthly journal *Hermandad* (begun in 1955), the provincial brotherhoods always maintained ample autonomy. They published bulletins that were seldom regular, with the exception of the monthly magazine *Blau División*, begun in 1957 by the Alicante brotherhood.[40]

The brotherhoods also demonstrated their convening power in October 1961, when an act of homage to Our Lady of the Pillar (Virgen del Pilar) in Zaragoza was organized for the twentieth anniversary of their baptism by fire on the Volkhov Front. A mantle with the BD emblem was placed on the Virgin, to be worn every 10 February on the anniversary of the Battle of Krasnyi Bor. Some four thousand ex-BD soldiers and their relatives attended, along with several FET leaders.[41] The vitality of the BD brotherhoods was reflected in their capacity to bring together a significant portion of the veterans in each province. Moreover, the social profile of BD brotherhoods was less middle-class coloured than that of other Francoist ex-combatant associations. Thus, the Santander brotherhood was founded in 1955 and boasted 186 members a year later, representing some 15–17 per cent of living BD veterans in that province. The middle and lower-middle strata were somewhat over-represented in the social origins of the 159 members who listed their profession, which accurately reflected the diversity of BD veterans: 54 (34 per cent) were employees, non-manual workers, and civil servants; 43 (27 per cent) were skilled labourers; 35 (22 per cent) were unskilled workers or day labourers; 10 (6.28 per cent) were members of the military; and 2 (1.35 per cent) were farmers.[42]

Except for the powerful Asturian association, most brotherhoods represented 15–33 per cent of BD returnees.[43] The president of the Albacete brotherhood claimed that this entity had gathered as many as 200 (38.1 per cent) of the 515 returnees to the province. The Guipúzcoa brotherhood, set up in 1961, had 120 members, which represented around 23 per cent of the returnees of the province. The Madrid brotherhood claimed two thousand members in 1958.[44] Other indicators place the influence of the brotherhoods at more modest levels. The Barcelona brotherhood distributed 2,940 copies of its bulletin (*Hermandad*) throughout Spain in December 1958, which corresponded to 7–8 per cent of all BD returnees.[45] The solid core of brotherhoods was much smaller: from 1957 to 2008 a total of 870 veterans were mentioned by name in *Blau División* as contributors, subscribers, associates, or simply references. This represented just over 2 per cent of the returned veterans.

Local brotherhoods were established on the initiative of BD veterans, who were generally well connected with local and provincial authorities, or by military garrison officers who had served on the Russian Front. All associations followed similar operational patterns: some published bulletins, several had social centres, and they dedicated part of their activities to achieving practical goals, such as interceding to obtain pensions for families of the fallen, seeking state subsidies for disabled veterans, and procuring subsidies for those in poverty.[46] They functioned as both mutual aid associations and informal employment agencies. They also mediated to secure access to union housing for the neediest, or to specific services such as participation in the state-sponsored leisure and recreational organizations.[47]

Solidarity among veterans also extended beyond associative spheres. Ties were maintained through informal social gatherings (*tertulias*) that

Fig. 7.4. Two returnees from Soviet captivity arrive at their hometown, April 1954 (AA)

brought together officers, surgeons, and simple soldiers. Their intense camaraderie was infused with bitter disenchantment: the BD were the "accursed heroes," or "a generation misunderstood today."[48] Many veterans knew that they could refer to these sentimental bonds when seeking employment or recommendations.[49]

The brotherhoods also assumed the task of maintaining the BD memory through a cult to the fallen. It was sustained by commemorative acts and Masses on specific dates, offerings at Civil War monuments, and collective participation in parades and commemorations of the regime. BD veterans also cultivated their own commemorative liturgy. On chosen anniversaries, they celebrated the memory of the departure of the "first division" in early July (1941), the arrival at the front on 12 October (1941), and especially the Battle of Krasnyi Bor (1943) on 10 February. The symbolic role of the families of the fallen remained significant, and specific celebrations were held for the mothers of fallen soldiers. Every year, on one of these three dates, a Catholic Mass would be said in several cities for the souls of those who are still "in Russia," followed by speeches. Wherever there was a close relationship with civil or military authorities, these acts included military reviews. However, in most provinces the local authorities gradually stopped attending.[50]

The veterans from the Russian campaign often complained about the scant visibility of the memory of their fallen comrades. No mausoleum equivalent to the majestic Valley of the Fallen, inaugurated in 1959, had been built for those who "are still in Russia." The monument to the Blue Division in Albacete, built in 1958 and now removed, was the only place where floral offerings were made on specific dates.[51] However, the number of streets and squares dedicated to the BD increased significantly during the late Franco years. Several towns, including Cuenca, Vitoria, Gijon, and Pontevedra, recognized all veterans as "adoptive sons" and named streets after the Blue Division in the early 1960s. Barcelona followed suit in 1966. Streets were named for General Muñoz Grandes in four cities, while squares and streets were named for local fallen heroes and BD officers in their hometowns. Madrid also inaugurated a street dedicated to the "fallen soldiers of the Blue Division" in 1958.[52] These local initiatives could be partly understood as a reaction by many Falange leaders who saw the political influence of the single party decreasing within the dictatorship. José M. Martínez-Val, a second head of the Falange in the Ciudad Real province and himself a BD veteran, wrote in 1968 that it should be compulsory to shout in the faces of the many former comrades who had politically deserted that the "Blue Division was no mistake at all." To him, the Division had been an entirely "national and Falangist" endeavour.[53]

Nonetheless, the BD memory in street names was significantly less present than the memory of the winners of the Civil War. Streets dedicated to 18 July, Franco, José Antonio Primo de Rivera, and several insurgent generals were far more frequent than urban reminders of the Blue Division. After the first democratic local elections in April 1979, their numbers decreased. In 1986, however, at least nineteen cities of more than fifty thousand inhabitants still had street names commemorating either the Blue Division, its fallen, or its "heroes."[54] They were still there in numerous towns at the beginning of the twenty-first century. Maintaining street names in memory of a unit of foreign volunteers in the Wehrmacht is truly exceptional in Western Europe. However, these constitute a trifling percentage of the Francoist symbols and places of memory that endured beyond 1978.[55]

The Blue Division Post-war Narrative

In addition to the publicity-oriented activity of the brotherhoods, an important percentage of the autobiographical narratives or BD-based fiction emerged from publishing houses linked to radical Falangist circles. Two such publishers were Caralt and Acervo, owned by

Fig. 7.5. Inauguration of calle División Azul (Blue Division street), Vitoria, 1961 (City Archive of Vitoria)

the Falangist Barcelona city councillor Luis de Caralt and the BD ex-combatant José Llorens Borrás, respectively. Borrás maintained close contact with several European fascist exiles in Spain (Horia Sima, Otto Skorzeny, Léon Degrelle) and published anti-Semitic and neo-Nazi material in the 1960s.[56]

In 1944, the Francoist regime began to downplay the memory of the BD. In the new rhetoric, dispatching the Blue Division to the Eastern Front had been a clever manoeuvre to appease Hitler while keeping Spain out of the conflict: a purely anti-communist enterprise and precursor to the Cold War. This diluted the Germanophilia of many BD members. From 1943 on, the change of direction began to surface subtly in some newspapers and was even defended by several BD veterans. Federico Izquierdo wrote in March 1945 that Franco had been right not to associate himself with Axis political formulas. "A handful of Spaniards, representatives of a national anti-communist feeling" had gone to Russia four years earlier, to carry on the fight of 1936, not out of "friendship with Germany."[57] Trinidad Nieto described reasons for celebrating the Allied triumph but lamented the possible "extermination" of the German people at Soviet hands. European civilization had been defeated by "abyssal Asia" and the United States.[58] Fifteen years later, Minister Fernando M. Castiella presented the Blue Division at Georgetown University as an eminently anti-communist enterprise, the price Spain had paid for its neutrality and a precursor to what the Cold War would represent.[59]

The BD memory is one of defeated winners; they failed to build an authentically fascist Spain and were defeated by the Soviet enemy, alongside their European allies. However, the BD is also important to the professional memory of the military establishment. There, a benign and idealistic interpretation of the Blue Division persisted until the end of the twentieth century. The BD experience has generated at least 150 memoirs, narratives, or biographical novels since 1942, with greatest intensity from 1954 to 1962, thanks to the public visibility that accompanied the return from the USSR of the prisoners of war aboard the ship *Semiramis* in April 1954. Officers Teodoro Palacios and Gerardo Oroquieta were exalted by the regime as heroic defenders of Christianity; they also emphasized the performance of the military over that of the Falangists, who saw their role in the Blue Division minimized.[60] Their long captivity inspired novels and plays focused on the suffering of their families in Spain.[61] Interest spiked with the fall of communist regimes in the early 1990s and again in the early 2000s, coinciding with a subliminal war of memory with the Spanish political left, which had launched the campaign for the recovery of the historical memory of the victims of Francoist repression.[62] To these we can add hundreds of short autobiographical or fictional stories and some cinematographic recreations, especially in the 1950s, when the BD occupied a more central or lateral position in the plot.[63]

Why was writing on this topic so prolific? Mainly due to the high percentage of survivors. Almost 90 per cent of the BD volunteers lived to tell the tale, because they were placed on a mostly stable front and withdrawn prior to the great Soviet offensives of 1944. The BD memory was never banned from the Spanish public sphere, and a considerable proportion of the volunteers were university students, intellectuals, or adept writers such as Ridruejo, Tomás Salvador, Castañón, and Rodrigo Royo, or journalists like Gómez-Tello and Trinidad Nieto, along with many others who stood out in the arts or sciences. The context was favourable for autobiographies, mainly those of educated Falangist volunteers. Their works constitute a subgenre in Spanish fascist literature. By 1975, a few BD-themed novels had also been published outside of Spain, though they departed from the usual tones.[64]

The BD memory underwent several renovations.[65] Though it was bothersome for Francoism between 1945 and 1950, it gradually adapted to the Cold War context. Spain was presented as a Catholic country and a forerunner in the fight against communism. A prime example of this was the autobiography of a BD veteran who was then a worker in Germany, Alberto de Lavedán. In April 1945, he escaped to Prague, where he witnessed the uprising against the Germans and the arrival of the Red Army. He identified with the Czech people as martyrs, emphasizing that the Blue Division had clearly pointed out the enemy when they confronted "the Soviet hordes ... with their red flags, their rapes, pillaging, mass murders." In his view, thousands of Spaniards had foreseen in 1936 "the tragic unrest of the current, dynamically aggressive COLD WAR that the Soviet Union is waging against the Christian world."[66] Thus, the leitmotif of BD literature consisted of highlighting how Spaniards fought *with* Germany, but not *for* the Third Reich, against a common enemy in the name of Western civilization and Catholic values, as a continuation of the Civil War and as a prelude to the Cold War.

The death of Franco provided non-conformist Falangists with a new motivation: to vindicate the legacy of the Blue Division as an example for new generations of neo-fascists and nostalgists, who were disoriented by the consolidation of democracy and their own electoral weakness. Many of them searched for a future in the past. New editions of memoirs of war veterans from the Eastern Front were now encouraged by marginal publishers such as García Hispán, which was owned by an ex-member of the neo-Nazi group CEDADE, and young propagandists aligned with revisionist tenets of the Holocaust or linked with attempts to renovate the ideology of Spanish fascism.[67] However, during the transition to democracy, interest increased in the plurality of motivations among the BD volunteers, who appeared as everything from anti-Francoists to adventurers of the Legion.[68]

The demise of the Soviet block and the USSR in 1991 helped to revive the interest of many ex-BD combatants in publishing their memoirs. This momentary resurgence of public interest in the Blue Division coincided with the intensification of the 2002–4 campaign in diverse sectors of Spanish civil society to recover from oblivion the memory of the defeated of 1939: it was the "return of historical memory." The social-democratic government of Rodríguez Zapatero (2004–11) partially assumed this task, provoking a parallel counter-offensive from intellectuals and writers linked to the most conservative sectors of the Popular Party (PP). They were joined by extreme right circles, traditional military historians, and a persistent, ultra-Catholic historiography, all of which consider the Blue Division as a sensitive touchstone of an alternative *historical memory*, that of the winners in the Civil War.[69]

Clichés in Blue Division Memory

The circumstances described here have conditioned the social frames of the collective and individual memory of the Blue Division.[70] The BD narrative mixes a performative reconstruction with factual reflections of events, combining remembering and forgetting. A set of narrative strategies, paratextual recourses, memoirs, novels, and films has forged a performative narrative about the individual experience of the BD volunteers that has been generalized to the whole Division as a collective. This interpretation has spread as the authentic *narrative* of the Blue Division: it became hegemonic during Francoism but also spread through the army and much of the Spanish public sphere after 1975.[71]

The main features of that narrative resemble those of the memorialistic works of German, Italian, or other soldiers in the Eastern Front. In broad strokes, their legitimizing discourse is also analogous to what was promoted by Wehrmacht veteran associations: Europeanism, anti-communism detached from Nazi expansionism, distancing from all complicity with the war crimes committed exclusively by SS units[72] What, then, were the most distinctive elements of the BD narrative on the Eastern Front? They can be summarized in four points.

a) *I had a disillusioned comrade.* Many narratives reveal a combination of rubber-stamp Falangist idealism and acrid disappointment, born

of the contrast between the virile, interclass environment of the
trenches and the hypocritical materialism of civilian life.[73] There was
also political disenchantment. The Francoist regime and its oppor-
tunist leaders had failed after 1945 to honour the sacrifice of the *divisionarios*. Many veterans presented themselves as the last Falangists,
holding high the flag of a pending revolution, only to become "out-
laws and outcasts." They were non-conformists, but unrepentant.
Ridruejo, Castañón, or Luis Romero evolved towards anti-Francoist
and democratic positions, yet they always maintained that the Blue
Division had represented the idealism of a "hypothetical Falange."
They were young men of "good will" who believed they were participating in "a movement to regenerate the country, as much in
terms of national empowerment as social reform," while the "real
Falange" had become "an essentially conservative power."[74]

b) *Morning stars and bloodied snow.* Most memoirs about the BD also
feature a striking realism, manifested in descriptions of the hardships of the war and a penchant for faithful descriptions of the
reality of combat and the trenches.[75] This had already appeared
in the literature on the Spanish Civil War or the Colonial War in
Northern Morocco, and coexisted with a rhetorical lyricism characteristic of the Falangist literary style. The result is a peculiar
mix of barracks language and beautiful literary images that evoke
the snowy Russian landscape in mystic terms or contemplate as
"morning stars" (*luceros*) the comrades who fell on starry nights
while on guard duty, a metaphor reminiscent of the Falangist anthem "Cara al sol."

c) *Cleaner than the "clean Wehrmacht."* As occurred with autobiographical testimonies of German and Italian combatants,[76] some taboos
were rarely broken. The "myth of the Wehrmacht" that was generated in the post-war public opinion of West Germany insisted
that the regular troops had served honourably, while SS and other
corps were exclusively responsible for the atrocities and crimes
against the civilian population.[77] This paradigm is reflected in
Spanish memorialistic works, with one nuance: the Blue Division
had behaved even more irreproachably. They distanced themselves
from the SS in general, though somewhat less from the Waffen-SS,
but their post-war discourse was strikingly similar to that of the
veterans of that organization.[78] What were those silences about?
Generally, about mistreatment of civilians, executions of prisoners
or commissars, desertions, abuse of civilian women, homosexual
relations between soldiers, the fight against partisans, and the Jewish question.

d) *A game of mirrors.* One extraordinary feature of BD memorialistic works is their recurrent appeal to national stereotypes: the delight in recreating the reactions of the *authentic* Spaniard through contrast between his idealized traits – southern, cheerful, gallant, and generous – and the collective psychology of the other peoples they encountered.[79] The numerous anecdotes thus acquire implicit meanings. They revealed the virtues of the Spanish race to the world: the "brown soldier, with a scent of carnations and the glory of the sun in his pupils" went to Russia to "mix on the hard ice of the damned steppe his hot blood full of passion and generosity with the blood of the German comrade."[80] This capacity for adapting to unforeseen circumstances in a hostile environment became a paramount expression of the qualities that had enabled Spaniards to conquer empires in times past:

> The scene of a Spanish *guripa* driving a sleigh, with his coat unbuttoned and hat to one side, is one of the most typical on the front ... These Andalusian comrades look as though they had been doing it all their lives though surely they had never seen a snowflake in their hometown ... Today the German comrades understand how a few handfuls of Spaniards, lost on a vast continent, managed to deeply implant their race, language, and religion.[81]

In combat, however, these jovial young men from the South amazed the Germans with their innate disregard for death. They were "Quixotes with machine guns", who, unlike cold German performance, fought according to their ancient *instinct*, "flirting with death."[82] This self-image had two additional functions. It turned frustration into symbolic victory: "General Winter" had proved too much for Napoleon, but not for Spanish mettle.[83] It also allowed them to contrast Spaniards and the rigid Germans who looked down on their exotic comrades. Therefore, the *divisionarios* became pseudo-victims of the Third Reich in the end.

An Unpleasant Topic: The Holocaust

With the Nuremberg trials and the Allies' efforts to broadcast the dimensions of Nazi racial extermination policies, the BD ex-combatants could not remain indifferent to this matter after May 1945. At first, they denied the existence of the Holocaust, at least as it was revealed to international public opinion beginning in 1945. There were attempts to dilute it through revisionist arguments that emphasized the crimes and rapes committed by the Red Army, or mass deaths from indiscriminate air raids on German cities. Even so, the Spanish veterans felt compelled to somehow justify their presence in the German Army. The Blue Division narrative began to distance itself from Nazi racism, partly through a selective accumulation of anecdotes that illustrated their disaffection with German anti-Semitism. They still held no sympathy for Jews as a collective and much less for the new state of Israel; its emergence was criticized in Falange publications.[84]

In the veterans' accounts published after 1945, the Jewish question was generally avoided. Some mention it superficially, pointing out that the Spanish soldiers had no knowledge of the Shoah, which was also the position of the Franco regime until mid-1944. In 1945, Antonio J. Hernández-Navarro presented the Jews of Grodno derogatorily in his autobiographic novel *Ida y vuelta* (Return trip). He described them as "unkempt and humble, entering their dark and mysterious houses with the humiliation and grime of centuries, like ants in an anthill; piling up spite and money, indifferent to the feet that tread upon them." These "scared and filthy Jews" were said to have caused a "slimy feeling" in the Spanish volunteers. The protagonist of this story, a Falangist from Madrid, is convinced that despite their obsequiousness, the Jews will cling to their grudges for generations, thirsting for vengeance on the goyim. They may even have caused the fall of the Third Reich:

> Today's Jews are as they were a thousand years ago and will be the same in another thousand years if the world lasts that long. And if the last one is victorious, all those who preceded him will rub their hands with glee in hell ... if the last brother of their race rips the skin off the last Christian.[85]

In his autobiographic novel *4 infantes 3 luceros* (4 infantry soldiers 3 morning stars), written in 1942, Jaime Farré recalled the encounter with Jewish girls in Grodno. Later, the protagonist of the novel, a Spanish Falangist, meets some Jewish girls in Riga, who tell him of the fate of their parents. When he finds a German sergeant who speaks Spanish, he asks why the Jews were persecuted. His partner explains to him the reason: the Jews were behind all conspiracies against Germany, and as a homeless people were opposed to patriotism. Afterwards he also describes how some BD volunteers came to hate a Baltic Jew who confessed to having fought with the International Brigades. At the end, the Spaniards' sense of distance from Nazi anti-Semitism was softened by the fact that they also shared the theory of a Jewish-Bolshevik conspiracy.[86]

From 1954 on, the Jewish question was approached from a more nuanced angle. In 1957, General Esteban-Infantes avoided making value judgements on these and other scenes observed by Spanish volunteers who had witnessed "the disagreeable spectacle of certain Lithuanian populations with a Jewish flavour and an air of destitution and sadness."[87] However, the writings of most veterans offered some value judgements regarding the treatment of Jews. Tomás Salvador wrote about the "poor, dirty, wretched" Jews he saw in Suwałki. It was plain that "the Germans carried their anti-Semitism to a point of twisting the truth," and the writer felt compassion for them.[88] Carlos M. Ydígoras recalled in his 1957 novel *Algunos no hemos muerto* (Some of us are not dead) the pitiful image of the Grodno Jews, the sexual attraction of Jewish women for Spanish volunteers, the clashes between Spaniards and SS soldiers, and a concentration camp full of Jewish prisoners that was allegedly discovered by a BD volunteer.[89] In 1960, Luis Riudavets de Montes took a bolder position:

> Some Jews, burdened by the star of Zion, also crossed the streets, silent, their heads hung low, perhaps ashamed; they were going to their work ... straight to the *ghetto*, which had been converted, by order of the German command, into an enormous camp for prisoners whose lives were not very safe. For Germany committed one of the greatest mistakes in pursuing the Jews with so much fury and lack of charity, many of whom they shot and sent to the gallows ... How many Jews had fallen in Vilnius, in Riga, in Kaunas? How many thousands, perhaps millions, were murdered by the SS? The number would be huge and the figures incredible.[90]

A similar narrative was reproduced in the ensuing years.[91] The best example was the short novel *El pan en el fango* (Bread in the mud, 1962), which received a literary award from a Catholic journal. The author, Manuel Bars Casamitjana, narrated how a Spanish soldier stood up to an SS patrol in Grodno that sought to stop him from sharing his rations with an elderly Jew. Both the Jew and the Spaniard die at the hands of these unflinching and merciless Teutonic soldiers, who "acted with a cold, metal fury, fulfilling their task with complete precision, like machines." The blood of the Spaniard and the Jew, shed together, symbolizes the true seeds of peace, a victory of Christian individualism over totalitarianism.[92] A similar message was reproduced by the novel *La última oportunidad* (The last chance, 1963), by Ramón Zulaica. In the end, a group of Spanish soldiers is shot alongside several elderly Jewish men who were forced to dig their own graves.[93]

There has been blanket denial that Spaniards had any knowledge of the persecution of Jews or the concentration camps. However, some accounts still contained anti-Semitic tones in occasional characterizations associated with the discursive tropes about the entanglement of

Judaism, Freemasonry, and communist leadership. Former BD chaplain Ildefonso Jiménez Andrades wrote about the contrast between the wretchedness of the civilian population of Minsk and the luxurious palaces of the Stalinist elites, most of them "Jewish leaders who lived in opulence."[94] Gómez-Tello, a leading Falangist journalist in the post-war period, ferociously criticized Israel on the occasion of the trial of Adolf Eichmann in 1961. He emphasized how the Jews shared the blame for past mass killings under Soviet communism.[95] Riudavets de Montes disdained biological racism but recalled that there had been a connection between Judaism and communism since Karl Marx. He lamented the persecution of the Jews, but was not fond of them:

> The old troikas crossed their streets and the Jews were still burdened by their enormous stars of Zion ... A lad just turned fourteen told me: "They are killing us mercilessly, Mr. Captain, and how is this my fault, being Jewish? What offence have I committed for them to kill me ...?"... Yes indeed, they were Jews, a cursed race able to destroy the world if a favourable occasion arose. They were the assassins of Jesus, the treacherous and deicidal people, that miserly and wretched people from whose ranks great thinkers would emerge, but also repugnant revolutionaries: Karl Marx, Hegel, Lenin ... However, a Christian spirit could not approve of that collective crime.[96]

In fact, post-war BD narratives attempted to maintain a difficult balance. On the one hand, they distinguished the behaviour of Spanish soldiers from that of their Wehrmacht comrades. The Spanish veterans admitted that many German soldiers were motivated by racist ideology, and that there were extermination camps. On the other hand, there was a desire to preserve a sense of loyalty towards former comrades-in-arms. Ángel Ruiz Ayúcar expressed this point of view in 1954:

> Much has been said about the concentration camps in this sad and spiteful post-war period. Everyone has thrown a stone at the fallen person without first checking to see if his own hands were clean ... But we will not join in this stoning. If we had any crimes that we wanted to reproach the Germans for, we would wait until they are powerful ... We will not fall into the aberration of insulting those who were our comrades in the past.[97]

This search for middle ground continued in the ensuing decades. Blue Division memoirs generally do recognize the Nazi crimes against Jews and Slavic war prisoners, though they dispute their quantitative dimension. The issue is dismissed with the worn-out argument that blame

Fig. 7.6. Spanish section of German military cemetery in Pankovka
(Novgorod AA)

falls on both sides of the conflict. During his visit to Auschwitz-Birkenau
in 1987, Pablo Castelo argued that the Soviets, with Katyn and their
Stalinist concentration camps, as well as the Allies, with their carpet
bombing of German cities and the two atomic bombs dropped on
Japan, had all committed atrocities against civilians, making them no
better than the Germans.[98]

Epilogue: "We Were Right!" The "Conversion" of Russia

A further, persistent feature of the Blue Division memoirs is their char-
acterization of the behaviour of the Spanish soldiers towards the Russian population as exemplary. As a veteran summarized in 1991, the
Spaniards had been "able to combine bravery with love" in their conduct. This interpretation became an efficient argument in presenting
the experience of the BD in Russia as a moral victory.[99]

The Soviet victory in May 1945 was mostly regarded by Spanish
veterans as their own and Europe's defeat. However, from 1954 on,
interest in the various forms of Orthodox worship and the memory of
the "rebirth" of religiosity among the Russian people during the Spanish occupation gave some veterans hope that Russia would overcome
communism. Certain among them even suggested the possibility of a

syncretistic fusion of Catholicism and Orthodoxy that could restore Russia to Christian civilization. The Russian people had rediscovered "their traditions, through the pain of communist persecution," with the help of the occupying forces.[100] In a parallel way, the language of social hygiene was replaced with a quasi-ethnographic interest in Russia. Some veterans collected popular legends and tales they had heard from the peasants of the Volkhov region. These stories conveyed bucolic images of a pre-revolutionary Russia full of religious apparitions and peasant customs.[101]

From 1950 on, nuances appeared that diverged from the overwhelmingly stereotyped image of the Soviet Union that was present in the media of the Franco regime. Among veterans, fascination for "the immense and mysterious Russia ... a strange people, introspective and religious in spite of the official atheism" grew, blending "love and hatred, tenderness and harshness."[102] Russian villagers were then remembered as the double victims of the Bolshevik terror and the rigours of German occupation. The anti-communist ideal of 1936–9 was reinforced by recalling the misery of Russian peasants. Veteran BD officers such as Colonel Díaz de Villegas offered training seminars for Falangist authorities on the effects of communism in Russia. He emphasized the evils of the communist system, which destroyed family ties and religion. Returning prisoners in 1954 used similar terms when remembering their dealings with Soviet civilians. However, some ex-Division members remained convinced that the Russian people could never change due to their history. Their "anthropological structure and racial composition" made them impermeable to Western values.[103]

Ramón Serrano Suñer, the former pro-Nazi Minister of Foreign Affairs and later a successful lawyer, emphasized in 1959 that the Spanish combatants had gone to the USSR to destroy Soviet communism but not the Russian people. Individually, they saw "the enemies they were facing more as victims of the ideological enemy than as the living incarnation of it." The Cold War had confirmed to them that Soviet communism was the main enemy of Western civilization, European culture, and Christian values. It remained an adversary that kept its own citizens in misery: an image confirmed in occasional travel narratives by former *divisionarios* who visited the USSR prior to 1989.[104]

Despite the fact that BD veterans had great difficulties coming to terms with the transition to democracy in Spain, the fall of the Berlin Wall, the reunification of Germany, and the full, almost immediate conversion of Russia and the other Eastern Bloc countries reinforced this line of argument. *We were right*, read the title of the memoirs of an active member of the BD Brotherhoods. After the fall of communism, former *divisionarios* re-encountered the Russian people and reaffirmed their convictions of 1941.[105] The "eternal Russia" had triumphed. This was the BD's ultimate victory, as one veteran expressed through a fictitious Russian pope, using the "old word" for it:

> Someday, God knows when, all this will end … and the eternal Russia will be rebuilt, though perhaps a bit smaller, reduced to what it was at the beginning of the sixteenth century … but more authentic. We have an old term to designate that rebirth, that reconstruction that will someday revive us: *perestroika*.[106]

With this, the memory of the Blue Division found closure. The veterans felt fully vindicated in their decision to volunteer fifty years earlier. This perception permeated Spanish public opinion and culture and has endured beyond the nostalgia for Francoism to the present day.

8 Conclusion: A Spanish Exception in the War of Extermination?

The German war of extermination in the East was not only a conflict between Germany and the Soviet Union. Nor were its consequences limited to the two main countries that took part in the hostilities. Thousands of Northern, Western, Southern, and Eastern Europeans took part in the war. They experienced the brutalization of the front to varying degrees. They witnessed or participated in war atrocities, rapes, and murders. Some were actively or passively involved in the Holocaust. Situational and structural factors conditioned the behaviour of national units on the front and in the rear. While some of their members were strongly motivated by fascism, anti-communism, and/or anti-Semitism, many others were simply conscripted soldiers, adventurers, or even apathetic warriors who had enlisted for different reasons. The type of war they conducted as well as the intensity of combat on the front line decisively influenced their behaviour and their perceptions of the conquered land and the enemy. It may also have contributed to the radicalization of attitudes towards Soviet civilians and partisans. In this respect, the same interpretative framework that has been applied to the study of the German Wehrmacht in the East can be extended to its foreign allies and collaborators, because the research questions are similar.

Were the divergent attitudes of the Spaniards with respect to the Wehrmacht an endorsement of the thesis that ideology and indoctrination of soldiers were the main prerequisite for their brutalization? Or were they a further example of how combat conditions and environment determined the combatants' behaviour? Evidence can be found to endorse both hypotheses. In contrast with the Germans, the Spaniards lacked strong racially oriented ideological indoctrination, but many aspects of their behaviour were not substantially different to ordinary German soldiers. However, the situationist hypothesis seems to better explain the differences that existed between Spaniards and Italians. The latter also lacked racial indoctrination, but had to fight in much worse conditions, and also carried out violent repressive measures against civilians.

Despite what post-war literature and veterans' accounts have instilled in the Spanish public sphere, there was no specifically "Mediterranean" pattern of war experience that corresponded to an epicurean nature, a peculiar type of fascism and/or anti-communist creed, or a lack of racial prejudice towards Jews and Slavs. On the contrary, the Blue Division was mainly and consistently composed of fascist and anti-communist volunteers, professional NCOs, and army officers. Their ideological cohesion was stronger than that of the Italian, Romanian, and Hungarian units on the Eastern Front, which predominately consisted of conscript soldiers. In many ways, this made the Blue Division more comparable to the ideological Western European volunteers in the Waffen-SS.

Assessments of Spanish conduct on the Eastern Front should fall somewhere between the "clean Blue Division" legend – as reproduced in the post-1945 narrative based on war veteran memoirs in more-or-less apologetic historical literature – and the general characteristics that apply to most German Wehrmacht troops, particularly in the northern sector of the Eastern Front. The Spanish 250th Division never had a central role in the war of extermination unleashed by the Wehrmacht on the Eastern Front, nor are there indications that the Spanish commanders knew of the long-term occupation schemes of the Third Reich leaders, which were implemented by the military. Unlike Hungarian soldiers in the Ukrainian and Romanian military police and combatants in Bessarabia, Bukovina, and Transnistria, Spaniards did not participate systematically or specifically in collective reprisals in the rearguard against Russian, Polish, Byelorussian, or Baltic civilians, or Jews.[1] Moreover, Spanish troops were not affected by strong ideological or sociocultural factors. Certainly, some racist undertones informed BD perceptions of the Russian other, whom they regarded as barbarian, Asiatic, and culturally inferior to "civilized" Western cultures. In their view, this presumed cultural inferiority had paved the way for the success of Bolshevism, which could only flourish on fertile soil. Spanish racial views were not completely void of biological elements, but were mostly shaped by historical, cultural, and geographical determinism. Since the mid-nineteenth century, Spanish anthropologists had considered their nation to be the outcome of a "racial alloy" that had continuity in the American colonies.[2]

In this respect, Spanish perceptions of the East had more in common with German and Austro-Hungarian perceptions of the Slavic enemy during the First World War.[3] Most Spanish volunteers had not been so-cialized in biological racism (in relation to Slavs and Jews). The fighting environment at the Volkhov Front, and later in Leningrad, did not fos-ter an accumulative radicalization of Spanish attitudes towards the en-emy or civilians. The north sector of the Eastern Front was more stable than the centre and south, with less partisan activity. Spanish soldiers had not been fighting for months before they arrived on the front, and they stayed less time on average than their German comrades. These factors decisively enhanced brutalization in the various Wehrmacht units, as has been demonstrated for the 121st, 123rd and 126th German Divisions of Army Group North.[4] The absence of these factors reduced the effects of steady brutalization in the Spanish Division.

Less certainty exists regarding other aspects, such as the treatment of prisoners and tactics applied in the anti-partisan fight.[5] General be-nevolence towards Soviet prisoners from December 1941 onwards was evident among Spanish soldiers, but there were also summary execu-tions and interrogations of prisoners during combat. Iberians were not especially effective, zealous, or cruel in reprisals or in the fight against partisans. They sometimes executed civilians accused of hiding par-tisans. However, there is no evidence to indicate that they engaged in collective killings or reprisals against entire villages. German re-ports scarcely mention Spanish participation in these activities. They do, however, reveal a certain lack of trust in the Spaniards to carry out rearguard population control and cleansing actions, given their demonstrated inefficacy in this area. The Blue Division's compliance with the Commissar Order also remains unclear. There is no mention of summary executions of Soviet commissars in Spanish memoirs or Blue Division archives. This does not necessarily mean it did not hap-pen, since that order would have been transmitted verbally to Wehr-macht combatants.

The attitudes of Spaniards towards civilians were more ambivalent than later narratives suggest. Eastern Front veteran Alberto Díaz ex-pressed years later how Spaniards got along "fairly well" with Russian civilians but "whoever says the Russians were bad is lying and who-ever says they were good is also lying and whoever says we Spaniards were saints lies too"; among the troops there were also "louts, rogues, opportunists, even criminals."[6] The image of Russia and the Russians that Spanish officers and volunteers had, or forged at the front, did not include racial hatred and contempt based on biological-genetic tenets. However, diaries, letters, published articles, and caricatures in the Fa-langist press from that time show a much more nuanced picture than the idyllic, harmonious coexistence described in memoirs and writings published after 1945. The misery of the Russian peasants, their humble and submissive character, were understood as the consequence of communist degeneration, de-Christianization, and a supposed destruction of basic moral values, such as respect for the family. However, climate, culture, land, and centuries of non-European tradition and despotic government were also perceived to be a decisive influence. Russians were an *Asian* people: bloated, lacking spiritual personality, telluric, and primitive, with amoral tendencies that predisposed them to being the propitiatory victim of communism.

This might be considered *cultural* racism, but it was not biological-genetic bigotry. It considered individuals to be determined by their cultural milieu, leaving little or no room for change.[7] Often, this was subliminally expressed in tones redolent of social hygiene: frequent allusions to their dirtiness and lack of personal or family hygiene helped undermine consideration of Russians as human beings and transform political or social arguments into biological ones. Such a mindset also festered in Spanish fascism, which considered the occupied peoples as spiritually and culturally inferior or "underage," though not as a biologically subhuman *Untermensch*. This peculiar vision of the enemy might incite commiseration and paternalism but never prevented Russian civilians from suffering requisitions and theft. Hierarchically uneven and logistically deficient troop provisioning was a factor from the moment the Spanish volunteers left their training camps in Germany. This was aggravated by organizational deficiencies and a lack of discipline among the BD troops, who were a heterogeneous mix of career officers, non-commissioned officers with little training, enthusiastic fascist volunteers, mercenary legionnaires, drafted soldiers who had been persuaded to go to Russia, adventurers, and, finally, unemployed workers seeking a living. From the moment they began to march in the summer of 1941, there were constant incidents involving the civilian population – all of which defy precise quantification – including requisitions, theft, sexual abuse, and even rape.

Spanish soldiers were not habitually involved in the homicide of Russian peasants; in fact, they coexisted reasonably well, given their condition as invading troops in a place such as the Eastern Front. A similar pattern of behaviour towards the civilian population was also displayed by other German divisions of Army Group North.[8] A few significant examples have revealed just how non-idyllic these relations were. Many Spanish officers had learned in the colonial wars in Northern Morocco to let their troops find provisions on location, a practice they repeated unscrupulously in Russia.[9] Colonel Díaz de Villages recalled the argument put forward by a Falangist volunteer engaged in a discussion with a German military policeman: "It would be absurd ... if after seeing so many of ours fall, after suffering such a difficult war, we could not even eat a Russian chicken."[10]

The complexity inherent in the presence of an occupying army among civilians led many Spanish soldiers and officers who lodged in the *izbas* to function as protectors of Russian families, which were mainly composed of women, children, and old men. The *divisionarios* would feed and protect them in exchange for services that ranged from lodging and laundry to sexual favours. The low intensity and even absence of biological racism led to a greater degree of familiarity between most Spanish soldiers and Russian civilians. Contrary to Romanian and Hungarian troops in Army Group Centre and Army Group South,[11] the Spaniards did not become involved in systematic reprisals or large-scale murders of civilians. They were, nonetheless, responsible for continual theft, requisitioning, and pillaging, along with occasional sexual abuse. This was typical of the experiences of other occupying Axis armies during the Second World War, such as the relatively benign presence of Germans in Norway, Denmark, and the Netherlands. In these countries, the experience of occupation was characterized by a low level of everyday tension, close interactions between occupiers and some segments of the occupied population, sporadic outbursts of violence, reprisals, and other incidents.[12] In the context of the Eastern Front, this was also somewhat characteristic of the occupation practices implemented by the Italian Army on the Don Front.[13] With regards to Spanish troop behaviour towards Russian civilians in the Volkhov and Leningrad area, what scandalized Army Group North – with its German military stereotypes – was not its lukewarm commitment to the Geneva Convention but the fact that Spanish soldiers were unsystematic in their pillaging. This negatively affected the immediate interests of the Wehrmacht in its attempts not to completely alienate the civilian population.

However, it must not be forgotten that the Blue Division effectively though indirectly aided a strategic action that served the mid-range plans for a war of extermination that had motivated the invasion of the USSR: the sentencing of three million people to death by starvation. Many Falangist volunteers, officers, and NCOs rejected Russia and the Russians as *Asian* people, whom they considered to be culturally and spiritually inferior. In addition to blaming Russia and communism for the misery of the peasants, many also accused the "submissive" and "brutish" Russians themselves. This view was permeated with commiseration and even empathy, not racial hatred. Spanish soldiers might commit excesses; they felt a certain sense of cultural superiority towards the enemy and civilians, akin to that experienced by North American soldiers facing the Japanese in the Pacific.[14] Nevertheless, the Blue Division – its commanders, many of its officers, and most of its soldiers – had not envisioned the mid-term extermination or subjugation of the Slavic population. Most were convinced that they had come to restore Christian faith and civilization in Russia by eradicating communism; the war they had to fight on the Eastern front was a different one.

Notes

1. Introduction: The Blue Division, the Franco Regime, and the Second World War

1 See Fernández Coppel (2007) and Escuadra (1998). All translations from foreign languages throughout this book are my own unless otherwise indicated.

2 See Núñez Seixas (2018d).

3 *El País* (11 and 12 October 2004).

4 Spain as a state did not participate in the conflict. This does not equate with neutrality, or non-alignment with any side in the war, at least until 1944.

5 Decades later, many war veterans still believed that their role had actually been to prevent Spain from entering the war on the Axis side. See, for example, J. de la Torre, "La División Azul," *Destino* (28 June 1975).

6 See, for example, Proctor (1972); Ruhl (1986); Bowen (2007); Moreno Juliá (2007), or the special issue on Spanish non-belligerency during the Second World War by Peñalba Sotorrio (2019).

7 See Preston (1995); Tusell (1995); Guderzo (1995); Payne & Contreras (1996); Thomàs (2016b).

8 See, for example, the extensive and well-documented monograph by Moreno Juliá (2004) that focuses more on operational and diplomatic aspects, as well as his detailed treatment of the Blue Legion (Moreno Juliá 2014). See also the monograph by Rodríguez Jiménez (2007a); the descriptive and uncritical study by the amateur military historian Caballero Jurado (2019); or the very specific treatment of chaplains and religiosity in the BD by Sagarra (2012). Within Russian historiography, some studies have appeared in recent years that stand apart from the international discussion on the Eastern Front. Their main merit undoubtedly lies in shedding light on some Soviet/Russian military archive sources that are

mostly unavailable to non-Russian historians: see Kovalev (2014) and Elpatevskij (2015).

9 See Hartmann (2009, 2013); Hartmann, Hürter, Lieb, & Pohl (2009); Fritz (2011).

10 See Kühne & Ziemann (2000) and Wette (1992).

11 However, a new generation of historians has dramatically revived the panorama of war studies in Spain. A good example is the *Revista Universitaria de Historia Militar* (www.ruhm.es), founded in 2012.

12 For refreshing perspectives on the military history of the Spanish Civil War, see Seidmann (2002), Matthews (2013, 2019), Hernández Burgos (2020) and Alcalde (2014). See also Esdaile (2020) for an updated review of recent studies.

13 See the classic study by Leed (1979: 1–38). Similarly, see Latzel (1997), Jasper (2011), Ziemann (2013), and Nübel (2014).

14 For the experience of the Condor Legion in the Spanish Civil War, see Schüler-Springorum (2010).

15 A model approach to this issue, for the Italian case, is examined in Giusti (2003). A descriptive (and passionately pro-Falangist) approach can also be found in Torres (2018).

16 See Ruhl (1986) and Moreno Juliá (2004, 2007)

17 See Wette (1992); Ulrich (1996); and Jasper (2011).

18 See Ulrich (1997); Epkenhans, Förster, & Hagemann (2006); Didczuneit, Ebert, & Jander (2011).

19 See Núñez Seixas (2018a: 355–87) for a comparative reflection.

20 Encinas Moral (2008).

21 See Juderías (1940); Martínez Martínez (1999).

22 Todorova (1997); Schenk (2002).

23 Elorza & Bizcarrondo (1999: 79–99); Fasey (2000).

24 See Núñez Seixas & Beyda (2019).

25 Cruz (1997); on the European context, see Klug (1987) and García (2005).

26 "El verdadero peligro ruso. La cabalgata asiática," *Arriba* (4 April 1935).

27 See Ventrone (2005) and Scoppola (2006).

28 See Núñez Seixas (2006: 177–305).

29 See Núñez Seixas & Beyda (2019: 7–36).

30 Serrano de Haro (1942: 289); De Castro Albarrán (1938: 156).

31 See, e.g., García Morente (1961: 20–1).

32 See "Por aquí pasó Rusia." *La Ametralladora* (17 October 1937); M. Somoza Polea, "Caballeros contra hordas," *La Ametralladora* (10 October 1937).

33 See Karl (1937: 161–96).

34 *Flecha* (25 July 1937); "Stalin, Miaja y sus charreteras," *La Ametralladora* (17 July 1938).

35 See examples in Núñez Seixas (2006a: 249–50).

36 J.M. Salaverría, "El ruso." *ABC* (20 December 1939); "Contra la URSS," *Mundo* (29 June 1941).

37 Peloille (2015).

38 See Tomasoni (2017).

39 See, e.g., L. Puértolas, "Un libro: Czech-Jochberg: Hitler, un movimiento alemán," *La Conquista del Estado*, 16 (27 June 1931); R. Bader, "El triunfo nacional socialista de Hamburgo," *La Conquista del Estado*, 21 (10 October 1931).

40 R. L[edesma] R[amos], "El nacional-socialismo alemán. El partido de Hitler," *La Conquista del Estado*, 2 (21 March 1931); "La liberación anti-marxista. Episodios del nacional-socialismo alemán," *Libertad*, 19 (19 October 1931); "En torno al nacional-socialismo," *Libertad* (9 November 1931).

41 R. Ledesma Ramos, "El nacional-socialismo en el poder. La ruta de Alemania," *JONS*, 1 (May 1933).

42 "Alemania," *FE*, 1 (7 December 1933); "El gesto de Alemania y la Sociedad de Naciones," *Arriba* (21 March 1935); "Ventana al mundo," *Arriba*, (16 and 30 May 1935); E. Gutiérrez-Palma, "Italia, Alemania, España," *Libertad* (24 September 1934).

43 See Thomàs (2019) and Gallego (2014: 181–7). See also Núñez Seixas (2019).

44 F. García Márquez, "La raza: fundamento de la comunidad," *JONS*, 11 (August 1934).

45 "Alemania: nazis y judíos," *FE* (11 January 1934); "Tribunales de Salud Pública," *FE* (22 February 1934).

46 The "pilgrimage" to Berlin was a rite of passage for many "little fascists" of the European periphery. See Reichel (2006); Bajohr & Strupp (2011); and Sallée (2014).

47 Gay (1934).

48 Beneyto Pérez (1934: 43–6, 113–18, 148–50).

49 Rato (1935; 1936: 119–23). The date 1492 refers to the year when the so-called Catholic Monarchs Fernando and Isabel expelled from a newly unified "Spanish" kingdom all Jews and Muslims who refused to convert to Catholicism.

50 O. Redondo, "Religión y política. Defensa de Hitler," *Libertad* (6 August 1934).

51 See R. de Maeztu, "Hitler: Su triunfo y su programa," *Acción Española* (16 May 1932). See also more examples in Hernández (2016: 777–8).

52 Morodo (1985: 114–24); Gallego (2014: 165–7).

53 Rosenberg's diaries, entry of 23 August 1936 (Matthäus & Bajohr 2015: 200).

54 Payne (1997: 261–7); Viñas (2001: 186–7).

55 Velarde Fuertes (2008).

56 Böcker (2000: 200, 230, 289–90); Álvarez Chillida (2002: 312–14).
57 Viñas (2001: 187–8); Morant i Ariño (2013: 136–7).
58 See Viñas (2001); Merkes (1961), and Schüler-Springorum (2010).
59 Ruiz Carnicer (1996: 156–61); Morant i Ariño (2013: 325–517).
60 For example, Dionisio Ridruejo visited Germany as Propaganda Chief in 1937 (Ridruejo 1976: 188–92).
61 See Brydan (2016, 2019b).
62 Schulze-Schneider (2004); Peñalba Sotorrio (2019).
63 See Ros Agudo (2002: 271–314); Janué i Miret (2008); and Sesma Landrín (2011). On the influence of Nazi law doctrines in Spain, see Rivaya (1998: 49–82), and Gallego (2014: 510–16, 740–7).
64 Bowen (2007).
65 Reports by the German vice-consul in Badajoz from 16, 17, and 20 August 1940 (PAAA, DBM, Reg. Pol. Allg. [RPA] 558/2, Box 767).
66 Alcalde (2014: 83–111).
67 See, for example, "El hombre y su estilo," *Arriba* (20 July 1940).
68 Reports by Löschner and Paul Winzer, Valencia, 28 April and 5 May 1941 (PAAA, DBM, RPA 557/2, Box 766).
69 Letter to von Stohrer, 13 July 1941 (PAAA, DBM, RPA 557/2, Box 766).
70 Richards (2010).
71 Reports from Löschner and Paul Winzer, Madrid and Valencia, 28 April 1941 (PAAA, DBM, RPA. 557/2, Box 766).
72 Report from Ambassador von Stohrer, Madrid, 17 July 1942 (PAAA, R-29744).
73 See Mazower (2000: 141–3).
74 Letter of M. D. Rius and C. Copa, Barcelona, 17 June 1940 (PAAA, DBM, RPA 558/2, Box 767).
75 Letter from Antonio Carreño, Madrid, 30 April 1941 (PAAA, DBM, RPA 555/1, Box 764).
76 Lazo (1998: 165–75).
77 Report from German consul in Bilbao, 1 July 1941, and letter signed by six *Requeté* officers, 29 June 1941 (PAAA, DBM, Box 796, Geheimakten, 6/9).
78 Letter (n.d., June 1941) signed by the five Requeté leaders from Navarre (PAAA, DBM, Box 796, Geheimakten, 6/9).
79 Letter signed by 19 Carlist officers and war veterans, Madrid, 3 August 1942 (PAAA, DBM, Geheimakten, Box 795, 6/2).

2. Russia Is Guilty!

1 Förster (1983); Wegner (1990).
2 Cited by Streit (1978: 34).
3 Wette (2002: 95–7).

4 Streit (1978: 29–30).
5 Hillberg (2005: 953–78); Snyder (2010).
6 Krausnick (1998: 123–30).
7 See Hilberg (2005: 1360–6) and Snyder (2010).
8 Hitler (1930: 751–53).
9 See the controversial Goldhagen thesis (1997). A criticism appears in Kühne (1999: 605–14) as well as in Browning (2002) and Böhler (2006: 17–19).
10 Pohl (2008); Hartmann (2009: 466–7).
11 Keller (2011: 320–3).
12 Krausnick (1977) and Römer (2008).
13 See Ueberschär & Wette (1984: 310–15); Bartov (2001: 106–7); Römer (2008: 133–58).
14 Römer (2008: 172–88).
15 See Wette (2002: 103–4) and Kershaw (2000: 357).
16 Bartov (1991, 2001); Rass (2003).
17 See Neitzel & Welzer (2011).
18 Römer (2012).
19 Hartmann (2009, 2013); Rutherford (2014).
20 Vehviläinen (2002); Kivimäki (2011); Kivimäki & Kinnunen (2012).
21 See Assworthy, Scafes, & Craciunoiu (1995) as well as Constantiniu, Dutu, & Retegan (1995), Rotari, Burcin, Zodian, & Moise (1999), and Filipescu (2006).
22 DiNardo (1996, 2005); Neitzel (2004); Cataruzza, Dyroff, & Langewiesche (2012).
23 Schlemmer (2005, 2009); Giusti (2016); Scianna (2019).
24 Kliment & Nakladal (1997: 65–89), Rychlik (2017).
25 Anderson (1999); Ungváry (2004, 2005a, 2005b); Romsics (2017).
26 Glantz (2001: 9).
27 Hausleitner, Mihok, & Wetzel (2001).
28 Ungváry (2005a: 99–100).
29 Stein (1966: 137–48); Wette (1984); Grunert (2012: 51–60).
30 Journal entries dated 23, 24 and 28 June 1941, quoted by Neitzel (2004: 137).
31 *Völkischer Beobachter* (28 June 1941).
32 García Pérez (1990); Kluke (1955); Mazower (2000: 221–2); Bruneteau (2003); Loff (2008); Grunert (2012); and Prévotaux (2010).
33 See Stein (1966); Wegner (1999: 112–29); Leleu (2007: 261–77); Rohrkamp (2011); Schulte, Lieb, & Wegner (2014); Böhler & Gerwarth (2016).
34 "Niederschrift über die Sitzung im Auswärtigen Amt vom 30. Juni 1941 über die Freiwilligen-Meldung in fremden Ländern für den Kampf gegen die Sowjetunion," 4 July 1941 (PAAA, Box 708, Geheimakten, 504/4);

"Richtlinien für den Einsatz ausländischer Freiwilliger im Kampf gegen die Sowjetunion," 6 July 1941 (BA-MA, RW 19/686).

35 *Toute l'Europe contre le Bolchévisme. 2ème anniversaire 22 Juin 1941–22 Juin 1943*, n.p.: C.E.A., n.d. [1943], 25–31.

36 See Ready (1987) and Müller (2007). For Western Europeans, see Estes (2003); Antoniou et al. (2016); and Alegre Lorenz (2017). For a non-exhaustive list of monographs on the different national units, see Bruyne (1991) as well as Bruyne & Rikmenspoel (2004) for the Walloons; Giolitto (2007), Carrard (2010), and Schöttler (2014) for the French; Pierik (2001) for the Dutch; Werther (2004), Smith, Poulsen, & Christensen (1999) as well as Christensen, Poulsen & Smith (2014) for the Danes; Figueiredo (2001) and Sorlie (2019) for the Norwegians; De Wever (1985, 1991), Carrein (1999), and Seberechts (2002) for the Flemish; Stein & Krosby (1966) for the Finns; Guerra (2012) for the Italians; Zaugg (2016) for the Albanians; and Motadel (2014) for other Muslim peoples.

37 Wegner (1999: 311); Neitzel (2004: 142).

38 Pierik (2001: 56–7); Christensen, Poulsen, & Smith (2014: 197).

39 Neitzel (2004: 149); Rohrkamp (2011: 14).

40 Luytens (2010); Guerra (2012); Milata (2009: 174–214; 2014).

41 The exact dimensions of these plans is little known. In this regard, Waffen-SS theorists and organizers such as Gottlob Berger and the *Germanische Leitstelle* expressed more pan-European ambition than Himmler. See Wegner (1999: 310–16) and Gutmann (2017).

42 In April 1945, 25 of the 38 Waffen-SS divisions (65.78%) were partially or entirely composed of non-German volunteers, though many divisions were very small (Rohrbach 2011: 604–6).

43 See *La SS t'appelle!*, n.p., 1943.

44 Zaugg (2016) and Petke (2014).

45 Golczewski (2003).

46 Hoffmann (1976); Motadel (2013; 2014: 133–77).

47 For Estonians, see Michaelis (2000) and Hiio (2014); for Latvians, Schill (1977) and Feldmanis (2005: 122–131); and Kott (2012).

48 Newland (1991: 122–37); Edele (2017); Petrov & Beyda (2017).

49 Andreyev (1987: 206–15); Hoffmann (1986).

50 Ridruejo (1978: 55–6).

51 Ruhl (1986: 22–24); Smyth (1994); Moreno Juliá (2004: 69–70).

52 Von Stohrer to Berlin, Madrid, 22 June 1941, and *Deutsche Informationsstelle* report, Madrid, 23 June 1941 (PAAA R.29741).

53 Ribbentrop to von Stohrer, Sonnenburg, 24 June 1941 (PAAA R.29741).

54 Report on the FET Political Council meeting, n.d. (June 1941), AHMC-FGV, C.115.

55 Moreno Juliá (2004: 65–6); secret reports, Berlin, 24 June 1941, and Madrid, 24 June 1941; von Stohrer to Berlin, Madrid, 25 June 1941 (PAAA R.29741). Letter n.d. (AHMC-FGV, C.115).

56 Reports from Krahmer, Madrid, 25 June 1941, and von Stohrer, 26 June 1941 (PAAA R.29741).

57 Reports from Eberhard von Stohrer, Madrid, 24 June 1941; Fritz Löwe, Tarragona, 26 June 1941; Rohrbach, Bilbao, 26 June 1941; von Knobloch, Alicante, 26 June 1941 (PAAA, Box 796, *Geheimakten* 6/9); reports from von Stohrer (24 June 1941), from consuls of Santa Cruz de Tenerife (25 June 1941), Málaga (26 June 1941), Alicante (27 June 1941), and Barcelona (26 June 1941), PAAA, Deutsche Botschaft Madrid, Box 766, Reg. Pol.Allg.

58 Telegrams from von Stohrer, 26 June 1941 (PAAA R.29741); copy of instructions to provincial head of the FET in Tétouan, n.d., and letter from the Spanish High Commissioner in Morocco to General Varela, 27 June 1941 (AHMC-FGV, C.588).

59 Andrés Saliquet to Varela, 30 June 1941, and Varela to Saliquet, 2 July 1941 (AHMC-FGV, C. 115). For a hagiographic approach to Muñoz Grandes, see Togores Sánchez (2007).

60 Ridruejo (1978: 57–9, entries of 4 and 12 July 1941).

61 Report by Heberlein, 2 July 1941 (PAAA R.29741).

62 Report on the meeting of German and Spanish Military Justice representatives on 19 August 1941 in Berlin (AGMAV 1978/8/2/1).

63 Von Weizsäcker to the German embassy in Madrid, Berlin, 3 July 1941 (PAAA, R-29742).

64 Report from Heberlein, Madrid, 9 July 1941 (PAAA, R. 29742); Kleinfeld & Tambs (1983: 42–5).

65 "Relación de voluntarios rusos" n.d. [July 1941], AGMAV 2005/3/2/3, see also the memoirs of the volunteer Vladimir Kovalevskii in Núñez Seixas & Beyda (2019).

66 Luis Aguilar, "Diario de mi campaña de Rusia," entry of 4 July 1941 (Parrilla Nieto 2018: 43).

67 Report from Heberlein, 17 July 1941 (PAAA, Madrid 553/3, Box 761); Lyautey (1942: 58–62).

68 M. Daranar, "El viaje a Rusia de los voluntarios falangistas," *ABC* (22 July 1941).

69 See reports from the 2nd section of General Staff, Grafenwöhr, 19 and 21 July 1941; and Commander Ramón Rodríguez Vita, n.d., in AGMAV, 2005/2/2; Muñoz Grandes's report to Varela, 29 July 1941 (AHMC-FGV, C.115).

70 Report from the BD General Staff to General Varela, 5 August 1941; report by the DGS, Irún, 8 August 1941, and Muñoz Grandes's report to Varela, 19 August 1941 (AHMC-FGV, C. 115).

71 Dionisio Ridruejo to Marichu de la Mora, Grafenwöhr, 9 August 1941 (AFRI); Captain surgeon Bernardino López Romero, *DEV. Hospital de Campaña 250. Memoria*, 20 August 1942, 7 (private archive of Carlos López del Río, Boiro/Madrid [ACLR]).

72 Dionisio Ridruejo to Marichu de la Mora, Grafenwöhr, 14 August 1941 (AFRI).

73 See Garriga (1977: 360–3); reports of von Stohrer, Madrid, 9 and 18 August 1941 (PAAA, R 29742).

74 See the exhaustive description by Caballero Jurado (2011).

75 Reports of the BD Chief of Military Police, Berlin, 12 and 23 May 1942 (AGMAV 1982/6/3).

76 Moreno Juliá (2004: 315); Caballero Jurado (2011: 211–17).

77 Ibáñez Hernández (1998); "Hoja de Campaña," *Blau División*, 266 (September 1981) and 273 (April 1982).

78 Report by Muñoz Grandes to General Varela, 1 August 1941, and translated copies of the speeches of Cochenhausen and Fromm (AHMC-FGV, C. 115).

79 Proctor (1972); Kleinfeld & Tambs (1983); Bowen (2000a). This tendency is noted in several local studies by amateur and neo-Francoist historians: see Negreira (2011); Torres (2014); and Caballero Jurado (2019).

80 Ellwood (1984: 145–6); Rodríguez Jiménez (2007a, 2009).

81 Ruhl (1986); Moreno Juliá (2004).

82 Dionisio Ridruejo to Marichu de la Mora, Grafenwöhr, 18 September 1941 (AFRI).

83 Levsen & Krüger (2010); Arielli & Collins (2013).

84 Aresti (2014). Regarding the German combatants, see Werner (2008).

85 Elster (1999, 2002).

86 Alfredo Rodríguez Pérez to his parents, Grafenwöhr, 25 July 1941 (AFN).

87 Skoutelsky (2006: 270–2); autobiography of J.M. Castañón, n.d., *c.* 1957–8 (RAH-FMD).

88 "¿Por qué fuimos allá?" *Blau División*, 21 (May 1961); Montes (2006: 23).

89 On the concept of "reference group," see Merton (1970: 228–386).

90 "I was not a Falangist, but I did what many of my friends and companions did," acknowledged Francisco Ruiz, who enlisted in 1942, when he was doing his military service (Pérez Maestre 2008: 125).

91 Letter from Pedro Luis Fajardo Biel, 12 August 1941 (AGA 51/20552).

92 Letter from Eduardo Aparisi, Valencia, n.d. (October 1941), PAAA, Box 796, *Geheimakten, 6/9*.

93 Licinio de la Huerga to Carlos Pinilla, Benavente, 11 July 1941 (CDMH, Carlos Pinilla's papers, Box 1448/1).

94 Quoted by López Villatoro (2012: 280).

95 Manuel S. y S. to Franco, Madrid, 21 July 1941. Other petitioners cited
    motives of avenging family members (such as the son of a lieutenant who
    had fallen in 1937) or anti-communism and patriotism (Cazorla Sánchez
    2014: 48–50).

96 Application of Isabel Salado Enríquez, Huelva, 13 December 1941 (AGA,
    51/20552).

97 From a sample of 61 volunteers in the Girona Militia, more than one-third
    (36%) were not born in Catalonia; almost 40% were skilled and unskilled
    workers, and one-fourth (24.6%) were low- and mid-ranking employees
    and civil servants, along with a significant number (6.5%) of liberal pro-
    fessionals, agricultural and industrial business owners. More than half
    were FET members, and others were right wing or traditionalists prior to
    1936. See also Gay (2002).

98 Reports from Samuel Hoare, Madrid, 8 July 1941 (NA-PRO 371/26940):
    Stille to German Foreign Ministry, Madrid, 8 July 1941 (PAAA, Sammlung
    der Lageberichte, Madrid 553/3, Box 761), and from the German consul in
    Barcelona, 10 July 1941 (PAAA, Box 796, *Geheimakten* 6/9); report by Am-
    bassador Foxá, Helsinki, 26 July 1941 (AMAE, R-2192, Exp. 31). The BBC
    service in Spanish reported that not only "misdirected" idealist volunteers
    joined the BD, but also ex-convicts and soldiers who had been forced to en-
    list. See report by Samuel Hoare, 14 September 1941 (NA-FO 371/26940).

99 Report by Major Mariano del Prado, Grafenwöhr, 21 July 1941 (AGMAV
    2005/272/23); Kleinfeld & Tambs (1983: 35–6).

100 Reports from the German ambassador in Madrid, and consuls in Bar-
    celona, Santa Cruz de Tenerife, Bilbao, Alicante, Málaga, Almería and
    other towns (PAAA, Deutsche Botschaft Madrid, Reg. Pol. Allg., Box 766);
    Moreno Juliá (2004: 98–100); Hoare to Foreign Office, 9 July 1941 (NA-
    PRO/FO 371/26940). See also Fernández Vicente (2019: 342).

101 Sánchez Brun (2002: 81).

102 Report from a *V-Mann* to Heberlein, Madrid, 3 July 1941 (PAAA, Box 796,
    Geheimakten 6/9).

103 "Parte mensual de FET," 1–30 June 1941 (AGA, 51/20557); Nicolás Marín
    (1982: 437–9); Alcalde (2012: 53–5).

104 "Parte mensual de FET," Asturias, June 1941 (AGA, 51/20565, Exp. 39).

105 Reports from Consul Richter, Tétouan, 5 and 10 July 1941 (PAAA, Box
    796, *Geheimakten* 6/9). Among the Moroccan soldiers stationed in Ibiza
    were 106 volunteers, all of whom were rejected; also, 490 Moroccan
    soldiers stationed in Tenerife volunteered (Negreira 1991: 97–8; list of
    names from 28 June 1941, in Negreira 2011: 20–2; Jiménez Soto 2015:
    161–2).

106 Cervera Gil (1998) and Ruiz (2012). An example was the Falangist
    Eduardo Díaz Infante (n.d.: 9–10).

107 Samuel Hoare to Anthony Eden, 2 July 1941 (cited by Palomares 1996: 35).

108 See Palacio Pilacés (2013, I: 271–9).

109 E. Haxel, *Zustandbericht über die span. Freiw. Div.*, 11 August 1943 (BA-MA, RH 24–50/59).

110 War diary of Enrique Sánchez Fraile, quoted by L. Ruiz, "Anotaciones de un soldado sobre la campaña de Rusia," unpublished paper, 2006. See also Viciana (2018: 236–7).

111 Unpublished statements by Dionisio Ridruejo (Morente 2006: 191).

112 "Diez respuestas a diez preguntas colocando los puntos sobre las íes," *Blau División*, 50 (October 1963).

113 Del Arco Blanco (2007); Alcalde (2014: 117–38; 2010).

114 Rodríguez Jiménez (2009: 276).

115 To avoid complications in the barracks under his command, in January 1942 the High Commissioner of Morocco, General Luis Orgaz, suggested that only Falangist volunteers be dispatched to replace those who returned from Russia; General Varela responded that "there are very few Falangist volunteers." Luis Orgaz to Varela, Tétouan, 10 January 1942, and Varela to Luis Orgaz, Madrid, 24 February 1942. The phrase referring to the FET volunteers in the letter from the Army Chief of Staff to Muñoz Grandes, Madrid, n.d., *c.* March 1942 (AHMC-FGV, C. 115).

116 Report by General Carlos Asensio, Army Central Staff, to Franco, Madrid, 9 February 1942 (AGMAV, C.2005/14/1/6).

117 Thomàs (2016b).

118 Rodríguez Jiménez (2007a: 311); Caballero Jurado (2004a: 30–1).

119 In the border town of Irún, the "first" BD volunteers who were returning to the front after leave or convalescence in Spain even asked not to share a train compartment with the replacements, as they were "not of the same class as those who went a year ago" (DGS report of 13 June 1942, AHMC-FGV, C.115).

120 For example, the Civil Guard Manuel Puentes in May 1942, also a Falangist, in a letter to Dionisio Ridruejo, 15 May 1942 (CDMH-FR, MF/R 5912).

121 Moreno Juliá (2004: 395–6); DGS reports, 24 and 28 February 1942 (AHMC-FGV, C.115). An Old Guard Falangist from Valencia volunteered in the late summer of 1942 while doing his military service in Barcelona. He had not been admitted one year before, but later "volunteers are lacking" and thus servicemen on duty were allowed to enlist (Georgacopulos 2015: 29).

122 Monthly report of the FET in Albacete, March 1942 (AGA, Presidencia, 51/20580).

123 Manuel Tarín Sala to Remedios Rebollo, 13 June 1942 (AFR).

124 Manuel Tarín Sala to Remedios Rebello, 12 July 1942, and to anonymous friends, 21 October 1942 (AFR).

125 Ursula to Corporal Antonio Herrero, Poznań, 13 September 1943, and Antonio Herrero to Ursula, Russia, 30 September 1943 (AA).

126 In Albacete, for example, 984 volunteers signed up at recruitment office in 1941. In March 1942, the number of enlistments was 132. See the monthly reports of the FET in Albacete, July 1941 and March 1942 (AGA, 51/20544 and 51/20580), and Alcalde (2012: 62).

127 Moscardó to Varela, Madrid, 20 July 1942 (AHMC-FGV, C. 115).

128 Rodríguez González (2003: 291); Negreira (2011: 129–200).

129 See Puente Fernández (2012: 195–7); Palacio Pilacés (2013, I: 482–6).

130 A soldier in Sant Sadurní d'Anoia refused to go to Russia, ignoring the suggestions of his superiors: J.J. Tharrats, "Sant Sadurní d'Anoia i la fil·loxera," *Diari de Girona* (11 October 1987).

131 Captain Federico Fuentes-Gómez de Salazar was called to formation in June 1942 on the courtyard of the Cadets Academy in Logroño. Those who *did not wish* to go do Russia were to take one step forward. Though almost all the cadets sympathized with the BD in theory, they had to make their decision in a matter of seconds (López-Covarrubias 2012: 16–17). Private José Linares García was recruited in a Moroccan barrack by an officer who sent eight soldiers for a physical exam, blurting out: "You are going to the Division, right?" By contrast, in neighbouring Tétouan "the colonel did not want anyone to 'volunteer' in that way" (Linares 2000: 23).

132 Interview with Joaquim M. Rosa de Oliveira, Lisbon, 17 October 2010 (courtesy of Mr. Ricardo Silva, Lisbon).

133 Muñoz Grandes to Varela, 10 May 1942; Varela to Muñoz Grandes, Madrid, 12 June 1942 (AHMC-FGV, C. 115); report by Sonnleithner, transmitted to Hitler and Ribbentrop, 4 September 1942 (PAAA R.29744); *O Independente*, 26 June 1992.

134 J. Farré de Calzadilla, "Legislación laboral protectora de los voluntarios de la División Azul," *Enlace*, 9 (20 September 1942).

135 ¡*Españoles!*, Murcia: Imp. Jiménez, n.d. [1942].

136 Letter by Captain Francisco González, Hof, 25 March 1942 (AHMC-FGV, C. 115).

137 Díaz Benítez (2005).

138 Marchena Cañete (2003: 49–50).

139 Cela (2010: 177–8).

140 Pérez Maestre (2008: 131–2).

141 Linares (2000: 30–1) indicated that in the 16th March Battalion (September 1942) there were many civilian volunteers, some seminary students and corporals and sergeants who regretted their decision to enlist back in 1941.

142 According to the recount by Moreno Juliá (2014: 505), as of the end of
1943, up to 42 per cent of Blue Division personnel had come from the
Falange. Yet no detailed sources are provided.

143 Such as the group of twenty-five members of the Franco's Youth Falange
from Almadén (Ciudad Real) who enlisted as volunteers in November
1942: *El Pirineo* (12 November 1942).

144 See *Boletín de Acción Católica*, Granollers (1 June 1942); *Cruzada* (1 March
1943); *FET y JONS* (3 February 1942, 10 November 1943 and 3 February
1944).

145 Report, n.d. (1943), CDMH, FNFF, MF/R 7256, Doc. 2595.

146 *Diario de operaciones e impresiones del teniente provisional Benjamín Arenales
en la campaña de Rusia*, unpublished war diary (1942), 1 and 31–2 (private
archive of Carmelo de las Heras, Madrid); war diary of Captain surgeon Manuel de Cárdenas Rodríguez (private archive of José Manuel de
Cárdenas, San Sebastián), p. 1; Miralles Güill (1981: 74–8); Castaño Doña
(1991); F. Cañas Estival, "Nochebuena en el frente ruso con mis camaradas," *Ofensiva*, 27 December 1942.

147 Ribbentrop to Adolf von Moltke, 11 February 1943; von Moltke to Ribbentrop, 12 February 1943 (PAAA, R.29747).

148 Memo of FET provincial leader Luis Julve, Huesca, 30 January 1942 (AGA
51/20665).

149 "Jerarquías de la Falange en Rusia," *Enlace*, II:13 (26 June 1943); A. Pozo
Zayas, "División Azul," *Nueva Alcarria* (27 February 1943).

150 Report of the FET Provincial Headquarters in Huelva, 2 June 1943 (AGA,
51/20613); notes of the British Vice-Consul in Granada, 28 February 1943;
report of the British embassy, 7 April 1943 (NA-PRO, FO 371/34813). In
July 1943 a rumour circulated that fourteen young men arrested in a police raid had been taken directly to Zaragoza and placed in the unit that
was leaving for the Russian Front. See British Vice-Consul report, Granada, 17 July 1943 (NA-PRO, FO 371/34813).

151 Hernanz Blanco (2013: 4, entry of 30 March 1942); M. Salvador Gironés,
"Cosas de por allá," *Blau División*, 59 (July 1964) and 80 (April 1966).

152 Reports from the military governor of Guipúzcoa, 16 April 1942, and the
DGS, San Sebastián, 4 March 1942 (AHMC-FGV, C. 115).

153 Report of the provincial delegate of the FET Office for Popular Education,
Logroño, 25 June 1943, and report of rumors, 25 October 1943 (AHPLR,
PP/20 and PP/20/8); Linares (2000: 30).

154 Muñoz Césaro (2011: 21, entry of 20 June 1942).

155 Cited in Rodríguez Jiménez (2009: 293). See also Linares (2000: 35).

156 Steengracht to Ribbentrop, Berlin, 1 October 1943, and memorandum
presented to the Spanish ambassador; report by Dieckhoff after a conversation with Jordana, Madrid, 2 October 1943 (PAAA, R.29750).

157 See, for example, AOK 16 to Army Group North, 7 February 1942, and the OKW report, Berlin, 8 April 1942 (BA-MA RH 19 III/493); reports of the German Foreign Ministry, 3 September 1942 (BA-MA, RH 20–18/1075).

158 Report of Obersturmführer Vey to Einsatzkommando I, 10 November 1943 (USHMM, Sp BD 11.001M.05).

159 Haxel, *Zustandbericht*, 11 August 1943.

160 The Catalan officer Daniel Torra expressed in July 1941 his discouragement at not having had the good fortune to go to the Russian Front, as the seventeen officer volunteers among from Reus and Tarragona exceeded the quota: "even those with connections are on the wait list. And here you have us thirteen left over, squirming like a basilisk and eager for some serious action or for new units to be organized." Letter from Daniel Torra, Tarragona, 6 July 1941 (Torra i Puigdellívol 2013: 35).

161 Letters from Captain Fernando Muñoz Acera to Muñoz Grandes, n.d. (AGMAV, 2003/4/2/1) and from José Salazar Melcón to Marisa Schütze Alonso, 14 October 1943 (MPA, R.4453/12).

162 Cuenca Toribio (2001: 25).

163 Instructions of the FET Office for Popular Education to the press, 29 June 1941 (AGA, SC, MIT, C. 76).

164 "Juventud y optimismo en el banderín de enganche," *Azul* (5 July 1941).

165 A sample of 122 soldiers from the Canary Islands who were recruited while doing their military service, and whose professions in civil life were known, also reports similar results: 40.16% were farmers, day labourers, and fishermen, while 14% were unskilled and skilled manual workers (Jiménez Soto 2015: 291).

166 Author's own estimates based on Ramírez-Copeiro del Villar (2001); Pérez Maestre (2008: 115–18, 217–86).

167 Moreno Juliá (2004: 395). The author, however, did not list the population sampled.

168 Ramos (1953: 6); González Pinilla (1987: 238); report by von Weizsäcker, 5 February 1943 (PAAA, R-29743).

169 Data has been compiled from diverse daily newspapers (*ABC, Arriba, Pueblo, Informaciones, La Vanguardia*), as well as from secondary sources, biographical reports on fallen Falangist soldiers and data compiled by the Spanish Army itself (AGMAV, C.3762/1 and C.3762/5).

170 Between January 1942 and December 1943, 214 obituaries with biographies of BD volunteers were published in the newspaper *ABC*. Sixty-five of the volunteers (30.3%) were from the Army. There were 56 FET members at that point (26.16%), 40 of whom (18.7%) were old shirts or *camisas viejas*. Along with these were 34 (15.88%) who had fought in the Civil War. There were 10 (4.67%) provisional ensigns and a small percentage

affiliated with Catholic Youth or other religious organizations (12, or 5.6%). Nine of the fallen (4.2%) were from families marked by repression in the Republican zone.

171 See lists of the fallen kept in the Fundación División Azul (Madrid), and data gathered from the discussion forum http://memoriablau.foros.ws

172 See Puente Fernández (2012: 179–80); author's estimates based on Palacio Pilacés (2013: II, 1083–1246); Viciana (2018: 242); Torres (2014: 183).

173 Von Stohrer, Madrid, 18 August 1941 (PAAA, Box 796, Geheimakten 6/9); Rühl (1986: 25–6) estimates this figure to be between 20% and 30%.

174 "Informe sobre la División Española de Voluntarios, llamada 'División Azul,' realizado con testimonios de prisioneros, desertores y diarios de campaña capturados por el Ejército Rojo," February 1942 (AHPCE, Box 104, Folder 1).

175 Some British reports mentioned this: Consul in Malaga, 10 July 1941 (NA-FO 371/26891).

176 "Informe sobre la División Española de Voluntarios," 4–8.

177 The efficacy of Falangist revolutionary rhetoric in attracting former members from the working-class left has been addressed, and to some extent overestimated, by Parejo (2008).

178 Monthly report July 1941, Murcia (AGA 51/20557); Torres (2014: 74, 183); Rodríguez González (2003: 251–5); Dolores Gancedo to Alberto Martín Gamero, Toledo, 27 October 1941 (AA).

179 Riudavets de Montes (1960). Some biographies in Parrilla Nieto (2007), and De la Iglesia & Burguete (2015).

180 Alcalde (2014: 101–2); J. Seoane Abella, "El Sargento Provisional en la División Azul," Blau División, 158 (September 1972).

181 See, e.g., Meliá Vila (2003).

182 Letters from Leopoldo Mulet, 21 October 1941, and from Julio González, 7 May 1942 (Ramón y Ortiz 2003: 345–8, 369–74).

183 Bellod Gómez (2004: 269–72).

184 The British ambassador surmised something similar: see the report of Samuel Hoare, 2 July 1941 (NA-FO 371/26940).

185 Georgacopulos (2015: 33, 40).

186 Arrese to Ridruejo, Madrid, 3 July 1941 (CDMH, Dionisio Ridruejo papers, MF/R 5912); Ridruejo (1978: 18–20, and 116); Blanco (1954: 8–10 and 34).

187 Diary of Enrique Menéndez Gundín, entry of 23 July 1941 (Cela 2010: 139).

188 "Informe de ambiente sobre la División Azul," Madrid, 7 July 1941 (AGA, Presidencia, 54/18950); 2nd Section of BD General Staff, n.d. [25 July 1941], AGMAV 2005/2/3/6.

189 War diary of Luis Aguilar, entries of 23 July 1941 and 3 August 1941, reproduced in Parrilla Nieto (2018: 49 and 53).

190 Dionisio Ridruejo to Marichu de la Mora, Grafenwöhr, n.d. [early August 1941], AFRI; Morente (2006: 294–5).

191 Dionisio Ridruejo to Marichu de la Mora, 25 October 1941, AFRI; "Diario de campaña de Salvador Zanón Mercado (1ª parte)" *Blau División*, 619 (February 2011), entry of 9 August 1941.

192 Sánchez Diana (1993: 95–8), memoirs of Private Enrique Murillo (Gragera Díaz & Infantes 2007: 146–9).

193 War diary of Federico Menéndez Gundín, entry of 8 September 1941 (Cela 2010: 142).

194 See examples in Linares (2000) and Sánchez Salcedo (2002).

195 Rodríguez Jiménez (2009: 285).

196 Order of BD Representation, 30 November 1942 (AGMAV 2006/8/3/1).

197 OKW to Army Group North, 8 June 1942, and Abwehr post report of the XIII Military District (Nuremberg), 28 June 1942, regarding Captain Juan Algarra, who was married to an English woman (BA-MA, RH 19 III/493).

198 Samuel Hoare to the Foreign Office, 6 August 1941 (NA-PRO, FO 371/26891).

199 Captain Collatz to LIV Army Corps, 26 October 1942 (BA-MA, RH 20–18/ 1075). There may have been more cases of desertion, as the BD Chiefs of Staff were reluctant to provide reliable data to the Germans. See report of General Hansen of the LIV Army Corps, to the 11th Army, 27 October 1942 (BA-MA, RH 20–18/ 1075).

200 According to reports by the BD General Staff (AGMAV, 3736/6), there were few proceedings for self-mutilation before the end of 1942: one in November 1941 and another in July 1942.

201 See four cases in Pinilla Turiño (1987: 261–3).

202 Report on the Blue Division, February 1942; a report to General Varela, n.d. (*c.* December 1941, AHMC-FGV, C. 115) indicated that there had been five desertions to date.

203 Moreno Juliá (2004: 202); Rodríguez Jiménez (2009: 329).

204 Author's own data based on orders of the BD General Staff between those dates (AGMAV, 3736/6).

205 See, for example, the report of the Intelligence section regarding Avelino Navarro, who had joined the BD while doing military service. He had been a Socialist, had served in the Republican Army, and was presumed to be "a Red Army sympathizer." The resolution was to watch him and deny him leave (report of Colonel S. Amado, 10 September 1943, AGMAV 1994/12/2).

206 Reports of the Commanding General of the 21st March battalion, 8 April 1943, and the 27th March Battalion, Hof, 18 October 1943 (AGMAV, 1989/5/4/3 y 1995/6/5/1).

207 See AOK 18 to Army Group North, 5 August 1942; OKH to Army Group North, 5 September 1942 and 15 September 1942 (BA-MA, RH 19 III/493).

208 Reports of Colonel Wilhelm Knüppel, 9 May 1943, and Lieutenant
     Förster, 9 July 1943 (BA-MA, RH 24–50/59).
209 The number of deserters in the International Brigades would be at least
     575 (of 32,256 total volunteers). See Skoutelsky (2006: 169, 266–74).
210 For instance, the Communist Julio Jiménez Gómez (2010), who deserted
     in January 1943.
211 Report of the Civil Governor of Barcelona, 9 July 1954 (AGMAV, C
     3770/1).
212 See, for example, Abwehrstelle Ostland to the OKW Amt Ausland/
     Abwehr, 24 January 1942 (BA-MA, RH 19 III/493) and report by the
     Generalkommando XXXVIII AK, Ic, *Unerlaubte Entfernungen-Fahnenflucht
     1.4.42–31.12.42* (BA-MA, RH 24–38/187).
213 Puente Fernández (2012: 87). For more cases, see AGMAV, C 3777/4.
214 Report by Sergeant Julio Luengo, Frankfurt a. M., 14 April 1943 (AGMAV
     C37777/4).
215 For example, Private Vicente Perales enlisted in June 1942. Upon being pun-
     ished by an officer, who sent him unarmed to the front lines, he deserted
     and was caught in a village in the rearguard and condemned to fifteen
     years of prison. See Court Martial of 13 May 1943 (AGMAV, 1990/5/5/12I).
216 Report of thé provincial head of the FET, Ourense, 16 October 1941 (AGA,
     21/20558).
217 Author's own estimates based on data by Puente Fernández (2012: 53–64)
     and Torres (2014: 120).
218 See, for example, the evocation of violence in 1936–7 in his hometown by
     BD volunteer Espinosa Poveda (1992: 32–5); or the brief autobiography of
     medical student Pau Arriaga (2003).
219 This was the case for Granada SEU leader Daniel Saucedo. An internal
     report stated that he should be dispatched to Russia to disprove his "fake
     Falangism" (Hernández Burgos 2013: 197–8).
220 See, for example, the series of articles published in the BD trench journal
     with the title *Mañana* [tomorrow]: *Hoja de Campaña*, 17 and 25 February
     1942 and 9 March 1942.
221 See, e.g., S. López de la Torre, "Dos años ya"; *Haz*, IV:6 (July-August
     1943); J. Hernández Bravo, "Un puesto de guardia sobre la nieve rusa,"
     Arriba (6 February 1942).
222 A. Aznar, "Fiesta de la Raza en Rusia," *Arriba* (11 October 1942); Ridruejo
     (2008: 123); J. Beneyto, "Paralelo oriental," *Haz* (19 August 1941).
223 Memorandum to the German ambassador in Madrid, 13 July 1941
     (PAAA, ADBM, Reg. Pol. Allg., 557/2, Box 766).
224 "Cartas desde Rusia," *Arriba* (16 January 1942); A. Abad Ojuel, "Los que
     vamos a la guerra," *ABC* (11 February 1942); A. Crespo, "Tiempos de
     juventud," *Juventud*, 23 (29 October 1942); F. Cañas Estival, "El Quinto

Aniversario de la muerte de José Antonio en las trincheras del Este de Europa," *Ofensiva* (19 November 1942).

225 "Hombres nuevos," *Hoja de Campaña* (4 November 1942); J.L. Gómez-Tello, "Con nuestros abuelos, contra nuestros padres," *El Español*, II:31 (29 May 1943); J. Sánchez Carrilero, "La paz no se encuentra; hay que ganarla," *Hoja de Campaña* (30 March 1942).

226 Ruiz Carnicer (1996: 143–7).; J. G. Landero, "El Sindicato Español Universitario. Su labor presente y sus anhelos futuros," *ABC* (2 November 1941); J.L.A. Bellogín, "De un camarada de la División Azul," *Haz* (14 October 1941); F. Sancho Ruano, "Evocación y recuerdo de la División Azul," *Horizontes*, 5 (31 January 1942).

227 Testimony by Luis García Berlanga in the film documentary by Javier Rioyo, *Extranjeros de sí mismos* (2001), available at: https://www.youtube.com/watch?v=EHOZ57wo45U (minute 58:30 onwards).

228 Diary of Enrique Menéndez Gundín, entries of 4 July 1941 and 26 October 1941 (Cela 2010: 137, 146); letters of five soldiers to Colonel Leandro García 13 October 1941, and from Sergeant Ríos, 12 December 1941 (FLGG-MPA).

229 Dionisio Ridruejo to Marichu de la Mora, 30 October 1941 and 17 December 1941 (AFRI); F. Izquierdo Luque, "La generación de los divisionarios," *Arriba* (9 February 1943); A. Tovar, "Cómo interpretamos el 25 de junio," *Haz*, IV:5 (June 1943).

230 War diary of Lt. Juan Romero Osende, entry of 29 October 1941 (private archive of Ana Romero, A Coruña). See also Andrés Oncala [D. Ridruejo], "La canción de la Falange en el frente ruso," *Arriba* (14 April 1942).

231 "Por la Navidad de los divisionarios," *Arriba* (17 November 1942); "Un cuadro legendario heroico," *Arriba* (25 February 1943); T. Nieto Funcia, "La salvación de los Catilinarios," *Arriba* (11 October 1942); D. Ridruejo, "La España del Wolchow," *Arriba* (18 July 1942).

232 See, e.g., letter of Manuel Tarín Sala to his grandfather, 10 April 1942 (AFR).

233 Castañón (1991: 81, 100); report by the British military attaché, Madrid, 9 July 1941 (NA-FO 371/26940).

234 See "Caídos de la División Azul: ¡Presentes!" *Nueva Alcarria* (11 April 1942).

235 Juan de Novgorod, "Paso a nuestra generación," *Hermandad*, III:8 (January–February 1959).

3. A Long March: From Central Europe to the Volkhov Front

1 J.M. Troncoso, "Con la División Española de Voluntarios en un campamento alemán," *Ejército*, 25 (February 1942).

2 Captain Bernardino López Romero, *Hospital de Campaña 250. Memoria. Desde el día 8 de septiembre al 1º de octubre de 1941*, 2 and 4–5 (ACLR).

3 War diary of the German liaison unit, entries of 26 and 31 August, 1 and 6 September 1941, BA-MA, RH 26–250/2; Rodríguez Jiménez (2007a: 118–19).

4 Muñoz Grandes to Varela, Minsk, 18 September 1941 (AHMC-FGV, C. 115).

5 Reizer (2009: 87, 96–7).

6 War diary of the 9th Army, entries of 24 and 25 September 1941, BA-MA, RH20–9/17; Kleinfeld and Tambs (1983: 102–3). This undid the initial plan of the 9th Army to deploy the Spanish Division in place of the 86th Division, which would have gone into the reserve.

7 War diary of Luis Aguilar, entry of 27 September 1941 (Parrilla Nieto 2018: 65–6).

8 Report by the quartermaster of the German liaison staff in the BD, *Bericht über die Erfahrungen beim Span.-Div.-Verplf. Amt Witebsk am 2.-10.10.41* (BA-MA, RH 19III/774).

9 War diary of Army Group North, vol. 4, entry of 10 October 1941 (BA-MA, RH 19III/168).

10 War diary of the German liaison unit, entries of 25 September and 1, 11, and 17 October 1941.

11 Dionisio Ridruejo to Marichu de la Mora, Grafenwöhr, 7 August 1941 (ARF); Vicente Rodríguez Vela to Colonel Leandro García, 22 March 1942 (MPA); Muñoz Césaro (2011: 30–1); Colonel Jesús Badillo to Varela, 16 August 1941 and 25 December 1941 (AHMC-FGV).

12 Recio Cardona (1998: 87–107); Ridruejo 1978: 119).

13 *Informe sobre la Sanidad de la División Azul*, Porkhov, 30 November 1941 (AGA, Presidencia 18950).

14 Sánchez Diana (1993: 158–9, 172); Díaz del Río (2011: 175–6).

15 Hernanz Blanco (2013: 254–5, entry of 9 November 1942); Farré Albiñana (1949: 187–90).

16 See Fritz (1995) and Kühne (2006).

17 See war diary of Manuel de Cárdenas, entry of 25 February 1942; similar accounts were collected by German diplomats in Spain among returned soldiers: report from Eberhard von Stohrer, Madrid, 1 June 1942 (PAAA, Deutsche Botschaft Madrid 553/3, Box 761).

18 Castaño Doña (1991: 60); Gragera Díaz & Infantes (2007: 76); Palacio Pilacés (2013: I, 388–9); War diary of Joaquín Cuerda Ros, entries of 19 and 22 September, 3 October, and 1 November 1941 (Cuerda Ros 2013: 38, 41, 46, 61–3); Anonymous, *Diario de un Soldado*, entry of 18 September 1941 (AGMAV, 46767/2/5).

19 A. Rugero Cozano, "Retazos," *Blau División*, 537 (April 2004).

20 *Tätigkeitsbericht des Gen, Kdo. LIV AK, Abt. Iva, für die Zeit vom 1.9–31 December 1942* (BA-MA, RH 24–54/ 235). German pilots of the Condor Legion held a similar view (Schüler-Springorum [2010: 152–7]).

21 See Hellbeck (2012: 507); DiNardo (1996: 711–30).

22 Reports of Captain Wessel, Dno, 2 October 1941 (BA-MA, RH 24–1/29); General von Chappuis, 8 December 1941 (BA-MA, RH 20–16/ 67); 16th Army to Army Group North, 18 November 1941 (BA-MA, RH 19III /774).

23 Ludwig Schwab, *Die Stadt Hof und die spanische Division im europäischen Freiheitskrieg*, 1944, 15 (SH-A, Manuskripte, M48).

24 Peter (1992: 180–4); *Spaniens Freiwillige an der Ostfront: Los voluntarios españoles en el frente. Ein Bildbuch von der Blauen Division*, Kaunas: Propaganda-Kompanie der Armee Busch, n.d. [1942].

25 Entries of 4 and 5 January 1942, in Jochmann (1982: 178). Hitler reproduced almost literally the views of the Prussian officer August Karl von Goeben, who fought in Spain as a mercenary in the mid-nineteenth century and penned two books: *Vier Jahre in* Spanien (1861) and *Reise- und Landbriefe aus Spanien und vom spanischen Heere in Marokko* (1863).

26 See for instance "Heldenkampf der Blauen Division," *Brüsseler Zeitung* (1 January 1942); "Moartea glorioasâ a Sefului. Escadrile Albastre," *Viata*, Bucharest (2 September 1942); "Die Blaue Division," *Pariser Zeitung* (3 October 1943).

27 Letters of Corporal Otto M., 30 October 1941, and Captain Hermann Sch., 5 November 1941 (BfZ-SS).

28 Author's interview of Dr. Christoph von Auer, Großburgwedel, 15 September 2002 (AA). See also "Las memorias de un capellán castrense," *Blau División*, 583 (February 2008), and the account by the former private of the 126th Infantry Division, H.-H. Kurz in *Blau División* (November-December 1987).

29 Letter from cavalry inspector Heinrich K., Brest-Litovsk, 30 April 1942 (BfZ-SS].

30 *Dos años de lucha. Estampas divisionarias*, Berlin: Gallus Druckerei AG, 1944, p. 5.

31 Hernanz Blanco (2013: 20).

32 A. Aragonés, "División Azul. Cartas de un voluntario," *Nueva Alcarria* (18 April 1942); Urquijo (1973: 320).

33 See, for example, the letters exchanged between the German soldier Alfons Littwin (15 December 1944) and the Spanish veteran Lidio Bengoa (Bilbao, 5 June 1944), GStA, I. Ha 218, Nr. 256.

34 War diary of Joaquín Ros, entry of May 1942 (Cuerda Ros 2013: 63); War diary of Manuel de Cárdenas, entry of 4 March 1942; Ydígoras (1984: 299); Meliá Vila (2003: 114).

35 "Alemanes y españoles ante Leningrado," *Hoja de Campaña* (31 November 1943); "Del 'landser' al 'guripa' pasando por Mestelewo," *Hoja de Campaña* (7 November 1943).

36 Jesús Martínez Tessier, *Diario de campaña*, entry of 24 September 1941 (private archive of Mr. Jorge Martínez Reverte, Madrid); "Informe sobre la División Española de Voluntarios," AHPCE, February 1942.

37 Report of the Feldgendarmerie of the 18th Army, 16–31 January 1943 (BA-MA, RH 20–18/ 1476); monthly report of the Hospitals' Inspection, June 1943 (AGMAV 29/7/49); Muñoz Césaro (2011: 53–4). Private Eugenio Rodríguez also described some quarrels between Spaniards and Germans, generally motivated by German behaviour towards civilians. See Pérez (2020: 187)

38 Report of lieutenant Benítez, Königsberg, 19 November 1943 (AGMAV, 1996/3/3/3).

39 Diary of Lidia Ósipova, entries dated 25 August 1942 and 8 January 1943 (Lomagin 2004: 464, 466–7).

40 Dionisio Ridruejo to Marichu de la Mora, 17 December 1941 (ARF); Muñoz Grandes to Varela, Minsk, 18 September 1941 (AHMC-FGV, C. 115).

41 Report form Oberführer SS Walther-Friedrich Schellenberg, Berlin, 4 January 1944 (PAAA, R-101143); Obersturmführer Vey to Einsatzgruppe I, 14 November 1943 (USHMM, Sp BD 11.001M.05).

42 See Aly (2005), as well as an updated synthesis in Herbert (2016: 105–15).

43 War diary of Manuel de Cárdenas, entry of 1 March 1942; Sanz Jarque (2010: 45–6); War memoirs of Benigno Cabo, 1944, 13–14 (private archive of Jorge Villena, Madrid).

44 Letter of Daniel Torra, 4 October 1941 (Torra i Puigdellívol 2013: 51).

45 *Arriba* (13 March 1942); Salas Iñigo (1988: 45).

46 G. Riera, "Crónica azul de guerra," *Hoja de Campaña* (5 September 1943).

47 Martínez-Mena (1991: 14–15).

48 Castañón (1991: 184–5, 187).

49 "El capitán Muñoz habla del heroísmo de los voluntarios de la División Azul," *El Alcázar* (3 February 1942).

50 Dionisio Ridruejo to Marichu de la Mora, Berlin, 21 August 1941 (ARF); Díaz del Río (2011: 210–11); the description of the bombardments in Berlin, in war memoirs of Benigno Cabo, 144.

51 "Cartas de Rusia," *Boletín del SEU de Madrid*, 12 (1942); "De la heroica División Azul," *Nueva Alcarria* (20 March 1943).

52 "Carta del camarada Gabriel Riera, voluntario en la División Azul," *Nueva Alcarria* (25 April 1942).

53 "Cartas de Rusia," *Boletín del SEU de Madrid*, 11 (1942).

54 Captain surgeon López Romero, *Hospital de Campaña 250. Memoria*, 9 (ACLR).

55 E. Nin de Cardona, "Regreso de un voluntario," *Nueva Alcarria* (14 March 1942); Muñoz Césaro (2011: 26, entry of 4 July 1942); Gómez-Tello (1945: 16); Riudavets de Montes (1960: 10).

56 Dionisio Ridruejo to Marichu de la Mora, Grafenwöhr, 7 August 1941 and
    Berlin, 21 August 1941 (ARF); Hernanz Blanco (2013: 38–9, entry of 25
    April 1942); war diary of Carlos Figuerola, entry of 17 June 1942 (Remírez
    de Esparza 2020: 27–8).
57 Vadillo (1967: 70–3, 101); Letter of Manuel Tarín Sala, 17 April 1942 (AFR);
    War diary of Arenales, 10–11. For more examples, see Núñez Seixas
    (2018b).
58 Interviews with Albert Lorenz (born 1927), Bernreuth, and Johann Leit-
    geb (born 1930), Auerbach, 17 May 2004, by Hans-Jürgen Kugler (AA).
59 Reports of the 2nd Section of the BD General Staff, 25 and 28 July 1941
    (AGMAV, 2005/2/3/7); Report of the 2nd Infanterie-Ersatzbattalion, Bay-
    reuth, 5 August 1942 (AGMAV, 1978/7/3/2); Diary of Joaquín Ros Cabo,
    entry of 10 September 1941, in Cuerda Ros (2013: 33).
60 Schwab, *Die Stadt Hof*, 20–1.
61 Paulus (2001: 73).
62 Notices of the commander of the 14th March Battalion, Hof, 31 August
    and 1 September 1942 (AGMAV, 1985/20/3 and 1984/12/1); report from
    Captain Antonio Villalobos, Hof, 6–7 July 1942 (AGMAV 1983/5/3).
63 Several examples in AGMAV 28/7/15/9.
64 Report from the Spanish military police, Berlin, 28 December 1942
    (AGMAV 1985/20/5); letter from General Muñoz Grandes to Alfredo
    Guedea, 28 October 1942 (AGMAV1985/8/4); *Inspección de Hospitales. In-
    forme mensual*, April 1943 (AGMAV 2025/6/1). See also Brydan (2019b).
65 Reports from Colonel Fernández de Landa, 20 July 1941, and Captain Víc-
    tor Hornillos, Grafenwöhr, 21 July 1941 (AGMAV 20052/2/21).
66 Letter from Alfredo Rodríguez Pérez to M. Rodríguez Dopazo, 20–1 July
    1941 (AXFN); letter from twelve volunteers to Colonel Leandro García,
    9 August 1941 (MPA); letter of Dionisio Ridruejo, Grafenwöhr, n.d. [c. 25
    July 1941], AFR.
67 See, e.g., Hernanz Blanco (2013: 24–5, entry of 9 April 1942).
68 M. Salvador Gironés, "Cosas de por allá," *Blau División*, 106 (June 1968);
    Muñoz Césaro (2011: 25).
69 War diary of Menéndez Gundín, entries of 10 and 29 October 1941 (Cela
    2010: 146–7).
70 Letter of Elisabeth Mees to corporal Antonio Herrero, Jöhlingen, 28
    March 1943 (AA).
71 See Morant i Ariño (2013: 422, 433–5), and Herzog (2007: 10–63).
72 Álvarez de Sotomayor (1991: 156).
73 "Crónica de Rusia," *Enlace*, 13 (29 November 1942).
74 D. Castro Villacañas, "Un soldado en Berlín," *Arriba* (26 March 1943).
75 J. Revuelta Imaz & F. Izquierdo Luque, "La partida," *Mensaje. Revista tri-
    mestral*, 1–2 (1943).

76 Report of the DGS, 19 January 1942 (AHMC-FGV, C.115); war memoirs of Benigno Cabo, 151.

77 See, e.g., Emmi Santter to Antonio Herrero, Brackenheim, 3 and 7 February 1943 (AA).

78 Nattermann (2011).

79 Sagarra (2012: 180–90).

80 Schwab, *Die Stadt Hof*, 22. One of these cases was Francisca Griessl (born 1943), who was told as a young adult that a Spanish soldier was her biological father. Many years later, she found that her father had been the pioneers' sergeant Francisco Suárez Ojeda (*Blau División*, 573, April 2007).

81 War diary of Manuel de Cárdenas, entries of 4 and 15 March 1942; war diary of J. Martínez Tessier, entries of 25–6 August 1941; *Diario de un Soldado*, entry of 29 August 1941.

82 Report from the director of the Spanish Hospital in Berlin, 6 February 1943 (AGMAV 1987/10/2/3); *Hoja de instrucción para los soldados españoles*, n.d. [1942], and DEV, 3d Section General Staff, *Instrucción general 3.054*, 18 May 1942 (AGMAV, 3736/5).

83 Leaflet *An alle Urlauber*, signed by the *Wehrmachtstandortältester Hof*, Hof: n.p., 1942, AA.

84 Vadillo (1967: 104–5, 110–11); reports from the 2nd Section of the General Staff, 28–9 July 1941 (AGMAV, 2005/2/3/7–8).

85 War Memoirs of Benigno Cabo, 14; Schwab, *Die Stadt Hof*, 21; Herrmann (2012: 95).

86 See the war diary of the Germain Liaison, 13 August 1941–24 July 1942, in BA-MA, RH 26–250/2, entries of 26 August and 1 September 1941. Martín Velasco also wrote that at times his motorized liaison group made off with more chickens than they could carry back to the camp (war diary of Martín Velasco, entry of 19 September 1941).

87 Reizer (2009: 96).

88 *Diario de un Soldado*, entry of 29 August 1941; Eizaguirre (1955: 17–19); Ridruejo (1978: 47–8).

89 See Núñez Seixas & Beyda (2019: 120–1, 126).

90 Transcribed letter of Private Carlos Juan, Minsk, 18 September 1941, in AHMC-FGV, C. 115).

91 Jasper (2011: 45); Böhler (2006).

92 Esteban-Infantes (1956: 50); Jiménez Andrades (1957: 38–47); Castelo Villaoz (1990: 55–6); Espinosa Poveda (1993: 9).

93 E. Borrás, "El heroísmo de la División Azul," *Mediterráneo* (26 February 1942); Sanz Jarque (2010: 77–82, 89).

94 M. Salvador Gironés, "Cosas de por allá," *Blau División*, 75 (November 1965).

95 Gómez-Tello (1945: 40).

96 L. Sánchez Maspons, "Crónica de un viaje a Rusia. La primera impresión al entrar en Ukrania," *Informaciones* (30 October 1941).

97 War diary of Martínez Tessier, entry of 29 August 1941; P. Carretero Vegas, "Suwalky o Sudauen, inicio de aquellas marchas," *Blau División*, 256 (November 1980).

98 War diary of Luis Aguilar, entry of 31 August 1941 (Parrilla Nieto 2018: 59).

99 Urquijo (1973: 261); J. Santamaría Díez, "Pieckzanka y Gasparone," *Blau División*, 271 (February 1982).

100 Report of the DGS, 28 April 1942 (FNFF 1992–4: 331–50).

101 Ursula [surname illegible] to Corporal Antonio Herrero Castellano, Poznań, 13 September 1943 (AA).

102 See B. Bengoa, "Polonia contra la hoz y el martillo," *Domingo. Semanario Naçional* (2 May 1937).

103 War diary of Martínez Tessier, entry of 8 September 1941; "División Azul," *Haz*, IV:4 (May 1943); Muñoz Césaro (2011: 126–7, 132–3, entries of 14 March and 16–17 March 1943).

104 Castañón (1991: 186); Reverte & Reverte (2001: 192).

105 M. Pombo Angulo, "La más bella oración," *ABC* (29 April 1943); E. Giménez Caballero, "Katyn o la venganza de Boris Godunof," *ABC* (2 May 1943); J. Arrarás, "Las fosas de Katyn y otras," *La Vanguardia Española* (15 May 1943).

106 Salvador (1962: 68–9, 73); Bars Casamitjana (1962: 1–2).

107 War diary of Martínez Tessier, entry of 8 September 1941.

108 War diary of Manuel de Cárdenas, entry of 16 March 1942.

109 War diary of Martínez Tessier, entry of 8 September 1941.

110 De la Vega (1998: 82); M. Salvador Gironés, "Cosas de por allá," *Blau División*, 153 (May 1972). See also the impressions written by Javier Urmeneta, reproduced in Jimeno Aranguren (2015: 112).

111 Report of the Spanish Military Gendarmerie in Riga, 6 August 1943 (AGMAV 1993/6/1/2); Meliá Vila (2003: 127); diary of Menéndez Gundín, entry of 4 November 1941 (Cela 2010: 148); Urquijo (1973: 325).

112 Cogollos Vicens (1985: 166–7); López-Covarrubias (2012: 322–4).

113 Errando Vilar (1942: 280–1).

114 Blanch Sabench (2010: 75); L. López Ballesteros, "Sur en el Norte," *El Español*, II:30 (22 May 1943); J.L. Gómez-Tello, "Veinticuatro horas en Riga," *El Español*, II:29 (15 May 1943).

4. The Blue Division on the Front

1 See Aly & Heim (1993: 381–5), Hürter (2001: 402–4), Ganzenmüller (2000; 2005: 19–40; 2014), Kilian (2012) and Rutherford (2014).

2 See Rössler & Schleiermacher (1993), as well as Madajczyk (1994).

3 Vehviläinen (2002).
4 General Busch, AOK 16, to Army Group North, 18 November 1941 (BA-MA, RH 20–16/66).
5 Glantz (2002: 287–304).
6 Ganzenmüller (2005) and Reid (2011).
7 Of the 1,311,000 inhabitants, 69% over fourteen years of age were women; those under fourteen and those over sixty totalled 46% (Kilian 2012: 94–6).
8 Hürter (2001); Hass (2002); and Kilian (2011).
9 Bordjugov (1999); Rass (2005: 80–90).
10 For a narration of the blockade, see Glantz (2002) and Salisbury (2003). On the daily life of those under siege, see the diary of Lena Muchina (2014) as well as Jarov (2013), Dobrotvorskaja (2013) and Adamowitsch & Granin (2018).
11 Ganzenmüller (2005: 279–313; 2011); Reid (2011: 143–71).
12 Reid (2011: 497–500); Voronina (2011).
13 The initial idea was for the BD to relieve two-thirds of the 126th Division, which would go into the reserves. See order of the 16th Army Command, 28 September 1941 (BA-MA RH 24–1/29).
14 Commander General of the I Army Corps to General Herrlein, 24 September 1941 (BA-MA, RH 24–1/37).
15 Diary of the German liaison corps, entries of 1, 4 and 11 October 1941 (BA-MA, RH 26–250/2). On Franz von Roques, see Hasenclever (2010: 108–20, 197).
16 Report of Spanish military attaché in Berlin, 7 November 1941 (AHMC-FGV, C. 115).
17 Report of Captain Collatz, n.d. [2 October 1941] (BA-MA, RH 24–1/29).
18 Report of Captain Wessel, Dno, 2 October 1941 (BA-MA, RH 24–1/29).
19 Report of the 16th Army to Army Group North, 10 October 1941 (BA-MA, RH 20–16/67); report of General von Roques, 20 October 1941 (BA-MA, RH 20–16/70).
20 War diary of Army Group North, entry of 23 October 1941 (BA-MA, RH 19III/168); Rutherford (2014: 122–8).
21 War diary of German liaison unit, entries of 9 November to 4 December 1941 (BA-MA, RH 26–250/2); Jesús Badillo to Varela, Novgorod, 24 October 1941 (AHMC-FGV, C. 115); *Diario de un Soldado*, entry in Sitno, 18 November 1941.
22 War diary of the XXXVIII Army Corps, entry of 7 December 1941 (BA-MA RH 24–38/51); War diary of Army Group North, entries of 7 and 8 December 1941 (BA-MA, RH 19III/769).
23 War diary of the XXXVIII Army Corps, entries of 8 and 9 December 1941.
24 See "Goluvaia Divizia istekaet krobiu," *Pravda* (17 January 1942).

25 War diary of the XXXVIII Army Corps, entries of 10, 11, 12 and 14 December 1941, also 9 and 13 January 1942; war diary of Army Group North, entry of 8 December 1941.

26 Reports from AOK 16, 6, 8, and 9 December 1941(BA-MA, RH 20–16/66).

27 Report to PCE, February 1942; Kovalev (2014: 124–231).

28 See, for example, F. M. Castiella, "¡Clavados al terreno!" *Informaciones* (20 January 1942).

29 According to data from the 16th Army, between 17 October and 21 December 1941, the BD suffered 509 deaths (6.41% of total deaths in the 16th Army) and 1,351 injured (4.52%). See *Verlustlisten*, BA-MA, RH 20–16/627.

30 Report by General Gómez Ulla, head of BD medical services, 10 March 1942 (AHMC-FGV, C.115).

31 Rutherford (2014: 200–2).

32 Report by Wilhelmi, 23 March 1942 (PAAA, Box 796, *Geheimakten 6/9*). That same month, Muñoz Grandes himself estimated 900 deaths and 1,000 wounded who were "irrecoverable" (Muñoz Grandes to Varela, Berlin, 16 March 1942, AHMC-FGV, C.115).

33 Army Group North, *Zahlenmässige Gesamtverluste bis 15.7.42*, 27 July 1942 (BA-MA, RH 19III/511).

34 War diary of Army Group North, entry of 14 December 1941.

35 Report of AOK 16, November 1941 (BA-MA, RH 19III/774); *Boletín de Información* of the 2nd Section of the BD General Staff, 17 January 1942 (AHMC-FGV, C.115).

36 DGS report, Irún, 17 January 1942 (AHMC-FGV, C. 115). Soon after, Esparza was relieved of his command and repatriated, apparently due to pressure from the Falange party.

37 Report of the 2nd Section of the XXXVIII Army Corps, 11 November 1941 to 31 March 1942 (BA-MA, RH 24–38/41). See also Pinilla (n.d.: 181–261).

38 F. Izquierdo Luque, "¡Otensky! ¡Possad!" *Hoja de Campaña* (1 July 1942); A. de Laiglesia, "Possad, el sublime martirio," *Hoja de Campaña* (24 June 1942); J.A. Villaescusa, "Nuestra primera operación," *Ofensiva* (18 October 1942).

39 The BD trench journal and the FET-JONS publication *Enlace*, published since mid-1942 for Spanish workers in Germany, began the mythification of these armed deeds. See E. G. R. I., "Soñando...," *Hoja de Campaña* (23 March 1942); L. Morcillo Díaz, "Heroísmo español en Tigoda," *Enlace* (1 November 1942).

40 See Carrera Buil & Ferrer-Dalmau (2003), and Román Jiménez (2011).

41 Jesús Badillo to Varela, 8 November 1941 and 24 November 1941 (AHMC-FGV, C. 115).

42 War diary of the AOK 16, 1st Section, entries of 16, 18 and 20 November 1941 (BA-MA, RH 20–16/49); reports of AOK 16th Army, signed by

Busch, 8 November 1941 and 14 December 1941 (BA-MA, RH 20–16/66); war diary of Army Group North, 9 December 1941.

43 Report of General von Chappuis, Grigorovo, 9 December 1941 (RH 20–16/ 67); War diary of Army Group North, entries of 9, 10, and 11 December 1941.

44 War diary of Army Group North, entries of 18, 20, 26, 28, and 29 December 1941.

45 War diary of the XXXVIII Army Corps, entry of 21 November 1941 (BA-MA RH 24–38/51).

46 Report of AOK 16 to Army Group North, 9 December 1941 (BA-MA RH 20–16/ 67).

47 War diary of the XXXVIII Army Corps, entry of 2 December 1941 (BA-MA RH 24–38/51).

48 War diary of the XXXVIII Army Corps, entry of 4 January 1942; Rutherford (2014: 197–9).

49 Lindemann to Army Group North, 3 October 1941, and reports by AOK 16, 17 November 1941 (BA-MA, RH 20–16/67); report of the 16th Army, 29 December 1941 (BA-MA, RH 20–16/90).

50 War diary of the XXXVIII Army Corps, entries of 24 January and 5 February 1942 (BA-MA RH 24–38/51).

51 Reports of von Weizsäcker, 10 and 16 January, 5, 13, 19, and 26 February 1942; report of von Stohrer, 27 February 1942; Ritter to the Secretary of State, 4 March 1942 (PAAA, R.29742); report of Spanish military attaché, Berlin, 1 February 1942 (AHMC-FGV, C.115).

52 Serrano Suñer to Ridruejo and Agustín Aznar, n.d. [winter of 1941], and to Dionisio Ridruejo, 6 April 1942 (Gracia 2007: 75–6, 79–80).

53 War diary of the XXXVIII Army Corps, entries of 10, 12, and 13 February 1942 (BA-MA RH 24–38/51).

54 See, for example, *España y Alemania. Fraternidad en el campo de batalla*, n.p., 1942; V. de la Serna, "El desfile del 42," *Enlace* (17 April 1943); *Schlacht am Wolchow*, 179–80; "Las hazañas de nuestros cruzados junto al lago," *El Alcázar* (13 February 1942). See also Aznar (1942) and Barrachina (1994).

55 Conversation between the Commander of the Army Group North and the Commander General of the XXXVIII Army Corps, war diary of the XXXVIII Army Corps, entry of 29 March 1942 (BA-MA RH 24–38/51).

56 According to the daily activity reports of the units under the command of the XXXVIII Army Corps between 1 April and 29 June 1942 (BA-MA, RH 24–38/180).

57 War diary of the XXXVIII Army Corps, entry of 27 May 1942 (BA-MA RH 24–38/51).

58 On the Volkhov Pocket combats, see Rutherford (2014: 240–6).

59 Combat reports of Colonel Hoppe, 24 June 1942; of Captain Schmidt-Liermann, 24 June 1942 (BA-MA, RH RH 24–38/55); of the SS Standanterführer Burk, 26 June 1942, and of Lieutenant Heinrichs, 24 June 1942 (BA-MA RH 26–126/49).

60 War diary of the XXXVIII Army Corps, entries of 22, 23, 24, and 26 June 1942 (BA-MA RH 24–38/51).

61 Report of AOK 16, 2 October 1942 (BA-MA RH 19III/693); report of Lt. von Uslar-Gleichen, Berlin, 25 July 1942 (BA-MA RH 19III/780). See also Rutherford (2014: 202–8).

62 See the album *Kampf und Sieg am* Wolchow (1942), BA-MA, RH 24–38/292.

63 Report of the XXXVIII Army Corps, IC Section, 13 July 1942 (BA-MA RH 24–38/137).

64 War diary of the XXXVIII Army Corps, entries of 6, 14, 19, and 31 July 1942 (BA-MA RH 24–38/51).

65 Letter from AOK 18 to the general in command of the XXXVIII Army Corps, 22 July 1942; letter from AOK 18 to Army Group North, 28 July 1942 (BA-MA, RH 19 III/493).

66 War diary of the XXXVIII Army Corps, entries of 7, 9, 13, and 21 August, 2 and 10 September 1942.

67 A BD report dated 7 December 1942 listed 7,252 men, an average of 348 soldiers/km of front, outnumbered only by the 1st German Infantry Division, which had 656 soldiers/km. The other divisions had fewer combatants per kilometre of front (*Stand 7.12.1942. Inf.-Gefechtsstärken der Div.-Abscnitte*, BA-MA RH 20–18/823).

68 The 121st Division also applied an iron-fisted occupation policy in Pavlovsk in the winter of 1941–2 (Rutherford 2014: 151–68, 287–8).

69 Most daily dispatches had "nothing special to report." See the war diary of the LIV Army Corps, October–November 1942 (BA-MA RH 24–54/60).

70 Note on the state of the horses of the LIV Army Corps, December 1943 (BA-MA RH 24–54/69).

71 In December 1942, the BD had a total of 7,242 combat-ready men, compared to 3,727 men the SS-Polizei Division and 3,944 in the 170th Division. Their light and heavy weaponry was quite similar. See reports of the LIV Army Corps, 7 December 1942 (BA-MA, RH 24–54/65).

72 Report of AOK 18 to Army Group North, 3 December 1942 (BA-MA RH 19III/708); weekly division reports of the LIV Army Corps, 5, 12, and 18 January 1943 (B-MA, RH 24–54/74).

73 Conversation between the commander general of Army Group North and the LIV Army Corps Command (war diary of the LIV Army Corps, entry of 31 December 1942 [BA-MA RH 24–54/60]).

74 Esteban-Infantes (1956: 136–7); Rutherford (2014: 283–5).

75 Lindemann to Army Group North, 9 December 1942, BA-MA, RH 20–18/1075.

76 Moreno Juliá (2007: 427–9).

77 Carrera Buil & Ferrer-Dalmau (2003: 227–36).

78 Rutherford (2014: 208–10); Moreno Juliá (2004: 186–7). For operational details, see Caballero Jurado (2004a) and Fontenla Ballesta (2012). See also report by Captain Alemany, 20 February 1942 (AGMAV c.2006/14/3/1).

79 War diary of the Army Group North, entries of 11 and 12 February 1943 (BA-MA, RH 19III/199); war diary of the L Army Corps, entries of 10 and 16 February and 2 March 1943 (BA-M, RH 24–50/35); war diary of the AOK 18, entries of 10 and 11 February 1943 (BA-MA, RH 20–18/470).

80 War diary of Army Group North, entries of 17 February and 7 March 1943 (BA-MA, RH 19III/200).

81 See, for example, L Army Corps to the 18th Army, 18 May 1943 (BA-MA, RH 24–50/65).

82 Conversation between General Kleffel and General Loch, 8 April 1943 (BA-MA, RH 24–50/64).

83 *Fahrtbericht 10 March 1943 250 (span.) Inf. Div.*, report to the L Army Corps, BA-MA, RH 24–50/49; *Fahrtbericht 24 March 1943* (BA-MA, RH 24–50/64).

84 "Befehl für die Umgliederung im Abschnitt des L. AK," 9 May 1943 (BA-MA, RH 24–50/65).

85 War diary of the L Army Corps, entries of 16 March, 8 and 18 April, 1, 9, and 17 May, 17 and 26 June 1943 (BA-MA, RH 24–50/57).

86 *Fahrbericht* of 26 June 1943 (BA-MA RH 24–50/65).

87 Order from the L Army Corps Command, 20 July 1943 (BA-MA, RH 24–50/66).

88 Order of the L Army Corps Command, 10 August 1943; report of García Navarro, 26 August 1943 (BA-MA RH 24–50/66).

89 Weekly reports to AOK 18, 16, and 22 March and 29 April 1943; liaison reports (Colonel Knüppel), 8 April 1943, 9 May 1943, 9 June 1943 (BA-MA, RH 24–50/59).

90 Liaison reports, 9 July and 11 August 1943 (BA-MA, RH 24–50/59).

91 Kleinfeld and Tambs (1983: 483–4); Moreno Juliá (1999, 2014); Wehrmacht General Staff report to the AOK 18, 28 September 1943 (BA-MA RH 19III/493).

92 Meeting of Lindemann and Esteban-Infantes, 13 October 1943; presentation of Esteban-Infantes to Lindemann, 14 October 1943 (BA-MA RH 24–50/84); Sonnleithner to Ritter, 3 October 1943, and to Ribbentrop, 9 October 1943 (PAAA, R.29750).

93 Esteban-Infantes to General Wegener, 13 November 1943 (PAAA, ADBM, Zusatz 12).

94 For thorough descriptions of the battles and the diplomatic circumstances surrounding the actions of the Blue Legion, see Pérez Rubio & Prieto Barrio (2014) and Moreno Juliá (2014).

95 General Order signed by A. García Navarro, 21 October 1943; and reply of the commander of the 250th Sappers' Battalion, 29 October 1943 (AGMAV 28/18/15/12).

96 Ibáñez Hernández (1997: 261–2); records of the conversation between Esteban-Infantes and Knüppel, 9 November 1943 (BA-MA, RH 24–50/84).

97 Testimony of Juan Ramírez de Verger, who volunteered in 1941 and was repatriated in May 1942 for being underage. He re-enlisted in the Blue Legion (Uriarte Arbaiza 2012: 113).

98 Report on re-enlistments dated 9 September 1943 (AGMAV, 1994/12/5/1). In the 2nd Company of the 26th March Battalion, for example, there were 23, all former volunteers from July 1941. There were 10 in the 3rd Company and 9 in the 4th Company. A relevant number were sergeants and corporals. The total amount of re-enlisments was 60, representing a small percentage of new arrivals.

99 War diary of the L Army Corps, entries of 5 and 30 October, 13 November, 10 and 12 December 1943 (BA-MA, RH 24–50/74); Knüppel to Esteban-Infantes, 13 November 1943 (BA-MA, RH 24–50/84).

100 M. Jiménez to Manuel Tarín, Kingisepp, 27 December 1943 (AFR).

101 Telegram from the 18th Army to the OKH, Dept. of Military Attachés, 27 January 1944, and 18th Army to Army Group North, 5 January 1944, both in BA-MA, RH 19III/774; Moreno Juliá (1999: 127).

102 Anonymous returned volunteer to Antonio Herrero Castellano, Logroño, 18 October 1943 (AA).

103 Vey to Einsatzkommando I, 23 November 1943 (USHMM, Sp BD 11.001M.05).

104 For further details, see Moreno Juliá (2014: 344–8), and Pérez Rubio & Prieto Barrio (2014: 144–50).

105 Report of the XXVI Army Corps to the 18th Army, 1 February 1944 (BA-MA, RH 24–26/115); war diary of the XXVI Army Corps, entry of 1 February 1944 (BA-MA, RH 24–26/113); Moreno Juliá (2014: 328–9); Report by Dieckhoff, Madrid, 11 February 1944 (PAAA, R-29751).

106 Commander of the Sicherungstruppen to Army Group North, 5 February 1944 (BA-MA, RH 19III/774).

107 Sonnleithner to the Secretary of State, Berlin, 20 February 1944; report by Steengracht, Berlin, 22 February 1944 (PAAA, R-29751).

108 Kleinfeld & Tambs (1983: 498–500); Moreno Juliá (2014: 368–9).

109 Dionisio Ridruejo to Marichu de la Mora, Grafenwöhr, 14 August 1941, AFRI.

110 Audoin-Rouzeau (1986: 53–6); Kühne (2006: 152–3).

111 War diary of Luis Aguilar, entry of 22 August 1941 (Parrilla Nieto 2018: 56–7).
112 Dionisio Ridruejo to Marichu de la Mora, 22 September 1941 (AFRI); letter from Daniel Torra, 19 December 1941 (Torra i Puigdellívol 2013: 57–8).
113 Audoin-Rouzeau (1986: 42–7) stated something similar about the French soldiers in the First World War. See also Nübel (2014: 42–788), and Knoch (1989).
114 Hernanz Blanco (2013: 123, 141, 162, 237); Merino Bravo (2007: 62–3).
115 War diary of Martín Velasco, entry of 2 November 1941.
116 "Diario de Salvador Zanón Mercado (5a parte)," *Blau División*, 623 (June 2011).
117 War diary of Enrique Sánchez Fraile, quoted by Martínez Reverte (2011: 430).
118 War diary of Martín Velasco, entry of 3 October 1941; A. Gaytan, "El frío en Rusia y el equipaje de la División Azul," *El Pirineo* (9 February 1942).
119 *Memoria sobre la influencia de las épocas de lluvias, fríos y deshielo en los servicios de guerra, en la campaña 1941–1942 en Rusia*, 10 May 1942 (BA-MA, RH 24–38/55). See also Brydan (2019a).
120 Alfredo Rodríguez Pérez to María-Luisa Pérez, 6 February 1942 (AFN); report of the chief doctor of the 16th Army, 30 December 1941 (BA-MA, RH 20–16/748); Rass (2003: 155).
121 Romero (1982: 135); A. Hernández-Navarro, "Camisa Azul en Nueva York," *Los Sitios* (12 February 1952).
122 Dionisio Ridruejo to Marichu de la Mora, 10 November 1941 (AFRI).
123 War diary of Daniel Torra, entry from 22 December 1941 (Torra i Puigdellívol 2013: 61).
124 M. Guijarro, "Mi primera aurora en Rusia," *Los Sitios* (7 September 1958).
125 War memoirs of Benigno Cabo, 1944.
126 Farré Palaus (1991: 86–7).
127 See, for example, the reports of the medical chief of the X Army Corps, 30 October 1941 (BA-MA RH 24–10/86).
128 See, e.g., Dionisio Ridruejo to Marichu de la Mora, 25 October 1941 (AFRI).
129 Hernanz Blanco (2013: 110–14, entry of 30 June 1942); Fritz (1995: 104–14); Lucas (2014: 71–91); F. Torres, "Ya se fueron los trineos," *La Voz de Galicia*, 15 April 1943.
130 Hernanz Blanco (2013: 88, 95–6, entries of 31 May 1942 and 1–3 June 1942). See also the war diary of Carlos Figuerola, 9 July 1942 (Remírez de Esparza 2020: 33–4).
131 J.M. Gutiérrez del Castillo, "El Aguinaldo de la División Azul," *Ofensiva* (3 December 1942).

132 Merridale (2005: 118–21). The Soviet soldiers had no source of indoor heating. Their winter equipment was better than that of the Germans, though not necessarily their food rations. Soviet industry could only provide one pair of boots for every three men.

133 War diary of the XXXVIII Army Corps, 11 November 1941 to 31 March 1942, entry of 20 February 1942 (BA-MA, RH 24–38/51).

134 Report of the XXXVIII Army Corps, 6 December 1941 (BA-MA, RH 20–16/ 67); see also Fritz (1995: 59–60) and Humburg (1999).

135 Alcalde (2014: 60–9).

136 Rosenthal (1990); Latzel (1997); Neitzel & Welzer (2011).

137 See, e.g., P. de la Llave Alas, "Juan," *Reconquista*, 352 (July 1979).

138 A good example of this was the account by Pioneers' sergeant Francisco Suárez Ojeda: see his war diary, 14–15 (private archive of Ms. María P. Suárez Medina, Gáldar, Gran Canaria).

139 See for instance the description of the daily routine by the soldiers of the 250th Transmissions Group, as reflected by the war diary of Private Carlos Orjales (Parrilla Nieto 2018: 147–8).

140 War diary of Martín Velasco, entries of 24 and 25 de October and 1 November 1941.

141 Farré Palaus (1991: 85).

142 See Maeland & Brunstad (2009: 3–4).

143 Letter from Daniel Torra, 19 December 1941 (Torra i Puigdellívol 2013: 57); war diary of Joaquín Ros Cabo, entry of July 1942 (Cuerda Ros 2013: 66); letters from private Antonio Quintana Lucas. n.d. (Quintana Solá 2020: 29–30, 36).

144 S. Zanón, "La campaña de Rusia, un año después (2)," *Blau División*, 612–13 (July–August 2010).

145 See, e.g., the memoirs of private Eugenio Rodríguez (July 1942), in Pérez (2020: 172–6).

146 War diary of Luis Aguilar, entry of 26 April 1942 (Parrilla Nieto 2018: 98).

147 Dionisio Ridruejo to Marichu de la Mora, Porchow, 17 December 1941 (AFRI).

148 War diary of Joaquín Ros Cabo (Cuerda Ros 2013: 62, entry of May 1942).

149 War diary of Benjamín Arenales, entries of 12 and 14 June 1942.

150 Hernanz Blanco (2013: 57, entry of 2 May 1942).

151 War diary of Daniel Torra, entries of 29 December 1941, 2 and 11 January 1942 (Torra i Puigdellívol 2013: 62–3).

152 War diary of Arenales, entries of 24 and 26 June 1942.

153 Hernanz Blanco (2013: 72–4, entry of 17 May 1942).

154 Letter from Daniel Torra, 1 April 1942 (Torra i Puigdellívol 2013: 82–5).

155 War diary of Arenales, entries of 28 June and 6 July 1942.

156 Hernanz Blanco (2013: 130 [entry of 17 July 1942], 138 [26 July 1942] and
     164–5 [17 August 1942]).
157 War diary of Daniel Torra, entries of 14 and 15 May 1942 (Torra i
     Puigdellívol 2013: 94).
158 L.M.D., "La hora del correo," ¡¡Arriba España!! (24 July 1943); Hernanz
     Blanco (2013: 60, 75–6, 97, 103, and 151).
159 War diary of Arenales, entry from 16 July 1942.
160 See examples in Puente Fernández (2012: 75, 83).
161 War diary of Arenales, entries of 26 July and 15 August 1942.
162 Hernanz Blanco (2013: 63, 80, entries of 8 and 24 May 1942).
163 Arenales' obituary was published some weeks later: see "Benjamín Are-
     nales Valcabado," Ofensiva (11 March 1943), and "Camarada Benjamín
     Arenales," Ofensiva (18 March 1943).
164 Hernanz Blanco (2013, 167–9, 212–13, entries of 19 August and 30
     September 1942).
165 See Remírez de Esparza (2020: 37–9 42, 47, 97–8).
166 Marchena Cañete (2003: 66); testimony of Valeriano Ruiz (Puente Fernán-
     dez 2012: 289–91).
167 Dionisio Ridruejo to Marichu de la Mora, Porkhov, 17 December 1941
     (AFRI).
168 A. Gaytan, "La guerra a retaguardia o los peligros de la ocupación,"
     El Pirineo (14 March 1942).
169 Sánchez Diana (1993: 111).
170 Sánchez Diana (1993: 128–9).
171 Testimony of Francisco Bergua, cited by Palacio Pilacés (2013, I: 475).
172 Ridruejo (1978: 302–3, entry of 19 November 1941). Romero (1982: 142–3)
     wrote that those soldiers returned "with swollen and febrile eyes [...]
     although some were eighteen and others up to thirty, they all seemed old.
     We saw them arrive through the fog, indifferent to danger and exhaus-
     tion; they lay down next to the first fire they found lit."
173 Dionisio Ridruejo to Marichu de la Mora, Porkhov, 17 December 1941.
     (AFRI).
174 Andrés Oncala [D. Ridruejo], "Cartas de la guerra. Nuestro vivir," Arriba
     (27 February 1942).
175 Dolores Gancedo to Alberto Martín Gamero, Toledo, 5 and 29 August
     1941 (AA).
176 N. Alcalá Arana, "Crónica de un día," Arriba (17 March 1942).
177 Ridruejo to Marichu de la Mora, 25 October 1941, and Grafenwöhr, 25
     July 1941 (AFRI).
178 Ridruejo to Marichu de la Mora, n.d. [early August 1941], 9, and 22
     August 1941 (AFRI).
179 J. Miquelarena, "Los voluntarios falangistas de la División Azul," ABC
     (4 August 1941); Muñoz Césaro (2011: 37, 65, 152).

180 On the strength of "primary groups" as a cohesive factor in the Wehrmacht, see Bartov (1991: 29–58). On the fusion of political cultures and social origins in the Wehrmacht, see Römer (2012, 2013).

181 Andrés de Oncala [D. Ridruejo], "El libro y la estatua," *Arriba* (13 January 1942).

182 See A. Aragonés, "División Azul. Cartas de un voluntario," *Nueva Alcarria* (25 April 1942).

183 Alfredo Rodríguez Pérez to his mother, 21 December 1941 (AFN).

184 M. M. Carrascosa, "Recuerdo a una fecha," *Ofensiva* (18 October 1942); M. Salvador Gironés, "Cosas de por allá," *Blau División*, 142 (June 1971); *El Norte de Castilla* (2 January 1942); Sanz Jarque (2010: 122).

185 See Núñez Seixas and Beyda (2018: 108).

186 *Diario de un Soldado*, entry from 1 September 1941.

187 Cases of soldiers repatriated for "homosexualism," in the DGS report, San Sebastián, 13 March 1942 (AHMC-FGV, C. 115). Martín Velasco echoed this in his war diary (entry of 4 November 1941).

188 Dionisio Ridruejo to Marichu de la Mora, 9 November 1941 (AFRI); L. Aguilar, "Diario de mi campaña en Rusia (IX)," *Blau División*, 604 (November 2009).

189 "Diario de campaña de Salvador Zanón Mercado (VI)," *Blau División*, 624–5 (July–August 2011).

190 Dionisio Ridruejo to Marichu de la Mora, 30 October 1941 and Porkhov, 17 December 1941 (AFRI).

191 Errando Vilar (1942: 105).

192 Linares (2000: 127).

193 Capdevila & Voldman (2002: 173–205; 2004); Koselleck & Jeismann (1994).

194 See Merridale (2005: 121–2) and Hill (2016).

195 Audoin-Rouzeau (1995: 176–9); Kühne (2006: 166–71). See further examples in B. Benítez, "A vosotros," *Ofensiva* (23 August 1942), and "Caídos de la División Azul," *Ofensiva* (28 October 1942).

196 V. de la Serna, "Presencia real de José Antonio en la División Azul," *Informaciones* (20 November 1941).

5. Occupation Practices of the Blue Division in Northwest Russia

1 *Directivas para la conducta de la tropa en Rusia*, 2nd Section of the General Staff., n.d., AGMAV/2003/5/1/4.

2 "Los comisarios de guerra en el Ejército soviético," *Pueblo* (26 November 1941).

3 *Instrucción general núm. 3.005*, 2nd and 3rd Sections of the BD General Staff, *Ampliación de normas jurídicas internas y de Derecho Internacional*, AGMAV 2005/4/2/1.

4 Order of the OKH, 2 October 1941 (BA-MA, RH 19II/123).

5 Römer (2008: 581–96; 2014); Rutherford (2014: 212).

6 2nd Section of the BD General Staff, *Instrucción n.º 2.018*, 12 May 1942 (AGMAV 2005/18/1/6).

7 Communication by the Chief of Staff of the L Army Corps, 3 May 1943 (AGMAV 2007/5/3/1).

8 On the importance of situational factors for the brutalization of German soldiers at the Eastern Front, see S. Neitzel & Welzer (2011), as well as Rutherford (2014). On indoctrination and its role in enhancing brutalization, see Bartov (2001) and Römer (2012, 2013).

9 Addendum to the report of Capitain Collatz for the XXXVIII Army Corps, 5 May 1942 (BA-MA, RH 26–250/3).

10 M. Salvador Gironés, "Cosas de por allá," *Blau División*, 166 (May 1973).

11 For example, the volunteer Salvador Zanón admitted that in the *izba* occupied by his group, potatoes would disappear from the family, but "they shared our bread, our rations and our mess portion." Two weeks later, he noted that the other soldiers had secretly entered a cellar where a Russian family stored their potatoes, though later they shared them with the same family. See "Diario de la Campaña de Salvador Zanón Mercado (Parte VI)," *Blau División*, 624–5 (July-August 2011), entries dated 22 and 24 December 1941, and 6 January 1942.

12 Salvador (1962: 355); Domingo (2009: 192–3).

13 "Crónica fácil. En la Calle del Pilar tiene usted su casa," *Hoja de Campaña* (31 October 1943).

14 Riudavets de Montes (1960: 45–50); "Cartas de Rusia," *Boletín del SEU de Madrid*, 12 (1942); J. E. Blanco, "Pioneros contra Dios. Sentido antirreligioso de la educación rusa," *Arriba* (29 April 1944).

15 *Instrucción general n.º 3.005*, 4 August 1941, AGMAV, 2005/4/2/1.

16 Ridruejo (1978: 157–8).

17 Gómez-Tello (1945: 39).

18 Díaz de Villegas (1967: 57–8).

19 D. Castro Villacañas, "Notas de hermandad. El teniente Rosse," *Enlace* (3 April 1943); Sánchez Carrilero (1992: 29); "La decisión, el valor y el entusiasmo de la gloriosa División Azul," *ABC* (25 January 1942).

20 Report by Colonel Jesús Badillo, n.d. (December 1941), AHMC-FGV, C. 115.

21 F. Prado Lerena, "Un enemigo vencido y otro que lo será," *Hoja de Campaña* (9 March 1942).

22 J. Martialay, "Más notas para un diario de guerra," *Nueva Alcarria* (14 February 1942); Audoin-Rouzeau (2008: 241–2). See also *Diario de un Soldado*, entry of 7 November 1941.

23 Quoted by Martínez Reverte (2011: 187).

24 See Merridale (2005: 315–16) and Hill (2019).

25 Audoin-Rouzeau (1986: 197–8).

26 "Encuentro con camaradas de la División Azul," *Informaciones* (24 january 1942); Alonso del Real [Fernando Ramos] (1953: 24); Esteban-Infantes (1956: 37); Royo Masía (1956: 213–14); Agustí Roca (2003: 106).

27 J. Martínez Tessier, "Termina el invierno en Rusia y se advierten síntomas de próximas operaciones," *Arriba* (9 April 1942).

28 This was affirmed by Enrique García Gallud in his unpublished memoirs (*Mis dos campañas militares, 1936–1942*); see Errando Vilar (1942: 89, 121–2, 204–5).

29 Bartov (2001: 76–87) and Knoch (2003). On Flemings, Norwegians, and Italians see De Wever (1985: 80), Sorlie (2014: 187–98), and Pannacci (2020).

30 For example, the watercolours *Portadores de una nueva cultura para Europa*, and *¡Europeos! Estos son los ojos que nos acechan*, en AGA, F/0474, IDD (03)003.000.

31 Boixcar (1954, 1955a, 1955b). For more details, see Núñez Seixas (2017).

32 For examples of caricatures of the Red Army, see the BD trench journal, *Hoja de Campaña*, 9 March 1942, depicting a Soviet patrol); 5 August 1942 (portraying prisoners); 10 September 1942 (Soviet tank crew member); 30 September 1942 (another prisoner); 3 October 1943, or 7 November 1943 (Soviet soldier). Only in one case (30 September 1942) do we find an aggressive depiction of the Soviet soldier. There are also the frequent caricatures of Stalin or Soviet communism, with Mongoloid or cadaverous features; or instead, those that evoke the Spanish Civil War, with Soviet soldiers wearing their unusual military cap, portrayed as abusing women (see *Hoja de Campaña*, 21 November 1943). Joaquín de Alba (*Kin*) also drew upon several of these themes for the exhibition *So were the Reds!*, as displayed in his waterproofs *Veinte años de estatuas libertarias*, *La igualdad o Sobre la miseria del pueblo, los soviets han construido sus "palacios"* (AGA, F/0474, IDD(03)003.000).

33 See "Una caricatura con moraleja," *Hoja de Campaña* (7 November 1943); "Los diez mandamientos del buen español," *Enlace* (29 November 1942).

34 "Crónica fácil. El prisionero," *Hoja de Campaña* (19 September 1943); Farré Albiñana (1949: 115).

35 Buchbender & Sterz (1982: 83–105); Latzel (2000b).

36 G. Gómez de la Serna, "La antigua voz del heroísmo en la estepa rusa," *Arriba* (5 May 1942); J. Revuelta, "De cómo Erich Maria Remarque no estuvo en la División Azul," *Haz*, IV:1 (February 1943).

37 Royo Masía (1956: 318).

38 *División Azul. 2.º Cuaderno*, Madrid: Vicesecretaría de Educación Popular, 1943; A. Abad Ojuel, "Hace un año que la División Azul combate," *El Pirineo* (13 July 1942).

39 See Bourke (1998: 175–91).

40 Sanz Jarque (2010: 123, 129). Colonel Esparza himself had ordered prisoners or wounded enemy soldiers to be shot: see the DGS report, 23 December 1941 (AHMC-FGV, C. 115).

41 *Diario de un Soldado*, entry of 3 November 1941.

42 On the practice of shooting prisoners in revenge for the mutilation of the bodies of fallen Spanish soldiers, see Sánchez Diana (1993: 118, 138, 144, and 146); the testimony of Alberto Díaz Gálvez, in Garrido Polonio & Garrido Polonio (2002: 168–9) and Viciana (2018: 227–8). See also López-Covarrubias (2012: 141, 223).

43 Sánchez Diana (1993: 109–10, 113–14, 144–6).

44 See for instance Errando Vilar (1942: 277). The reference to mutilations, which are not corroborated by other sources, is found in Kleinfeld & Tambs (1983: 245).

45 Some testimonies in Sagarra (2012: 628–30). A similar incident was also described by Pioneers' sergeant Francisco Suárez Ojeda in April 1942 (war diary, p. 6).

46 Diary of the Health Unit 2nd Company, written by the military surgeon Luis Rodríguez de la Borbolla (quoted in Rodríguez Jiménez (2007a: 226); DGS report, undated (end of September 1941), AMC-FGV, C.115; *Diario de un soldado*, entry of 11 September 1941. Some days later, he reported in Borisov (19 September 1941) that in a nearby Soviet prisoner camp, the Germans would kill "100–200, as reprisals for the snipers."

47 DGS report, San Sebastián, 29 January 1942 (AHMC-FGV, C.115).

48 War diary of Federico Menéndez Gundín, entry of 30 August 1941 (Cela 2010: 140).

49 Report by military attaché Roca de Togores, Berlin, 30 October 1941 (AGMAV, DEV 29/3/52).

50 War diary of Martínez Tessier, entry of 29 August 1941; Hernández Navarro (1971: 48–9); Gómez-Tello (1945: 169–71).

51 Ydígoras (1984: 52–3); Urquijo (1973: 268).

52 F. Torres, "El sargento Gil," *ABC* (6 March 1943).

53 E. Feijoo García, "Ramón García Pinto, voluntario de la División Azul," *Mediterráneo* (7 February 1942).

54 Pinilla Turiño (1987: 271–4); 2nd Section of General Staff, *Instrucción general, num. 2.019*, 31 May 1942, AGMAV 2005/18/1/8.

55 "En un hospital de campaña de la División Azul," *Arriba* (13 March 1943); A. Gaytan, "Mischka, soldado soviético, en la División Azul," *El Pirineo* (11 March 1942); A. Andújar, "Nuestro ruski ha sido herido," *Hoja de Campaña* (8 August 1943); F. Torres, "El prisionero de Kopino," *La Voz de Galicia*, 16 March 1943.

56 Lomagin (1998: 14–16); war diary of Army Group North, entry of 19
    October 1941 (BA-MA, RH 19III/168).

57 As was even pointed out in the propaganda book published in 1943:
    *Balance de heroísmo. La División Española de Voluntarios en el Frente del Este,
    Invierno 1942–1943, Rusia*, Tallin: n.p., 1943, 19; likewise, Blanco (1954: 33).

58 De Andrés (2004: 143–4); Ruiz Ayúcar (1981: 158–61). Further cases were
    the deserter Pablo S. Alexandrovich, who was protected by officers of
    the Spanish General Staff, and later adopted by a major who took him
    to Spain, and Serguei D. Marchenko, born in 1926, was an assistant cook
    in the BD medical corps and, under the protection of some officers was
    taken to Seville, where he settled. Furthermore, the eighteen-year-old
    Walter Jamsa from Pushkin, an assistant of a Spanish officer, lived in
    April 1944 in Ciudad Real. See J. M. García Setién, "Pablo Sakienko Alex-
    androvich. Un ruso de la División Azul," *Blau División*, 602 (September
    2009); "Un joven ruso se bautizará en Sevilla," *Los Sitios de Gerona* (24
    May 1944), and C.L.P., "Un muchacho ruso en Ciudad Real," *Lanza* (22
    April 1944).

59 M. Salvador Gironés, "Cosas de por allá," *Blau División*, 87 (November
    1966).

60 In September 1942, the BD Service Corps had 45 Soviet prisoners in its
    service in its baking, supply, and meat companies: the number had de-
    screased to 34 in 1943. See also the report by the Service Corps Comman-
    dant, 29 September 1942 (AGMAV 2006/3/2/3), and reports by Captain
    Rafael González Fernández, 27 February 1943 (AGMAV 1987/15/1/2).

61 Díaz del Río (2011: 172–3).

62 Instruction concerning Prisoners of war, 2.ª Sección de EM, 16 July 1942,
    AGMAV 2006/1/3/1.

63 Reports to the Sicherheitspolizei und SD-Aussenstelle Puschkin, 7
    November 1942, Central State Archive of Saint Petersburg (TsGA SPB).
    Fund 9788, Opis 1. Delo 31, List 21.

64 See, e.g., Ebert & Peukert (2006).

65 Romeu Fernández (2007: 66–7). See also the testimony of the nurses Aure-
    lia Segovia and Teresa Valderrama, in López-Covarrubias (2012: 249–51).

66 Order by OKH, 4 May 1943, *Hoja de instrucción sobre el tratamiento de evadi-
    dos (para la tropa)* (AGMAV 2007/7/1/11).

67 General orders n. 20 (21 May 1943) and 22 (9 May 1943), AGMAV,
    2007/7/1/22 and 2007/7/1/17.

68 Instruction by L Army Corps to BD, 2 September 1943, AGMAV
    2008/13/2/1.

69 General Order, 2nd General Staff Section, 19 May 1943, in AGMAV
    2007/9/3/1.

70 J. Miquelarena, "El hotel Smolensko, hotel moderno," *ABC* (16 August 1941).

71 "División Azul," *Nueva Alcarria* (15 November 1941).

72 See the comic strips *Felicidad en los hogares* and *Apenas pisamos la primera carretera rusa, camino del frente, ya vemos lo que es el adelanto soviético*, in AGA, F/0474, IDD (03) 003.000.

73 *El Alcázar* (3 February 1942).

74 J. Fuertes, "Lo que nos llega de Rusia a los falangistas. Sacrificio y entusiasmo de la División Azul," *Arriba* (1 January 1942).

75 EL CORREO DEL ZAR, "División Azul. Comentario," *Nueva Alcarria* (21 February 1942).

76 J.L. Gómez-Tello, "La aldea rusa," *Enlace* (20 September 1942); F. Izquierdo Luque, "Una casa colectiva en Rusia," *Pensamiento Alavés* (22 May 1942).

77 Postcards from BD volunteers, 22 October 1941 and 19 December 1941 (Vázquez Enciso 1995: 133–5); Vicente Rodríguez Vela to Colonel Leandro García, 22 March 1942 (MPA-FLGG).

78 War diary of Juan Romero Osende, entries from 24 August 1941 and 17 October 1941.

79 War diary of Martínez Tessier, entry from 14 September 1941.

80 War diary of Arenales, entry of 25 May 1942.

81 Gómez-Tello (1945: 51); "Cómo hablan del Mando los voluntarios de la 'División Azul,'" *Informaciones* (26 February 1942).

82 "La gloriosa División Azul," *El Norte de Castilla* (24 February 1942).

83 Fernández Velasco (1943: 9–11); "Información de la provincia," *Nueva Alcarria* (11 April 1942).

84 Theleweit (1995).

85 Romeu Fernández (2007: 57, entry dated 16 October 1941); Gómez-Tello (1945: 50).

86 "Diario de un voluntario. Notas de mi macuto," *Nueva Alcarria* (20 December 1941); "División Azul. Cartas de un voluntario," *Nueva Alcarria* (21 March 1942); Farré Albiñana (1949: 92).

87 Memoirs of Joaquín Montaña, in Cela (2010: 249–50).

88 Bellod Gómez (2004: 199–200); J. de la Cruz Lacacci, "La casa de Nicolai Frederich," *Reconstrucción*, 34 (June-July 1943).

89 Raimundo Sánchez Aladro to Joaquina Cabero, 17 February 1943 (MPA, R.6410, A6/15–5); V. de la Serna, "Notas de un viaje a la División Azul," *Informaciones* (12 December 1941); Crespo (1945: 178).

90 Vid. "Lo que vimos en Rusia," *Hoja de Campaña* (23 May 1943); "Miseria sobre miseria (El ayer de Rusia)," *Hoja de Campaña* (20 June 1943); C. Lamela, "Yo era oficial del Zar," *Hoja de Campaña* (8 August 1943).

91 *Arriba* (13 March 1942); M. Timmermans, "Recuerdos de un invierno en Rusia," *Arriba* (4 August 1942).

92 S. Zanón, "La campaña de Rusia, un año después (III)," *Blau División*, 615 (October 2010); war diary of Ramón Abadía, cited by Palacio Pilacés (2013: I, 549).

93 Ridruejo (1978: 172–3). Other testimones were rather discordant: see Larraz Andía & Sierra-Sesúmaga (2010: 371–2).

94 Dionisio Ridruejo to Marichu de la Mora, 19 September 1941 (AFRI); Jiménez Andrades (1957: 39, 51); Sánchez Carrilero (1992: 25–7); Vascano (1960: 84).

95 Benz (1996: 9–18).

96 E. Montes, "Drama y grandeza. De Dostoievski a Stalin," *Domingo. Semanario Nacional* (2 May 1937).

97 Dionisio Ridruejo to the editorial board of *Escorial*, 22 September 1941 (CDMH-FR, MF/R 5912).

98 Gómez-Tello (1945: 52, 111–13).

99 A. de Laiglesia, "Estampas de la División Azul. La única retaguardia," *Enlace* (28 June 1942) and "La leyenda partida," *Hoja de Campaña* (4 February 1942).

100 D'Ors Pérez (1960); Errando Vilar (1942: 255–6, 260); *Hermandad*, II:4 (July-August 1958). See also Pérez (2020: 146).

101 Letter of Dolores Gancedo to A. Martín Gamero, Toledo, 22 and 23 October 1941 (AA). The Chekhov story she refers to is *Ward no. 6*.

102 War diary of Manuel de Cárdenas, entry dated 21 April 1942.

103 War diary of Menéndez Gundín, entry dated 18 September 1941 (Cela 2010: 143).

104 "¿Cuántos comunistas hay en Rusia?" *Hoja de Campaña* (3 October 1943); Gómez-Tello (1945: 124–6); R. de Gonzalo, "La conquista de la aldea," *Ofensiva* (9 August 1942).

105 "Carta de Rusia," *Voluntad* (8 February 1942).

106 *Odiel* (15 January 1942).

107 See, e.g., "Charlando con un labrador ruso. Impresiones de un soldado en la Rusia liberada," *Hoja de Campaña* (26 September 1943).

108 Hispanus, "Cartas desde Rusia. Crisis moral," *Lucha* (7 July 1943).

109 See, for example, *Hoja de Campaña* (13 December 1941; 11 January 1942; 5 August 1942; 19 August 1942; 26 August 1942; 18 November 1942; 21 March 1943; 31 March 1943, and 11 April 1943) (figures 3 and 4).

110 Hernanz Blanco (2013: 46–47, entries dated 27–30 April and 1 May 1942).

111 Letter of Manuel Tarín to Remedios Rebollo, 5 June 1942 (AFR).

112 A. de la Iglesia, "Para la historia de nuestra División Azul. Su paisaje," *ABC* (17 May 1942); Díaz de Villegas (1967: 45–6); Errando Vilar (1942: 61–2, 113 and 233).

113 See Latzel (2000: 145–56); Müller (2007: 175–94); and Kipp (2014: 47–110). See also Corni (2010; 2012: 37–8) and Vettorazzo (2004).

114   Nerín (2005: 204–6).
115   F. Torres, "La campaña de invierno para el ejército ruso," *ABC* (26 January 1943).
116   "División Azul. Cartas de un voluntario," *Nueva Alcarria* (21 March 1942); P. Salvador, "División Azul: Voz española en la batalla del mundo," *Hoja de Campaña* (9 May 1943).
117   Riudavets de Montes (1960: 21, 77).
118   Errando Vilar (1942: 112–13); J. Revuelta Imaz, "Camisas azules en Nowgorod," *Pueblo* (28 July 1942).
119   Fritz (1995: 195–203).
120   Letter of Raimundo Sánchez Aladro, 10 December 1943 (MPA, R 6410/A6/15–2).
121   Thus, Montserrat Romeu (2007: 67) described a tailor in Porkhov as "the classic Russian with small spectacles, a Russian blouse and Jewish look."
122   War diary of Martínez Tessier, entry dated 19 September 1941. See also J. Martínez Tessier, "Desde la División Azul. Estampas soviéticas," *SI. Suplemento semanal de Arriba*, 37 (13 September 1942).
123   J. González Muñoz, "Los que regresan del otro lado. Un voluntario de la División Azul habla para EL CORREO GALLEGO," *El Correo Gallego*, 30 August 1942.
124   See Liulevicius (2000; 2006) and Dornik (2013).
125   Letter of Carlos Juan, Minsk, 18 September 1941 (AHMC-FGV, C. 115).
126   Dionisio Ridruejo to Marichu de la Mora, 19 September 1941 (AFRI); Andrés Oncala [D. Ridruejo], "Paisaje de la batalla," *Arriba* (10 January 1942). See also Ridruejo (1978: 225–30).
127   A. Aragonés, "De la División Azul. Carta de un voluntario," *Nueva Alcarria* (3 January 1942).
128   Errando Vilar (1942: 250–1); "Crónica fácil. Un concierto," *Hoja de Campaña* (30 May 1943); J. L. Gómez Tello, "Nowgorod, la ciudad blanca de los españoles," *El Español*, II:16 (6 February 1943).
129   M. Bendala, "Política y guerra en el mundo. La juridicidad en la guerra de Rusia," *Juventud* (30 April 1942).
130   "Rusia vista desde fuera," *Juventud* (7 May 1942).
131   M. Bendala, "Rusia como misión europea," *Haz*, IV:5 (June 1943).
132   D. Lagunilla, "Los instintos primitivos de la raza eslava," *El Español*, II:15 (6 February 1943).
133   S.M.C.: "La morbosidad de la Rusia soviética," *Hoja de Campaña* (5 September 1943).
134   Letters of the Juventud de Acción Católica to Muñoz Grandes, Sigüenza, 20 November 1941 (AGMAV 1979/6/1/5), and from Private Carlos Juan, 18 September 1941.

135 "La raza," *Hoja de Campaña* (10 October 1943); G.G.R.: "Los bolcheviques, la imprenta y la religión," *Hoja de Campaña* (14 November 1943); "El comunismo, interpretación materialista de la vida," *Hoja de Campaña* (21 November 1943); Martínez Cruces (1942: 110–11).

136 "Sangre ibérica sobre el hielo de Rusia," *Arriba* (29 July 1942). For utopias based on the German "cultural mission" in Russia, consisting in bringing "order" to the East, see Kipp (2014: 139–46, 176–82).

137 C. Alonso del Real, "Diálogo sobre tema ruso," *El Español*, II:48 (25 September 1943).

138 Álvarez Chillida (2014).

139 Maeztu (1941: 67–8).

140 See some examples in Stargardt (2015: 207–8).

141 See Ayçoberry (2003) and Quinkert (2014).

142 Regarding the supposed German commitment to re-Christianize Russia, see F. de Bolinaga, "La ayuda a la Religión en Rusia y la aportación de la Iglesia española," *Lucha* (20 August 1943).

143 See "Han matado a una niña," *Hoja de Campaña* (15 August 1943); Sánchez Carrilero (1992: 91–3). F. Torres, "Rusos en la retaguardia," *Lucha* (15 July 1943).

144 See also Núñez Seixas (2018c).

145 *Directivas para la conducta de la tropa en Rusia*, G. S. 2nd section, n.d., AGMAV, 2003/5/1/4.

146 DEV General Staff, *Ampliación de Normas Jurídicas internas y de Derecho Internacional*, AGMAV 2005/4/2/1.

147 Römer (2008: 581–96).

148 2nd Section of DEV General Staff, *Instrucción num. 2018*, 12 May 1942, AGMAV 2005/18/1/6.

149 Comuniqué of the Head of General Staff of Army Corps L, 3 May 1943, AGMAV 2007/5/3/1.

150 Kilian (2012: 189–240).

151 See some observations concerning Soviet women during the occupation in Rebrova (2014).

152 See the report of Sicherungsregiment 107, 8 March 1942 (BA-MA, RH 20–16/99).

153 Edict by Muñoz-Grandes, 3 September 1941 (AGMAV 1978/13/5/1).

154 Report by Sonderführer Walter, Bautrupp II, 29 September 1941 (BA-MA, RH 19III/774).

155 See the order of the local Novosokol'niki command, 5 October 1941; reports of station officer Seifert, 13 October 1941, and the Vilnius Transport Command, 16 October 1941; reports of Local Command I (V) 293 Novosokol'niki and V 181, 21 and 22 October 1941; and Military Police report, Novosokol'niki, 20 October 1941 (BA-MA, RH 19III/774).

156 DEV, 2nd Section GS, General Instruction 2009, 19 October 1941 (AGMAV 3736/5).

157 However, these reports tended to blame foreign allies or neighbouring divisions for bad behaviour, which could have been the doing of Germans. See Kilian (2012: 218–19).

158 Gregori to Luis Romero, 8 November 1942 (UCSD-MS 563).

159 Dionisio Ridruejo to Marichu de la Mora, 24 October 1941 (AFRI).

160 See reports by liaison officer Dr. Gutzschebauch, 2–10 October 1941, as well as reports to the IA department of the Army Group North, 2 November 1941, OKH to Army Group North, 3 November 1941, and of General von Chappuis to the Supreme Command of the 16th Army, Grigorovo, 17 November 1941 (BA-MA, RH 19 III/774).

161 This point was also pointed out by Vladimir Kovalevskii (Núñez Seixas & Beyda 2019: 152–3).

162 Kilian (2012: 215–17); Palacio Pilacés (2013, I: 548).

163 Report of Group IV W of 16th Army, 29 October to 21 December 1941 (BA-MA, RH 20–16/1100); Hasenclever (2010: 305–9); Army Group North war diary, entry dated 24 October 1941 (BA-MA, RH 19III/168).

164 Urquijo (1973: 283); information note of the General Staff 2nd section, 28 December 1941, AGMAV 2005/8/3/1.

165 Captain Collatz to Army Group North, 23 October 1941 (BA-MA, RH 19III/774).

166 Collatz to Army Group North, 5 November 1941 (BA-MA, RH 19III/774). For testimonies of sexual assault on Russian women by Germans and Spaniards, see the war memoirs of Francisco Manero (Palacio Pilacés 2013, I: 551–2), and Benigno Cabo, 132. See also some Russian eyewitness accounts in Kovalev (2014: 347).

167 Only one occurred between November 1941 and August 1942 (General Staff Order 103, 16 July 1942, AGMAV 3736/6).

168 Secret report by a surgeons' commission that visited Germany and Poland, December 1941 (FNFF 1992: 404–19); report to Varela, 22 December 1941 (AHMC-FGV, C. 115).

169 Testimonies of A.P. Jaschin, S.V. Aleksandrovna, and G. Ivanovna (Kovalev 2014: 354–9).

170 *¿Qué ha pasado con el Aguinaldo?* N.d. [February/March 1942], AGMAV 2005/16/2/13.

171 Reports of General von Chappuis, 8 December 1941, and General Busch, 4 December 1941 (BA-MA, RH 20–16/67).

172 Bartov (1991: 76–8); Kilian (2012: 220–5). As with the case of Hungarian soldiers, German reports tended to exaggerate their concern for the civilian population whenever others were responsible for misconduct (Anderson 1999; Ungváry 2005).

173 Núñez Seixas & Beyda (2019: 208–9); war diary of the XXXVIII. Army Corps, entry dated 18 November 1941 (BA-MA, RH 24–38/51). The detainee was condemned and repatriated in January of 1942 (DGS report, Madrid, 27 January 1942, AHMC-FGV, C.115).

174 War diary of the XXXVIII. Army Corps, entry from 2 December 1941 (BA-MA, RH 24–38/51).

175 *Tätigkeitsbericht der Abt. III des Gen.Kommandos des XXXVIII A. K. für die Zeit vom 11.XI.1941 bis 31.III.1942* (BA-MA, RH 24–38/253).

176 Kilian (2012: 225–33).

177 Cogollos Vicens (1985: 115); Hernanz Blanco (2013: 220, entry from 6 October 1942).

178 F. Torres, "Bombardeo de San Petersburgo," *ABC* (4 June 1943); Esteban-Infantes (1956: 128).

179 Monthly report of the Wirtschaftskommando Krasnogwardeisk for April 1942 (BA-MA, RH 20–18/1358); Pardo Martínez (2005: 118).

180 Cárdenas, *Diario*, entry from 1 September 1942.

181 See J. Santamaría Díez, "Sdrinoga," *Blau División*, 179 (June 1974); D'Ors Pérez (1960).

182 War diary of Manuel de Cárdenas, entry from 3 June 1942.

183 See *Instrucción general 2.016*, 4 May 1942 (AGMAV, 28/28/18); for the written responses of officers to the memo of General Esteban-Infantes dated 27 May 1943, see AGMAV, 2007/12/2/5.

184 See, e.g., the account by Vladimir Rudinski, a Soviet citizen who worked for the Spaniards as an interpreter: V. Rudinski, "Ispantsy Goluboi divizii," *Nasha strana* (8 September 2007) and "Patriarkh russkoi zarubezhnoi publitsistiki," *Nasha strana* (6 August 2011).

185 Díaz del Río (2011: 202–3); testimony of A. Vallejo, in Larraz & Sierra-Sesúmaga (2010: 373).

186 "Diario de la campaña de Salvador Zanón Mercado (V)," *Blau División*, 623 (June 2011), entry from 22 December 1941.

187 Kovalev (2014: 330–2).

188 Interview with Vasíly P. (born 1928), Podberez'e, 29 April 2003 (AA); testimony of a peasant girl from Trubitchino, in Garrido Polonio & Garrido Polonio (2002: 90–1).

189 Diary of Lidia Ósipova, entries dated 25 August, 17 September, 30 September, 1 and 5 October 1942 (Lomagin 2004: II, 464–6).

190 Report to the Sicherheitspolizei und SD-Aussenstelle Puschkin, 2 November 1942 (TsGA SPB, Fund 9788. Opis 1. Delo 31. List 29).

191 This occurred a few months after the Spaniards arrived in Pavlosk, when a group of seven soldiers entered the lodgings of Russian civilian Catarina Malischeva. The accused were condemned to six months' incarceration (AGMAV, C. 3777/2).

192 Letter from Lieutenant P. Emerich, Ortskommandantur II (351),
     22 September 1942 (BfZ-SS).
193 De Andrés (2004: 25); Pardo Martínez (2005: 118).
194 General Instruction 2016, 4 May 1942 (AGMAV 28/28/18/3).
195 In October 1943 a similar instruction outlined the same terms (GS Order
     1 February 1943, AGMAV, 28/29/11/7). More examples in Bowen (2000:
     114–15).
196 Roberto Rivero to Carmen Sánchez, 26 August 1942 (De Ramón & Ortiz
     2003: 355–6).
197 War memoirs of Benigno Cabo, 128–9; García-Izquierdo (2009: 333–5).
198 Chicharro-Lamamié de Clairac (2001: 42). Love affairs between occupy-
     ing soldiers and Soviet women normaly had one real function: to find an
     illusory refuge from the hardships of war: see Fritz (1995: 78–9); Ruther-
     ford (2014: 166–7), and Mühlhäuser (2010: 159, 216).
199 OKH to Army Group North, 20 May 1942, and 18th Army to Army
     Group North, 12 June 1942 (BA-MA, RH 19III/ 493). Some examples are
     described by Díaz Infante (n.d.: 49).
200 Pardo Martínez (2005: 133); Palacio Pilacés (2013, I: 552).
201 D. Ramírez Morales, "Notas de un diario," *Juventud*, 29 (5 November 1942).
202 Raimundo Sánchez to Joaquina Cabero, 18 January 1943 (MPA, R.6410,
     16/15–3). See also M. Salvador Gironés, "Cosas de por allá," *Blau Di-
     visión*, 85 (September 1966).
203 War diary of Martínez Tessier, entry from 14 September 1941.
204 "Cartas de Rusia," *Boletín del SEU de Madrid*, 11 (1942).
205 War diary of Arenales, entry dated 5 June 1942. See also "Lo que cuentan
     los voluntarios de la División Azul," *El Progreso*, 7 February 1942.
206 See e.g. the unpublished novel *Recuerdos* by the BD veteran Óscar Rey,
     which narrates a story of love and jealousy between two Spanish soldiers
     and a Russian girl (personal archive of Carlos Rey, A Coruña).
207 *Diario de un Soldado*, entry from 28 October 1941.
208 J. Santamaría Díez, "Anecdotario del Dr. Payno," *Blau División*, 183
     (October 1974). See also the memoirs of Private Eugenio Rodríguez,
     who referred openly to the existence of Russian and Polish prostitutes in
     Novgorod and other places close to the front line (Pérez 2020: 151, 165).
209 Private Eugenio Rodríguez recalled in his memoirs that he and his
     comrades often found shelter and female company at a family's *izba*, in
     exchange for protection and food. One night, they even witnessed how
     the family hid two partisans who were searched by a German patrol. See
     Pérez (2020: 166–8).
210 *Diario de un Soldado*, entries from 2, 3, and 8 December 1941. Such con-
     duct was also common among German soldiers (Rutherford 2014: 187–9;
     Mühlhäuser 2010: 251–2).

211 Antonio Herrero to his mother, 25 April 1943 (AA); war diary of Manuel de Cárdenas, entry from 20 May 1942; Jiménez Malo de Molina (1943: 176).

212 Pardo Martínez (2005: 123); note of the DGS, 9 December 1941 (AHMC-FGV, C. 115). Some Russian mothers hid their daughters from the Spanish officers (Kovalev 2014: 365).

213 Álvarez de Sotomayor (1991: 162–3); Royo Masía (1956: 88–9); García Luna (1959: 32, 113); Sanz Jarque (2010: 330).

214 Testimony of A. Davichenko, reproduced in the documentary *The Siege of Leningrad* (Saint Petersburg local TV, 2007); diary of Lidia Ósipova, entries dated 25 August and 5 October 1942 (Lomagin 2004, 2: 464–6).

215 Untitled memoirs of Evdokiia Bogacheva-Baskakova (1970), pp. 29 and 32–5 (Museum of Russian Culture, San Francisco, Manuscript Collection, Box 2, Folder 4).

216 See record of the court martial and sentence, 7 April 1942, as well as reports by attorney officer of the BD, 7 March 1942 and 17 April 1942 (AGMAV C.3791/30).

217 "Al amparo paterno," *Hoja de Campaña* (15 August 1944); J. Martialay, "Nueva primavera," *Nueva Alcarria* (23 May 1942).

218 Puente (1954: 157–8); J. Martialay, "Horas y horas en el descanso," *Nueva Alcarria* (7 March 1942).

219 War diary of Martín Velasco, entry from 3 October 1941.

220 Interviews with Lidia N. Yerofejeva, Posad, 27 February 2015, and the priest of Korotskoe, 27 February 2015 (AA); Kovalev (2014: 336, 372–3).

221 See, for example, Montes (2006: 93–6, 113–17). On the overabundance of orphan children in the rearguard, see the report of the Wirtschaftskommando Krasnogwardeisk, 20 April 1942 (BA-MA, RH 20–18/1358).

222 *Blau División*, 50 (October 1963); Miralles Güill (1981: 88–90).

223 See, for example, Puente Fernández (2012: 125–8). A Russian child, Boris S. Nikolaievich, was taken to Santiago de Compostela by an artillery officer and adopted by a local family, which baptized him as a Catholic (*El Compostelano*, 7 June 1944).

224 Ydígoras (1984: 26, 53, 59–60, 68–9, 71–3).

225 DEV, 2nd Section, 17 October 1941 (AGMAV 3736/5); testimonies of Juan Luis Pacheco, Francisco Tarrés, Pedro Bejarano, Adolfo de Montagut, and Guillermo González de Canales, numbered in Sagarra (2012: 643–4); Luis Aguilar, "Diario de mi Campaña de Rusia (3)," *Blau División*, 603 (2009), entry from 18 September 1941; Urquijo (1973: 272).

226 War diary of Martínez Tessier, entry dated 28 September 1941.

227 Jiménez Malo de Molina (1942: 178–9, 187–8).

228 Vadillo (1967: 347–53).

229 Sánchez Diana (1993: 132).

230 On Soviet partisans, see Slepyan (2006), Hill (2005), and Musial (2009).

231 Hasenclever (2010: 371–7, 410–17, 448–55); Rutherford (2014: 145, 215).
     Some attributed it to the lack of a mounted section (cavalry) in the BD,
     which had been replaced with a bicycle section that could not carry out its
     duties in forested or marshy areas. See the IC section report of the XXXVIII
     Army Corps, 13 July 1942 (BA-MA, RH 24–38/164); J. Martínez Esparza,
     "Los 'partisanes' y otros rusos," *Hoja de Campaña* (15 December 1943).
232 General Instruction 2007, 17 October 1941 and 2007B, 28 October 1941
     (AGMAV, 2005/5/5).
233 General Instruction 2023, 7 July 1942 (AGMAV, 2006/1/1/7); OKW or-
     der from 20 August 1941 (BA-MA, RW 19/686). Testimony of one such
     reprisal was narrated by repatriated soldiers in a DGS report, San Se-
     bastián, 30 January 1942 (AHMC-FGV, C.115); *Tätigkeitsbericht der Abt.
     Ic/A. O. für die Zeit von 1. bis 22 November 1941* (BA-MA, RH 20–16/473).
234 García Hispán (1992: 46–7); Kovalevskii's memoirs, in Núñez Seixas &
     Beyda (2019: 254–73).
235 High Command of the XXXVIII Army Corps, 5 January 1942 (BA-MA,
     RH.24–38/34).
236 For a comparative discussion, see Heuser (2013: 142–215).
237 See Kovalevskii's memoirs, in Núñez Seixas & Beyda (2019: 129–45).
238 Píoneers' Battalion 250 to the captain of the 1st Company, 5 October
     1942 (AGMAV 1985/3/5/1); Army Corps L, Order dated 10 July 1943
     (BA-MA, RH 24–50/66).
239 Muñoz Césaro (2011: 158, 183, entries from 29 May and 31 October 1943).
240 Obersturmführer Vey to Einsatzkommando 1, 6 November 1943
     (USHMM, Sp BD 11.001M.05).
241 Daily report of 250th Division to the XXXVIII Army Corps, 18 December
     1941 (BA-MA, RH 24–38/171).
242 Interrogations of a Spanish soldier of the 10th Company, Regiment 269;
     of a soldier of the 3rd Company of the same regiment, and another of the
     Reconnaissance Batallon: Gatchina Naval Archive, 102.o.1.d.354.ll.71–4,
     110–13, and 146–9.
243 Testimony of Anselmo Pérez Gómez (Pérez Maestre 2008: 161–3); Sanz
     Jarque (2010: 239); Diary of Private Pedro Solé, entry from 25 March 1942
     (http://www.miabueloenrusia.com).
244 Daily Report of 250th Division to XXVIII Army Corps, 21 November
     1941, 3 and 4 December 1941 (BA-MA, RH 24–38/171); see also the report
     of the 16th German Army, *Partisanenbekämpfung in der Armee in der Zeit
     vom 6–12 December 1941* (BA-MA, RH 20–16/99).
245 Interview of Lidia Nikolaévna, Rogavka, 28 March 2004 by Pavel Ten-
     dera (Author's Archive), and annex to the report of the 16th Army High
     Command to the Army Group North, 13 February 1942 (BA-MA, RH
     20–16/99).

246 Kipp (2007, 2014).

247 For a synthesis of the anti-Semitic rhetoric and contents of Spanish fascism and early Francosim, see Álvarez Chillida (2002: 381–420). See also Böcker (2000); Palmero Aranda (2016); and Schammah-Gesser (2007).

248 Rother (2005: 53–77); Rozenberg (2010: 213–48); and Herrman & Brenneis (2020).

249 Von Stohrer to Auswärtiges Amt, Madrid, 28 February 1941 (PAAA, R 29741); report from the German embassy in Madrid, 7 November 1941, quoted by Rozenberg (2010: 179).

250 See Cuartero (1941: 23–5) and Carrión (1941).

251 Quoted by Tranche & Sánchez Biosca (2011: 69, 440–1).

252 E. Blanco B., "El verdadero enemigo," *Hoja de Campaña* (4 May 1942): "We know you! Your surnames are Democracy, Marxism and Plutocracy, and your first name is unmistakable: Judaism." See also "España defiende Europa contra sus tres enemigos aliados: bolchevismo, judaísmo, masonería," *Hoja de Campaña* (15 December 1943); "Los bolcheviques, la imprenta y la religión," *Hoja de Campaña* (14 November 1943); and "El comunismo interpretación materialista de la vida," *Hoja de Campaña* (21 November 1943).

253 "¿Cuántos comunistas hay en Rusia?" *Hoja de Campaña* (3 October 1943).

254 "La raza," *Hoja de Campaña* (10 October 1943).

255 A. Gaytan, "Cante jondo en el Frente del Este," *Hoja de Campaña* (25 May 1942).

256 Muñoz Grandes criticized some members of the General Staff and labelled them despectively as "Jews" (Pardo Martínez 2005: 142). See also Martínez Cruces (1932: 28).

257 Bowen (2007).

258 L. Sánchez Maspons, "Camino de Rusia. El paso por Cracovia y la Polonia Oriental," *Informaciones* (28 October 1941).

259 Report by the DGS, 28 April 1942, reproduced in FNFF (1992–94: III, 331–50).

260 *ABC* (26 April 1945); Garriga (1983: 41–43); Rother (2005: 125–9).

261 Krausnick (1998: 154–5); Kovalev (1998: 43); Hill (2005: 25–37); Hasenclever (2010: 548–50); Kilian (2012: 95).

262 *Instrucción general 2010*, 28 October 1941, AGMAV/2005/5.

263 News of the atrocities perpetrated against the Soviet civilians and Jews often spread as rumours propagated by soldiers on trains or on leave from the front (Humburg 2011; Jasper 2011: 79–82).

264 Arad (2009: 196–7); Rutherford (2014: 159–60).

265 Domingo (2009: 190–1).

266 M. Martínez-Mena, "España se adelantó al tiempo en que vivía," *Blau División*, 36 (August 1962).

267 Cholawski (1998: x–xxvii, 3–31); see also Ackermann (2011: 93–127), and the testimony of Chasia Bornstein-Bielicka (2008: 51–96).
268 Klarsfeld (1980); Fatal-Knaani (1995, 1996); Ackermann (2011: 158–72).
269 A. Gaytan, "La guerra a retaguardia o los peligros de la ocupación," *El Ideal Gallego* (13 March 1942).
270 Errando Vilar (1942: 20).
271 M. Nofuentes, "Las marchas de la División en tierra rusa," *Juventud*, 2 (30 April 1942); S. Zanón, "La campaña de Rusia, un año después (1st part)'; Jiménez Malo de Molina (1943: 37–41); war diary of González de Canales, quoted by Sagarra (2012: 598).
272 See the war diary of Luis Aguilar, entry of 10 September 1941.
273 Tych (2005). On silence as a usual form of reaction by the *bystanders*, see Barnett (1999: 125–8). Examples of silence were captain Urmeneta (Jimeno Aranguren 2015: 111–12) and Private Quintana Lucas (Quintana Solá 2020: 26, 53).
274 *Diario de un Soldado*, entries of 1 and 3 September 1941; Ridruejo to Marichu de la Mora, 22 September 1941 (AFRI); war diary of Menéndez Gundín, entries of 31 August and 6 September 1941 (Cela 2010: 140–1); Palacio Pilacés (2013, I: 379, 383–4).
275 Blanco (1954: 17–19); Royo Masía (1956: 267); Urquijo (1973: 264); Ydígoras (1984: 61–2).
276 On Baltic anti-Semitism in 1940–5, see Felder (2009: 172–5) and Weiss-Wendt (2009).
277 Arad (2009: 144–6); Dieckmann (2011: 892–6, 967–1008).
278 War diary of Martínez Tessier, diary entry of 8 September 1941.
279 Quoted in Palacio Pilacés (2013, I: 382).
280 Gómez Tello (1945: 12–13).
281 Cholawsky (1998: 231–2) and Arad (2009: 261–2).
282 Gómez Tello (1945: 64–73).
283 Ridruejo (1978: 40, 42–3, 53, 60–4, and 80–1).
284 Castañón (1991: 127).
285 See Muñoz Césaro (2011: 187, entry dated on 9 November 1943).
286 Gutman (2005) and Friszke (2005).
287 Ridruejo (1978: 42–3). On Polish -Semitism, see Musial (2002: 71–8), Pufelska (2007); and Gross (2002).
288 Some testimonies in Klarsfeld (1980). See also Bornstein-Bielicka (2008: 98–120).
289 Bornstein-Bielicka (2008: 35); letter from Chasia Bornstein-Bielicka, Kibutz Lehavot Habaschan (Israel), 23 August 2009 (AA).
290 Jiménez Malo de Molina (1943: 38–9); Klovsky (2003: 22); interview with Bronka Klibanski, available at http://collections.ushmm.org/search/catalog/irn502736 (last seen on 11 December 2015).

291 Captain Collatz to Army Group North, 23 October 1941 (BA-MA, RH 19-HI/774); war diary of the Germain Liaison section, entries of 26 August, 1 and 6 September 1941 (BA-MA, RH 26–250/2); *Diario de un Soldado*, entries of 3 and 4 September, 1941.

292 Note from the Local *Kommandantur* of Grodno, 26 August 1941, AGMAV, 1978/7/4.

293 Von Bock (1995: 268, 281), entries of 3 and 20 September 1941.

294 Ridruejo (1978: 64–5).

295 Cf. A. Dalmau, "Rússia es culpable!" *El Diumenge* (28 July 1991); interview with Manuel Grande by X. M. Núñez Seixas, Ourense, 27 December 1987 (AA).

296 Meliá Vila (2003: 75–6).

297 Blumstein (2002: 71–3).

298 Reizer (2009: 86–7).

299 Zandman (1995: 42).

300 Moshe Berkowitz's handwritten memoirs are kept at the Yad Vashem Museum, Jerusalem. See a poorly edited Spanish translation by revisionist amateur historians, alongside an introduction by Berkowitz's grandson, in Berkowitz & Fontenla Ballesta (2019: 85–7).

301 Quoted by Muszynski (2002: 19–20).

302 Romeu Fernández (2007: 37–8). Photo on p. 4: a group of Jews walking away, with the six-point star on their backs, in a snowy urban setting.

303 See, for example, the notes by Manuel de Cárdenas on Spanish hospital personnel in Vilnius (war diary, entry of 19 March 1942), as well as Pardo Martínez (2005: 189).

304 Urquijo (1973: 326); war diary of Menéndez Gundín, entry of 7 May 1942 (Cela 2010: 154–5); Blanco (1954: 57).

305 See memoirs of Bemigno Cabo (1944) as well as Sagarra (2012: 600).

306 Memoirs of Private Emilio Murillo (Gragera Díaz 2004: 170).

307 García-Izquierdo (2009: 185).

308 Hilberg (1992: 195–268); Barnett (1999); Cesarini & Levine (2002).

309 Mendel (1972: 218). The author, however, provides no further details. Another attempt at escape by a group of Jews from the Riga ghetto involved bribing a Luftwaffe officer to take them to Sweden; unfortunately, he was in fact a Gestapo agent.

310 Edvarson (2008: 59–60); Hilberg (1992: 156–7).

311 Bowen (1998).

312 Anderson (1999), Hausleitner, Mihok, & Wetzel (2001), see also Ungváry (2002–3).

313 Michaelis (1978: 321) and Wette (2002: 135–40). The myth of the pro-Jewish nature of the Italian occupation in Russia and the Balkans is nonetheless subject to debate (Rodogno 2005; 2006: 107–51).

314 Romero (1982: 139).

315 Friedländer (2007).

316 See Rass (2005); Wette (2003); and Hartmann, Hürter, Lieb, & Pohl (2009).

317 Cataruzza (2006); Bajohr, & Löw (2015).

318 Caballero Jurado (2004b).

319 Kovalev (2014: 379–93) arrives at a similar conclusion in describing the reaction of the BD volunteers to the Jewish question, based on some testimonies regarding Riga that partially coincide with ours here.

320 Reverte & Reverte (2001: 193–5).

321 K., "La marmita," *Hoja de Campaña* (10 February 1942).

6. The Last Crusaders of the Nazi New Order (1944–5)

1 Obersturmführer Vey to Einsatzkommando I, 29 November 1943, and Sturmbahnführer Gotard to Chef of SD "Ostland," Gatchina, 11 December 1943 (USHMM, Sp BD 11.001M.05).

2 *Inland II* to Ribbentrop, Berlin, 29 January 1944; notice by Ribbentrop, 1 February 1944 (PAAA-R.101143).

3 German miilitary attaché, Madrid, 13 January 1944 (BA-MA, RW 5/430); Winzer to Reichssicherheitshauptamt, Madrid, 4 February 1944 (USHMM, Sp BD 11.001M.05).

4 Notice by Colonel Kurmmacher, 19 January 1944; order by foreign section of Abwehr, 19 January 1944; German Occupation Authority in France, 17 January 1944 (BA-MA, RW 5/430).

5 Report by Samuel Hoare, 25 March 1944 (Grandío Seoane 2017: 127).

6 Memorandum by Walter Schellenberg, 2 June 1944 (BA-MA, RW 5/430).

7 Minute by OKH, 19 July 1944; report of Sonderstab F, 7 July 1944; notices of 3, 8, and 10 September 1944; minutes from *Allgemeines Heeresamt*, 29 July 1944 (BA-MA, RW 5/431); minutes of the meeting of Colonel Rudolf Major, Major Umé (ag. Ausland-Abwehr) amd Sonderführer Keller (Sonderstab F), 5 August 1944; Oberkommando der Wehrmacht to Sonderstab F, 12 August 1944 (BA-MA, RW 5/431).

8 See Hitler's private conservations, entries of 7 June and 7 July 1942 (Conversaciones 2004: 411–12, 415–16, 451).

9 Reports of Spanish ambassador in Berlin, 18 August 1944, and Spanish ambassador in Slovakia, Bern, 21 April 1945 (AMAE, R-2299/2 and R-2192/36); Janué i Miret (2014).

10 Norling (2007); Ezquerra (1947).

11 See Bowen (2001); Gil Martínez (2011); Sourd (2007); Palacio Pilacés (2015: 194–7); and Kocjancic (2016).

12 W. Vopersal, *Freiwilligen-Kompanie (span.) 101*, BA-MA N 756. Examples of desertion in letter of José Luis Ibáñez, Hollabrunn, 27 February 1945

(GstA, I. HA 218/536), and minutes from 15 January 1945 (GStA I. HA 218/467).

13 See J. Tomás Giner, *Informe sobre diversos asuntos en Berlin en relación con Falange*, 16 May 1946 (Archive of the FUE, Madrid, Archivo del Gobierno de la República en el Exilio, Ministerio de Gobernación, 103–4).

14 A few Spaniards were scattered through diverse units, such as the South-Tyrolean SS-Polizei Freiwilligen Battallion Posen, and even the special battalion Dirlewanger (Sourd 2007: 90–5).

15 Thus, Corporal Julio García Aguilar, who volunteered for the BD in 1943, remained in the Blue Legion and, after returning to Spain, crossed the Pyrenees in May 1944. In June 1945, he showed up at the Spanish consulate of Bratislava, then fled to Vienna, Belgrade, and finally reached Italy, where he managed to contact the Spanish consulate in Rome. Finally, he was repatriated by the consulate (see the report in AGA, 52/2289).

16 Details of the participation of Spanish soldiers at the Battle of Berlin are little known. However, see the unreliable narration of Ezquerra (1947).

17 Some of them seem to have been killed by Spanish Republican volunteers of the Leclerc Division, as they entered Berchtesgaden; see the war diary of Lucas Camón Portillo, 7 May 1945 (Coale 2014: 422–3).

18 See letters from Leo García, SS-Lazarett Starkenbach, 14 January 1945, 16 January 1945, and 22 January 1945 (GStA, I.Ha 218 / 586).

19 For further information on this, see Núñez Seixas (2012: 156–62).

20 Grunert (2012).

21 See *La Joven Europa (1942–1943). Antología de textos divisionarios y españoles*, Molins de Rei: Eds. Nueva República, 2010.

22 "Socialismo europeo," *Enlace* (21 December 1944).

23 See "Obreros como mercancía humana," *Enlace* (23 November 1944), and "Habla un refugiado," *Enlace* (20 January 1945).

24 "Raza y Revolución," *Enlace* (15 October 1944).

25 For further details, see Núñez Seixas (2005).

26 See Bowen (2001: 196–219), and Leleu (2007: 261–77).

27 See Ezquerra (1947); Parrilla (2002); Puente (1954: 16–22); Eizaguirre (1955: 32–48). See also the biographies of some of them collected in report dated on 24 September 1954 (AGMAV, C.3770/2).

28 J.M. Pons Mascaró, "¡Españoles...'" *Enlace* (29 January 1945).

29 J.L. Ibáñez Pajares, "Horas decisivas," *Enlace* (23 November 1944).

30 Letter signed by Jesús Ochoa Miranda and six more Spaniards, St. Valentin (Vienna), 8 January 1945, GGstA, I. Ha 318 / 586.

31 Letter of José Ignacio Imaz, Braunschweig, 29 December 1944 (GStA, I. Ha 318 / 586).

32 Adolfo González Almenara to Arrizubieta, Kratzan, 7 January 1945 (GStA, I. Ha 218 / 586).

33 David Gómez to Arrizubieta, Chemnitz, 25 December 1944, GStA, I. Ha
    318 / 586.
34 Antonio Lucena to Arrizubieta, Kornwestheim, 7 January 1945 (GStA, I.
    Ha 318 / 586).
35 Letter of a Spanish volunteer of the Waffen-SS, Berlin, 28 April 1945
    (Vázquez Enciso 1995: 261).
36 Pedro Portela to Arrizubieta, Stockerau, 10 January 1945 (GStA, I. Ha 318
    /586).
37 Letters by Juan Sánchez Peñalver, Reservelazarett Rinteln, 15 March 1945,
    and by Jesús Corral Martín, 6 January 1945, to Arrizubieta (GStA, I. Ha
    318 / 586).
38 Puente (1954: 20–2). See also EL LEGIONARIO, "Por qué luchamos," *Enlace*
    (6 January 1945).
39 "Amigos de Enlace," *Enlace* (23 November 1944).

7. War Veterans and Memories from the Eastern Front in Franco's Spain (1942–75)

1 DGS report, 19 December 1941 (AHMC-FGV, C. 115).
2 Sicherheitsdienst director and the Sicherheitspolizei to the Foreign Ministry, Berlin, 9 April 1942; German Foreign Ministry to embassy in Madrid,
   13 May 1942; report from German consul in San Sebastián, 21 May 1942
   (PAAA, R-101144, and Geheimakten, Box 796).
3 DGS reports, 26 and 27 May 1942 (AHMC-FGV, C. 115).
4 Alcalde (2014: 169–70).
5 Reports from Rohrbach, 23 July 1942 and 22 August 1942 (PAAA, Box 796,
   Geheimakten, 6/9).
6 Notice on the meeting of von Stohrer with Serrano Suñer, 25 July 1942
   (PAAA, Box 796, Geheimakten, 6/9).
7 Letter from the Civil Governor of Málaga to the German consul, 19 January 1944, in PAAA, Deutsche Botschaft Madrid, Zusatz 91.
8 Alcalde (2014: 268–78). See also Núñez Seixas (2018d).
9 AGMAV, C.3770/1 and C.3770/2; Merino Izquierdo (2017: 179–82).
10 "La generación de los divisionarios," *El Español* (2 January 1943). See also
   J. Moya Gómez, "Algo sobre heroicidad," *Ofensiva* (26 November 1942).
11 "Los de Rusia," *Hoja de Campaña* (18 November 1942).
12 D. Castro Martínez, "Nuevamente dispuestos a las órdenes de Franco,"
   Lanza (26 March 1946).
13 Salvador (1971).
14 *Boletín Oficial del Estado*, 22 January and 5 February 1942, 8 and 17 May 1942.
15 Alcalde (2014: 177–8); Palacio Pilacés (2013, II: 886–92).
16 *Blau División*, 104 (April 1968).

17 Bernal García (2010: 276–86).

18 For the case of the region Castile-La Mancha, see González Madrid (2007).

19 For example, in the south-eastern city of Alicante, five ex-BD volunteers served as town councillors in 1963, and two in 1967. See *Blau División*, 44 (March 1963) and 89 (January 1967).

20 Pinilla (n.d.: 170–2); *Blau División*, 598 (May 2009), reported that 40 ensigns became lieutenants, 154 lieutenants became captains, 15 captains became commanders, and 7 commanders became lieutenant colonels.

21 Cuenca Toribio (2001: 43).

22 See García Hispán (1991: 77–80); "Los generales de la División Azul," *Blau División*, 539 (June 2004).

23 Echternkamp (2000); Echternkamp & Hettling (2008); Manig (2004) and Schwelling (2010).

24 Report from Gardemann, Madrid, 2 January 1942 (PAAA, Botschaft Madrid, Box 796, *Geheimakten*, 6/9).

25 DGS reports from 9, 13, 18, and 20 June 1942 assumed the existence of an ex-BD "organization" under the command of a "second José Antonio [Primo de Rivera]" that sought to reorient the regime and vindicate Morocco, Portugal, Andorra, and Gibraltar (AHMC-FGV, C. 115).

26 See several examples in PAAA, ADBM, *Zusatz 91. Betr.: von den Alliierten gefertigte Verzeichnisse (Inventarlisten u.a.)*.

27 Moreno Juliá (2009: 90; 2014: 429–30); report from Dieckhoff, 9 June 1944 (PAAA, R-29752).

28 Dolores Gancedo to A. Martín Gamero, Toledo, 1 November 1941 (AA).

29 Telegram from von Stohrer, Madrid, 28 October 1941 (PAAA, Box 796, Geheimakten, 6/10).

30 DGS report, 21 June 1942 (AHMC-FGV, C. 115).

31 Uriarte Arbaiza (2012: 172–3); Sagarra (2012: 655–60); *La Vanguardia Española* (11 July 1943).

32 *La Vanguardia Española* (2, 3, and 4 April 1954); Rodríguez Jiménez (2008); Segador (2019: 90–3).

33 Richards (2013: 150–5).

34 Lehmann (2006: 182–95).

35 As, e.g., in Ciudad Real: see "Nota para los excombatientes de la División Azul," *Lanza* (27 April 1954).

36 *La Vanguardia Española* (9 January 1956).

37 *Hermandad*, 7 (August-September 1956).

38 Alcalde (2014: 280–2). According to Sagarra (2012: 985–7), 40 brotherhoods existed between 1943 and 2012.

39 In 1959, the National BD Brotherhood petitioned the Ministry of Foreign Affairs to authorize its affiliation with the Verband Deutscher Soldaten

(VDS), to request aid from the FRG for mutilated veterans and families of the fallen. Inclusion became effective in January 1960. Two years later, an agreement on war pensions was signed, and was ratified by the Bundestag in 1965 (Aschmann 1999: 385–91).

40 See *Blau División*, 534 (January 2004); Sagarra (2012: 985–7) identifies 21 publications. Some local newspapers also reserved regular space for the provincial BD Brotherhood.

41 Sagarra (2012: 674–5); "Juntas Consultivas," *Hermandad*, 8 (March–April 1959).

42 Author's own estimation based on Puente Fernández (2012: 210–13, 226–7) and the brochure *Hermandad de Excombatientes y familiares de caídos de la "División Azul". Santander. Índice de afiliados. Mayo 1956*, n.p., 1956.

43 In 1974 (Rodríguez Jiménez 1997: 361–4, 396), the BD brotherhood would have numbered 12,550 ex-combatants, or almost a third of the survivors. Sagarra (2012: 664) stated that there were 10,000 (almost 25%). Both figures seem inflated.

44 L. Parreño, "50.° aniversario de la División Azul," *La Tribuna* (7 April 1991); Archive of the *Registro de Asociaciones*, San Sebastián (courtesy of Dr. Amaia Lamikiz); Alcalde (2014: 281).

45 "Tirada y difusión de Hermandad," *Hermandad*, 6 (November-December 1958).

46 "Actividades," *Hoja de Campaña. Órgano de actividades de la "División Azul" de Valencia*, 9 (March 1961).

47 *Hermandad*, 19 (April–May 1961). Examples of intercession to secure work for BD veterans in *Blau División*, 2 (July 1957), and 4 (November 1957).

48 "Mirador nacional. A tumba abierta," *Los Sitios* (11 July 1971); "Treinta años de una gesta," *Los Sitios* (24 October 1971).

49 The BD veteran Ángel Marchena, after being a rural warden in his village, did odd jobs and leveraged his condition to obtain letters of recommendation from former BD officers. Through these, he accessed housing in Barcelona. Years later, he passed a medical examination to migrate to Germany because the surgeon also was a veteran of the Russian Front (Marchena Cañete 2003: 116–20, 124–7).

50 S. Nieva Yarritu, "Seguimos solos y aislados," *Hermandad*, 16 (October-November 1960).

51 See "Se conmemora en Albacete el XXVI aniversario de la entrada en combate de la División Azul," *Los Sitios*, 13 October 1967; "Ciudad Real. Homenaje a la División Azul," *Lanza* (11 February 1968).

52 See *Blau División*, 11 (January 1960) and 31 (March 1962); López de Maturana (2014: 272–7); *La Vanguardia Española* (11 February 1966).

53 J.M. Martínez Val, "Memoria de la División Azul," *Lanza* (10 February 1968).

54 *Guía Código Postal-España,* Ministerio de Transportes, Turismo y Teleco-municaciones, Madrid, 1986.

55 Duch i Plana (2002).

56 Rodríguez Jiménez (1997: 402).

57 See, for example, "Para ser inexpugnables," *La Vanguardia Española* (24 February 1943); F. Izquierdo Luque, "La victoria de la paz de Franco," *El Español,* 127 (31 March 1945).

58 T. Nieto Funcia, "Razones españolas sobre la paz," *El Español,* 133 (12 May 1945).

59 *Los Sitios* (25 March 1960).

60 Luca de Tena & Palacios (1955); Eizaguirre (1955); Calavia & Álvarez Cosmen (1956); Oroquieta & García Sánchez (1958); Negro Castro (1959); Poquet Guardiola (2001); Salamanca & Torres García (2002).

61 For example, J. Salom, *El mensaje* (Madrid 1963); J.L. Martín Vigil, *La muerte está en el camino* (Barcelona 1956); C. Kurtz, *El desconocido* (Barcelona 1956).

62 Until 1988, there were at least 136 titles including books, pamphlets, novels, films, and autobiographies focused on the Blue Division (Caballero & Ibáñez 1989). See also Núñez Seixas (2006).

63 In addition to *Embajadores en el infierno* (Ambassadors to hell, José M.[a] Forqué, 1956), we can recall *La patrulla* (The patrol, Pedro Lazaga, 1954), *La espera* (The wait, Vicente Lluch, 1956), and *Carta a una mujer* (Letter to a woman, Manuel Iglesias, 1961). After a long pause, the topic was re-addressed in the ambitious, but failed, movie *Silencio en la nieve* (Silence in the snow, Gerardo Herrero, 2011). See Ibáñez Hernández (2001).

64 For example, see Alvarellos (1948) or the 1959 work of Hanns Maassen, a former combatant of the International Brigades who became a writer in the German Democratic Republic. See also Paniagua (1961).

65 See Possi (2016, 2017), as well as Guzmán Mora (2016).

66 Lavedán (1959: 12).

67 Casals (1995: 177, 315–16).

68 See Cogollos Vicens (1985) and Linares (2000).

69 See Bullón de Mendoza & Togores (2011), as well as many of the presentations at the conference held in Madrid in 2011 for the seventieth anniversary of the Blue Division (http://www.congresoladivisionazul.com). For some interesting sources, though mostly treated acritically, see Sagarra (2012) and Caballero Jurado (2019).

70 Halbwachs (2004).

71 For more details, see Núñez Seixas (2006b).

72 Rochat (1982); Mondini (2008: 157–218); Osti Guerrazzi (2010: 266–79; 2011); Corni (2012: 45–9); Focardi (2013); Carteny (2013). Regarding the Italian memoirs and autobiographic writings on the Eastern Front, see the

bestsellers by Bedeschi (1994) and Revelli (2013). For the French combatants, see Carrard (2010).

73 See Salvador (1975); Urgoiti y Bas (1987); Royo Masía (1944: 157–9).

74 Castaño Doña (1991: 104); Ridruejo (1976: 438–9); Romero (1982: 143).

75 Rodríguez Puértolas (1986: 556–65).

76 Epkenhans, Förster, & Hagemann (2006); Wette (2002: 180–1); Corni (2012).

77 Heer (1999: 180–8); Pätzold (2000), see also Bald, Klotz, & Wette (2001).

78 Wilke (2011: 17); Werther & Hurd (2014: 334–5). However, the brotherhoods joined the first acts of fraternizing with veterans of the Waffen-SS in the mid 1960s, such as the gathering of former SS in Rendsburg in October 1965: see "Foto con pie," *Blau División*, 76 (December 1965).

79 An early example in A. Marquerie, "Ejercicios de la División Azul," *Informaciones* (6 August 1941). Memoirs of French SS volunteers provide similar examples (Carrard 2010: 119–22).

80 *División Azul. 2° Cuaderno*, n.p.

81 "Los transportes en la División Azul," *Hoja de Campaña* (16 March 1942). See also J. R. Masoliver, "Los Guzmanes no han muerto," *Destino*, 305 (22 May 1943).

82 Ydígoras (1984: 302); Á. de Laiglesia, "Un Quijote ha muerto en Rusia," *El Español* (27 February 1943).

83 "La infantería española," *Hoja de Campaña* (6 April 1942); R. Garriga, "Nuestros voluntarios, invictos también del frío," *La Vanguardia Española* (14 January 1942).

84 On the reception in Spain of the Nuremberg trials, see Palmero Aranda (2016: 241–52).

85 Hernández Navarro (1971: 57–60).

86 Farré Albiñana (1949: 90, 250–5).

87 Esteban-Infantes (1956: 50).

88 Salvador (1962: 73).

89 Ydígoras (1984: 57–8, 62–9).

90 Riudavets de Montes (1960: 13–14). Before leaving for Russia, he stated that a Jewish conspiracy had existed in Spain; see his "Riesgo y ventura de la raza hispana," *El Alcázar* (14 February 1942).

91 See Vadillo (1967: 134–5, 156, 159–66, 180, 186–94); V. Lor Fernández, "Lia, la enfermera polaca," *Hermandad*, 5 (September–October 1958); Castelo Villaoz (1990: 45); Sánchez Salcedo (2002: 44), Linares (2000: 110).

92 Bars Casamitjana (1962: 6–12).

93 Zulaica (1963).

94 Jiménez Andrade (1957: 50–1).

95 *Arriba* (14 April 1961).

96 Riudavets de Montes (1960: 18–19, 40–1, 155–6).

97 Ruiz Ayúcar (1981: 156).
98 Castelo Villaoz (1992: 87–8).
99 Vidal y Gadea (1991: 63); A. Medina León, "Españoles y rusos," *El Español*, 159 (30 October 1965).
100 G. Alonso del Real, "Un sargento español ante la Virgen de Kazán," *ABC* (21 May 1955); M. Atienza, "Recuerdos de Rusia," *Hermandad*, 17 (December 1960–January 1961).
101 See, for example, Bendala (1944).
102 Álvarez de Sotomayor (1991: 160–1). See also the impressions written by captain Javier Urmeneta in 1942, reproduced by Jimeno Aranguren (2015: 121).
103 Díaz de Villegas (1950; 1951); García Luna (1959: 38–9, 121); M. Martínez-Mena, "Pensar y vivir de un pueblo, con el cual los divisionarios simpatizamos," *Blau División*, 56 (April 1964).
104 R. Serrano Suñer, "Hacia un patriotismo europeo," *ABC* (29 September 1959); M. Salvador Gironés, "Cosas de por allá," *Blau División*, 54 (February 1964); J. A. Vidal y Gadea, "Notas de un viaje a la URSS (III y último)," *Blau División*, 197 (December 1975); V. Mas, "Dos viajes a Rusia," *Blau División*, 537 (April 2004).
105 Espinosa Poveda (1993); Tremlett (2008: 59–60), reproduces similar views expressed by the president of the BD Brotherhood at that time, Juan Chicharro-Lamamié de Clairac.
106 De la Vega (1999: 33–4).

8. Conclusion: A Spanish Exception in the War of Extermination?

1 See Anderson (1999). Studies on the brutalization of Romanian warfare in the war against the Soviet Union mostly focus on its participation in the deportation of the Jewish and Gypsy populations See Hausleitner, Mihok, & Wetzel (2001), as well as Heinen (2007: 109–49), and Deletant (2006: 150–204).
2 For the emergence and development of racial thought in Spain, see Goode (2009).
3 See Liulevicius (2000) and Dornik (2013).
4 Rutherford (2014: 115–52, 240–79).
5 Russian testimonies after 1944 only indicate that a Spanish lieutenant in Korotskoe was responsible for some shootings of peasants (Kovalev 2012: 369).
6 Domingo (2009: 158).
7 See Wievorka (2009: 42–7) and Kallis (2009: 26–84).
8 As Rutherford (2014: 280–302) suggests for the German 121st and 126th Divisions, while battle conditions fostered greater brutalization among the soldiers of the 123rd Division.

9 Balfour (2002: 215–33); Nerín (2005: 280–3).
10 Sánchez Carrilero (1992: 124).
11 See Anderson (1999) and Ungváry (2005).
12 See Bohn (1997); Poulsen (1991); and Foray (2010).
13 Schlemmer (2005: 368–97; 2009); a different perspective on the Italian treatment of civilians, based on Soviet documents, is offered by Scotoni (2013: 218–23, 286–300), who underlines the benign charcter of Italian occupation in comparison with German behaviour towards civilians and prisoners of war. See also Scianna (2019: 229–66) and Pannacci (2020).
14 Schrijvers (2002).

Sources and References

Primary Sources

Public and Private Archives

Archive of the FUE, Residencia de Estudiantes, Madrid
Archivo General de la Administración, Alcalá de Henares (AGA)
Archivo General Militar, Ávila (AGMAV)
Archivo Histórico Municipal de Cádiz, Fondo General Varela (AHMC-FGV)
Archivo del Ministerio de Asuntos Exteriores, Madrid (AMAE)
Author's Archive (AA)
Bibliothek für Zeitgeschichte, Stuttgart, Sterz Collection (BfZ-CS)
Bundesarchiv-Militärarchiv, Freiburg im Breisgau (BA-MA)
Central State Archive of Saint Petersburg (TsGA SPB)
Centro Documental de la Memoria Histórica, Salamanca (CDMH)
City Archive Hof/Stadtsarchiv Hof (SH)
Feldpostarchiv, Museum für Kommunikation, Berlin
Geheimes Staatsarchiv Preussischer Kulturbesitz, Berlin (GHSta)
Historical Archive of La Rioja/Archivo Histórico Provincial de la Rioja, Logroño (AHPLR)
Historical Archive of Spanish Communist Party/Archivo Histórico Partido Comunista de España, Madrid (AHPCE)
Museo del Pueblo de Asturias, Gijón (MPA), Leandro García González Papers (FLGG)
National Archives – Foreign Office, Surrey, London (NA-FO)
Naval Archive, Gatchina (Russian Federation)
Political Archive of the German Ministry of Foreign Affairs/Politisches Archiv des Auswärtigen Amtes, Berlin (PAAA)
Private Archive of Mr. Xosé Fernández Naval, Santiago de Compostela (AFN)
Private Archive of Mr. Carlos López del Río, Boiro/Madrid (ACLR)

Private Archive of Dr. María-Xesús Nogueira (Santiago de Compostela)
Private Archive of Mr. Francisco Rebollo, Torrevieja (AFR)
Private Archive of Mr. Carlos Rey (A Coruña)
Private Archive of Ridruejo Family, Barcelona (AFRI)
Real Academia de la Historia, Santiago Montero Díaz Papers, Madrid
    (RAH-FMD)
United States Holocaust Memorial Museum, Archive Collections, Washington
    (USHMM)
University of California San Diego – Manuscripts Section (UCSD-MSS)

Unpublished War Diaries and Memoirs

Diario de un Soldado, anonymous, AGMAV 46767/2/5
Diario de operaciones e impresiones, Lieutenant Benjamín Arenales (private
    archive of Carmelo de las Heras, Madrid)
Memoirs of Evdokiia Bogacheva-Baskakova, 1970 (Museum of Russian
    Culture, San Francisco, Manuscript Collection, Box 2, Folder 4)
Memoirs of Private Benigno Cabo, 1944 (private archive of Mr. Jorge Villena,
    Madrid)
War diary of medical captain Manuel de Cárdenas (private archive of José
    Manuel de Cárdenas, San Sebastián).
War diary of Jesús Martínez Tessier (private archive of Martínez-Reverte
    family, Madrid)
War diary of Ensign Juan Romero Osende (private archive of Ana Romero
    Masiá, A Coruña)
War diary of Pioneers' Sergeant Francisco Suárez Ojeda (private archive of
    María P. Suárez Medina, Gáldar, Gran Canaria)
War diary of private Martín Velasco Carvajal (private archive of Mr. Pablo
    Velasco, Toledo)

References

Guerra psicológica sobre la División Azul (Rusia, 1941–1944). (n.d.). n.p.
Ackermann, F. (2011). *Palimpsest Grodno. Nationalisierung, Nivellierung
    und Sowjetisierung einer mitteleuropäischen Stadt, 1919–1991*. Wiesbaden:
    Harrasowitz.
Alcalde, A. (2012). Cultura de guerra y excombatientes para la implantación
    del franquismo en Albacete (1939–1945). *Al-Basit, Revista de Estudios
    Albacetenses, 57*, 37–69.
Alcalde, A. (2014). *Los excombatientes franquistas (1936–1965)*. Zaragoza: PUZ.
Adamowitsch, A., & Granin, D. (2018). *Blockade Buch. Leningrad 1941–1944*.
    Berlin: Aufbau Verlag. (Original work published 2014)

Agustí Roca, C. (2003). *Rússia és culpable! Memòria i record de la División Azul.* Lleida: Pagès.

Alegre Lorenz, D. (2017). *Experiencia de guerra y colaboracionismo político-militar: Bélgica, Francia y España bajo el Nuevo Orden (1941–1945).* PhD Thesis, Autonomous University of Barcelona.

Alvarellos, F.J.G. (1948). *Legionarios españoles contra Rusia.* Buenos Aires: Emecé.

Álvarez Chillida, G. (2002). *El antisemitismo en España. La imagen del judío (1812–2002).* Madrid: Marcial Pons.

Álvarez Chillida, G. (2014). Epígono de la Hispanidad. La españolización de la colonia de Guinea durante el primer franquismo. In S. Michonneau & X.M. Núñez Seixas (Eds.), *Imaginarios y representaciones de España durante el franquismo* (pp. 103–25). Madrid: Casa de Velázquez.

Álvarez de Sotomayor, M. (1991). *Generación puente* Alicante: García Hispán.

Aly, G. (2005). *Hitlers Volksstaat. Raub, Rassenkrieg und nationaler Sozialismus.* Frankfurt a. M.: Fischer.

Aly, G., & Heim S. (1993). *Vordenker der Vernichtung: Auschwitz und die deutschen Pläne für eine neue europäische Ordnung.* Frankfurt a. M.: Fischer.

Anderson, T.G. (1999). A Hungarian *Vernichtungskrieg*? Hungarian troops and the Soviet partisan war in Ukraine, 1942. *Militärgeschichtliche Mitteilungen,* 58, 345–66.

Andreyev, C. (1987). *Vlasov and the Russian liberation movement. Soviet reality and émigré theories.* Cambridge: Cambridge UP.

Antoniou, G., Carrard, Ph., Dordanas, S., Gentile, C., Hale, Ch., & Núñez Seixas, X.M. (2016). Western and Southern Europe: The cases of Spain, France, Italy, and Greece. In J. Böhler & R. Gerwarth (Eds.), *The Waffen–SS* (pp. 76–119). Oxford: Oxford UP.

Arad, Y. (2009). *The Holocaust in the Soviet Union.* Lincoln/Jerusalem: University of Nebraska Press/Yad Vashem.

Aresti, N. (2014). The Battle to define Spanish Manhood. In A. G. Morcillo (Ed.), *Memory and cultural history of the Spanish Civil War* (pp. 147–77). Leiden/Boston: Brill,

Arielli, N., & Collins, B. (Eds.). (2013). *Transnational soldiers: Foreign military Enlistment in the moderneEra.* Basingstoke: Palgrave Macmillan.

Armada, A. (1983). *Al servicio de la Corona,* Barcelona: Planeta.

Aschmann, B. (1999). *"Treue Freunde..."? Westdeutschland und Spanien 1945–1963.* Stuttgart: Franz Steiner.

Assworthy, A., Scafes, C., & Craciunoiu, F. (1995), *Third axis, fourth ally: Romanian armed forces in the European war, 1941–1945.* London: Arms and Armours.

Audoin-Rouzeau, S. (1986). *14–18. Les combattants des tranchées à travers leurs journaux* Paris: Armand Colin.

Audoin-Rouzeau, S. (2008). *Combattre. Une anthropologie historique de la guerre moderne (XIX–XXIe siècle)*, Paris: Le Seuil.

Ayçoberry, P. (2003). Der Bolschewik. In E. Francois & H. Schulze (Eds.), *Deutsche Erinnerungsorte* (pp. 455–68). Munich: Beck.

Aznar, M. (1942). *Un episodio de la compañía de esquiadores en el lago Ilmen*. Madrid: Dédalo.

Bajohr, F., & Löw, A. (Eds.). (2015). *Der Holocaust. Ergebnisse und neue Fragen der Forschung*. Frankfurt a. M.: Fischer.

Bajohr, F., & Strupp, Ch. (Eds.). (2011). *Fremde Blicke auf das "Dritte Reich." Berichte ausländischer Diplomaten über Herrschaft und Gesellschaft in Deutschland 1933–1945*. Göttingen: Vandenhoeck & Ruprecht.

Bald, D., Klotz, J., & Wette, W. (2001). *Mythos Wehrmacht. Nachkriegsdebatten und Traditionspflege*. Berlin: Aufbau.

Balfour, S. (2002). *Deadly Embrace: Morocco and the road to Spanish Civil War*, Oxford: Oxford UP.

Barnett, V.J. (1999). *Bystanders: Conscience and complicity during the Holocaust*. Newport, CT/London: Praeger.

Barrachina Juan, E. (1994). *La batalla del lago Ilmen*. Barcelona: PPU.

Bars Casamitjana, M. (1962). *El pan en el fango*. Olot: Biblioteca Olotina.

Bartov, O. (1991). *Hitler's army: Soldiers, Nazis, and war in the Third Reich*. New York/Oxford: Oxford UP.

Bartov, O. (2001). *The Eastern Front, 1941–45, German troops and the barbarization of warfare*. Houndmills/New York: Palgrave Macmillan. (Original work published 1985)

Bartov, O. (2003). *Germany's war and the Holocaust: Disputed histories*, Ithaca/London: Cornell UP.

Beck, B. (2004). *Wehrmacht und sexuelle Gewalt. Sexualverbrechen vor deutschen Militärgerichten 1939–1945*. Paderborn: Schöningh.

Bedeschi, G. (1994). *Centomila gavette di ghiaccio*. Milan: Mursia. (Original work published 1963)

Beevor, A. (1998). *Stalingrad: The fateful siege, 1942–1943*. New York: Penguin.

Beevor, A. (2002). *Berlin. La caída: 1945*. Barcelona: Crítica.

Bellod Gómez, A. (2004). *Soldado en tres guerras. Campaña de África. Guerra civil española. División Azul en Rusia*. Madrid: San Martín.

Bendala, F. (1944). *Leyendas del lago Ilmen*. Madrid: Viuda de Juan Pueyo.

Beneyto Pérez, J. (1934). *Nacionalsocialismo*. Barcelona: Labor.

Benz, W. (1996). *Feindbild und Vorurteil. Beiträge über Ausgrenzung und Verfolgung*. Munich: DTV.

Berkowitz, A., & Fontenla Ballesta, S. (2019). *La División Azul ante el Holocausto*. Lorca: Fajardo el Bravo.

Bernal García, F. (2010). *El sindicalismo vertical. Burocracia, control laboral y representación de intereses en la España franquista (1936–1951)*. Madrid: CEPC.

Birn, R.B. (2009). Die SS–Ideologie und Herrschaftsausübung. Zur Frage der Inkorporierung von "Fremdvölkischen." In J.E. Schulte (Ed.), *Die SS, Himmler und die Wewelsburg* (pp. 60–75). Paderborn: Schöningh.

Bishop, Ch. (2005). *SS Hitler's foreign divisions: Foreign volunteers in the Waffen-SS 1940–1945.* Staplehurst: Spellmount.

Blanch Sabench, J.M. (2010). *Memorias de un soldado de la División Azul.* Madrid: Galland Books.

Blanco, J.E. (1954). *Rusia no es cuestión de un día.* Madrid: Publicaciones Españolas.

Blumstein, A. (2002). *A little house on Mount Carmel.* London: Valentine Mitchell.

Böcker, M. (2000). *Antisemitismus ohne Juden. Die Zweite Republik, die antirepublikanische Rechte und die Juden. Spanien 1931 bis 1936.* Frankfurt a. M.: Peter Lang.

Böhler, J. (2006). *Auftakt zum Vernichtungskrieg. Die Wehrmacht in Polen 1939.* Frankfurt a. M: Fischer.

Bohn, R. (Ed.). (1997). *Die deutsche Herrschaft in den "germanischen" Ländern, 1940–1945.* Stuttgart: Steiner.

Boixcar. (1954). "Sinfonía en rojo y azul," *Hazañas bélicas, 118.* Barcelona: Toray.

Boixcar. (1955a). "Sucedió en Rusia," *Hazañas bélicas, Almanaque.* Barcelona: Toray.

Boixcar. (1955b). "El cerco de Leningrado," *Hazañas bélicas, 121.* Barcelona: Toray.

Böhler, J., & Gerwarth, R. (Eds.). (2016). *The Waffen SS: A European history.* Oxford: Oxford UP.

Bordjugov, G. (1999). Terror der Wehrmacht gegenüber der russischen Zivilbevölkerung. In G. Gorzka & K. Stang (Eds.), *Der Vernichtungskrieg im Osten–Verbrechen der Wehrmacht in der Sowjetunion aus Sicht russischer Historiker* (pp. 53–68). Kassel: Kassel UP.

Bornstein–Bielicka, Ch. (2008). *Mein Weg als Widerstandskämpferin.* Munich [Tel Aviv]: DTV. (Original work published 2003)

Bourke, J. (2008). *Sed de sangre: historia íntima del combate cuerpo a cuerpo en las guerras del siglo XX.* Barcelona: Crítica.

Bowen, W.H. (1998). "A great moral victory": Spanish protection of Jews on the Eastern Front, 1941–1944. In R. Rohrlich (Ed.), *Resisting the Holocaust* (pp. 195–211). Oxford/New York: Berg.

Bowen, W.H. (2000a). *Spaniards and Nazi Germany: Collaboration in the New Order.* Columbia: Missouri UP.

Bowen, W.H. (2000b). The Last Defenders of the New Order: Spaniards and Nazi Germany, August 1944–May 1945. In C. Kent et al. (Eds.), *The lion and the eagle: Interdisciplinary essays on German-Spanish relations over the centuries* (pp. 397–422). New York/Oxford: Berghahn.

Bowen, W.H. (2001). The ghost battalion: Spaniards in the Waffen-SS, 1944–1945. *The Historian, 63*(2), 373–85. https://doi.org/10.1111/j.1540-6563.2001.tb01471.

Bowen, W.H. (2007). Spain and the Nazi occupation of Poland, 1939–44. *International Social Science Review, 82*(3–4), 135–48. *JSTOR*, www.jstor.org /stable/41887323. Accessed 18 July 2021.

Browning, Ch. (2002). *Aquellos hombres grises. El batallón 101 y la solución final en Polonia*. Barcelona: Edhasa. (Original work published 1992)

Bruneteau, B. (2003). *"L'Europe nouvelle" de Hitler. Une illusion des intellectuels de la France de Vichy*. Paris: Éditions du Rocher.

Bruyne, E. de (1991). *Les wallons meurent à l'Est. La Légion Wallonie et Léon Degrelle sur le Front russe 1941–1945*. Brussels: Didier–Hatier.

Bruyne, E. de, & Rikmenspoel, M. (2004). *For Rex and for Belgium: Léon Degrelle and political & military collaboration 1940–45*. Solihull: Helion and Company.

Brydan, D. (2016). Axis Internationalism: Spanish Health Experts and the Nazi "New Europe," 1939–1945. *Contemporary European History, 25*(2), 291–311. http://dx.doi.org/10.1017/S0960777316000084.

Brydan, D. (2019a). Transnational Exchange in the Nazi New Order: the Spanish Blue Division and its medical services. *Journal of Contemporary History, 54*(4), 880–901. http://dx.doi.org/10.1177/0022009418786789

Brydan, D. (2019b). *Franco's internationalists: social experts and Spain's search for legitimacy*. Oxford: Oxford UP.

Buchbender, O., & Sterz, C. (Eds.). (1982). *Das andere Gesicht des Krieges. Deutsche Feldpostbriefe 1939–1945*. Munich: Beck.

Bullón de Mendoza, A., & Togores, L.E. (Eds.). (2011). *La otra memoria*. Madrid: Actas.

Buschmann, N., & Carl, H. (Eds.). (2001) *Die Erfahrung des Krieges. Erfahrungsgeschichtliche Perspektiven von der Französischen Revolution bis zum Zweiten Weltkrieg*. Paderborn: Schöningh.

Caballero Jurado, C. (2004a). *"Morir en Rusia." La División Azul en la batalla de Krasny Bor*. Valladolid: Quirón.

Caballero Jurado, C. (2004b). Erich Rose, el trágico destino de un oficial "judío" de la División Azul. *Revista Española de Historia Militar, 54*, 3–15.

Caballero Jurado, C. (2011). *División Azul: estructura de una fuerza de combate*. Madrid: Galland Books.

Caballero Jurado, C. (2019). *La División Azul. De 1941 a la actualidad*. Madrid: La Esfera de los Libros.

Caballero Jurado, C., & Ibáñez, R. (1989). *Escritores en las trincheras. la División Azul en sus libros, publicaciones periódicas y filmografía (1941–1988)*. Madrid: Barbarroja.

Calavia, E., & Álvarez Cosmen, F. (1956). *Enterrados en Rusia*. Madrid: Sasso.

Capdevila, L., & Voldman, D. (2002). *Nos morts. Les sociétés occidentales face aux tués de la guerre*. Paris: Le Grand Livre du Mois.

Capdevila, L., & Voldman, D. (2004). Rituels funéraires de sociétés en guerre (1914–1945). In S. Audoin-Rouzeau, A. Becker, Ch. Ingrao, & H. Rousso

(Eds.), *La Violence de guerre 1914–1945* (pp. 289–311). Paris: Éditions Complexe/IHTP.

Carles de Alcázar, M. (1941). *Romance a la División Azul*. Barcelona: Imprenta del Regimiento de Infantería no. 50.

Carrard, Ph. (2010). *The French who fought for Hitler: Memories from the outcasts*. Cambridge: Cambridge UP.

Carrein, K. (1999). De Vlaamse Oostfronters: Sociaal Profil en wervingsverloop, november 1941–augustus 1944. *BEG-CHTP, 6*, 107–49.

Carrera Buil, F.J., & Ferrer-Dalmau, A. (2003). *Batallón Román. Historia fotográfica del 2.º Batallón del Regimiento 269 de la División Azul*. Madrid: Fundación División Azul.

Carrión, D. (1941). *¡Voluntariado español!*. Quintanar de la Orden: Imprenta Nacional.

Carteny, A. (2013). La memorialistica italiana della Campagna di Russia (Bedeschi, Rivelli, Rigoni Stern). In A. Biagini & A. Zarcone (Eds.), *La campagna di Russia* (pp. 269–74). Rome: C Cultura.

Casals, X. (1995). *Neonazis en España. De las audiciones wagnerianas a los skinheads (1966–1995)*. Barcelona: Grijalbo.

Castaño Doña, R. (1991). *Legionario en Rusia*. Alicante: García Hispán.

Castañón, J.M.ª (1991). *Diario de una aventura (con la División Azul 1941–1942)*. Gijón: Fundación Dolores Medio.

Castelo Villaoz, P. (1990). *Aguas frías del Wolchow*. Villena: García Hispán.

Castelo Villaoz, P. (1992). *URSS: Un rayo de luz y esperanza*. Alicante: García Hispán.

Castro Albarrán, A. de (1938). *Guerra santa, el sentido católico del movimiento nacional español*. Burgos: Editorial Española.

Cataruzza, M. (2006). The historiography of the Shoah – An attempt at a bibliographical synthesis. *Totalitarismus und Demokratie, 3*(2), 285–321. http://dx.doi.org/10.7892/boris.20572.

Cataruzza, M., Dyroff, S., & Langewiesche, D. (Eds.). (2012). *Territorial revisionism and the allies of Germany in the Second World War: Goals, expectations, practices*. Oxford/New York: Berghahn.

Cazorla Sánchez, A. (2014). *Cartas a Franco de los españoles de a pie (1936–1945)*. Barcelona: RBA.

Cela, R. (2010). *En Rusia con la División Azul*. Ponferrada: Peñalba.

Cesarini, D., & Levine, P.A. (2002). Introduction. In D. Cesarini & P.S. Levine (Eds.), *Bystanders to the Holocaust: A re-evaluation* (pp. 1–27). London/Portland, OR: Frank Cass.

Chicharro Lamamié de Clairac, J. (2001). *Diario de un antitanquista en la División Azul*. Madrid: Fundación Don Rodrigo/Fundación División Azul.

Cholawsky, S. (1998). *The Jews of Belorussia during World War II*. Ámsterdam: Harwood Publishers.

Christensen, C.B., Poulsen, N.B., & Smith, P.S. (2014). Dänen in der Waffen-SS 1940–1945. Ideologie, Integration und Kriegsverbrechen im Vergleich mit anderen "germanischen" Soldaten. In Lieb, Schulte, & Wegner (Eds.), *Die Waffen-SS. Neue Forschungen* (pp. 196–215). Paderborn: Schöningh.

Coale, R.S. (2014). *Un républicain espagnol dans la Deuxième division blindée française: Le journal de guerre de Lucas Camons Portillo (1939–1948).* Habilitation thesis, Paris. Université Sorbonne Nouvelle-Paris 3.

Cogollos Vicens, J. (1985). *¿Por qué? Y ¿para qué?.* Valencia: n. ed.

Constantiniu, F., Dutu, A., & Retegan, M. (1995). *România în razboi (1941–1945). Un destin în istorie.* Bucharest: Editura Militara.

Conversaciones (2004). *Las conversaciones privadas de Hitler.* Barcelona: Crítica.

Corni, G. (2010). Briefe von der Ostfront. Ein Vergleich deutscher und italienischer Quellen In L. Klinkhammer, A. Osti Guerrazzi, & Th. Schlemmer (Eds.), *Die "Achse" im Krieg. Politik, Ideologie und Kriegführung 1939–1945* (pp. 398–432). Paderborn: Schöningh.

Corni, G. (2012). *Raccontare la guerra. La memoria organizzata.* Milan/Torino: Bruno Mondadori.

Crespo [Villoldo], A. (1945). *De las memorias de un combatiente sentimental.* Madrid: Ediciones Haz.

Cruz, R. (1997). "¡Luzbel vuelve al mundo! Las imágenes de la Rusia soviética y la acción colectiva en España. In R. Cruz & M. Pérez Ledesma (Eds.), *Cultura y movilización en la España contemporánea* (pp. 273–303). Madrid: Alianza.

Cuartero, A. (1941). *Los que se marchan. La División Azul.* Madrid: Nuevas Gráficas.

Cuenca Toribio, J.M. (2001). *Conversaciones con Alfonso Armada. El 23F.* Madrid: Actas.

Cuerda Ros, C. (2013). *Diario de la División Azul. Un músico en el frente ruso.* Carena: L'Eliana.

D'Ors Pérez, J.P. (1960). *Diario de un médico español en Rusia.* Madrid: Ediciones Deportivas.

De Andrés, A. (2004). *Artillería en la División Azul (Krasny Bor).* Madrid: Fundación Don Rodrigo.

De la Iglesia, J.A., & Burguete, D. (2015). *Suboficiales españoles en Rusia. Brigadas y sargentos en la División Azul.* Valladolid: Galland Books.

De la Vega, E. (1998). *Arde la nieve. Un relato histórico sobre la División Azul.* Sevilla: Barbarroja.

De la Vega, E. (1999). *Rusia no es culpable. Historia de la División Azul.* Madrid: Barbarroja.

De Wever, B. (1985). *Oostfronters. Vlamingen in het Vlaams Legioen en de Waffen SS.* Tielt/Weesp: Launoo.

De Wever, B. (1991). Rebellen an der Ostfront. Die flämischen Freiwilligen der Legion "Flandern" und der Waffen-SS. *Vierteljahrshefte für Zeitgeschichte*, 39(4), 589–610.

Del Arco Blanco, M.A. (2007). Hombres nuevos. El personal político del primer franquismo en el mundo rural del sureste español (1936–1951). *Ayer*, 65, 237–67. http://hdl.handle.net/10481/17341.

Deletant, D. (2017). Romania. In D. Stahel (Ed.), *Joining Hitler's Crusade* (pp. 46–78).

DiNardo, R.L. (1996). The dysfunctional coalition: The Axis powers and the Eastern Front in World War II. *The Journal of Military History*, 60(4), 711–30.

DiNardo, R.L. (2005). *Germany and the Axis powers. From coalition to collapse.* Lawrence: Kansas UP.

Díaz Benítez, J.J. (2005). Voluntarios de la zona aérea de Canarias y África occidental en la Wehrmacht. *Historia Social*, 53, 47–62.

Díaz de Villegas, J. (1950). *Lo que vi en Rusia*, s. ed. [Imp. Pueyo], Madrid.

Díaz de Villegas, J. (1951). *Rusia vista por dentro*. Madrid: n.p.

Díaz de Villegas, J. (1967). *La División Azul en línea*. Barcelona: Acervo.

Díaz del Río, G. (2011). *Los zapadores de la División Azul. Rusia 1941–1942.* Madrid: Actas.

Díaz Infante, E. (n.d.). *Los recuerdos tatuados*. n.p.

Didczuneit, J., Ebert, J., & Jander, Th., eds. (2011). *Schreiben im Krieg, Schreiben vom Krieg. Feldpost im Zeitalter der Weltkriege.* Essen: Klartext.

Dieckmann, Ch. (2011). *Deutsche Besatzungspolitik in Litauen/2.* Göttingen: Wallstein.

Dobrotvorskaja, K.A. (2013). *Blokadnye devocki.* Moscow: Novoe Izdatélsky.

Domingo, A. (2009). *Historia de los españoles en la II Guerra Mundial. Sus peripecias en todos los frentes y bajo todas las banderas.* Córdoba: Almuzara.

Domínguez Arribas, J. (2009). *El enemigo judeo-masónico en la propaganda franquista, 1936–1945.* Madrid: Marcial Pons.

Dornik, W. (2013). "Ganz in den Rahmen dieses Bildes hinein passt auch die Bevölkerung." Raumerfahrung und Raumwahrnehmung von österreichisch-ungarischen Soldaten an der Ostfront des Ersten Weltkrieges. In B. Bachinger & W. Dornik (Eds.), *Jenseits des Schützengrabens Der Erste Weltkrieg im Osten: Erfahrung – Wahrnehmung – Kontext* (pp. 27–43). Innsbruck/Vienna/Bolzano: Studienverlag.

Duch i Planas, M. (2002). Toponimia franquista en democracia. In C. Forcadell et al. (Eds.), *Usos públicos de la Historia* (Vol. I) (pp. 377–90). Zaragoza: AHC.

Ebert, J., & Peukert, S., eds. (2006). *Briefe einer Rotkreuzschwester von der Ostfront.* Göttingen: Wallstein.

Echternkamp, J. (2000). Mit dem Krieg seinen Frieden schließen-Wehrmacht und Weltkrieg in der Veteranenkultur (1945–1960). In Th. Kühne (Ed.), *Von der Kriegskultur zur Friedenskultur? Zum Mentalitätswandel in Deutschland seit 1945* (pp. 80–95). Münster: Lit.

Echternkamp, J., & Hettling, M. (Eds.). (2008). *Bedingt erinnerungsbereit. Soldatengedenken in der Bundesrepublik.* Göttingen: Vandenhoeck & Ruprecht.

Edele, M. (2017). *Stalin's defectors: How Red Army soldiers became Hitler's collaborators.* Oxford: Oxford UP.

Edvarson, C. (2008). *Gebranntes Kind sucht das Feuer.* Munich: Dtv [Stockholm 1984].

Eizaguirre, R.P. (1955). *En el abismo rojo: Memorias de un español, once años prisionero en la U.R.S.S..* Madrid: Artes Gráficas Rehyma.

Ellwood, Sh. (1984). *Prietas las filas. Historia de Falange Española.* Barcelona: Crítica.

Elorza, A., & Bizcarrondo, M. (1999). *Queridos camaradas. La Internacional Comunista and España, 1919–1939.* Barcelona: Planeta.

Elpatevskij, A.V. (2015). *Golubaja divizija: voennoplennye i internirovannye ispancy v SSSR.* Saint Petersburg: Aletejja.

Elster, J. (1999). *Alchemies of the mind: Rationality and the emotions.* Cambridge: Cambridge UP.

Elster, J. (2002). *Ulysses unbound: Studies in rationality, precommitment, and constraints.* Cambridge: Cambridge UP.

Encinas Moral, A.L. (2008). Rusia vista por los diplomáticos españoles del siglo XIX (1801–1835) en el escenario de las relaciones hispano-rusas. In M. Cortés Arrese & J.A. Mancebo Roca (Eds.), *El viaje a Rusia* (pp. 131–52). Murcia: Nausícaä.

Epkenhans, M., Förster, S., & Hagemann, K. (Eds.). (2006). *Militärische Erinnerungskultur. Soldaten im Spiegel von Biographien, Memoiren und Selbstzeugnissen.* Paderborn: Schöningh.

Errando Vilar, E. (1942). *Campaña de invierno.* Madrid: José G. Perona.

Escuadra, A. (1998). *Bajo las banderas de la Kriegsmarine. Marinos españoles en la Armada alemana.* Madrid: Fundación Don Rodrigo.

Esdaile, Ch. (2020). Recent writings on the military history of Spain's civil war. *European History Quarterly, 50*(2), 331–44. DOI: 10.1177/0265691420913496.

Espinosa Poveda, A. (1992). *Artillero 2.º en la gloriosa División Azul (4 julio 1941–18 abril 1943).* Madrid: Fundación División Azul.

Espinosa Poveda, A. (1993). *¡¡Teníamos razón!! Cuantos luchamos contra el comunismo soviético.* Madrid: Fundación División Azul.

Esteban-Infantes, E. (1956). *La División Azul: Donde Asia empieza.* Barcelona: AHR.

Estes, K.W. (2003). *A European Anabasis – Western European volunteers in the German Army and SS, 1940–1945.* n.p.: Gutenberg-e/Columbia UP (available at www.gutenberg-e.org/esk01/main.html).

Ezquerra, M. (1947). *Lutei até ao fim: Memórias dum voluntário espanhol na Guerra 1939–1945*. Lisbon: Astória.

Farré Albiñana, J. (1949). *4 infantes, 3 luceros*. Tétouan: Librería Escolar.

Farré Palaus, R. (1991). *Impresiones. Centinela junto al Ilmen*. Alicante: García Hispán.

Fasey, R.J. (2000). The presence of Russian revolutionary writing in the literary climate of pre-Civil War Spain, 1926–1936. *Forum for Modern Language Studies, 36*(4), 402–11. https://doi.org/10.1093/fmls/XXXVI.4.402.

Fatal-Knaani, T. (1996). Grodno. In S. Spector & B. Freundlich (Eds.), *Lost Jewish worlds: The communities of Grodno, Lida, Olkieniki, Vishay* (pp. 15–190). Jerusalem: Yad Vashem.

Felder, B.M. (2009). *Lettland im Zweiten Weltkrieg. Zwischen sowjetischen und deutschen Besatzern 1940–1946*. Paderborn: Schöningh.

Feldmanis, I. (2005). Waffen-SS units of Latvians and other non-Germanic peoples in World War II: Methods of formation, ideology and goals. In *The hidden and forbidden history of Latvia under Soviet and Nazi occupations 1940–1991* (pp. 122–231). Riga: Institute of the History of Latvia.

Fernández Coppel, J. (2007). *La escuadrilla azul: Los pilotos españoles en la Luftwaffe*. Madrid: La Esfera de los Libros.

Fernández Velasco, A. (1943a). *Apuntes de la División Azul*. La Felguera: Imp. La Torre.

Fernández Vicente, I. (2019). *El proyecto fascista en el País Vasco, 1933–1945*. PhD Dissertation, University of the Basque Country.

Figueiredo, I. de (2001). De norske frontkjemperne-hva litteraturen sier og veien videre. *Historisk Tidsskrift, 80*, 531–51.

Filipescu, M.T. (2006). *Reluctant Axis. The Romanian Army in Russia, 1941–1944*. n.p.

Focardi, F. (2013). *Il cattivo tedesco e il bravo italiano. La rimozione delle colpe della seconda guerra mondiale*. Bari: Laterza.

Fontenla Ballesta, S. (2012). *Los combates de Krasny Bor*. Madrid: Actas.

Foray, J.L. (2010). The "clean *Wehrmacht*" in the German-occupied Netherlands, 1940–5. *Journal of Contemporary History, 45*(4), 768–87. http://dx.doi.org/10.1177/0022009410375178.

Förster, J. J. (1980). "Croisade de l'Europe contre le bolchévisme": La participation d'unités de volontaires européens à l'opération "Barberousse" en 1941. *Revue d'Histoire de la Deuxième Guerre Mondiale, 30*(118), 1–26.

Förster, J.J. (1983). Das Unternehmen "Barbarossa" als Eroberungs-und Vernichtungskrieg. In Militärgeschichtliches Forschungsamt (Ed.), *Das deutsche Reich und der zweite Weltkrieg. Bd. 4: Der Angriff auf die Sowjetunion* (pp. 413–47). Stuttgart: DVA.

Förster, J.J. (2005). Hitlers Verbündete gegen die Sowjetunion 1941 und der Judenmord. In Ch. Hartmann, J. Hürter, & U. Jureit (Eds.), *Verbrechen der Wehrmacht. Bilanz einer Debatte* (pp. 91–7). Munich: Beck.

Friedländer, S. (2007). *The years of extermination: Nazi Germany and the Jews, 1939–1945*. New York: Harper Collins.

Friszke, A. (2005). Actitudes hacia los judíos de la prensa del movimiento polaco en la clandestinidad, 1939–1944. In D. Bankier & I. Gutman (Eds.), *La Europa nazi y la solución final* (pp. 221–37). Madrid: Losada.

Fritz, S. (1995). *Frontsoldaten: The German soldier in World War II*. Lexington: The University Press of Kentucky.

Fritz, S. (2011). *Ostkrieg: Hitler's war of extermination in the East*. Lexington: The University Press of Kentucky.

Fundación Nacional Francisco Franco [FNFF] (1992). *Documentos inéditos para la historia del Generalísimo Franco, Vol. II-2*, Madrid: FNFF.

Gallego, F. (2014). *El evangelio fascista. La formación de la cultura política del franquismo (1930–1950)*. Barcelona: Crítica.

Ganzenmüller, J. (2000). "… Die Stadt dem Erdboden gleichmachen." Zielsetzung und Motive der deutschen Blockade Leningrads. In S. Creuzberger et al. (Eds.), *St. Petersburg-Leningrad-St. Petersburg. Eine Stadt im Spiegel der Zeit* (pp. 179–95). Stuttgart: DVA.

Ganzenmüller, J. (2005). *Das belagerte Leningrad 1941–1944. Die Stadt in den Strategien von Angreifern und Verteidigern*. Paderborn: Schöningh.

Ganzenmüller, J. (2011). Mobilisierungsdiktatur im Krieg. Stalinistische Herrschaft im belagerten Leningrad. *Osteuropa, 61*(8–9), 117–34.

Ganzenmüller, J. (2014). Hungerpolitik als Problemlösungsstrategie. Der Entscheidungsprozess zur Blockade Leningrads und zur Vernichtung seiner Zivilbevölkerung. In Quinkert & Morré (Eds.), *Deutsche Besatzung* (pp. 34–53).

García, A.M. (2001). *"Galubaya Divisia": crónica de la División Azul*. Madrid: Documedia.

García, H. (2005). Historia de un mito político: el *peligro comunista* en el discurso de las derechas españolas, 1918–1936. *Historia Social, 51*, 3–20.

García Hispán, J. (1991). *La Guardia Civil en la División Azul*. Alicante: García Hispán.

García Luna, J. (1959). *Las cartas del Sargento Basilio*. Barcelona: Pentágono.

García Morente, M. (1961). *Idea de la Hispanidad*. Madrid: Espasa-Calpe. (Original work published 1938)

García Pérez, A. (1942). *Héroes de España en campos de Rusia 1941–1942*. Madrid: Camarasa.

García Pérez, R. (1990). La idea de la "Nueva Europa" en el pensamiento nacionalista español de la inmediata postguerra 1939–1944. *Revista del Centro de Estudios Constitucionales, 5*, 203–40.

García-Izquierdo Sánchez, D. (2009). *El último divisionario en Possad. Batallón de Transmisiones en la División Azul*. Granada: García Hispán.

Garrido Polonio, F., & Garrido Polonio, M.A. (2002). *Nieve Roja. Españoles desaparecidos en el frente ruso*. Madrid: Oberon.

Garriga, R. (1977). *La España de Franco, vol. 1: Las relaciones con Hitler*. Madrid: G. del Toro.

Garriga, R. (1983). *Berlín, años cuarenta*. Barcelona: Planeta.

Gay, J.V. (2002). Els gironins de la División Azul. *Revista de Girona, 215*, 39–47. https://www.raco.cat/index.php/RevistaGirona/article/view/94778.

Gay, V. (1934). *La revolución nacionalsocialista*. Barcelona: Librería Bosch.

Gentile, C. (2012). *Wehrmacht und Waffen-SS im Partisanenkrieg: Italien 1943–1945*. Paderborn: Schöningh.

Georgacopulos Teja, C. (2015). *Un artillero de trinchera. Memorias de un divisionario valenciano*. Valencia: Vicente J. Sanjuán Eds.

Gil Martínez, E.M. (2011). *Españoles en las SS y la Wehrmacht 1944–1945. La Unidad Ezquerra y la batalla de Berlín*. Madrid: Almena.

Giolitto, P. (2007). *Volontaire français sous l'uniforme allemand*. Paris: Perrin.

Giusti, M.ᵃT. (2003). *I prigionieri italiani in Russia*. Bologna: Il Mulino.

Giusti, M.ᵃT. (2016). *La campagna di Russia*, Bari: Laterza.

Glantz, D. (2001). The Soviet-German War 1941–1945: Myths and realities: A survey essay. *Publications*. 217. https://tigerprints.clemson.edu/sti_pubs/217.

Glantz, D. (2002). *The Battle for Leningrad 1941–1944*. Lawrence, Kansas: University Press of Kansas.

Golczewski, F. (2003). Die Kollaboration in der Ukraine. In Babette Quinkert, Christoph Dieckmann, & Tatjana Tönsmeyer (Eds.), *Kooperation und Verbrechen. Formen der "Kollaboration" im östlichen Europa 1939–1945* (pp. 151–82). Göttingen: Wallstein Verlag.

Goldhagen, D.J. (1997). *Los verdugos voluntarios de Hitler. Los alemanes corrientes y el Holocausto*. Madrid: Taurus. (Original work published 1996)

Gómez-Tello, J.L. (1945). *Canción de invierno en el Este. Crónicas de la División Azul*. Barcelona: Luis de Caralt.

González Madrid, D. (2007). *Los hombres de la dictadura. Personal político franquista en Castilla-La Mancha, 1939–1945*. Ciudad Real: Almud.

González Pinilla, A. (1999). Españoles en la Wehrmacht y las Waffen-SS (1944–1945). In R. Recio Cardona (Ed.), *Españoles en la Segunda Guerra Mundial (el frente del Este)* (pp. 134–9). Madrid: Vandalia.

Goode, J. (2009). *Impurity of blood: Defining race in Spain, 1870–1930*. Baton Rouge: Louisiana State UP.

Gracia, J. (2007). *El valor de la disidencia. Epistolario inédito de Dionisio Ridruejo, 1933–1975*. Barcelona: Planeta.

Gracia, J. (2008). *La vida rescatada de Dionisio Ridruejo*. Barcelona: Anagrama.

Gragera Díaz, F. (2004). *Los quintos del pelargón*. Madrid: Oberon.

Gragera Díaz, F., & Infantes, D. (2007). *Rumbo a Rusia. Los voluntarios extremeños de la División Azul.* Madrid: Oberon.

Gross, J.T. (2000). *Vecinos. El exterminio de la comunidad judía de Jedwabne (Polonia).* Barcelona [Cracow]: Crítica. (Original work published 2000)

Grunert, R. (2012). *Der Europagedanke westeuropäischer faschistischer Bewegungen, 1940–1945.* Paderborn: Schöningh.

Guerra, N. (2012). *I volontari italiani nelle Waffen-SS. Il pensiero politico, la formazione culturale e le motivazioni al volontariato. Una storia orale.* Turku: Turun Yliopisto.

Guderzo, M. (1995). *Madrid e l'arte della diplomazia. L'incognita spagnola durante la seconda guerra mondiale.* Florence: Manent.

Gutman, I. (2005). Las relaciones entre judíos y polacos a la luz de las actitudes políticas de los polacos en período bélico. In Bankier & Gutman (Eds.), *La Europa nazi y la solución final* (pp. 199–219). Madrid: Losada.

Gutmann, M.R. (2017). *Building a Nazi Europe: The SS's Germanic Volunteers.* Cambridge: Cambridge UP.

Guzmán Mora, J. (2016). *Visiones de Rusia en la narrativa española. El caso de la División Azul.* PhD Thesis, University of Salamanca.

Halbwachs, M. (2004). *La memoria colectiva.* Zaragoza: PUZ [Paris 1925].

Hartmann, Ch. (2009). *Wehrmacht im Ostkrieg: Front und militärisches Hinterland 1941/42.* Munich: Oldenbourg.

Hartmann, Ch. (2013). *Unternehmen Barbarossa. Der deutsche Krieg im Osten 1941–1945,* Munich: Beck.

Hartmann, Ch., Hürter, J., Lieb P., & Pohl, D. (2009). *Der deutsche Krieg im Osten 1941–1944. Facetten einer Grenzüberschreitung.* Munich: Oldenbourg.

Hasenclever, J. (2010). *Wehrmacht und Besatzungspolitik in der Sowjetunion. Die Befehlshaber der rückwärtigen Gebiete 1941–1943.* Paderborn: Schöningh.

Hass, G. (2002). Deutsche Besatzungspolitik im Leningrader Gebiet 1941–1944. In B. Quinkert (Ed.), *"Wir sind die Herren dieses Landes." Ursachen, Verlauf und Folgen des deutschen Überfalls auf die Sowjetunion.* Hamburg: VSA, 64–81.

Hausleitner, M., Mihok, B., & Wetzel, J. (Eds.). (2001). *Rumänien und der Holocaust. Zu den Massenverbrechen in Transnistrien 1941–1944.* Berlin: Metropol Verlag.

Heer, H. (1999). *Tote Zonen. Die deutsche Wehrmacht an der Ostfront.* Hamburg: Hamburger Editionen.

Heinen, A. (2007). *Rumänien, der Holocaust und die Logik der Gewalt.* Munich: Oldenbourg.

Hellbeck, J. (2012). *Die Stalingrad Protokolle. Sowjetische Augenzeugen berichten aus der Schlacht.* Frankfurt a. M.; Fischer.

Herbert, U. (2016). *Das Dritte Reich: Geschichte einer Diktatur.* Munich: Beck.

Hernández, C.G. (2016). *Manuel Delgado Barreto (1878–1936).* PhD Thesis, Universidad San Pablo-CEU.

Hernández Burgos, C. (2013). *Franquismo a ras de suelo. Zonas grises, apoyos sociales y actitudes durante la dictadura (1936–1976)*. Granada: Universidad de Granada.

Hernández Burgos, C. (Ed.). (2020). *Ruptura: The impact of nationalism and extremism on daily life in the Spanish Civil War (1936–1939)*. Brighton: Sussex Academic Press.

Hernández Navarro, A.J. (1971). *Ida y vuelta*. Madrid: Espasa-Calpe. (Original work published 1946)

Hernanz Blanco, G. (2013). *Diario de Guillermo en Rusia, 1942*. n.p.: RH+ Ediciones.

Herrmann, A. (2012). *Kleine Hofer Stadtgeschichte*. Regensburg: Verlag Friedrich Pustet.

Herrmann, G., & Brenneis, S. (Eds.). (2020). *Spain, World War II and the Holocaust: History and representation*. Toronto: University of Toronto Press.

Heuser, B. (2013). *Rebellen-Partisanen-Guerilleros. Asymmetrische Kriege von der Antike bis heute*. Paderborn: Schöningh.

Herzog, D. (2007). *Sex after fascism. Memory and morality in twentieth-century Germany*. Princeton, NJ: Princeton UP.

Hiio, T. (2014). Estnische Einheiten der Waffen-SS. Vorgeschichte, Rekrutierung, Zusammensetzung. In Schulte, Lieb, & Wegner (Eds.), *Die Waffen-SS. Neue Forschungen* (pp. 138–59). Paderborn: Schöningh.

Hilberg, R. (1992). *Perpetrators, victims, bystanders: The Jewish catastrophe 1933–1945*. New York: Harper Collins.

Hilberg, R. (2005). *La destrucción de los judíos europeos*. Madrid: Akal. (Original work published 1961)

Hill, A. (2005). *The war behind the Eastern Front: Soviet partisans in North-West Russia, 1941–1944*. London: Frank Cass.

Hill, A. (2019). *The Red Army and the Second World War*. Cambridge: Cambridge UP. (Originally published in 2016)

Hitler, A. (1930). *Mein Kampf*. Munich: Verlag Franz Eher Nachfolger. (Original work published in two volumes 1925, 1927)

Hoffmann, J. (1976). *Die Ostlegionen. 1941–1943. Turktataren, Kaukasier und Wogafinnen im deutschen Heer*. Freiburg i. Br.: Rombach Verlag.

Hoffmann, J. (1986). *Die Geschichte der Wlasow-Armee*. Freiburg i. Br.: Rombach.

Humburg, M. (1999). Siegeshoffnungen und "Herbstkrise" im Jahre 1941. Anmerkungen zu Feldpostbriefen aus der Sowjetunion. *Werkstattgeschichte, 22*, 25–40.

Humburg, M. (2011). "Jedes Wort ist falsch und falsch-das ist das Wesen des Worts." Vom Schreiben und Schweigen in der Feldpost. In Didczuneit, Ebert, & Jander (Eds.), *Schreiben im Krieg-Schreiben vom Krieg* (pp. 76–85).

Hürter, J. (2001). Die Wehrmacht vor Leningrad. Krieg und Besatzungspolitik der 18. Armee im Herbst und Winter 1941/42. *Vierteljahrshefte für Zeitgeschichte, 49*(3), 377–440.

Hürter, J. (2006). *Hitlers Heerführer: Die deutschen Oberbefehlshaber im Krieg gegen die Sowjetunion 1941/42*. Munich: Oldenbourg.

Ibáñez Hernández, R. (1997). La División Azul, elemento de negociación diplomática. In J. Tusell (Ed.), *La política exterior de España en el siglo XX* (pp. 253–70). Madrid: UNED.

Ibáñez Hernández, R. (1998). Prensa española de trinchera en el frente del Este. *Aportes, XIII*(2), 105–29.

Ibáñez Hernández, R. (2001). La cruzada antibolchevique en las pantallas. La División Azul en el cine y la televisión. *Aportes, XVI*(2), 36–53.

Iglesias-Sarria Puga, M. (1987). *Mi suerte dijo sí. Evocación autobiográfica de Guerra and Paz (1918–1945)*. Madrid: San Martín.

Jacobson, M.F. (2009). Looking Jewish, seeing Jews. In L. Back & J. Solomos (Eds.), *Theories of race and racism: A reader* (pp. 303–17). London/New York: Routledge.

Janué i Miret, M. (2008). Un instrumento de los intereses nacionalsocialistas durante la Guerra Civil española: El papel de la Sociedad Germano-Española de Berlín. *Iberoamericana, 31*, 27–44. https://doi.org/10.18441 /ibam.8.2008.31.27-44.

Janué i Miret, M. (2014). "Woe betide us if they win": National Socialist treatment of the Spanish "volunteer'" workers. *Contemporary European History, 23*(3), 329–57. http://dx.doi.org/10.1017/S0960777314000174.

Jarov, S. (2013). *Povsednevnaja zizn' blokadnogo Leningrada*. Moscow: Molodaja Gvardija.

Jasper, A. (2011). *Zweierlei Weltkriege? Kriegserfahrungen deutscher Soldaten in Ost und West 1939 bis 1945*. Paderborn: Schöningh.

Jiménez Andrades, I. (1957). *Recuerdos de mi campaña en Rusia*. Badajoz: Diputación Provincial.

Jiménez Malo de Molina, V.J. (1943). *De España a Rusia. 5.000 kilómetros con la División Azul*. Madrid: Imprenta de Madrid.

Jiménez Soto, F. (2015). *Voluntarios de Canarias en la División Azul*. PhD Thesis, University of Las Palmas.

Jimeno Aranguren, R. (2015). *Miguel Javier Urmeneta (1915–1988). Segunda República, Franquismo y Transición*. Pamplona: Pamiela.

Jochmann, W. (Ed.). (1982). *Adolf Hitler. Monologe im Führerhauptquartier 1941–1944*. Munich: Heyne.

Juderías, J. (1940). *Rusia contemporánea: estudios acerca de su situación actual*. Madrid: Fortanet.

Kallis, A. (2009). *Genocide and fascism: The eliminationist drive in fascist Europe*. London: Routledge.

Karl, M. (1937). *Técnica del Komintern en España*. Badajoz: Tip. Gráfica Corporativa.

Keller, R. (2011). *Sowjetische Kriegsgefangene im Deutschen Reich 1941/42.* Göttingen: Wallstein.

Keller, S. (2014). Elite am Ende. Die Waffen-SS in der letzten Phase des Krieges 1945. In Schulte, Lieb, & Wegner (Eds.), *Die Waffen-SS, Neue Forschungen* (pp. 354–73). Paderborn: Schöningh.

Kershaw, I. (2000). *Hitler 1936–1945.* Barcelona: Península.

Kilian, J. (2011). "Der Russe braucht einen Herrn über sich": Die Wehrmacht im Leningrader Gebiet. *Osteuropa, 61*(8–9), 65–74.

Kilian, J. (2012). *Wehrmacht und Besatzungsherrschaft im Russischen Nordwestern 1941–1944. Praxis und Alltag im Militärverwaltungsgebiet der Heeresgruppe Nord.* Paderborn: Schöningh.

Kipp, M. (2007), The Holocaust in the letters of German soldiers on the Eastern Front (1939–1944). *Journal of Genocide Research, 9*(4), 601–15. https://doi.org/10.1080/14623520701644424.

Kipp, M. (2014). *"Großreinemachen im Osten." Feindbilder in deutschen Feldpostbriefen im Zweiten Weltkrieg.* Frankfurt a. M./New York: Campus Verlag.

Kivimäki, V. (2011). Entre la victoria y la derrota: La memoria de la II Guerra Mundial en Finlandia. *Historia Social, 71,* 41–58.

Kivimäki, V., & Kinnunen, T. (Eds.). (2012). *Finland in World War II: History, memory, interpretations.* Leiden/Boston: Brill.

Klarsfeld, S. (Ed.). (1980). *Documents concerning the destruction of the Jews of Grodno 1941–1944, vol. I. A: Accounts by Jewish survivors residing in the West. B: Accounts recorded in Poland and the Soviet Union.* New York: The Beate Klarsfeld Foundation.

Kleinfeld, G.R., & Tambs, L.A. (1983). *La División Española de Hitler.* Madrid: San Martín.

Kliment, C., & Nakladal, B. (1997). *Germany's first ally: Armed forces of the Slovak state 1939–1945.* London: Schiffer Publ.

Klovsky, D. (2003). *The Road from Grodno,.*Samara: OFORT Press.

Klug, E. (1987). Das "asiatische" Russland. Über die Entstehung eines europäischen Stereotyps. *Historische Zeitschrift, 245,* 265–89.

Kluke, P. (1955). Nationalsozialistische Europaideologie. *Vierteljahrshefte für Zeitgeschichte, 3,* 240–70.

Knoch, P. (1989). Kriegsalltag. In Knoch (ed.), *Kriegsalltag. Die Rekonstruktion des Kriegsalltages als Aufgabe der historischen Forschung und der Friedenserziehung* (pp. 222–51). Stuttgart: J.B. Metzlersche Verlagsbuchhandlung.

Knoch, P. (2003). Das Bild des russischen Feindes. In W. Wette & G.R. Ueberschär (Eds.), *Stalingrad. Mythos und Wirklichkeit einer Schlacht* (pp. 160–7). Frankfurt a. M.: Fischer.

Kocjancic, K. (2016). Španci v nemški službi na Slovenskem med drugo svetovno vojno. *Prispevki za novejšo zgodovino, 56*(2), 7–21.

Koselleck, R., & Jeismann, M. (Eds.). (1994). *Der politische Totenkult. Kriegerdenkmäler in der Moderne* Munich: Wilhelm Fink Verlag.

Kott, M. (2012). Rekrutierung der Waffen-SS im Reichskommissariat Ostland: Der Versuch einer schwer fassbaren Synthese. In *Reichskommissariat Ostland: Tatort und Erinnerungsobjekt* (pp. 117–45). Paderborn: Schöningh.

Kovalev, B. (1998). Nazi collaborators in the Soviet Union during and after World War II. *Refuge, 17*(2), 43–9. https://doi.org/10.25071/1920-7336.21967

Kovalev, B. (2009). *Kollaborat's'ionizm v Rossii v 1941–1945 gg.: Tipy i formy.* Novgorod: NovGU imeni I'A' roslava Mudrogo.

Kovalev, B. (2011). *Povsednevnai'a zhizn naseleniia Rossii v period natsistskoi okkupatsii.* Moscow: Molodai'a gvardiija.

Kovalev, B. (2014). *Dobrovol´ci na cyzoj voyne. Ocerki istorii golyboj divizii.* Novgorod: Novgorodskij gosydarstveii´j universitet.

Krausnick, H. (1977). Kommissarbefehl und "Gerichtbartskeiterlass Barbarossa" in neuer Sicht. *Vierteljahrshefte für Zeitgeschichte, 25*, 682–738.

Krausnick, H. (1998). *Hitlers Einsatzgruppen. Die Truppe des Weltanschauungskrieges 1938–1942.* Frankfurt a. M.: Fischer. (Original work published 1981)

Kühne, Th. (1999). Der nationalsozialistische Vernichtungskrieg und die "ganz normalen Deutschen." Forschungsprobleme und Forschungstendenzen der Gesellschaftsgeschichte des Zweiten Weltkrieges. Erster Teil. *Archiv für Sozialgeschichte, 39*, 580–662.

Kühne, Th. (2006). *Kameradschaft. Die Soldaten des nationalsozialistischen Krieges und das 20. Jahrhundert.* Göttingen: Vandenhoeck & Ruprecht.

Kühne, Th., & Ziemann, B. (Eds.). (2000). *Was ist Militärgeschichte?* Paderborn: Schöningh.

Larraz Andía, P., & Sierra-Sesúmaga, V. (2010). *Requetés. De las trincheras al olvido.* Madrid: La Esfera de los Libros.

Latzel, K. (1997). "Vom Kriegserlebnis zur Kriegserfahrung. Theoretische und methodische Überlegungen zur erfahrungsgeschichtlichen Untersuchung von Feldpostbriefen. *Militärgeschichtliche Mitteilungen, 56*, 1–30. https://doi.org/10.1524/mgzs.1997.56.1.1.

Latzel, K. (2000a). *Deutsche Soldaten-nationalsozialistischer Krieg? Kriegserlebnis-Kriegserfahrung 1939–1945.* Paderborn: Schöningh.

Latzel, K. (2000b). Kollektive Identität und Gewalt. In P. Jahn & U. Schmiegelt (Eds.), *Foto-Feldpost. Geknipste Kriegserlebnisse 1939–1945* (pp. 13–22). Berlin: Museum Karlshorst.

Lavedán, A. de (1959). *Un español tras el telón de acero.* Barcelona: Mateu.

Lazo, A. (1998). *La Iglesia, la Falange y el fascismo (un estudio sobre la prensa española de posguerra).* Seville: Universidad de Sevilla.

Leed, J. (1979). *No man's land. Combat and identity in World War I*. Cambridge: Cambridge UP.

Lehmann, W. (2006). *Die Bundesrepublik und Franco-Spanien in den 50er Jahren: NS-Vergangenheit als Bürde?* Munich: Oldenbourg.

Leleu, J.-L. (2007). *La Waffen-SS. Soldats politiques en guerre*. Paris: Perrin.

Levsen, S., & Krüger, Ch. (Eds.). (2010). *War volunteering in modern times*, Basingstoke: Palgrave.

Linares, V. (2000). *Más que unas memorias. Hasta Leningrado con la División Azul*. Madrid: Barbarroja.

Liulevicius, V.J. (2000). *War land on the Eastern Front: Culture, national identity, and German occupation in World War I*. Cambridge: Cambridge UP.

Liulevicius, V.J. (2006). Der Osten als apokalyptischer Raum. Deutsche Fronterfahrungen im und nach dem Ersten Weltkrieg. In G. Thum (Ed.), *Traunland Osten. Deutsche Bilder vom östlichen Europa im 20. Jahrhundert* (pp. 47–65). Göttingen: Vandenhoeck & Ruprecht.

Llorens Borrás, J.A. (1958). *Crímenes de guerra*. Barcelona: Acervo.

Loff, M. (2008). *"O nosso século é fascista!" O mundo visto por Salazar e Franco (1936–1945)*. Porto: Campo das Letras.

Lomagin, N.A. (1998). *Soldiers at war: German propaganda and Soviet Army morale during the Battle of Leningrad 1941–1944*. Pittsburgh: The Center for Russian and East European Studies (The Carl Back Papers in Russian and European Studies, no. 1306).

Lomagin, N.A. (2004). *Neizvéstnaya blocada*. Saint Petersburg: Izdatelsky dom Neva. 2 vols.

López de la Torre, S. (1964). *El robo del Jordán*. Madrid: Gráficas Norte.

López de Maturana, V. (2014). *La reinvención de una ciudad: Poder y política simbólica en Vitoria durante el franquismo (1936–1975)*. Leioa: UPV/EHU.

López Villatoro, F. (2012). *La Falange republicana en Andalucía. Guerra Civil, Movimiento y División Azul. Córdoba 1931–1945*. Córdoba: A. C. Cantamara.

López-Covarrubias, J.A. (2012). *Toledanos en la División Azul. Entre la memoria y el olvido*. Argés: Covarrubias.

Luca de Tena, T., & Palacios Cueto, T. (1955). *Embajador en el infierno.Memorias del capitán Palacios: once años de cautiverio en Rusia*. Madrid: Kamerad.

Lucas, J. (2014). *War on the Eastern Front. The German soldier in Russia, 1941–1945*. Barnsley: Frontline Books.

Luytens, D.-C. (2010). *SS Wallons. Témoignages. Récits de la 28e division SS de grandiers volontaires Wallonie*. Brussels: Jourdan.

Lyautey, P. (1942). *Espagne d'aujourd'hui*. Paris: Sequana.

Maassen, H. (1959). *Die Messe des Barcelo*. Halle/Saale: Mitteldeutscher Verlag.

Mabire, J. (1975). *Mourir à Berlin*. Paris: Fayard.

Machcewicz, P., & Persak, K. (2002). *Wokol Jedwabnego*. Warsaw: Instytut Pamieci Narodowej. 2 vols.

Madajczyk, C. (Ed.). (1994). *Vom Generalplan Ost zum Generalsiedlungsplan*. Munich: Saur.

Maeland, B., & Brunstad, P. (2009). *Enduring military boredom: From 1750 to the present*. Palgrave: Basingstoke.

Maeztu, R. (1941). *Defensa de la Hispanidad*. Buenos Aires: Poblet (Original work published 1934)

Manig, B.-O. (2004). *Die Politik der Ehre. Die Rehabilitatierung der Berufssoldaten in der frühen Bundesrepublik*. Göttingen: Wallstein.

Marchena Cañete, A. (2003). *La vida de un luqueño. Memorias de Ángel Marchena*. Luque: Ayuntamiento de Luque/Diputación de Córdoba.

Martínez, T. (1997). *Albacetenses de la diáspora*. Albacete: Diputación Provincial.

Martínez Cruces, P. (1942). *La Nueva Cruzada. División Española de Voluntarios*. Madrid: Impr. Viuda de Juan Pueyo.

Martínez Esparza, J. (1943). *Con la División Azul en Rusia*. Madrid: Ediciones Ejército.

Martínez Martínez, R. (1999). *Sofía Casanova: mito y literatura*. Santiago de Compostela: Xunta de Galicia.

Martínez Reverte, J. (2011). *La División Azul*. Barcelona: RBA.

Martínez-Mena, M. (1991). *Las "batallitas" de mi abuelo*. Alicante: García Hispán.

Massie, S. (1999). *Pavlovsk: The life of a Russian palace*. Boston: Little Brown & Co.

Matthäus, J., & Bajohr, J. (Eds.). (2015). *Alfred Rosenberg. Die Tagebücher von 1934 bis 1944*. Frankfurt a. M.: Fischer.

Matthews, J. (2013). *Soldados a la fuerza. Reclutamiento obligatorio durante la Guerra Civil, 1936–1939*. Madrid: Alianza.

Matthews, J. (Ed.). (2019). *Spain at war: Society, culture, and mobilization, 1934–44*. London: Bloomsbury.

Mazower, M. (2000). *Dark continent: Europe's twentieth century*. London: Penguin.

Medina Mercado, H. (1942). *Voluntarios españoles contra Rusia: Comedia en tres actos y cuatro cuadros*. Murcia: n.p.

Meliá Vila, J. (2003). *Bajo 6 banderas con la muerte en los talones. Año 1936 a Diciembre de 1943*. n.p. [Valencia]: n.p.

Mendel, B. (1972). *Yidin in Letland*. Tel Aviv: Reshafim.

Merino Bravo, F. (2007). *Pacofunker. "Un guripa en la estepa."* n.p.: Author's edition.

Merino Izquierdo, R. (2017). *Los niños de Rusia. La verdadera historia de una operación retorno*. Barcelona: Crítica.

Merkes, M. (1961). *Die deutsche Politik gegenüber dem spanischen Bürgerkrieg 1936–1939*. Bonn: Röhrscheid.

Merridale, C. (2005). *Ivan's war: The Red Army 1939–1945*. London: Faber and Faber.

Merton, R.K. (1970). *Teoría y estructura sociales*. Mexico City: FCE. (Original work published 1949)

Michaelis, M. (1978). *Mussolini and the Jews: German–Italian relations and the Jewish question in Italy, 1922–1945*. Oxford: Clarendon.

Michaelis, R. (2000). *Esten in der Waffen-SS: die 20. Waffen-Grenadier-Division der SS (Estnische Nr. 1)*. Berlin: Michaelis.

Milata, P. (2009). *Zwischen Hitler, Stalin und Antonescu. Rumäniendeutsche in der Waffen-SS*. Cologne/Weimar/Vienna: Böhlau.

Milata, P. (2014). Motive rumäniendeutscher Freiwilliger zum Eintritt in die Waffen-SS. In Schulte, Lieb, & Wegner (Eds.), *Die Waffen-SS. Neue Forschungen* (pp. 216–29). Paderborn: Schöningh.

Miralles Güill, J. (1981). *Tres días de guerra y otros relatos de la División Azul*. Ibi: García Hispán.

Mondini, M. (2008). *Alpini. Parole e immagini di un mito guerriero*. Bari: Laterza.

Montes, J.R. (2006). *El búnker*. Barcelona: Inédita.

Morant i Ariño, T. (2013). *Mujeres para una "Nueva Europa." Las relaciones y visitas entre la Sección Femenina de Falange y las organizaciones femeninas nazis, 1936–1945*. PhD Thesis, University of Valencia.

Moreno Juliá, X. (1999). La Legión Azul. In Recio Cardona (Ed.), *Españoles en la Segunda Guerra Mundial* (pp. 123–33).

Moreno Juliá, X. (2004). *La División Azul. Sangre española en Rusia, 1941–1945*. Barcelona: Crítica.

Moreno Juliá, X. (2007). *Hitler y Franco*. Barcelona: Planeta.

Moreno Juliá, X. (2014). *Legión Azul y Segunda Guerra Mundial. Hundimiento hispano-alemán en el Frente del Este, 1941–1944*. Madrid: Actas.

Morente, F. (2006). *Dionisio Ridruejo: del fascismo al antifranquismo*. Madrid: Síntesis.

Morodo, R. (1985). *Los orígenes ideológicos del franquismo. Acción Española*. Madrid: Alianza.

Motadel, D. (2013), Islam and Germany's war in the Soviet borderlands, 1941–5. *Journal of Contemporary History*, 48(4), 784–820. https://doi.org/10.1177%2F0022009413493948.

Motadel, D. (2014). *Islam and Nazi Germany's War*. Cambridge (MA)/London: The Belknap Press of Harvard UP.

Muchina, L. (2014). *Lenas Tagebuch. Leningrad 1941–1942*. Berlin: List.

Mühlhäuser, R. (2010). *Eroberungen: Sexuelle Gewalttaten und intime Beziehungen deutscher Soldaten in der Sowjetunion 1941–1945*. Hamburg: Hamburger Edition.

Müller, R.-D. (2007). *An der Seite der Wehrmacht. Hitlers ausländische Helfer beim "Kreuzzug gegen den Bolschewismus" 1941–1945*. Berlin: Ch. Links.

Müller, S.-O. (2007). *Deutsche Soldaten und ihre Feinde. Nationalismus an Front und Heimatfront im Zweiten Weltkrieg*. Frankfurt a. M.: Fischer.

Muñoz Césaro, J.S. (2011). *Yo fui legionario de Europa*. Salobreña: Alhulia.

Musial, B. (2002). *"Konterrevolutionäre Elemente sind zu erschiessen." Die Brutalisierung des deutsch-russischen Krieges im Sommer 1941*. Vienna/Munich: Propyläen.

Musial, B. (2009). *Sowjetische Partisanen 1941–1944: Mythos und Wirklichkeit*. Paderborn: Schöningh.

Muszynski, W.J. (2000). *W Walce o wielka Polske*. Warsaw: Rekonkwista-Rachocki i Slka.

Muszynski, W.J. (2002). *Blekitna dywizja. Ochotnicy Hiszpanscy na froncie wschodnim 1941–1945*. Warsaw: Idem im Me.

Nattermann, R. (2011). Politische Beobachtung im "tono fascista": Italienische Konsularberichte über das Dritte Reich. In Bajohr & Strupp (Eds), *Fremde Blicke* (pp. 304–48).

Negreira, J. (Ed.). (2011). *Los divisionarios: Soldados baleares en la División Azul (1941–1944)*. Palma de Mallorca: Lleonard Muntaner.

Negro Castro, J. (1959). *Españoles en la URSS*. Madrid: Escelicer.

Neitzel, S. (2004). Hitlers Europaarmee und der "Kreuzzug" gegen die Sowjetunion. In M. Salewski & H. Timmermann (Eds.), *Armeen in Europa-Europäische Armeen* (pp. 137–50). Münster: Lit.

Neitzel, S., & Welzer, H. (2011). *Soldaten. Protokolle von Kämpfen, Töten und Sterben*. Frankfurt a. M.: Fischer.

Nerín, G. (2005). *La guerra que vino de África*. Barcelona: Crítica.

Newland, S.J. (1991). *Cossacks in the German Army, 1941–1945*. Portland, OR: Frank Cass.

Nicolás Marín, M.ªE. (1982). *Instituciones murcianas en el franquismo (1939–1962)*. Murcia: Editora Regional.

Norling, E. (2007). The story of a Spanish Waffen-SS Officer: SS-Obertsturmführer R. Luis García Valdajos. *Siegrunnen*, *79*, 7–16.

Nübel, Ch. (2014). *Durchhalten und Überleben an der Westfront. Raum und Körper im Ersten Weltkrieg*. Paderborn: Schöningh.

Núñez Seixas, X.M. (2005). ¿Un nazismo colaboracionista español? Martín de Arrizubieta, Wilhelm Faupel y los últimos de Berlín (1944–1945). *Historia Social*, *51*, 21–47.

Núñez Seixas, X.M. (2006a). *¡Fuera el invasor! Nacionalismos y movilización bélica durante la guerra civil española, 1936–1939*. Madrid: Marcial Pons.

Núñez Seixas, X.M. (2006b). "Russland war nicht schuldig." Die Ostfronterfahrung der spanischen Blauen Division in Selbstzeugnissen und Autobiographien, 1943–2004. In Epkenhans, Förster, & Hagemann (Eds.), *Soldat und Gesellschaft* (pp. 236–67).

Núñez Seixas, X.M. (2012). *La sombra del César. Santiago Montero Díaz, una biografía entre la nación y la revolución*. Granada: Comares.

Núñez Seixas, X.M. (2017). Russia and the Russians in the eyes of the Spanish Blue Division soldiers, 1941–4. *Journal of Contemporary History, 52*(2), 352–74. http://dx.doi.org/10.1177/0022009416647118.

Núñez Seixas, X.M. (2018a). *El frente del Este. Historia* y memoria de la guerra germano-soviética, 1941–1945. Madrid: Alianza.

Núñez Seixas, X.M. (2018b). Wishful thinking in wartime? Spanish Blue Division's soldiers and their views of Nazi Germany, 1941–44. *Journal of War & Culture Studies, 11*(2), 99–116.

Núñez Seixas, X.M. (2018c). Good invaders? The occupation policy of the Spanish Blue Division in Northwestern Russia, 1941–1944. *War in History, 25*(3), 361–86.

Núñez Seixas, X.M. (2018d). Inconvenient heroes? War veterans from the Eastern Front in Franco's Spain (1942–1975). In A. Alcalde & X.M. Núñez Seixas (Eds.), *War veterans and the World after 1945: Cold War politics, decolonization, memory* (pp. 187–202). London: Routledge.

Núñez Seixas, X.M. (2019). Spanish views of Nazi Germany, 1933–45: A fascist hybridization? *Journal of Contemporary History, 54*(4), 858–79. http://dx.doi.org/10.1177/0022009417739366.

Núñez Seixas, X.M., & Beydá, O. (Eds.). (2019). *Un ruso blanco en la División Azul. Memorias de Vladímir Kovalevski (1941).* Barcelona: Galaxia Gutenberg.

Oroquieta Arbiol, G., & García Sánchez, C. (1958). *De Leningrado a Odesa.* Barcelona: Marte.

Osti Guerrazzi, A. (2010). *"Noi non sappiamo odiare": L'esercito italiano tra fascismo e democracia.* Turin: UTET.

Osti Guerrazzi, A. (2011). "Wir können nicht hassen." Zum Selbstbild der italienischen Armee während des Krieges und nach dem Krieg. In H. Welzer, S. Neitzel, & Ch. Guderius (Eds.), *"Der Führer war wieder viel zu human, viel zu gefühlvoll." Der Zweite Weltkrieg aus der Sicht deutscher und italienischer Soldaten* (pp. 350–91). Frankfurt a. M.: Fischer.

Palacio Pilacés, L.A. (2013). *Tal vez el día. Aragoneses en la URSS (1937–1977), el exilio y la División Azul.* n.p. [Zaragoza]: Comuniter. 2 vols.

Palacio Pilacés, L.A. (2015). *El horizonte infinito. Los cuatro nacimientos de Isidoro Lahoz.* n.p. [Zaragoza]: Comuniter.

Palmero Aranda, F. (2016), *El discurso antisemita en España (1936–1948).* PhD Thesis, Universidad Complutense de Madrid.

Palomares, C. (1996). *The reaction of the Allies to Franco's pro-Axis moves during the summer of 1941.* MA Thesis, Cambridge University.

Paniagua, E. (1961). *Los hombres se matan así.* Madrid: Lorenzana.

Pannacci, R. (2020). Il nemico "rosso." I soldati sovietici nell'immaginario italiano e nella pratica della guerra combattuta. Campagna di Russia 1941–1943. *Mondo Contemporaneo, 1,* 53–83. DOI: 10.3280/MON2020-001002.

Pardo Bazán, E. (1987). *La revolución y la novela en Rusia*. Madrid: Tello, 3 vols.

Pardo Martínez, S. (2005). *Un año en la División Azul*. Valladolid: AF Ediciones.

Parejo, J.A. (2008). *Señoritos, jornaleros y falangistas*. Sevilla: Bosque de Palabras.

Parrilla Nieto, M. (2002). Pedro Portela Ovalle. Un combatiente europeo superviviente del asalto al tren de repatriados en Chambéry-Alta Saboya. *Boletín Informativo de la Hermandad Nacional de Sargentos Provisionales en los Tres Ejércitos y Guardia Civil*, 113, 7–16.

Parrilla Nieto, M. (2007). *Sargentos para la Historia. 25 biografías del período 1936–1943*. Madrid: Hermandad Nacional de Sargentos Provisionales.

Parrilla Nieto, M. (2018). *Grupo de Transmisiones 250*. Finestrat: Vicente J. Sanjuán Eds.

Pätzold, K. (2000). *Ihr waret die besten Soldaten. Ursprung und Geschichte einer Legende*. Leipzig: Militzke Verlag.

Pau Arriaga, A. (2003). *Memoria de dos guerras*. Madrid: A. Pau Pedrón.

Paulus, H. (2001). Das Wirken des Sondergerichts Bayreuth von 1942–1945 im Landgerichtsbezirk Hof. In *Miscellanea curiensia: Beiträge zur Geschichte und Kultur Nordoberfrankens und angrenzender Regionen*, 3, 61–86.

Payne, S.G. (1997). *Franco y José Antonio. El extraño caso del fascismo español*. Barcelona: Planeta.

Payne, S.G., & Contreras, D. (Eds.). (1996). *España y la Segunda Guerra Mundial*. Madrid: Editorial Complutense.

Peloille, M. (2015). *Positionement politique en temps de crise: Sur la réception du fascisme italien en Espagne, 1922–1929*. Uzés: Inclinaison.

Peñalba Sotorrio, M. (2019). Beyond the war: Nazi propaganda aims in Spain during the Second World War. *Journal of Contemporary History*, 54(4), 902–26. https://doi.org/10.1177%2F0022009418761214.

Pérez, D., ed. (2020). *Los diarios de Karagandá (de Eusebio Rodríguez)*. Madrid: Actas.

Pérez Caballero, R. (1986). *Vivencias y recuerdos: Rusia 1941–1943*. Madrid: Novograph.

Pérez Maestre, A. (2008). *La División Azul de Huelva 1941–1943*. Huelva: Diputación Provincial.

Pérez Rubio, M., & Prieto Barrio, A. (2014). *Legión Española de Voluntarios en Rusia. Los últimos de la División Azul*. Madrid: Actas.

Peter, A. (1992). *Das Spanienbild in den Massenmedien des Dritten Reiches 1933–1945*. Frankfurt a. M. et al.: Peter Lang.

Petke, S. (2014). Militärische Vergemeinschaftungsversuche muslimischer Soldaten in der Waffen-SS. Die Beispiele der Division "Handschar" und des "Osttürkischen Waffenverbandes der SS." In Schulte, Lieb, & Wegner (Eds.), *Die Waffen-SS, Neue Forschungen* (pp. 248–66). Paderborn: Schöningh.

Petrov, Y., & Beyda, O. (2017). The Soviet Union In D. Stahel (Ed.), *Joining Hitler's Crusade* (pp. 369–425). Cambridge: Cambridge UP.

Pierik, P. (2001). *From Leningrad to Berlin: Dutch volunteers in the service of the German Waffen-SS 1941–1945*. Soesterberg: Aspekt. (Original work published 1995)

Pinilla, A.G. (n.d.). *Héroes entre valientes. Los condecorados en la División Azul*. Madrid: Ágora.

Pinilla Turiño, C. (1987). *Como el vuelo de un pájaro*. Madrid: Publisalud.

Pohl, D. (2008). *Die Herrschaft der Wehrmacht. Deutsche Militärbesatzung und einheimische Bevölkerung in der Sowjetunion 1941–1944*. Munich: Oldenbourg.

Polonsky, A., & Davies, N. (1991). *Jews in Eastern Poland and the USSR, 1939–1946*. London: Macmillan.

Poquet Guardiola, J. (2001). *Once años de cautiverio en Rusia. Diario de un prisionero de la División Azul*. Valencia: n. ed. (Original work published 1955)

Possi, V. (2016). La narrativa testimoniale nella letteratura spagnola e italiana sulla campagna di Russia. *Artifara, 16*, 203–16.

Possi, V. (2017). Idealismo e imaginario falangista en las primeras novelas de la División Azul. *Castilla. Estudios de Literatura, 8*, 216–57. http://dx.doi.org/10.24197/cel.8.2017.216-257.

Poulsen, H. (1991). Die deutsche Besatzungspolitik in Dänemark. In R. Bohn, J. Elvert, H. Revas, & M. Salewski (Eds.), *Neutralität und totalitäre Aggression: Nordeuropa und die Großmächte im Zweiten Weltkrieg* (pp. 369–80). Stuttgart: Steiner.

Prego, A. (1954). *Héroes de España en Rusia*. Madrid: Publicaciones Españolas.

Preston, P. (1995). *Franco: A biography*. London: Fontana Press.

Prévotaux, J. (2010). *Un Européisme nazi: Le Groupe Collaboration et l' idéologie européenne dans la Seconde Guerre Mondiale*. Paris: F.X. de Guibert.

Proctor, R. (1972). *Agonía de un neutral: las relaciones hispanoalemanas durante la segunda guerra mundial y la División Azul*. Madrid: Editora Nacional.

Puente, M. (1954). *Yo, muerto en Rusia (Memorias del alférez Ocañas)*. Madrid: Eds. del Movimiento.

Puente Fernández, J.M. (2012). *Cántabros en la División Azul (1941–1944)*. Torrelavega: Librucos.

Pufelska, A. (2007). *Die Judeo-Kommune-Ein Feindbild in Polen. Das polnische Selbstverstaendnis im Schatten des Antisemitismus*. Paderborn: Schöningh.

Quinkert, B. (2014). Aufruf zur Kooperation. Die deutsche Propaganda gegenüber sowjetischen Soldaten und Zivilisten. In Quinkert & Morré (Eds.), *Deutsche Besatzung* (pp. 196–215).

Quinkert, B., & Morré, J. (Eds.). (2014). *Deutsche Besatzung in der Sowjetunion 1941–1944. Vernichtungskrieg, Reaktionen, Erinnerung*. Paderborn: Schöningh.

Quintana Solá, C. (2020). *Cartas desde el frente ruso. La vida cotidiana de un soldado de la División Azul*. Lorca: Fajardo el Bravo.

Ramírez-Copeiro del Villar, J. (2001). *Huelva en la Segunda Guerra Mundial: Espías y neutrales*. Valverde: Author's edition.

Ramón, M. de, & Ortiz, C. (2003). *Madrina de guerra. Cartas desde el frente.* Madrid: La Esfera de los Libros.

Ramos, F. (1953). *División Azul.* Madrid: Publicaciones Españolas.

Rass, Ch. (2003). *"Menschenmaterial": Deutsche Soldaten an der Ostfront. Innenansichten einer Infanteriedivision, 1941–1945.* Paderborn: Schöningh.

Rass, Ch. (2005). Verbrecherische Kriegsführung an der Front. Eine Infanteriedivision und ihre Soldaten. In Hartmann, Hürter, & Jureit (Eds.), *Verbrechen der Wehrmacht* (pp. 80–90).

Rato, R. de (1935). *Vagabundo bajo la luna. Rápida visión de Europa y sus problemas.* Madrid: E.P.C.

Rato, R. de (1936). *Una generación a la intemperie. Perfil juvenil de Europa.* Madrid: A.B.F.

Ready, J.L. (1987). *The forgotten Axis: Germany's partners and foreign volunteers in World War II.* Jefferson, NC/London: McFarland & Co.

Rebrova, I. (2014). Überlebensstrategien von Frauen in den besetzten Gebieten und in Partisaneneinheiten. Kriegsalltag und genderspezifische Erinnerung. In Quinkert & Morré (Eds.), *Die deutsche Besatzung* (pp. 276–95).

Recio Cardona, R. (1998). *El Servicio de Intendencia de la División Azul. La vida cotidiana de los expedicionarios (1941–1943).* Madrid: Fundación Don Rodrigo.

Reichel, P. (2006). *Der schöne Schein des Dritten Reiches. Gewalt und Faszination des deutschen Faschismus.* Hamburg: Ellert & Richter.

Reid, A. (2011). *Blokada. Die Belagerung von Leningrad, 1941–1944.* Berlin: Berlin-Verlag.

Reizer, L. (2009). *In the struggle: Memoirs from Grodno and the forests.* New York/Jerusalem: Yad Vashem/The Holocaust Survivors Memoirs Project.

Remírez de Esparza, I. (2020). *Capitán Figuerola, caído en Rusia. Diario de Campaña.* Valladolid: Galland Books.

Revelli, N. (2013). *Mussolini's death march: Eyewittness accounts of Italian soldiers on the Eastern Front.* Lexington: University Press of Kansas.

Reverte, J.M., & Reverte, J. (2001). *Soldado de poca fortuna: Jesús Martínez Tessier.* Madrid: Aguilar.

Richards, M. (2010). Antonio Vallejo Nágera: Heritage, psychiatry and war. In M.A. del Arco Blanco & A. Quiroga (Eds.), *Right-wing Spain in the civil war era: Soldiers of God and apostles of the fatherland, 1914–1945* (pp. 195–224). London: Bloomsbury.

Richards, M. (2013). *After the civil war: Making memory and re-making Spain since 1936.* Cambridge: Cambridge UP.

Ridruejo, D. (1976). *Casi unas memorias. Con fuego y con raíces.* Barcelona: Planeta.

Ridruejo, D. (1978). *Los cuadernos de Rusia. Diario.* Barcelona: Planeta.

Ridruejo, D. (2008). *Escrito en España* (J. Gracia, Ed.). Madrid: CEPC.

Riudavets de Montes, L. (1960). *Estampas de la Vieja Rusia (recuerdos de un voluntario de la División Azul)*. Madrid: Imprenta Héroes.

Rivaya, B. (1998). *Filosofía del Derecho y primer franquismo*. Madrid: CEPC.

Rochat, G. (1982). Memorialistica e storiografia sulla campagna italiana di Russia 1941–1943. In *Gli italiani sul fronte russo* (pp. 465–84). Bari: ISR Cuneo.

Rodogno, D. (2005). *Italiani brava gente?* Fascist Italy's policy toward the Jews in the Balkans, April 1941–July 1943. *European History Quarterly, 35*(2), 215–40. http://dx.doi.org/10.1177/0265691405051464.

Rodogno, D (2006). *Fascism's European empire: Italian occupation during the Second World War*. Cambridge: Cambridge UP.

Rodríguez Jiménez, J.L. (1994). *Reaccionarios y golpistas. La extrema derecha en España: del tardofranquismo a la consolidación de la democracia (1967–1982)*. Madrid: CSIC.

Rodríguez Jiménez, J.L. (1997). *La extrema derecha española en el siglo XX*. Madrid: Alianza.

Rodríguez Jiménez, J.L. (2007a). *De héroes e indeseables. La División Azul*. Madrid: Espasa-Calpe.

Rodríguez Jiménez, J.L. (2007b). Propuesta de revisión de la historia oficial de la División Azul. Los temas ocultos. *Cuadernos de Historia Contemporánea*, special issue, 321–32.

Rodríguez Jiménez, J.L. (2008). El papel de las familias en las gestiones para la liberación de los prisioneros de la División Española de Voluntarios en la URSS. *Historia del Presente, 11*, 141–64.

Rodríguez Jiménez, J.L. (2009). "Ni División Azul, ni División Española de Voluntarios: el personal forzado en el cuerpo expedicionario enviado por Franco a la URSS. *Cuadernos de Historia Contemporánea, 31*, 265–96.

Rodríguez Puértolas, J. (1986). *Literatura fascista española* (Vol. I). Madrid: Akal.

Rohr, I. (2007). *The Spanish Right and the Jews, 1898–1945: Antisemitism and opportunism*. Brighton: Sussex Academic Press.

Rohrkamp, R. (2011). *"Weltanschaulich gefestigte Kämpfer": Die Soldaten der Waffen-SS 1933–1945. Organisation-Personal-Sozialstruktur*. Paderborn: Schöningh.

Román Jiménez, M. (2011). *"... Que en Rusia están." Historia del II Batallón del 269 (Rusia, 1941–1942)*. Valladolid: Galland Books.

Römer, F. (2008). *Der Kommissarbefehl. Wehrmacht und NS-Verbrechen an der Ostfront 1941/42*. Paderborn: Schöningh.

Römer, F. (2012). *Kameraden. Die Wehrmacht von innen*. Munich/Zürich: Piper.

Römer, F. (2013). Milieus in the military: Soldierly ethos, nationalism and conformism among workers in the Wehrmacht. *Journal of Contemporary History, 48*(1), 125–49.

Römer, F. (2014). Der Kommissarbefehl bei den Frontdivisionen des Ostheeres 1941/42. In Quinkert & Morré (Eds.), *Deutsche Besatzung* (pp. 95–112).

Romero, L. (1957). *Tudá*. Barcelona: Acervo.

Romero, L (1982). Recuerdos de un Divisionario Azul: la Historia se hace recuerdo. *Tiempo de Historia, VIII* (92–3), 132–43. http://hdl.handle.net/10366/29222.

Romeu Fernández, M.M. (2007). *Relato de un viaje*. Ronda: Picaflor.

Romsics, I. (2017). Hungary. In Stahel (Ed.), *Joining Hitler's Crusade* (pp. 79–106).

Ros Agudo, M. (2002). *La guerra secreta de Franco*. Barcelona: Crítica.

Rosenthal, G. (1990). Biographische Verarbeitung von Kriegserlebnissen. In G. Rosenthal (Ed.), *"Als der Krieg kam, hatte ich mit Hitler nichts mehr zu tun." Zur Gegenwärtigkeit des "Dritten Reiches" in Biographien*. Opladen: Leske+Budrich (pp. 7–25).

Rössler, M., & Schleiermacher, S. (1993). *Der "Generalplan Ost": Hauptlinien der nationalsozialistischen Planungs- und Vernichtungspolitik*. Berlin: Akademie-Verlag.

Rotari, J., Burcin, O., Zodian, V., & Moise, L. (1999). *Maresalul Antonescu la Odessa*. Bucharest: Paideia.

Rother, B. (2005). *Franco y el Holocausto*. Madrid: Marcial Pons.

Royo Masía, R. (1944). *¡Guerra! Historia de la vida de Luis de Pablos*. Madrid: Gráficas Ultra.

Royo Masía, R. (1956). *El sol y la nieve*. Madrid: Cíes.

Royo Masía, R. (1976). *El sepulturero*. Madrid: Sedmay.

Rozenberg, D. (2010). *La España contemporánea y la cuestión judía*. Madrid: Marcial Pons/Casa Sefarad.

Ruhl, K.-J. (1986). *Franco, Falange y III Reich. España durante la II Guerra Mundial*. Madrid: Akal.

Ruiz Ayúcar, A. (1981). *La Rusia que yo conocí*. Madrid: FN. (Original work published 1954)

Ruiz Carnicer, M.A. (1996). *El Sindicato Español Universitario (SEU), 1939–1965: La socialización política de la juventud universitaria en el franquismo*. Madrid: Siglo XXI.

Rutherford, J. (2014). *Combat and genocide on the Eastern Front: The German infantry's war, 1941–1944*. Cambridge: Cambridge UP.

Rychlik, J. (2017). Slovakia. In Stahel (Ed.), *Joining Hitler's Crusade* (pp. 107–33).

Sagarra, P. (2012). *Capellanes en la División Azul. Los últimos cruzados*. Madrid: Actas.

Salamanca, A., & Torres García, F. (2002). *Esclavos de Stalin: el combate final de la División Azul (memorias de un prisionero en la URSS)*. Madrid: FN.

Salas Iñigo, J. (1988). *Aquella Rusia*. Zaragoza: Mira.

Salisbury, H.E. (2003). *The 900 days: The siege of Leningrad*. Cambridge, MA: Da Capo Press. (Original work published 1969)

Sallée, F. (2014). *Sur les chemins de terre brune: voyages et voyageurs dans l'Allemagne nationale-socialiste (1933–1939)*. PhD Thesis, Université de Grenoble.

Salvador, T. (1962). *División 250*. Barcelona: Acervo. (Original work published 1954)

Salvador, T. (1971). La División 250, llamada "Azul." *Historia y Vida, 35*, 102–13.

Salvador, T. (1975). *Camaradas 74*. Barcelona: Plaza & Janés.

Sánchez Brun, G.J. (2002). *Instituciones turolenses en el franquismo 1936–1961. Personal y mensaje políticos*. Teruel: Instituto de Estudios Turolenses.

Sánchez Carrilero, J. (1992). *Crónicas de la División Azul*. Albacete: Gráficas Albacete.

Sánchez Diana, J.M. (1993). *Cabeza de puente. Diario de un soldado de Hitler*. Granada: García Hispán.

Sánchez Salcedo, E. (2002). *Framan (de Serrablo a Leningrado)*. Sabiñánigo: Ayuntamiento de Sabiñánigo/IEA/Museo Ángel Orensanz.

Sanz Jarque, J.J. (2010). *Alas de águila. La División Azul en Rusia*. Madrid: Actas

Schammah-Gesser, S. (2007). La imagen de Sefarad y los judíos españoles en los orígenes vanguardistas del fascismo español. In R. Rein (Ed.), *España e Israel veinte años después* (pp. 67–88). Madrid: Dykinson/Fundación Tres Culturas.

Schenk, F.B. (2002). Mental Maps. Die Konstruktion von geographischen Räumen in Europa seit der Aufklärung. Literaturbericht. *Geschichte und Gesellschaft, 28*(3), 493–514.

Schill, P. (1977). *Die Geschichte der lettischen Waffen-SS*. Ettlingen: P. Schill.

Schlemmer, Th. (2005). *Die Italiener an der Ostfront 1942/1943. Dokumente zu Mussolinis Krieg gegen die Sowjetunion*. Munich: Oldenbourg.

Schlemmer, Th. (2009). *Invasori, non vittime. La campagna italiana di Russia 1941–1943*. Bari: Laterza.

Schlemmer, Th. (2010). Gefühlsmassige Verwandtschaft? Zivilisten, Kriegsgefangene und das königlich-italienische Heer im Krieg gegen die Sowjetunion 1931 bis 1943. In Klinkhammer, Osti Guerrazzi, & Schlemmer (Eds.), *Die "Achse" im Krieg* (pp. 368–97).

Schöttler, P. (2014). Trois formes de collaboration: L'Europe et la réconciliation franco-allemande – à travers la carrière de Gustav Krukenberg, chef de la Division Charlemagne." *Allemagne d'aujourd'hui, 207*, 225–46.

Schrijvers, P. (2002). *The GI war against Japan: American soldiers in Asia and the Pacific during World War II*. Basingstoke: Palgrave.

Schüler-Springorum, S. (2010). *Krieg und Fliegen. Die Legion Condor im spanischen Bürgerkrieg*. Paderborn: Schöningh.

Schulte, J.E., Lieb, P., & Wegner, B. (Eds.). (2014). *Die Waffen-SS. Neue Forschungen*. Paderborn: Schöningh.

Schulze-Schneider, I. (2004). Alemania y la guerra civil española: información y propaganda. *Spagna Contemporanea, 26*, 57–84.

Schwelling, B. (2010). *Heimkehr – Erinnerung – Integration. Der Verband der Heimkehrer, die ehemaligen Kriegsgefangenen und die westdeutsche Nachkriegsgesellschaft*. Paderborn: Schöningh.

Scianna, B.-M. (2019). *The Italian war on the Eastern Front, 1941–1943. Operations, myths and memories*. Basingstoke: Palgrave Macmillan.

Scoppola, P. (2006). Aspetti e momenti dell'anticomunismo. In A. Ventrone (Ed.), *L'ossessione del nemico. Memorie divise nella storia della Repubblica* (pp. 71–8). Roma: Donzelli.

Scotoni, G. (2013). *Il nemico fidato. La guerra di sterminio in URSS e l'occupazione alpina sull' Alto Don*. Trento: Panorama.

Seberechts, F. (2002). *Tussen Schelde en Wolchow. Vlaanderen en het Oostfront*. Brussels/Antwerp: Globe & Perspectief Uitgaven.

Segador, A. (2019). *Memoria y experiencia de los prisioneros de guerra de la División Azul en la Unión Soviética (1941–1954)*. MA Thesis, University of Santiago de Compostela.

Seidmann, M. (2002). *Republic of egos: A social history of the Spanish Civil War*. Madison: University of Wisconsin Press.

Sesma Landrín, N. (2011). Importando el Nuevo Orden. El Instituto de Estudios Políticos y la recepción de la cultura fascista y nacionalsocialista en España (1939–1943). In F. Gallego & F. Morente (Eds.), *Rebeldes y reaccionarios. Intelectuales, fascismo y derecha radical en Europa* (pp. 243–79). Barcelona: El Viejo Topo.

Shepherd, B. (2004). *War in the ild East: The German Army and Soviet Partisans*. Cambridge, MA: Harvard UP.

Shils, E.A., & Janowitz, M. (1948). Cohesion and Disintegration in the Wehrmacht in World War II. *Public Opinion Quarterly, 12*, 280–315.

Skoutelsky, R. (2006). *Novedad en el frente. Las Brigadas Internacionales en la guerra civil*. Madrid: Temas de Hoy.

Slepyan, K. (2006). *Stalin's guerrillas: Soviet partisans in World War II*. Lawrence: University Press of Kansas.

Smith, P.S., Poulsen, N.B., & Christensen, C.B. (1999). The Danish volunteers in the Waffen SS and German warfare at the Eastern Front. *Contemporary European History, 1*, 73–96. http://dx.doi.org/10.1017/S0960777399000144.

Smyth, D. (1994). The dispatch of the Spanish Blue Division to the Russian Front: Reasons and repercussions. *European History Quarterly, 24*(4), 537–53.

Snyder, T. (2010). *Bloodlands. Europe between Hitler and Stalin*. New Haven: Yale UP.

Sorlie, S. (2019). *Sonnenrad und Hakenkreuz. Norweger in der Waffen-SS 1941–1945*. Paderborn: Schöningh.

Sourd, J.P. (2007). *Croisés d'un idéal. Volontaires espagnols de la Waffen SS, Heer et Kriegsmarine (1944–1945).* n.p.: Dualpha.

Stahel, D. (Ed.). (2017). *Joining Hitler's Crusade.* Cambridge: Cambridge UP.

Stargardt, N. (2015). *Der deutsche Krieg 1939–1945.* Frankfurt a. M.: Fischer.

Stein, G.H. (1966). *The Waffen-SS: Hitler's elite guard at war, 1939–1945.* Ithaca, NY: Cornell UP.

Stein, G.H., & Krosby, H.P. (1966). Das Finnische Freiwilligen Bataillon der Waffen-SS: Eine Studie zur SS-Diplomatie und zur ausländischen Freiwilligen-Bewegung. *Vierteljahrshefte für Zeitgeschichte, 14,* 413–53.

Streit, Ch. (1978). *Keine Kameraden. Die Wehrmacht und die sowjetischen Kriegsgefangenen 1941–1945.* Stuttgart: DVA.

Theleweit, K. (1995). *Männerphantasien.* Munich: DTV. 2 vols.

Thomàs, J.M. (Ed.). (2016a). *Estados Unidos, Alemania, Gran Bretaña, Japón y sus relaciones con España entre la guerra y la postguerra (1939–1953).* Salamanca: Universidad Pontificia Comillas.

Thomàs, J.M. (2016b). *Franquistas contra franquistas. Luchas por el poder en la cúpula del régimen de Franco.* Barcelona: Debate.

Thomàs, J.M. (2019). *José Antonio Primo de Rivera: The Reality and Myth of a Fascist Spanish Leader.* New York/Oxford: Berghahn.

Todorova, M. (1997). *Imagining the Balkans.* New York: Oxford UP.

Togores Sánchez, L.E. (2007). *Muñoz Grandes, héroe de Marruecos, general de la División Azul.* Madrid: La Esfera de los Libros.

Tomasoni, M. (2017). *El caudillo olvidado. Vida, obra y pensamiento de Onésimo Redondo (1905–1936).* Granada: Comares.

Torra i Puigdellívol, M. (2013). *Ideals i desenganys. Cartes des de Rússia a un germà (1941–1942).* n.p.: Mecenix.

Torres, F. (2014). *Soldados de hierro. Los Voluntarios de la División Azul.* Madrid: Actas.

Torres, F. (2018). *Cautivos en Rusia. Los últimos combatientes de la División Azul.* Madrid: Actas.

Tranche, R.R., & Sánchez Biosca, V. (2011). *El pasado es el destino. Propaganda y cine del bando nacional en la Guerra Civil.* Madrid: Cátedra/Filmoteca Española.

Tremlett, G. (2008). *Ghosts of Spain: Travels through Spain and its silent past.* New York: Walker & Company.

Tusell, J. (1995). *Franco, España y la Segunda Guerra Mundial. Entre el Eje y la Neutralidad.* Madrid: Temas de Hoy.

Tych, T. (2005). Presenciando el Holocausto: Diarios polacos, memorias y recuerdos. In Bankier & Gutman (Eds.), *La Europa nazi* (pp. 239–72).

Ueberschär, G.R., & Wette, W. (Eds.). (1984). *"Unternehmen Barbarossa." Der deutsche Überfall auf die Sowjetunion 1941. Berichte, Analyse, Dokumente.* Paderborn: Schöningh.

Ulrich, B. (1996). Militärgeschichte von unten: Anmerkungen zu ihren Ursprüngen, Quellen und Perspektiven im 20. Jahrhundert. *Geschichte und Gesellschaft, 22*, 473–503.

Ulrich, B. (1997). *Die Augenzeugen. Deutsche Feldpostbriefe in Kriegs- und Nachkriegszeit, 1914–1933*. Essen: Klartext.

Ungváry, K. (2002–3). Ungarische Besatzungskräfte in der Ukraine 1941–1942. *Ungarn-Jahrbuch, 26*, 125–63.

Ungváry, K. (2004). Robbing the dead: The Hungarian contribution to the Holocaust. In B. Kosmala & F. Tych (Eds.), *Facing the Nazi Genocide* (pp. 231–62). Berlin: Metropol.

Ungváry, K. (2005a). Das Beispiel der ungarischen Armee. Ideologischer Vernichtungskrieg oder militärisches Kalkül? In Hartmann, Hürter, & Jureit (Eds.), *Verbrechen der Wehrmacht* (pp. 98–106).

Ungváry, K. (2005b). *A magyar honvédség a második világháborúban*. Budapest: Osiris.

Urgoiti y Bas, C. (1987). *Prólogo al tema Amistad*. Madrid: Dédalo.

Uriarte Arbaiza, I. (2012). *Las mujeres de la División Azul. Una valerosa retaguardia*. Madrid: Barbarroja.

Urquijo, A. de (1973). *Cuando empuñamos las armas. La pequeña historia de una familia numerosa entre 1936 y 1942*. Madrid: Moneda y Crédito.

Vadillo, F. (1967). *Orillas del Volchov*. Barcelona: Marte.

Vadillo, F. (1971). *Arrabales de Leningrado*. Barcelona: Marte.

Vadillo, F. (1975). *Y lucharon en Krasny Bor*. Barcelona: Marte.

Vascano, J.L. (1960). *Infierno en la estepa*. Valencia: Valenciana.

Vázquez Enciso, M. (1995). *Historia postal de la División Azul. Españoles en Rusia*. Madrid: Lindner Filatelia Ibérica.

Vehviläinen, O. (2002). *Finland in the Second World War: Between Germany and Russia*. Basingstoke: Macmillan.

Velarde Fuertes, J. (2008). *Antonio Bermúdez Cañete: Periodista, economista y politico*. Madrid: Actas.

Ventrone, A. (2005). *Il nemico interno: immagini, parole e simboli della lotta politica nell'Italia del Novecento*. Rome: Donzelli.

Vettorazzo, G. (2004). *Cento lettere dalla Russia 1942–1943*. Rovereto: Museo Storico Italiano della Guerra.

Viciana, A. (2018). *700. Los almerienses en la División Azul*. Almería: Instituto de Estudios Almerienses.

Vidal y Gadea, E. (1991). *Breves notas sobre la División Azul*. Alicante: García Hispán.

Viladot Fargas, J. (2000). *El espíritu de la División Azul: Possad*. Madrid: Barbarroja.

Viñas, Á. (2001). *Franco, Hitler y el estallido de la guerra civil. Antecedentes y consecuencias*. Madrid: Alianza.

Von Bock, F. (1995). *Zwischen Pflicht und Verweigerung: Das Kriegstagebuch.* Munich: Herbig.

Voronina, T. (2011). Heroische Tote. Die Blockade, die Opferzahl und die Erinnerung. *Osteuropa, 61*(89), 155–68.

Wegner, B. (1990). Der Krieg gegen die Sowjetunion 1942/43. In Militärgeschichtliches Forschungsamt (Ed.), *Das deutsche Reich und der zweite Weltkrieg. Bd. 6: der globale Krieg. Die Ausweitung zum Weltkrieg und der Wechsel der Initiative* (pp. 761–1102). Stuttgart: DVA.

Wegner, B. (1999). *Hitlers Politische Soldaten: Die Waffen-SS, 1933–1945.* Paderborn: Schöningh. (Original work published 1986)

Weiss-Wendt, A. (2009). *Murder without hatred: Estonians and the Holocaust.* New York: Syracuse UP.

Werner, F. (2008). "Hart müssen wir hier draußen sein": Soldatische Männlichkeit im Vernichtungskrieg 1941–1944. *Geschichte und Gesellschaft, 34*(1), 5–40.

Werther, S. (2004). *Dänische Freiwillige in der Waffen-SS.* Berlin: Wissenschaftlicher Verlag.

Werther, S., & Hurd, M. (2014). Go East, old man: The ritual spaces of SS veterans' memory work. *Culture Unbound, 6,* 327–59. http://dx.doi.org/10.3384/cu.2000.1525.146327.

Wette, W. (1984). Die propagandistische Begleitmusik zum deutschen Überfall auf die Sowjetunion am 22. Juni 1941. In Ueberschär & Wette (Eds.), *Unternehmen Barbarossa* (pp. 111–29).

Wette, W. (Ed.). (1992). *Der Krieg des kleinen Mannes. Eine Militärgeschichte von unten.* Munich/Zürich: Piper.

Wette, W. (2002). *Die Wehrmacht. Feindbilder, Vernichtungskrieg, Legenden.* Frankfurt a. M.: Fischer.

Wette, W. (Ed.). (2003). *Retter in Uniform. Handlungsspielräume im Vernichtungskrieg der Wehrmacht.* Frankfurt a. M.: Fischer.

Whealey, R.H. (1989). *Hitler and Spain: The Nazi role and the Spanish Civil War 1936–1939.* Lexington: The University Press of Kentucky.

Wievorka, M. (2009). *El racismo: una introducción.* Barcelona: Gedisa.

Wilke, K. (2011). *Die "Hilfsgemeinschaft auf Gegenseitigkeit" (HIAG) 1950–1990. Veteranen der Waffen-SS in der Bundesrepublik.* Paderborn: Schöningh.

Ydígoras, C.M. (1984). *Algunos no hemos muerto.* Madrid: Cyr [1957].

Zandman, F. (1995). *Never the last journey.* New York: Schocken Books.

Zaugg, F. (2016). *Albanische Muslime in der Waffen-SS. Von "Großalbanien" zur Division "Skanderberg."* Paderborn: Schöningh.

Zulaica, R. (1963). *La última oportunidad.* San Sebastián: Ágora.

Index

Toronto Iberic

CO-EDITORS: Robert Davidson (Toronto) and Frederick A. de Armas (Chicago)

EDITORIAL BOARD: Josiah Blackmore (Harvard); Marina Brownlee (Princeton); Anthony J. Cascardi (Berkeley); Justin Crumbaugh (Mt Holyoke); Emily Francomano (Georgetown); Jordana Mendelson (NYU); Joan Ramon Resina (Stanford); Enrique García Santo-Tomás (U Michigan); H. Rosi Song (Durham); Kathleen Vernon (SUNY Stony Brook)

1 Anthony J. Cascardi, *Cervantes, Literature, and the Discourse of Politics*
2 Jessica A. Boon, *The Mystical Science of the Soul: Medieval Cognition in Bernardino de Laredo's Recollection Method*
3 Susan Byrne, *Law and History in Cervantes'* Don Quixote
4 Mary E. Barnard and Frederick A. de Armas (eds), *Objects of Culture in the Literature of Imperial Spain*
5 Nil Santiáñez, *Topographies of Fascism: Habitus, Space, and Writing in Twentieth-Century Spain*
6 Nelson Orringer, *Lorca in Tune with Falla: Literary and Musical Interludes*
7 Ana M. Gómez-Bravo, *Textual Agency: Writing Culture and Social Networks in Fifteenth-Century Spain*
8 Javier Irigoyen-García, *The Spanish Arcadia: Sheep Herding, Pastoral Discourse, and Ethnicity in Early Modern Spain*
9 Stephanie Sieburth, *Survival Songs: Conchita Piquer's Coplas and Franco's Regime of Terror*
10 Christine Arkinstall, *Spanish Female Writers and the Freethinking Press, 1879–1926*